1990.

Michael.
Herr.

Love from
Sheila.

EQUUS:
THE HORSE IN THE ROMAN WORLD

Ann Hyland

EQUUS:
THE HORSE IN THE ROMAN WORLD

B. T. Batsford Ltd, London

© Ann Hyland, 1990
First published 1990

All rights reserved. No part of this publication
may be reproduced, in any form or by any means,
without permission from the Publisher.

ISBN 0 7134 6260 4

Photoset by Deltatype Ltd, Ellesmere Port, Cheshire
Printed and bound in Great Britain by
Biddles, Guildford

for the publishers B. T. Batsford Ltd
4 Fitzhardinge Street, London W1H 0AH

*To my generous friends
Stephen Jenkins and Peter Connolly
who gave me much encouragement and help during the writing
of this book.*

Contents

Foreword by Professor John Mann — ix
Acknowledgements — xi
List of plates — xiii
Introduction — 1

PART ONE:
Basic Principles of Roman Horsemastership

1 Breeding — 5
2 Stud management and practices — 30
3 Veterinary medicine — 49

PART TWO:
The Roman Cavalry Horse

Introduction — 63
4 Psychology and physiology of the Roman battle charger — 66
5 Supply of equines to the Roman army — 71
6 Cavalry logistics — 87
7 The horse's education — 101
8 Rider training — 111
9 Hazards and health — 122
10 Military equipment: the horse's tack — 130
11 Military equipment: the horse's armour — 145
12 Practicalities — 157
13 External influences — 170
14 Development of cavalry — 187

PART THREE:
The Horse in State and Civilian Use

15 The Roman circus	201
16 Daily life	231
17 Transport and the *Cursus Publicus*	250
Select glossary of Roman and equine terms	263
Horse breeds noted in classical literature	266
Bibliography	267
Index	275

Foreword

Too often, the historian or archaeologist, when faced with a problem in a specialized field of which he has no first-hand knowledge, is prepared, whether through arrogance or ignorance, to put forward theories which merely arouse derision in the specialist in that field. For example, the study of Hadrian's Wall has been bedevilled by the half-baked views of archaeologists on military tactics. The work of specialists is vital if studies of the past are to have any value.

But the specialist, if he or she is to contribute meaningfully to the study of the past, also needs to take account of what the student of the past – however tall and ethereal his ivory tower – has to say. In the case of Hadrian's Wall again, modern military writers have gone astray through a failure to take into account what we know about the Roman army.

It is with great pleasure then that one turns the pages of Ann Hyland's book. Not only has she a profound knowledge and understanding of horses, and not least of what they can or cannot do, but she has also consulted historians with a wide and real knowledge of the Roman army, and of Roman life in general. Any scholar worth his salt is pleased to have his brains picked by one who is determined to get things right, and one of Ann Hyland's qualities is certainly determination. This is what gives this work its authority. It is a most percipient study of the horse in the Roman world, and its authority is what makes it so enjoyable to read.

J. C. Mann

Acknowledgements

In writing this book I have been helped by many people in a variety of ways. Encouragement for tackling such an unusual aspect of Roman history has come from many friends, most notably from Peter Connolly, who also gave a large measure of practical help with the loan of Roman equipment – saddles, armour, bit – and many of the photographs. Stephen Jenkins spent untold hours helping with the first translation into English of our mutual friend who came to be known as 'Mr Pelagonius', Roman veterinary surgeon and shedder of light on to much of Roman horselore and racing tactics. Professor John Mann read the typescript for error and was persuaded to write a foreword. Additionally he also offered valuable advice, many additions for inclusion, and pointers towards research areas, as well as checking some Latin translations. I would like to thank my veterinary surgeon, Russell Lyon, MRCVS, for reading the veterinary chapter to check for any modern mistakes. He is not responsible for Mr Pelagonius' errors. Others have helped by supplying me with a great number of articles of interest which I might not otherwise have had access to: Mike Bishop, Dr Margaret Roxan, Mark Hassell, Mike Macdona, and in particular Dr Graham Webster, whom I would also like to thank for his very sympathetic historical editing of the book. I am grateful to Pat Brett for discussions on homoeopathic veterinary medicine; Mrs M. Painter, Librarian of Isle of Ely College, Wisbech, who obtained many obscure titles for research; and Henry Deptford, Dr Marjorie Barr, and Jim Chapman for discussions over modern farming, modern medicine, and horse equipment.

The author and publishers wish to thank the following for making photographs available and for permission to reproduce them: *Maps and line illustrations*: 1, Janet Wheeler, from A. Hyland, *Beginner's Guide to Western Riding*, Pelham, 1971; 4, J. F. Coates; 5, L. E. Ross; 6, from Williams, 1985; 7, from Frend, 1956. *Plates*: 1, Peter Connolly; 3, M. Fiennes; 5, 6 and 7, Peter Connolly; 8 and 9, Janet Harrison; 10,

11 and 12, Anna Oakford; 13, 14, 15 and 16, Janet Harrison; 18, The Vindolanda Trust; 19, Janet Harrison; 20, Peter Jugurtha; 21, Ecole Française d'Archaéologie; 22, The Mansell Collection; 23, Musée de la Civilisation Gallo-Romaine, Lyon; 24, The Vienna Kunsthistorisches Museum; 25, 26 and 27, The Sousse Museum, photographs by Ann Hyland; 28, The Bardo Museum, photograph by Alan Raistrick; 29, The Ashmolean Museum, Oxford; 30; 31, The Mansell Collection.

Lastly, though he would rather be given a packet of Polo mints, thanks to Katchina who put up with the many odd experiments to see what equine reactions would be, and who had to work with the considerable extra weight of arms and armour. Some of this work was conducted at speed, some was truly experimental and there were a few anxious moments along the way. Without the field trials much of what follows would have been speculative. Katchina made them positive.

List of Plates

1 Long-reining: Longinus Biarta, an *eques* of the *Ala Sulpiciana*
2 Method of holding the reins in the same hand as the shield
3 The quarter turn in modern Western riding
4 Vonatorix, a member of the *Ala Longiniana*, in a typical pose
5 The small horned Roman saddle with breast and haunch breeching
6 A close-up of the rider's position in the small horned saddle
7 A canter on the right lead
8 A close-up of the rider's position in the large horned saddle
9 A modern Western bit
10 A facsimile of the Newstead curb bit
11 A horse's skull with the Newstead bit in place
12 The Newstead bit in action
13 The Newstead bit with no pressure applied
14 The Newstead bit with pressure applied
15 A modern Western bit and drop noseband
16 A snaffle bridle and headpiece
17 A metal parade chamfron
18 A facsimile of the Vindolanda chamfron
19 A leather chamfron
20 Roman cavalrymen riding down four Britons
21 The Battle of Pydna
22 Detail of horses ready for battle
23 The Lyon Circus mosaic
24 The wreck of a chariot
25 Mosaics depicting racehorses Adorandus and Crinitus
26 Four racing stallions
27 A pastoral scene of mares with foals and youngtock
28 Hare hunting with hounds
29 A hunting scene
30 Travelling
31 A hunting scene

Introduction

Despite the mountain of literature on all aspects of the Roman world, the place of the horse has so far attracted little attention. In the martial sphere we read that cavalry horses were small, quick and ugly; that certain tribes excelled as horsemen; that cavalry detachments were deployed in such and such a battle; or that the reason for a Roman defeat was the enemy's superior cavalry. Yet the picture was so much fuller than the mere sketch we are shown. With the legions rode the cavalry *alae* mounted on horses from many nations, some bred in Rome's provinces renowned for producing quality horseflesh, some levied from tribute-paying allies. Within the protection provided by military chargers and tramping legionaries plodded thousands of baggage mules laden with supplies, and mules harnessed to *carroballistae* hauling the machines of war.

On the racing side the fever heat of Rome on holiday at the circus is often colourfully depicted. Of the important equine element we are usually left ignorant, except for a vague picture of galloping horses and the all too frequent *naufragii* of chariot collisions. The human element of top racing drivers notching up a cricket score of wins, many achieving their centuries, is given more coverage than the animals they drove. On the racetrack Rome displayed the finest horseflesh that a long tradition, inherited from and influenced by the Greeks, could produce. It was an industry just as important to the Romans, and touching their economy even more, than that of the modern racing world.

In many ways we are the inheritors of Roman expertise. The Romans still influence us in several areas. With regard to the horse there are many links in the way we ride him, the equipment we use, the veterinary care he receives, his nutrition and his general care. Most telling is the way he was trained, particularly for military use: his display of talent on the parade ground, the elaborate tack he carried, the very considerable weight of rider and armour under which he was expected to perform to optimum efficiency. Today many riders, particularly those practising American stock-seat (Western) riding, benefit from the methods used to train the Roman cavalrymen and their mounts to a high degree of proficiency.

The *Equidae*, the family of horses, donkeys, and their indispensable hybrid offspring the mules, had a little recognized but for all that immense impact on Roman life. Without its mule-borne baggage the legions would have found it virtually impossible to operate. As frontiers extended cavalry increasingly became a military arm of both size and importance. Without the racing fraternity and their passionate addiction to the sport the circus would not have existed. Efficient transport haulage by land would have been non-existent, hampered and slowed to oxen pace. The cities' bakery mills would have lacked motive power and bread risen in price. Rapid communications, so vital in a military state, would have been absent.

In some spheres the *Equidae* put a massive strain on the Roman economy; in others the economy would have ground to a halt without them.

In the following pages I shall draw together the threads of Rome's equine history, culled largely from the ancient sources. These passages speak clearly to a horseman with a sense of history. To historians I hope a horsewoman's interpretation will be a valuable addition to their current store of knowledge, and maybe fill a gap and answer some questions.

Part One

BASIC PRINCIPLES OF ROMAN HORSEMASTERSHIP

1
Breeding

The ideal horse

In any comprehensive work on horses, and their kin such as mules and donkeys, the starting point is a study of breeds, the methods employed in selecting suitable stock, and the stud practices used to achieve successful parturition. We are fortunate in possessing considerable literature from Roman times, in particular the works of poets such as Virgil, Oppian, Nemesian and Gratius Faliscus; the geographer Strabo; the gentleman farmers Varro and Columella; and that inveterate unknown traveller writing to his son in the work known to us as the *Expositio Totius Mundi et Gentium*. Pliny the Elder also throws a little light on to areas concerning horsebreeding, and later on his nephew described the facilities owned by gentleman riders, as well as the string of ponies owned by a fortunate child.

Perhaps the best place to begin, before discussing individual breeds, is with a description of the Romans' ideal horse, and the reasons for such a horse being favoured. There is a handful of descriptions of the conformation of horses, ranging from that of Varro written in 37 BC, followed by that contained in Book III of Virgil's *Georgics*. These are followed in the Christian era by those of the first-century writers Calpurnius Siculus and Columella. Two poets in the second century, Oppian and Nemesian, give a detailed description of the hunting horse in their *cynegetica*. In the fourth century two veterinary practitioners laid down their requirements for a good, sound horse. Apsyrtus was veterinary surgeon at the court of Constantine the Great, and Pelagonius was a practitioner engaged in maintaining the health and tending the ailments and injuries of circus horses competing in the exciting but dangerous sport of chariot racing.

Three main categories of horse are described: the warhorse of Virgil; the hunting horses of Nemesian, Oppian and Gratius Faliscus; and the racehorses of Pelagonius. There is a close resemblance in the main points of ideal conformation in these categories. In each field of endeavour the horses were put under great stress in the execution of their work.

The recommendations of Columella and Pelagonius could have been written by the same man, yet three centuries separate their publication. There is possibly blatant plagiarism, but it does show a continuity of ideals. Below is Pelagonius' description of the ideal stallion (*Ars Vet.*):

> Small head, black eyes, nostrils open, ears short and pricked up; neck flexible and broad without being long; mane thick and falling on the right side; broad and muscular chest, big straight shoulders, muscles sticking out all over the body, sides sloping in, double back, small belly, stones small and alike, flanks broad and drawn in; tail long and not bristly, for this is ugly; legs straight; knee round and small, and not turned in; buttocks and thighs full and muscular; hoofs black, high and hollow, topping off with moderate sized coronets. He should in general be so formed as to be large, high, well set up, of an active look, and round-barrelled in the proportion proper to his length. (quoted in Morgan 1962, p. 115)

With two exceptions, this describes a horse that today's horseman would agree possessed good conformation, as well as being structurally adapted to withstand the rigours of hard, stressful work. On analysing each point it can be appreciated why it was necessary to breed horses of this calibre.

A small head is one of the hallmarks of good breeding. Coarse, heavy-headed horses nearly always have ill-proportioned bodies with a resulting propensity for poor action and leg ailments when the animal is put under stress. Black eyes, or rather the appearance of having black eyes which most horses give, are the norm, with the exception of horses of certain colours such as golden dun which sometimes have tiger-like eyes with a dark surround and amber iris. Others such as cremello and albino horses frequently have blue eyes. Some have what is known as a 'wall eye', 'glass' or 'watchet eye'. This is a light-coloured, glassy eye which is the result of lack of pigment. Although such eyes have been, and to some extent still are, discriminated against there is no clinical proof that they are inferior. Any cloudiness or spotting of the eye, however, indicates incipient trouble.

Open nostrils, or rather nostrils capable of extreme dilation, are absolutely vital for an adequate intake of air, and the dissipation of heat via hot breath, especially for horses used in any type of work requiring endurance. Battle chargers used by Roman cavalry on extensive campaigns were true endurance mounts, and some of the conditions met with in arid areas would cause a horse to 'tie up' if he could not regulate his heat build-up.

Short ears are another sign of good breeding. Long, broad, lop ears

1 Points of the horse

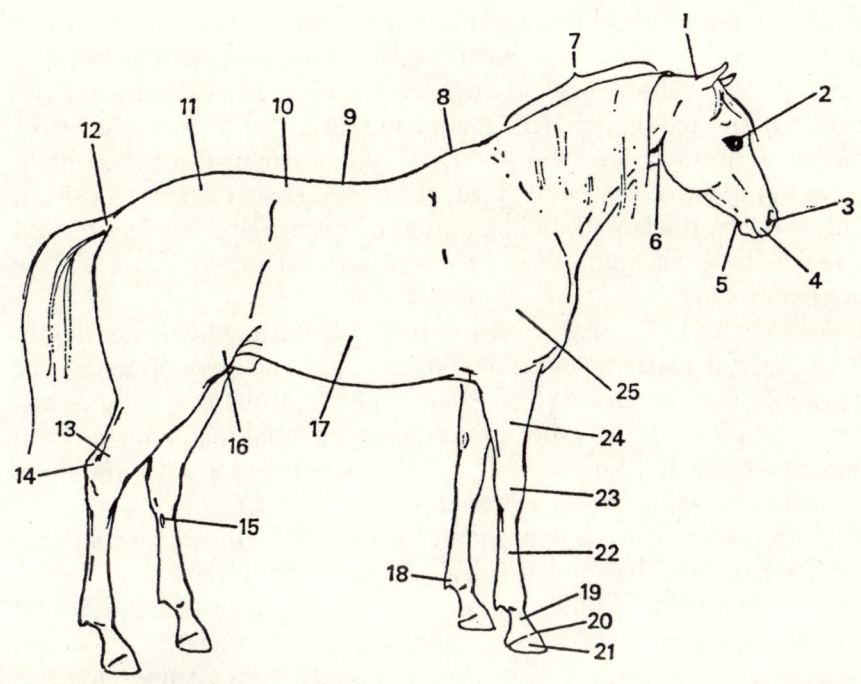

1 Poll
2 Eye
3 Nostril
4 Muzzle
5 Chin groove
6 Throatlatch (gullet)
7 Crest (of neck)
8 Withers
9 Back
10 Loins
11 Point of croup
12 Dock
13 Hock
14 Point of hock
15 Chestnut
16 Stifle
17 Barrel
18 Fetlock
19 Pastern
20 Coronet
21 Hoof
22 Cannon bone
23 Knee
24 Forearm
25 Shoulder

generally go with a heavy head. The forward-pricked 'to attention' ear position shows alertness and also gives a clue to disposition. Ears neither pricked forward nor laid back nor turned back to listen indicate relaxation and calm disposition, and while desirable when the horse is at rest, during work would probably indicate inertia, dullness and poor responses. The laid-back ear indicates bad temper. These traits are not desirable in a horse expected to give of its best. Under extreme pressure of a hard gallop, however, the ears do lie flat back along the neck.

A flexible neck of adequate width is desirable. The spinal column needs flexibility to enable the animal to perform to maximum efficiency, and the neck is used as a balancing mechanism when the horse is manoeuvring. A horse held on a tight rein is not nearly so balanced as an animal permitted enough freedom of rein. Too long a neck would distort the ideal proportions and therefore the attainment of maximum efficiency in movement. This is true to an even greater degree of a short, thick neck. A thick mane falling to the right is merely a convention and one which is still followed today by people striving for correct show presentation.

A broad and muscular chest is a necessity for any horse needing to work to full capacity, whether on extended marches or under the pressure of the racetrack. Such a chest gives adequate heart and lung room, and good heart and respiration are essential requirements for a horse to reach full fitness. Without adequate internal space optimum performance will never be achieved.

The requirement of straight shoulders is the major divergence between the Roman and the modern ideal. Straight shoulders give a stilted, upward motion that under certain conditions such as the pomp of a parade can appear quite extravagant and flashy, and therefore attractive. In practice, however, a sloping shoulder tends to give a smoother ride and puts less stress on the limbs. The angle of the shoulder is normally followed through in the angle of the pastern and that of the hoof. Straight pasterns and upright hoofs lead to concussion, which in turn leads to leg and hoof ailments and breakdowns.

Nemesian mentions the sloping shoulder when commenting on the Libyan horse (*Cynegetica*): 'No need to repine at their ugly head and ill shapen belly, or at their lack of bridles or because both breeds [Libyan and Moorish] have temper of freedom or because long manes lash sloping shoulders.' Both breeds excelled in endurance, and a prime requisite for an endurance horse is a good shoulder. One reason why the Romans probably preferred a straighter shoulder, apart from the raised action, is because such animals tend to have the more rounded conformation so desirable to the Romans. This made possible the comfortable sitting place, whereas the sloping shoulder is more often found on horses with a more streamlined frame. The heavy musculature is also a trait of the stockier type of riding horse. Sides sloping in is a rather confusing description, but does convey the picture of a fit, athletic horse.

The double back, which many modern riding horses possess when in good to heavy flesh, is merely the raising of the muscle and fat on either side of the spine. For the majority of Roman horsemen, who used a blanket or pad saddle, a horse possessing a well-padded sitting place would offer comfort and some security. The military, from early in the

Principate, and possibly even earlier if they followed the methods of some of the Asiatic and Celtic tribes, had the benefit of a more rigid saddle constructed to offer seat security even without the benefit of stirrups. Considering that hard-worked chargers must frequently have been in rather poor flesh due to living off the land when on extended marches and campaigns, it was essential that the cavalry adopt some form of proper saddle, both to save themselves from the excruciating pain of riding a horse with a bony backbone, and also to prevent fistulous withers occurring as a result of friction on a horse which lacked fatty accretions around the wither. This condition would render the horse temporarily unusable.

A small belly would denote a well-bred, fit animal. A belly distended by bad conformation often goes with a coarse, unwieldy build. 'Stones [testicles] small and alike' are essential in a stallion. Irregular sizing of testicles could indicate less than perfect reproductive organs. Until recently the British Ministry of Agriculture, Fisheries and Food licensed all stallions, and a horse with disparate testicles had to be gelded by law; most breed societies today will not accept such horses for breeding. 'Flanks broad and drawn in' denotes a horse of good proportions that is not grossly overweight. A tail which is long and 'not bristly' suggests good breeding, as well-bred animals invariably have silky-textured mane and tail hairs.

Straight legs are essential in the horse, as any crookedness in their formation puts undue stress on the limbs and joints and predisposes the animal to breaking down. However, the advice that a horse should have small knees is the other major divergence from the modern ideal, as it is now thought preferable to have all joints of adequate size, neither gross nor too small, and that they should be flat at the front, not round. The recommendation to have knees 'not turned in' is sound, for the same reason that straight legs are desirable.

Full and muscular buttocks and thighs give power and thrusting ability to the horse. In the two main areas of hard use – the military and the racetrack – a horse with powerful quarters had a distinct advantage over his leaner, more spindly counterpart. A battle charger needed powerful haunches to give a strong support base to manoeuvres with the forehand raised, either facilitating a rapid turn over the hocks in a tight space, or giving added height and poundage for a downward thrust from *spatha* or lance accompanied by the aggressive use of teeth and forelegs. On the racetrack powerful quarters enabled that extra thrust in a race for the line, and a solid support base in the many turns around the central *spina*. Any weakness in the hindquarters would hasten a breakdown on the track. This weakness is a very common failing with racehorses today, and according to Pelagonius' *Ars Veterinaria* it was all too common in the circus too.

Black hooves are frequently far tougher than the indeterminate greyish-black feet of many chestnuts, or the whitish horn of the white-legged or totally grey horses. Solid bay horses with no white markings always have black hooves and are well known to have far fewer hoof problems than horses of other colours, as are dun horses which also have black legs and hooves. As the Romans lacked iron horseshoes, it would be imperative for their horses, particularly a military horse on the march, to remain soundfooted over extended periods. Gratius Faliscus (*Cyn.* 150–541) says that in a hunter the colour is more important than the breed and advises choosing brown steeds and those whose backs resemble spent embers. He is describing the two colours bay and dun with a dorsal stripe.

In addition to Pelagonius and other writers, Palladius, writing in the middle of the fourth century AD, gives specific recommendations for choosing a stallion, and his advice to look for 'shape, colour, action and beauty' (quoted Morgan 1962, p. 116) is still relevant, although colour is mainly a matter of personal choice. However, in certain pure breeds an undesirable colour or marking could suggest an admixture of non-pure blood. For example, purebred Suffolk Punches are always chestnut, and purebred Arabians are never pie or skewbald. As for the other criteria, a horse can never possess good action if his conformation is bad, and if he answers to Pelagonius' description, with the exceptions mentioned, he would be beautiful in both the accepted Roman sense and in modern eyes as well. Two of the most popular modern breeds fill most of the Roman criteria. One is the good Arabian who, when in prime condition, is a beautiful horse with an extremely ancient lineage and antecedents who had a possible, indeed probable, impact on Roman breeding. The other is the heavier but refined American Quarter Horse, which has been evolved over the past two centuries, but became a fixed type and breed in the middle of this century. He owes much to the English Thoroughbred and through him to the Arabian. Many Quarter Horses mirror Pelagonius' description.

Palladius recommends that broodmares should possess the same attributes as the stallion, and in addition have 'large long barrels and bodies' – a tenet hard to fault as the mare needs ample room for the growing foetus, which at birth in a robust horse of 15 hands (152 cm), the approximate maximum height of most Roman horses, would weigh in the region of 90–100 lb (40–45 kg).

Breeds and their evolution

The majority of breeds take their names from the locality where they were first produced over a sufficient span of time to fix breed characteristics and define performance specialities. With few exceptions this was so in the Roman era. As with the descriptions of the ideal horse there are several lists of breeds with their merits and demerits recorded. Information on specific breeds has come from a very great number of classical sources, in particular the Greek and Roman poets, and some of it is very clear, although not all writers are in agreement as to each breed's merits. Some information is confusing in the way it is presented, but in general we get a fairly good idea of what was on offer. Some writers give one or two references in passing to certain breeds and their utility. Others expound on one type only. In other texts the abilities and characteristics of a breed can be inferred from the context in which they appear. The most revealing as well as the most numerous passages on specific breeds are found in the works of the poet Oppian, the geographer Strabo, the veterinary practitioner Pelagonius, and the writer on veterinary matters Vegetius Publius Renatus. Other writers give valuable titbits.

Modern considerations when purchasing a horse are: its breed, size (particularly if a crossbreed), colour, sex, capabilities and price. Roman descriptions appear altogether more general, but it has to be borne in mind that a prospective Roman breeder or purchaser would be far more familiar with equine characteristics than the average person today because certain classes were required to possess horses (Suetonius, *Aug.* 38). The military needed them, and the racing fraternity, as is still customary but no longer obligatory, inherited their job with a faction (*Codex Theo.* 15.7.7). They were in compulsory service and were bound by their profession (ibid., 14.3.21).

Nearly fifty breeds, and maybe more, are mentioned by name, and can be garnered in clusters or singly from writings spanning nearly a thousand years. Greece has by far the largest number of breeds when assembled into major groups, followed by Italy and the adjacent islands, Spain, Africa, the many countries of Asia Minor, Persia and Parthia, and there were individual breeds in a number of Roman provinces. Breeds that stand out by the frequency with which they appear in ancient sources are the Libyan (or Numidian), the Spanish, Parthian (or Persian), Thracian, Cappadocian and Thessalian.

Libyan

References are made to Libyan, Numidian and African horses interchangeably, so I take them to be the same breed. The Libyan/Numidian

MAIN BREEDS OF HORSE AND BREEDING PROVINCES MENTIONED IN ROMAN AND GREEK LITERATURE

— Frontier
---- Provincial Boundary

2 Map showing the main breeds of horse mentioned in Roman and Greek

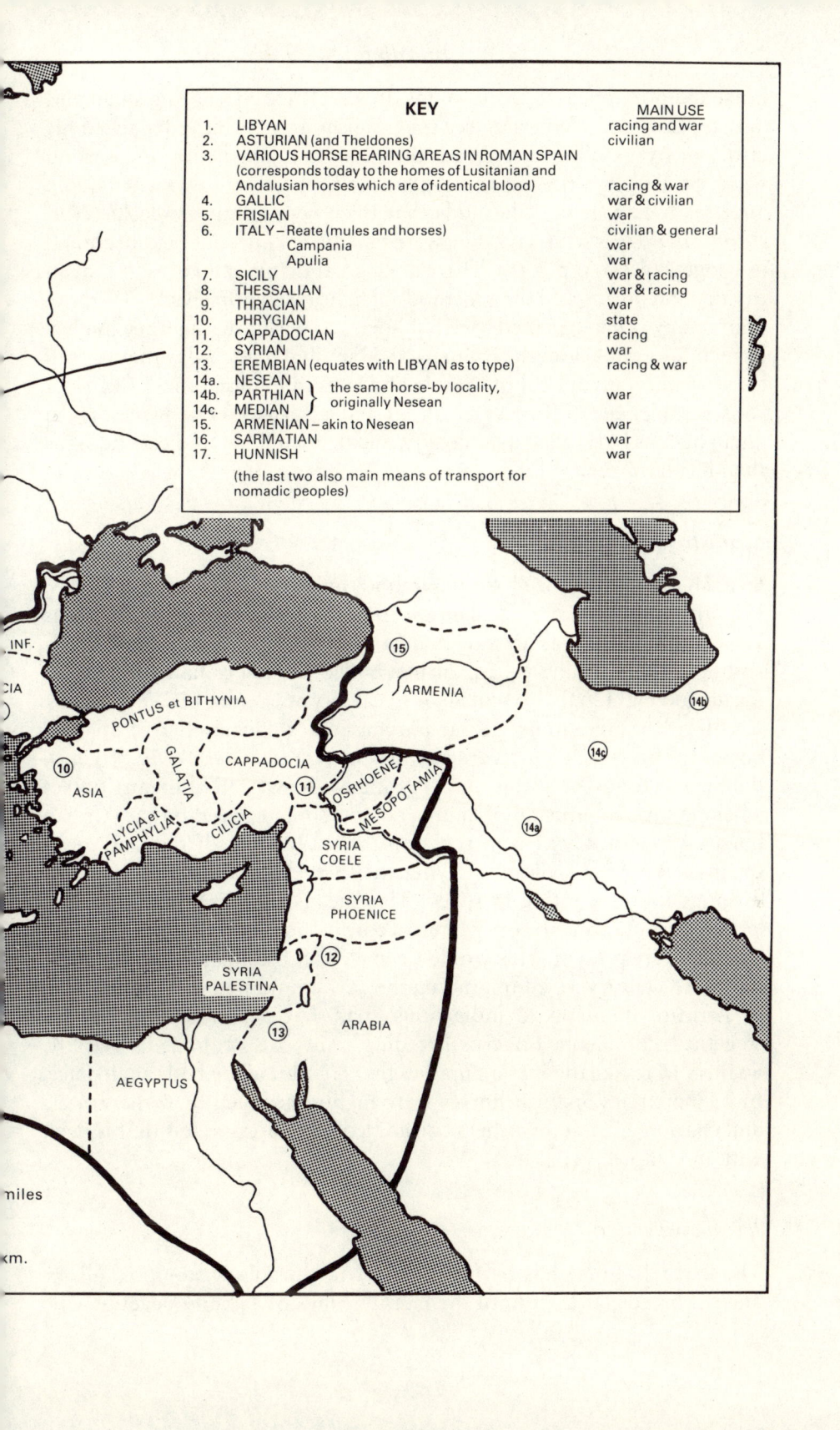

	KEY	MAIN USE
1.	LIBYAN	racing and war
2.	ASTURIAN (and Theldones)	civilian
3.	VARIOUS HORSE REARING AREAS IN ROMAN SPAIN (corresponds today to the homes of Lusitanian and Andalusian horses which are of identical blood)	racing & war
4.	GALLIC	war & civilian
5.	FRISIAN	war
6.	ITALY – Reate (mules and horses)	civilian & general
	Campania	war
	Apulia	war
7.	SICILY	war & racing
8.	THESSALIAN	war & racing
9.	THRACIAN	war
10.	PHRYGIAN	state
11.	CAPPADOCIAN	racing
12.	SYRIAN	war
13.	EREMBIAN (equates with LIBYAN as to type)	racing & war
14a.	NESEAN	
14b.	PARTHIAN } the same horse-by locality, originally Nesean	war
14c.	MEDIAN	
15.	ARMENIAN – akin to Nesean	war
16.	SARMATIAN	war
17.	HUNNISH	war

(the last two also main means of transport for nomadic peoples)

horse did not appeal to the Romans. It was criticized as being small and ugly by Livy and Nemesian (see p. oo), although the latter balanced his criticism by extolling its virtues of endurance, obedience and second wind. Strabo says they were usually small, obedient, and swift (*Geog.* 17.3.7). Aelian agrees and adds that they were lightly made (*de Nat. Anim.* III.2). Apsyrtus says they were like the Spanish but better (quoted in Ridgeway 1905, p. 253). There are a great many references to Libyan cavalry and horses and their methods of fighting on horseback – far more than to any other specified breed of horse, so we know that they made a tremendous impact on the Romans. In Hannibal Barca's day they caused the Romans a great deal of trouble and later in Imperial times formed a considerable part of Roman cavalry. I shall return to the Libyan horse in later pages as he has had a far greater impact in military and genetic areas than has been realized.

Spanish

Spanish horses were well known in both military and racegoing circles. Military records frequently mention Spanish cavalry. For instance, it was known that there was an interchange of cavalry between North Africa and Spain in the days when Carthage held the lower half of Spain in thrall, and Hannibal also had Spanish cavalry at Cannae in 216 BC (Livy, XXIII. 46). Later Julius Caesar purchased a great number of Spanish horses for his war against Vercingetorix in 52 BC (*de Bello Gall.* VII. 55). Publius Vegetius confirms the crossing with African (Libyan) horses when he says an infusion of Spanish blood confers speed on the African horses. Oppian (*Cyn.*) comments on the speed, lack of size and weak spirit of the Spanish horse, saying they were cowardly and in a few furlongs found wanting in speed. This means they were sprinters and lacked stamina, yet a century later, according to Nemesian, courage and stamina were present. This would tie in well with Gallienus' policy in the mid third century AD of upgrading the cavalry mounts with an infusion of African blood on to indigenous Spanish types, and with Publius Vegetius' comments on crossbreeding. Apsyrtus' comment that the Spanish were like the Libyan implies that crossbreeding had taken place. In racing circles Spanish horses were highly esteemed by some writers and charioteers, and by others considered second-class, but that is dealt with in Chapter 15.

Parthian/Persian

The Parthian horse has by far the most favourable write-up of all the ancient breeds, at least until the later writings of Publius Vegetius who admires him as a riding horse but does not place him at the top of the list. Along with the Parthian I include the Nisaean, Median, and the very closely linked Armenian and Cappadocian, as in the height of the Achaemenid era (sixth century BC) the Nisaean horse was paramount of all breeds in Asia Minor. He was bred on the Nisaean Plains of Media. The Armenians and Cappadocians at that time paid yearly tribute of horses to the Persians so that there was an infusion into the Persian breed from both these countries and vice versa – Persian blood on to Armenian and Cappadocian stock. Both these countries were Persian satrapies, so there was a two-way traffic in horseflesh. Only satraps (governors) and their high-ranking staff were entitled to Nisaean horses, which were reserved for the nobility. The Apadana frieze at Persepolis gives a very clear idea of the conformation of these horses – heavy, slightly convex headed, high crested, solid fleshed and well-muscled animals of considerable height, going from the handlers walking alongside them (Hyland 1988, p. 9). These and similar types were much prized by the Romans. Oppian says of the Parthian, 'He is eminently handsome and the only one to stand up to a lion', and of the Nisaean, 'most beautiful, gentle to ride, obedient to the bit, small head'; of the Armenian and Cappadocian horses, 'Swift, spirited, warlike and strong.' Nemesian comments that the Cappadocians have good conformation, are huge and high mettled. Publius Vegetius extols them as high-bred racehorses (*Mulom*. III.VI).

Strabo gives us the information which clinches the connections between the Nisaean, Median, Persian, Parthian and Armenian horses – neighbouring Cappadocia, with similar tribute to Armenia and, according to Nemesian, 'huge' horses, obviously had a mingling of breeds, especially in breeding establishments closer to the borders. On Media, Strabo says:

> In the time of the Persians 50,000 mares belonging to the Kings pastured there. As for the Nesean horses which kings used because the best and largest, some say they came from there [Media], others that they came from Armenia. They are characteristically different in form [i.e. in conformation] as also are the Parthian horses, as they are now called as compared with the Helladic and the other horses in our country [Greece]. (*Geog*. 11.13.7)

He continues on Armenia, saying: 'It is good for horse pasturing and Nesean horses are also bred there and are not inferior to those of Media' (ibid., 11.14.9). A final comment on Armenia from Strabo informs us that the style of horsemanship in Armenia, Thessaly and Media is similar, bringing Thessaly into the sphere of Persian influence (ibid., 11.14.12).

Thracian

As long ago as Homer's day, when most horses were what we would term pony-sized, Thrace was producing 'huge' white horses (*Iliad*). Even taken in context this implies a superior horse in size and stamp. Later, Gratius Faliscus comments that they were 'easy keepers and excellent performers but with ugly necks and thin spine curving along their backs'. This is a picture of the typical ewe-necked, roach-backed horse which is most unattractive. The Thracian animal was, however, very capable (*Cyn.* 150–541). Great importance was placed on the horse in Thracian culture as is shown by the constant depiction of the mounted hero. In Thracian religion the horse stood high, white horses being sacrificed to the sun. Votive tablets from Thrace are the only depictions of Apollo on horseback.

Thrace and Persia had a history of mutual trade (Fol & Marazov 1977, p. 118), and I would hazard that the 'huge' size of Thracian horses was probably a result of commerce with peoples of the Median plains. Stockbreeding has always been the major occupation of nomadic tribes, and in most instances is the reason they are nomadic, other than enforced migration. Such tribes follow the grazing from high to low lands and back again on a seasonal basis. The Persians acquired Nisaean horses as an established breed from the Medes along with their stamping grounds, so they had already exerted genetic influence by crossbreeding on to other stock. There are other links between Thracian and Persian horses: white horses were also sacred to the Persians and on occasion were sacrificed in propitiation to the Strymon (Herodotus, VII. 113). Another Thracian link was with Greece (Fol & Marazov 1977, p. 140), and what more natural quality product to trade in than prized horseflesh. The Mycenean horses were known to Gratius Faliscus as grey (another way of describing white, as grey horses lighten with age), huge and supreme racers.

Thessalian

Thessalian horses, which were considered the best in Greece, were no match for the Persian stock raced against them by Xerxes in an interlude on his march to Greece (Herodotus, VII. 196). Later, disaffected Thessalian cavalry joined Xerxes' army. In the countdown to the final days of Persian dominance in Greece the Persian land forces and cavalry wintered in Thessaly, and the following year at Plataea were routed in one of history's bloodiest battles (Hyland 1988, p. 13). From a breeding point of view the thousands of Nisaean chargers wintering in Thessaly must have given a prodigious boost to the quality of Thessalian stock, particularly influencing the size of future horses. At Plataea the loose mounts of fallen Persian cavalry would have continued the work of upgrading other Greek horses under their new ownership.

From bone evidence it is known that early Greek horses were small (Karageorghis 1967, pp. 154–80). Only parts of Greece have soil fertile enough for quality fodder to be raised. Lack of adequate balanced feeding has a great bearing on the eventual size of any horse, regardless of its inherent genetic potential. Although the introduction of horses with not only greater height but bulkier conformation went a long way to improve many of the breeds in Greece, it was the introduction of medick (lucerne or alfalfa; see Ch. 2) which allowed these genetic impulses to be released. All the breeds of horses that have been given the title 'huge' by the Roman and Greek writers had, somewhere in their pre-Roman history, received a hefty input of Persian/Nisaean blood, and in the passage of centuries the size and individual characteristics of indigenous stock in a particular region became fixed into a specific breed.

Later, when Italy, or Magna Graecia as it was known, came into the Greek sphere of influence, the improved Greek stock had been established for long enough to fix individual types in each region of the Greek mainland. These in turn had a further influence on the upgrading of Italian breeds. The well-known fertile areas of Italy that produced good horses, such as Tuscany, Apulia and Reate, would also have been able to produce fodder of a higher nutritive quality, thus enhancing the growth of their bloodstock. Strabo has a tale to tell of Venetian (Henetian) horses known as the Wolf Breed that by his time had disappeared, but in their heyday had been highly sought after. It bears re-telling in Strabo's words and then unravelling the implications it had on future generations of equines.

> A prominent man among the Heneti gave bail for some hunters for a wolf, agreeing to settle any damage the released wolf did . . . and the wolf when set free drove off a considerable herd of unbranded horses and brought them to the steading of the man who was fond of giving bail; and the man who received the favour not only branded all the mares with a wolf, but also called them the wolf breed, mares exceptional for speed rather than beauty; and his successors kept not only the brand but also the name for the breed of the horses and made it a custom not to sell a mare to outsiders, in order that the genuine breed might remain in their family alone, since horses of that breed had become famous. But at the present time, as I was saying, the practice of horse breeding has wholly disappeared. (*Geog.* 5.1.9)

Strabo also has this to say on the Venetian horses of Cispadana:

3 Map showing the main areas from which Roman cavalry was drawn

KEY

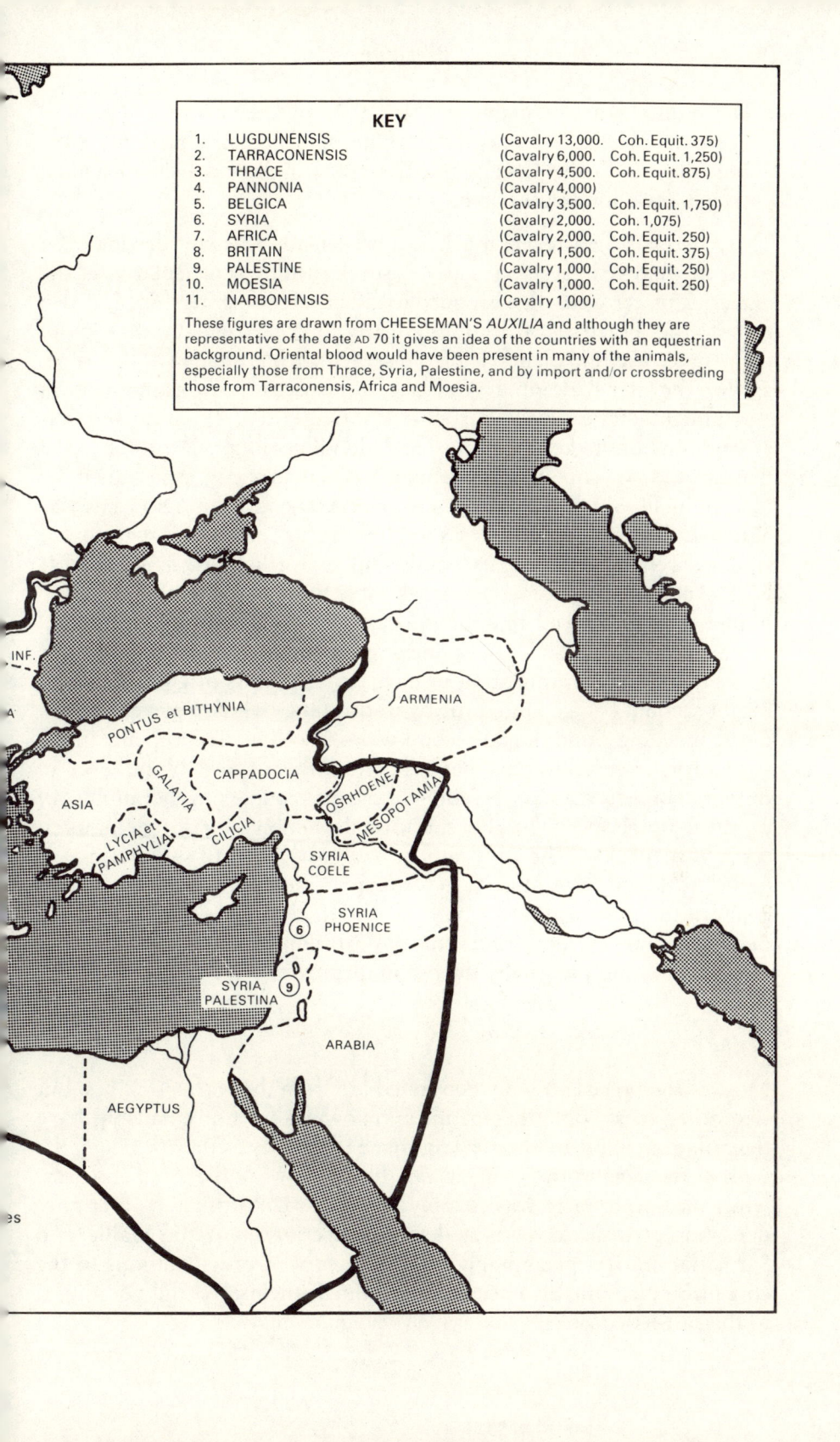

1.	LUGDUNENSIS	(Cavalry 13,000.	Coh. Equit. 375)
2.	TARRACONENSIS	(Cavalry 6,000.	Coh. Equit. 1,250)
3.	THRACE	(Cavalry 4,500.	Coh. Equit. 875)
4.	PANNONIA	(Cavalry 4,000)	
5.	BELGICA	(Cavalry 3,500.	Coh. Equit. 1,750)
6.	SYRIA	(Cavalry 2,000.	Coh. 1,075)
7.	AFRICA	(Cavalry 2,000.	Coh. Equit. 250)
8.	BRITAIN	(Cavalry 1,500.	Coh. Equit. 375)
9.	PALESTINE	(Cavalry 1,000.	Coh. Equit. 250)
10.	MOESIA	(Cavalry 1,000.	Coh. Equit. 250)
11.	NARBONENSIS	(Cavalry 1,000)	

These figures are drawn from CHEESEMAN'S *AUXILIA* and although they are representative of the date AD 70 it gives an idea of the countries with an equestrian background. Oriental blood would have been present in many of the animals, especially those from Thrace, Syria, Palestine, and by import and/or crossbreeding those from Tarraconensis, Africa and Moesia.

Dionysus, Tyrant of Sicily [430–367 BC], collected his stud of prize horses from here. Not only did the fame of Henetian [Venetian] foal breeding reach the Greeks but the breed itself was held in high esteem for a long time. (ibid., 5.1.4)

These two passages reveal much to a horseman. The wolf driving off a band of mares suggests an early case of rustling, particularly as the maverick mares were then branded to indicate legal ownership, and also proves the practice of branding early on. It suggests that more importance was laid on descent from the female line, at least at that time, as with the later Bedouin in Arabia, possibly because the dam is certain and it might not be certain, particularly if range bred, who is the sire. It is an early attempt to keep the breed and bloodlines intact. Refusal to sell a mare would prevent outsiders gaining access to progeny, especially if the male animals which were sold were gelded. The fact that Dionysus was able to collect his stud of horses implies that at some point mares were sold as well as stallions, as 'stud' implies further breeding whereas 'stable' might not. The fact that Strabo says 'Greeks' rather than 'Greece' implies that the breed may have been renowned only in the Italian/Magna Graecian sphere, not on the Greek mainland. One reason for the breed dying out, or appearing to have done so in its original Venetian locality, could be accounted for by in-breeding (which I prefer to term incest breeding) if no outside blood was allowed in. To keep any breed strong it is essential to have periodic outcrosses of fresh blood, even in purebred breeding. Incest breeding in the first couple of generations *can* produce superb specimens, but the normal reaction is for degeneration to set in very quickly. The bad traits have a nasty habit of smothering the good. Although occasional sales of mares – accepting that the Sicilian deal was not the only one – would allow diffusion of the pure bloodlines on to other horses, imparting some of the original 'wolf breed' qualities, this breed would eventually die out in its purest form.

Gallic

Most of the breeds already mentioned are from the warmer climes, but two other areas, or rather peoples, renowned for horsemanship have their place in the Roman breed jigsaw, particularly as they provided the bulk of the cavalry in auxiliary *alae* from Early Empire days onwards, when the cavalry arm was steadily increased. Unfortunately, literature does not provide us with a detailed description of the Gallic and Sarmatian horses, presumably because they were fringe nations to the core of Empire, and also because the animals themselves did not appeal to the aesthetic tastes of the writers on equine matters.

What we do know of the Gauls is that they were better as cavalry than as infantry. Reputedly the best cavalry force the Romans had came from Gaul (Strabo, *Geog.* 4.4.2). In *de Bello Gallico*, Caesar makes frequent reference to levies of horses from different tribes. He also made heavy use of cavalry, often sending it out in advance both in large contingents and small groups. His cavalry was composed in the main of the native mounts which various auxiliaries brought with them, of Spanish and Italian horses specially purchased, and of German horses for his special shock force of German cavalry. We learn a little of the Gallic and German horses from Caesar (*de Bello Gall.*, IV. 1–2), for he tells us that the Gauls take delight in importing draught horses at great expense, but the Germans make do with their homebred animals, which were inferior and ill-favoured but which through regular exercise were toughened into top endurance horses. Obviously for the Romans, who were not gifted horsemen as a rule, the visual aspect of a horse's conformation overrode its innate ability to perform.

As early as 170 BC Cincibulus, a king of the Gauls, was intent on improving the Gallic horse. On an embassy to Rome to complain of Roman depredations in his Alpine territory he was appeased by rich presents of gold and silver and two caparisoned horses (*equi phalerati*). Striking while the diplomatic iron was hot his two brothers also requested the right to buy ten horses each and export them from Italy (Livy, XCIII.5; Ridgeway 1905, p. 101). This clearly indicates that Italian horses had reached a very high standing in Roman life, that it was illegal to export without permission, and that the Romans were well aware of the implications of allowing neighbouring peoples to upgrade their own stock for cavalry use. The information in this passage plus that Caesar gives sheds considerable light on Gallic breeds. In his exhaustive survey of the origins of various breeds Prof. Ridgeway emphasizes the small indigenous Gallic types. Crossed with the imported Italian horses which already had considerable height through earlier infusions of outside blood, it would not take long using 20 stallions to upgrade the indigenous stock. Granted the passage does not say 'stallions' but 'horses', but the Latin texts when mentioning equines always indicate male or female except in a collective sense, and the practice when upgrading any breed is to buy in outside male blood. A mature stallion of four years of age would be quite capable of covering at least 20 mares with a reasonable rate of conception each year, and if he ran with a herd would have the chance of considerably more foals each year. The horse is not the most fertile of animals, with a conception rate of approximately 60 per cent, but this is an average which allows for the infertile stallion, the non-cycling mare, and the mare who does not carry to term. With good stud management many stallions have a near 100 per cent fertility rate, and it is almost always the mare's fault if conception does not occur when she is put to a known fertile stallion.

Regarding Caesar's comment on the Gauls importing draught horses, this does not mean the modern type of draught horse which weighs in the region of one ton, but the smaller types which we would now term ride and drive – a well set up, very chunky horse with plenty of substance about him. To a people possessing small, pony-type horses the Roman ideal would have seemed a giant.

Sarmatian

The literary description we have of the nomadic Sarmatians' horses stops after telling us they were small, swift, and hard to manage, and that males were gelded (Strabo, *Geog.* 7.4.8). Pliny the Elder enlarges a little, saying that the Sarmatians rode mares and travelled 150 miles (240 km) a day (*Nat. Hist.* VIII). Pliny of course exaggerated, but he was on the right track about distances covered, as the Mongols in later centuries could cover 80 miles (130 km) a day on an indefinite basis if necessary. Fortunately, archaeology has provided us with several clues about the ancestors of the Sarmatian horses of Strabo's era, which are not as straightforward as his description of them as small, quick and wilful.

The Pazyryk burials of the fifth century BC are one of a number of finds attributable to early Sarmatian, proto-Sarmatian and neighbouring peoples (Sulimirski 1970, p. 23). The barrows at Pazyryk have yielded the largest number of horse carcasses so far found. There are also skeletons. Both groups are buried with their masters to assist him in the afterlife. Additional grave goods include imports from China and Persia, suggesting trade on a regular basis. The most remarkable thing about the horses, apart from the state of preservation of the carcasses, is the size of some of them, with many reaching 15 hands (152 cm) and more (Rudenko 1970, p. 56). The translation of this Russian work states that they were 'thoroughbreds, powerful cantering animals and typical riding horses'. In essence this means that they were of powerful physique allied with considerable size, quality and body mass. The use of the word 'thoroughbred' must be discounted in this context as it is misleading, today's meaning being a specific breed not then in existence. Taken in conjunction with the Persian imports it would seem that trade could also have supplied the typical horse of Achaemenid times. A later tenuous but probable link is the known importation of Ferghana horses in 102 BC by the Han Dynasty Emperor Wu Ti, who wished to upgrade his small Chinese horses to combat the superior cavalry of the Huns (Hyland 1988, p. 22). The Altai people also had trade links with China, whose merchants would have known of the provenance of the superior Altai horses. By the time of Wu Ti the Sarmatians of the Altai had moved out, taking their herds with them.

The colouring of the carcasses in the Pazyryk burials was mostly chestnut, brown, sometimes with golden hues (which suggests to me a link with the horse known today as one of Russia's toughest horses, the Akhal-Teke), and less commonly bay. White legs and pale hooves were absent. A Russian authority on horses, V. O. Vitt, explains this as a way of avoiding a brightly coloured hoof which easily breaks. In essence this is close to the truth. As we saw when discussing the Roman and Greek descriptions, dark hooves on brown, bay and dark chestnut horses have tougher and more resilient horn, less susceptible to cracks and abrasion than lighter hooves.

Rudenko reports that both the larger horses and the smaller ponies buried at Pazyryk were without exception gelded. He also says that the number of high quality horses in the chieftains' tombs was so large that it must have been an established practice to breed horses of this stamp. This implies that there was a sufficiency of good, sizeable stock in the early Sarmatian herds, and even if the genetic pool had become depleted by Strabo's time not all the Sarmatian mounts would have been small. As ancient writers rarely tell us what they mean by small, moderate or large, their statements can only be assessed with reference to other breeds known to the writer. Strabo comments on the Parthian horses as being the largest. We do not know the exact height of Parthian horses but from the bone evidence in the early Pazyryk burials, where some Sarmatian horses were in excess of 15 hands (152 cm), the Parthian horses must have been between 15 and 16 hands (152–163 cm) in order to be described as 'large'. They may have grown even taller due to the good grazing on the Median plains. A 14 to 14.2 hand (142–147 cm) animal would seem small to Strabo in comparison, particularly if he was in lean condition from foraging for himself while constantly on the move – a 14 hand animal in heavy flesh from good stable care and high feeding will seem large in comparison with the same sized but lean animal of nomadic peoples. A certain size would have been required to carry the rider plus the typical Sarmatian war gear of body armour, plus its own protective trappings for which we have pictorial though somewhat exaggerated proof in Trajan's Column. Since Tacitus tells us that the protective body armour worn by Sarmatians was restricted to the chieftains and nobles (*Hist.* 1.79), and presumably their horses, we can assume that their horses would need to be bigger than those carrying unarmoured warriors. This would tie in with the two sizes of animal found in the Pazyryk burials, and also gives a hint that the Persian habit of the best stock going to the nobility carried through to the Sarmatians.

The modern Arab

In 125 BC, when the Romans were having trouble with the Gauls around Arles, it was a Numidian cavalry force attached to the legions that bailed them out. Fulvius Flaccus, the Roman commander, proceeded to occupy the territory and the modern Camargue pony is said by French writers to have descended from indigenous stock crossed with the Numidian horses of the auxiliaries. Later, when the Roman presence was augmented by the establishment of the colony of Arles, further upgrading of stock was achieved by infusions of blood from the accompanying Roman horses (Ridgeway 1905).

Thus we come full circle, back to the Libyan/Numidian horse that has more specific references accorded it in connection with the early military sphere than any other breed. Earlier I said that it also had a tremendous genetic influence on breeding in general over a very long period. Prof. Ridgeway (1905, p. 245) points out that Egypt acquired her horses from Libya in Muhammad's time. Many centuries earlier Sophocles commented on the two Libyan teams in the races at Delphi (*Electra*, 699ff), and Herodotus tells us that Libyan chariot horses were in Xerxes' forces in his march to Greece (*Hist.* 7.88). From the descriptions of both looks and performance given by several writers, the Libyan horse is very closely akin to the Arabian, which today is thought by many to be the most beautiful and the toughest horse of all. The characteristics disliked by the Romans – the sloping shoulder, the ugly head, the gaunt belly – were those points which did not accord with their ideal of a straight-shouldered rather more substantially fleshed horse. The Romans preferred the straighter or slightly convex head of the Parthian/Persian horse (which can be seen on many of the quality sculptures of the Roman era) to the concave skull of high caste Arabians, which today is considered a hallmark of beauty.

There is no agreement as to where the Arabian sprang from. Purists like to say that he rose phoenix-like from the deserts of Arabia. Other more sensible theories admit to mystery, and although discounted by modernists I find Prof. Ridgeway's theory of the Libyan ancestry for the modern Arabian very attractive. I believe that movement was to Arabia, rather than from Arabia.

There are various indications that the Arabian horse, though going by other names, had already developed by Roman times. However, purists say he was not yet a recognized breed in the early centuries of the Christian era. Some quote Strabo as saying there were no horses in Arabia then, but this is only part of his reference. He does say that Nabatea had no horses (*Geog.* 16.4.18), yet in the same passage he says Nabatea had mules! Mules are of course the offspring of donkeys and horses. On Arabia, Strabo gives a very confused tale of horses there being driven out by a lion to an offshore island and from there being driven to Persia across the Red Sea (ibid., 16.4.20). Obviously there was a semi-historical legend of horses in Arabia at one time. In 1983, fossilized remains of horses were found in eastern Arabia, but news of this discovery only reached the horsebreeding section of Arabian horse-owners a few years later (*AHS News* 1987). Further research is being undertaken by P. J. Whybrow, head of the Palaeontology Department of the British Museum.

Far clearer than Strabo is Oppian's statement (*Cyn.*) that Aristarchus of Samothrace (217/215–145/143 BC), head of the Alexandrian Library and founder of scientific scholarship, mentions the Erembian horse. Oppian himself, in another section of his *Cynegetica* on types of animal hunted, mentions the Erembian lion of Arabia Felix which would have been hunted from horseback.

To me the most fascinating nugget and the one that ties the ancient Libyan horse in with the horse we know today as the Arabian was found in Newstead, Scotland. In his book *A Roman Frontier Post and its People*, James Curle records that:

> the auxiliaries . . . had 14 hands horses as fine in head and limbs as modern high-caste Arabs. The skull of one of these slender-limbed 14 hands horses is almost identical with the skull of an Arab mare (Jerboa, by Maidan out of Jerud) in the British Museum. That they closely agree is especially suggested by the frontal index. (Curle 1911, p. 368)

The measurements given by Curle are as follows:

Length in mm   Jerboa 368   Newstead 372
Width in mm   Jerboa 205   Newstead 201

The implication is that the heads in Roman times were as fine as now. Skulls and limb bones from Newstead show:

(1) broad-browed big-boned ponies of the 'forest' or *robustus* type from 11 to 12.2 hands;
(2) slender-limbed ponies of the 'Celtic' variety, of the 'plateau' type, from 11.2 to 12.2 hands, and 14 hands ponies of the 'Libyan' variety of the 'plateau' type built on the lines of the finer kinds of desert Arabs. (ibid.)

There were also the bones of some horses of nearly 15 hands.

The analysis of the bone finds of all animals found at Newstead was conducted by Prof. James Ewart, F.R.S., Regius Professor of Natural History in the University of Edinburgh. James Curle's book was published five years after Prof. Ridgeway's theory of the Libyan ancestry of the Arabian horse was put forward.

In Flavian/Trajanic times an *ala* of African cavalry was sent from Africa to the Rhine (Holder 1980). Although the ethnic composition of the *alae* changed, by the time of Trajan an *ala* travelling from Africa, whatever its human makeup, would be mounted on horses indigenous to the area in which it was raised and stationed. Hence a large number of horses of Libyan blood would be coming into the European sphere, to add to the genetic pool already present from earlier Numidian cavalry in the Roman army. If troops in those days were anything like the youth of today, some extra cash would be very attractive to those who rode stallions and could hire their services out, albeit on the quiet. Also, retired cavalry horses capable of breeding would almost certainly be used in a civilian capacity to raise remounts, if not by the military themselves. Another African *ala* in Europe was the *Ala Flavia Afrorum* (Holder 1980).

The reason I have devoted so much space to one breed of horse, the Libyan/Arabian, is that the Arabian has certain qualities inherent in its makeup that would have been very beneficial to Roman stock. Though some may have disliked their looks, the military recognized the Numidians and by extension their mounts as superior. Libyan horses were frequently crossed on to Spanish to improve the latter. The Arabian, though he is a smallish horse himself, even today, has a very prepotent trait. For instance, when an Arabian is crossed on another horse of a different breed but similar in size to himself, the offspring is frequently very much larger than either parent. Prof. James Ewart ascertained this as long ago as 1905 and from my own experience I have found this to be corroborated. (My stallion Nizzolan, a 15 hand (152 cm) purebred Arabian, has almost without exception produced stock larger than either parent when put to non-Arab mares the same height as himself. The resulting offspring range from 2½ to 6 in. (6–15 cm) taller at the withers. When crossed on to ponies the resulting foal matures at approximately 6 in. (15 cm) taller than its dam. When bred to a purebred Arabian mare the offspring retains the normal Arabian height range of its parents. On checking with other Arabian owners I have found similar cases.) In Roman days this one factor must have made the Libyan horse a very attractive breeding prospect, particularly when size to carry an armoured cavalryman was essential, and quality was also desirable.

The other very favourable trait of Libyan/Arabian horses is their virtual indestructibility. Throughout the centuries they have become known as the toughest, most enduring horses in existence, capable of carrying great weight in proportion to their size, and remaining healthy on relatively little fodder in comparison to other breeds. They are also very fast, which is probably why the African horse was so highly favoured on the Roman racetrack. Their speed is not that of a sprinter, but the sustained momentum of the best stayers.

Where the Libyans originally got their horses from is another matter. Bones of domesticated horses are found in the Middle East from 2000 BC onwards, and martial conquest and the peregrinations of nomadic herdsmen have both been responsible for the horse spreading throughout the ancient world. Breed and type fixation happens when a specific nation capitalizes on such an acquisition and incorporates selective breeding for desirable qualities. The next step is for the result of this selection to become known by the name of the people who implemented the intensive breeding programme.

Hunnish

Before closing the survey of breeds available to the Roman horseman, especially the military man, one other conformation description must be mentioned. It comes from the closing years of the Roman Empire when the pressure from barbarian tribes was foreshadowing the Empire's downfall. It is given to us by Publius Vegetius (*Mulom.* III. VI), who places the Hunnish horse at the top of his list for use in war. He follows this with the Thuringian, Burgundian and Frisian. He then goes on and lists saddle and racehorses in a similar way to the earlier writers, but his description of the Hunnish horse is a true nightmare of an equine, suitable to Don Quixote's Rosinante, or the rouncy in Albrecht Dürer's superb portrait of a *Landsknecht* and his mount drawn in 1499. But in spite of its ugliness the Hunnish horse had other qualities that made it eminently suitable for war:

> The Hunnish horses are large, roman nosed, with staring eyes, a narrow nose, broad jaw, strong and stiff neck. The mane hangs down to the knees and he has long sides [i.e. he is long bodied], a bent back [i.e. roach backed], thick tail, strong cannons, small base [i.e. stands over a little ground, which as he had already been described as long bodied means he was narrow], dinner plate hooves, hollow flanks. The whole body is angular, with skinny haunches, scrawny muscles. In length it is great, in height of great stature, with a gaunt belly, big bones. He is thin and his beauty is distinguished by being deformed [i.e. he is ugly]. (ibid.)

On the credit side, 'his temperament is moderate [i.e. equable], calm, he endures wounds, is teachable, up to work, and withstands cold and hunger' (ibid.).

The sum gives a very real picture of a passive, spiritless creature that is undernourished and ill kempt. But from a trooper's point of view it was quite capable of carrying him from A to B, and was probably too dejected to put up a struggle. Some horses lack spirit and perform like automatons, and the intelligence of others is so limited that they would not recognize danger until it hit them. They were definitely not the type the Romans admired. They are also the most unrewarding types to work with – insensitive and with not much between the ears but bone. The narrow frontal plane of the Hunnish horse's face allows little area for the brain, unlike the broad brow of the Libyan/Arabian, and it is a proven fact that the Arabian, renowned for his intelligence, does have a larger brain than other equines.

Conclusion

The Romans had an extremely wide choice for their equine companions. Some breeds were more suited to the track, others, particularly those denoted as large, found their metier in the field of war. On the whole the Romans did not have the same attitude to purity of breed prevalent amongst serious breeders today. They bred for the job and, particularly in the military, state studs crossbred on a very large scale to produce the desired goods. Certain breeds excelled as racehorses and they also travelled from course to course. Both colts and fillies were used as racehorses, and it is clear from charioteer inscriptions that the racing stallion was used at stud during his racing career. Once he had finished his track life he retired to stud in the country (Dio, LXXIV. 4.1–4).

The peripatetic nature of most horses' work meant that there were constant infusions of new blood, and a continuous mixing of breeds, throughout the Roman era. One way to start a new breed (and a fairly common way, especially in America), is for certain individuals that excel in one particular, usually a specific mode of performance, to be bred from and the blood kept fairly concentrated over a period long enough to establish the type. In the process the animals that will be used to impart new blood are not always the very top performers, but the stock that passes the required characteristics on in sufficient strength to fix them. The racing field has many examples of this, where one animal was so prepotent that he sired mirror images of himself, and in performance passed on his own speciality. Other cases exist where a moderate individual sires exceptional stock in sufficient number to make his genes highly desirable. A horse has a very long breeding life and if he proves himself at stud early enough several generations of top-rate performers will be recognized and his gene bank and that of his offspring can be capitalized on. Eventually outside blood is desirable to keep the breed strong.

The Romans, though not known as eminent horsemen, did make the best use of what was available and in their expanding cavalry ranks had to resort to outcrossing. For the track they set up state studs where they kept the top breeds. We know from one charioteer inscription that many breeds were used (see Ch. 15), but by the Late Empire it was found necessary to pass laws concerning the future of ex-racehorses, the best from Cappadocia being retired with full fodder, and the inferior from Spain being sold off (*Codex Theo.*, 10.15.10.1).

2
Stud management and practices

Principles of breeding

Stud management includes all the practices that govern rearing, maintenance, general care and basic education of horses in the Roman world. The two main sources for stud practices and management are Varro and Columella, with Cato the Elder supplying a little information, although he was more concerned with cattle and slaves and, being the hard man he was, getting the most out of both. He would not have approved of pensioning off the Cappadocian racehorses, but would rather have been in favour of the treatment the Spanish ones received. For more specialized knowledge, Virgil gives us some very important information in Book III of his *Georgics* which, in the author's opinion, is far more salient than the dry facts of the gentleman farmer's almanacs. Many of Virgil's recommendations find positive echoes in today's selection and training of horses, and quite a few important comments relating to cavalry confirm research and answer some questions about the horses used. He also gives a very clear and frightening description of rabies in horses (ibid., III. 497–524).

At the beginning of the Empire, Columella wrote that there were three classes of horses being raised: the first or 'Noble Horse' was for the circus and the Sacred Games; the second class was for breeding mules, whose price matched those of the Noble Horse; the third class was of common horses which produced ordinary stock. Three centuries later, with the almost incessant wars and external pressures from barbarian hordes threatening on many fronts, the main concern of the state was to breed enough mounts for the cavalry, and to augment the supply by compulsory purchase and taxation. From Augustan days to the third and fourth centuries the cavalry had steadily grown from a supporting force to constituting approximately one-third of the army's strength. In Diocletian's time there were 70 *vexillations* of approximately 500 men each in the eastern sector alone (Jones 1964). That is a large number of horses, considering a possible 25 per cent turnover each year.

Stallions used for producing ordinary horses ran out with their mares. No specific covering season was kept to, but it can be assumed that it was generally around mid-spring, with the bulk of coverings taking place over a two-month span. Varro says that a mare carries her foal until the tenth day of the twelfth month (*de Re Rust.*), which is absolutely correct! A mare normally carries her foal just a few days short of eleven and a half months, with successful foaling possible a couple of weeks either side of this (the longest I have had a mare carry her foal is 12 months, 4 days). The two-month span allows for two heat cycles (at three-weekly intervals) should the mare not conceive on what is known as the foaling heat, which occurs approximately a week to ten days after foaling. This is not the optimum time for conception, although it used to be so considered. The Noble mares, and one must assume also the ones used for raising mules, were covered at the spring equinox (21 March) according to Columella, and between the spring equinox and the summer solstice according to Varro. Noble mares were only expected to produce one foal every two years. Some breeders still follow this practice, and some mares when lactating will not conceive another foal anyway. As we have seen, the horse is not the most fertile of animals, with an average success rate of 60 per cent. So in Roman times, without modern drugs to help achieve maximum productivity, a foal must have been a very expensive commodity.

Virgil describes how mares in oestrus seek out a stallion, and even gives the visual sign of a vaginal discharge to pinpoint the exact time to cover the mare (*Georgics* III.271–82). He relates a story which Varro and the Elder Pliny also tell about some mares, particularly those in Roman Spain (Olisipo, or modern Lisbon in Portugal), being impregnated by the west wind. This is not as far-fetched as it seems if explained in logical terms. Favonius, the west wind, begins to blow about six weeks before the spring equinox, which is the time of lengthening days and increasing warmth. Length of day and sunlight have a direct bearing on a mare's coming into oestrus for the first time each year. Another point worth mentioning is that horses always turn their tails to the wind if turned loose to graze and the wind is strong. Thus the story is obviously an easy way to explain something not fully understood, particularly if horses ranged freely and coverings were unmonitored. Mares in oestrus going crazy is also not so far fetched, as some mares are particularly difficult, and often spiteful with heels at pasture, when just coming into and just going out of season.

Columella says that a stallion denied mares also goes crazy. This behaviour can be explained by the increase of certain hormones during the covering season. With some stallions I have handled I have noticed a change for the worse in their amenability as spring approaches. It used to be considered, and still is in some areas, that stallions are difficult to handle, and this is true of some. Under certain conditions when correct discipline and firm handling is absent they can be decidedly dangerous, particularly when covering mares and if the groom is ignorant or negligent. Varro recommends covering the mare twice a day and in hand (i.e. a groom handling the stallion and another the mare), as the Roman idea was that repeated coverings were necessary. Even today this is believed by some who do not understand the mare's cycle.

Lucilius, as well as his friend Atticus, kept one stallion to every ten mares; he says, 'which I keep for breeding as Atticus does one [stallion] to every ten mares'. This implies it to be fairly general practice for breeding better quality stock, and also suggests that those colts not used for breeding – i.e. the inferior stock – were gelded. This is backed up by one of the few remarks on horses made by Cato the Elder (*de Agri Cult.*), who says that a man renting out his land for winter pasture can keep two oxen and one gelding of his own on it. Columella gives the stallion a much larger band of mares – between 15 and 20. This would approach modern practice more closely, if the stallion owner is lucky enough to attract this number for his horse. To help minimize the stallion frustrations with mares not yet receptive, a teaser was used (Columella, *de Re Rust.*). This is still the practice on large studs, particularly Thoroughbred establishments. A less valuable stallion, frequently a pony, is used to visit the mares and establish, through their behaviour, whether or not they are ready to be covered. The teaser may occasionally be allowed his own pony mare so he does not go completely beserk.

Columella says a stallion can cover between the ages of 3 and 20. Varro is silent on the subject. Pliny the Elder (*Nat. Hist.* VIII), as usual, has some facts mixed up with his myths, saying that a stallion goes on covering until he is 33 and does not retire to stud until he is 20; and that one at Opais covered a mare at the age of 40, albeit needing a bit of help in mounting. He comments that few animals are as infertile as the horse, and that a stallion cannot serve 15 times a year. Also he says that mares foal yearly up to the age of 40. Today a very few exceptional stallions may go on covering an extremely limited number of mares in their late twenties, and it is possible (just) that a covering could be effected at 33 if the horse were lucky to live so long, but normally at that age he would be sterile and find it impossible to mount the mare. Not retiring to stud until aged 20 did not necessarily mean his stud life started then, as active racing stallions had progeny racing during their own track life. Pelagonius (among others) says that many racehorses stay on the track until they are 20, often still being very capable (*Ars Vet. Int.* 1). Pliny's information on mares is very inaccurate. Columella and Varro are nearer the mark, Columella saying that covering starts at two and they are no good after age ten because foals of old mares are slow and lazy. Varro recommends three years as the earliest age to cover and ten as the sensible upper age limit. No doubt this was exceeded in many cases, but it does give us a broad outline of the breeding life of both stallions and mares. I have found that older mares, particularly those who have bred irregularly or are still maiden at 14, are very hard to get in foal (my veterinary surgeon confirms that without modern hormone and fertility drugs *many* mares' breeding life would be finished by 14 years of age). Stallions remain potent longer. Potency does diminish with age but a stallion should remain fertile into his twenties. Virgil (*Georgics* III) is far more accurate concerning aspects of breeding. He says that a stallion should be pensioned off when old and that in old age he is impotent (ibid., 96–7); that in war he maintains his spirit but performance flags (ibid., 99). He also recommends that the prime breeding criteria should be the parents' performance record (ibid., 101).

Genetics as such were not understood, but obviously the principles were. Oppian in his *Cynegetica* tells us that when a 'coloured' foal is desired the stallion should be decked in 'false colours' so that the mare is influenced into producing a 'coloured' foal of the desired coat pattern. He also gives much the same advice for breeding variegated pigeons. Varro, in an isolated statement in the *Lingua Latina*, says: 'as we say that some horses of the same appearance are not alike, if by breed they are different on the sire's side'. In other words, in a breeding context, different animals which may look alike have inherited different characteristics from the breed of their sire. This implies that in Varro's day a horse's breeding was usually identified from the sire's pedigree more than from the mare's unlike the female descent of Strabo's 'Wolf Breed' (see Ch. 1). This is also the case today. It is normal to upgrade a breed by introduction of new blood through the stallion, using good blood on the 'topside'. Obviously one stallion can influence a breed much more quickly than a single mare can.

When man interferes with nature in the breeding of any animal species, and particularly the horse because of his many desirable qualities, he tends to choose for his foundation stock and for subsequent infusions of new blood animals that would not necessarily be successful breeders in the wild. There the stallion that succeeds is the most aggressive, regardless of other qualities. Under controlled conditions a temperament that will make him readily subservient to man is a prime requisite. In Roman times, when animals tended to be smaller, size would also have been a very important factor and the choicest animals would be considered those approximating to the Roman ideal conformation, coupled with size and an amenable disposition.

Prior to and during the breeding season stallions were fed a high grain ration and first-rate fodder (Virgil, *Georgics* II.124–8), whereas broodmares were kept on the lean side (ibid., III.129) on the very reasonable assumption that conception in fat mares was difficult. Stallions naturally need a higher ration in active breeding months, particularly when coping with two or three coverings a day, and in the Roman tradition twice every day during the week-long heat cycle for each mare. On a stud of any size, and even with a limited number of up to 20 mares, there would be several mares coming into season at the same time. Keeping mares lean to aid conception is good advice today, as overweight mares are frequently difficult to settle in foal. Virgil also implies that the mares are worked until the latter stages of pregnancy, either ridden or yoked in harness (ibid., III.139–40). Varro recommends that the mare do no work. Today there are conflicting opinions. Some studs do not work their broodmares at all, but that is usually where the only activity on the stud is raising stock. Others more sensibly keep the mares in moderate work until the latter stages of pregnancy. This is usually done where the mare is normally a riding horse but is also used to rear the occasional foal; or where, as in rural areas of continental Europe, horses are used in general agricultural work, foal and quickly return to work while in foal for the following year. The current foal runs alongside the dam while she is working. In the Roman world the method practised must also have been according to the stud owner's financial standing – large estate, large herd and wealthy owner, or small-time farmer with a few mares he also worked.

Varro quotes one tale he calls 'incredible' (*de Re Rust.*). It is worth remembering because it appears in Oppian and other sources as well, and so must have been Roman farming folklore. It concerns the mare put to her own son, and is the Romans' way of putting across their horror at incest breeding, whether animal or human. A stallion when presented in the covering yard was expected to cover his own dam. He refused, and so the groom covered his head and the covering was effected. On removing the blindfold and seeing what he had done he savaged his groom. An eminent equine veterinary practitioner specializing in stud work confirms that left to their own devices in the wild horses rarely practise incest breeding (John Broughton MRCVS, pers. comm.). It is occasionally used for various reasons in stud work. As for tricking the horse by blindfolding, it is possible to trick a stallion that refuses to cover a particular mare (and this does happen) by substituting another and removing her in just in time so that the appropriate one can be covered (S. A. Mardon, pers. comm.). Occasionally stallions are so violent that they have killed their handlers, even in modern times (Joan Fox, pers. comm.). Generally, though, a stallion fairly and sympathetically handled is a delight to work with and very honest.

Mule breeding was an enormous farming industry in Roman times. Not much information is available to us, as the mule was a humble creature in comparison with the horse who held a very exalted position in the Roman mind. The best and largest mules in Italy were bred in Reate (Varro, *de Re Rust.*), and on more than one occasion Varro said that mule foals were sold 'even to the Arcadians' who were considered to have the best mules in the Peloponnese, and by inference these were usually better than Reatine. To achieve size in the offspring it was better to put a jack donkey on to a horse mare, the resulting foal being termed a *mulus*, while a horse stallion on to a donkey mare resulted in a *hinnus*. As we are told almost nothing more about mules we can only speculate as to their real size, but the jacks can hardly have been of the familiar small 'burro' type, especially as Reatine mules were considered larger. Centuries of poverty rations and overwork no doubt stunted the poor donkey. Once good stud management was introduced into herds of breeding jacks and horse mares, or donkey mares and horse stallions, genetic potential would begin an upwards trend again. (In America today some breeds of draught mules are huge, standing 16 hands (163 cm) and more with massive bulk. Others are about 15 hands (152 cm). The jackass used to cover mares is a large 15 hand ass with very coarse conformation. American riding mules are also about 15 hands and I recall riding one very refined animal. In Australia the top mileage champion in endurance in 1988 was Patsie Sinfield's Juanita, a molly (female) mule who stands 14 hands (142 cm).) There is pictorial representation of mules on mosaics and on various columns, most notably the mules drawing a heaped baggage wagon on the Igel monument and the *ballistae* mules of Trajan's Column. Though not to be trusted for exact proportions, it is reasonable to assume that should the respective artists and stonemasons have been shown a diminutive beast they would not have translated it into a horse-sized animal.

The idea of a mule foaling crops up repeatedly in the literature. The superstitious Romans were much influenced by portents foretelling various disasters, whether military or political debacles or adverse natural phenomena. A mule giving birth was considered miraculous, because it is theoretically a sterile animal unable to reproduce. However, there are 14 recorded cases of mules foaling in America (Hyland 1988, p. 12). With the tens of thousands of mules in the Roman Empire it would be very odd if the occasional mule did not foal, because its ability to do so is a question of chromosome count. The mule is a hybrid, and if the chromosome count of both parents divided by two comes to an odd number the animal is sterile. In rare instances where the division results in an equal number that animal can be fertile (Dent 1977, p. 18). Put to another fertile specimen, horse or ass, young can be produced. It would also be possible, going one step further, that should there be the extremely rare instance of two fertile mules of opposite sexes present in the same herd they too could reproduce.

The ass or donkey generally receives bad press in Roman literature, although a few comical proverbs were written about him. His lot in life was to be treated harshly, as he still is today in many Mediterranean countries where he is half starved and much overburdened.

Routine care

Care of equines depended to a large extent on the resources available to the owner, from the small provincial farmstead yielding only a few yoke of oxen, one stallion, and a few race mares for breeding (which Juvenal (*Sat.* VIII) mockingly describes as being confiscated by the taxman), to the spreading acres of the rich landowner who had large *latifundia* in the most fertile regions of Italy and the provinces.

The herds of wealthy owners with large acreage and corresponding grazing rights were driven to the mountains in summer. This had the triple benefit of preserving the lowland grazing for a further period into the season of restricted growth, utilizing the mountain pastures, and accustoming the stock to rocky going. The latter was essential in the days before the use of iron horseshoes. Dry, rocky conditions gradually toughen a horse's hooves, whereas damp conditions lead to a spongy hoof where the sole can be bruised and cut very easily and the outer horn, on which the horse actually stands, abrades far more quickly. Conditions in the military meant that a horse had to have hard, sound hooves to be worth using. On the racetrack the friction of pounding hooves against the hard-packed sand of the arena would also abrade a hoof very quickly. Many years ago I noticed a marked change for the worse when I brought two horses from America to England. In America the ground they worked over was mostly sandy and relatively dry and they were never shod, even though one horse was competing in 100 mile rides and undergoing many hundreds of miles of training. In Britain the continually soggy underfoot conditions softened even these tough hooves so that the horses could not be worked for more than a few days without shoeing, and this was irrespective of whether they were on roads or not. One horse was chestnut with good feet, the other bay with very hard black hooves. The old proverb 'no hoof no horse' was never more applicable than in Roman times when the Empire spread over such diverse territories and terrains. It is significant that nailed-on iron shoes were developed by the Celts in the softer conditions they had to ride in.

The concern to maintain a hard-hoofed horse is also shown in the construction of the stabling used. Varro recommends that a good floor should be laid in all stables to keep the hoof from rotting, and Pelagonius states that it is of prime importance to keep a horse in a dry stable, because the hooves become wet with dampness (*Ars Vet.* II.30). He is talking of incipient thrush, an unpleasant rotting hoof condition occasioned by damp, dirty stables and foul bedding. He recommends a flooring of planks which must be kept clean of damp and dung, as 'the soundness of the feet is of prime importance' (ibid., XV.226). He obviously recognized the truth of the old saw. The bedding he advises, admittedly for a sick animal, is deep litter of chaff or straw (ibid., XXVII.363). Columella also recommends keeping a sick animal on a deep bed.

The rest of the stable construction, at least on Varro's estate, seems to have been separate stalls for the mares so that they can be kept warm and dry. In frosty weather the stables were kept shut and a fire lit inside. Possibly the reference is to a brazier, but even that is a dangerous practice in a highly inflammable environment. Some idea of actual stables can be gathered from Pompeii where the house of Popidius Secundus has stabling of four stalls, with masonry stall dividers, leading on to a court. At Mondeleia in Syria a stable with mangers and tie rings attached to a rock wall has been found (Vigneron 1968). As there are words in Latin for both loose box (*equile*) and stall (*stabulum*), it is obvious that there were diverse methods of keeping equines. Added to these were ways of keeping them *en masse* which can be inferred from a passage in Pelagonius on racing stock (*Ars Vet.* XIII.213). This would be the method used when horses were housed in their hundreds. In marching camps the cavalry used a picket line (*Polybius, Hist.* VI.33).

Varro recommends that grooms should have the many diseases and treatment written out. This implies the ability to read and write and thus a relatively high standing and educational level in the stud groom. He must have filled a similar position to that occupied today by a head lad in a racing stable or a stud manager, with the overall day-to-day management under his care, as well as the slaves who did the actual work. Veterinary surgeons, of whom there were some in private practice, would have been called in rarely and then only by the wealthy. Their normal location would have been in a fairly populous area — in a town or adjacent urban districts — where they could expect to make a decent living. The day-to-day care of any farm animal must have depended on a knowledgeable stud groom being able to recognize and treat most ailments. He would have been a very valuable asset to an estate owner who had invested in a sizeable breeding establishment. Stud grooms would have been expected to be able to cope with a horse suffering from worms, colic, various lamenesses, muscle strains, mange, loss of hair, coughs, poisonous bites, and so on. The stable medicine chest must have contained a wide array of drenches, potions and salves for internal and external application. Many of the practices and recommendations contained in Varro, Columella, and at greater length in Pelagonius would have been readily recognized by grooms of even fifty years ago.

Some common causes of colic are ingesting mouldy feed, impaction and parasites in the intestines. All three could be dealt with by the groom. Owing to the disjointed way in which Pelagonius imparts information, his 'colic signs' are scattered in no particular order, as if they were so familiar to him that he assumed the reader could sort them out for himself, but he is accurate nonetheless: 'A colic sufferer has staring eyes, is restless with an uncertain gait, may fall as if in epilepsy [this describes the sudden rolling and thrashing about of a colicky horse]. This will be followed by pain and he suddenly throws himself down. He may sweat, pant, and quiver' (*Ars Vet.* XXI.291). Any good groom will recognize these signs, particularly the getting up and down and violent movement as the pain stabs. Until very recently, most stables kept colic drenches but now modern medicine cures colic more rapidly with injected drugs. Pelagonius recommends various drenches, some with a multitude of herbal components, one of which was ground pine seeds (ibid., XXI.288). These were reputed to be capable of producing an abortion and thus were assumed also to eliminate the cause of the colic. Additionally he recommends blanketing the horse and taking it out for a walk: keep it warm and keep it moving (ibid., XXI.289). It is often the practice today to keep the horse walking in order to stop it thrashing about in case of a fatal twisted gut. Pelagonius gives a very simple remedy for severe colic caused by impaction (ibid., VII.130): dose the horse with wild rue seed potion and pull the tail up under the stomach (which action, I am told, has the effect in oxen of opening the sphincter!!).

Columella (*de Re Rust.*) gives a very accurate description of a horse with colic caused by worms – in this case maw-worms and tapeworms and therefore visible to the naked eye. He says the horse rolls in pain, brings his head near his belly, and flicks his tail. He recommends removing the dung by hand and washing the bowel with salt water, and then giving the horse a drench of caperbush and vinegar to kill the worms. The first part of the treatment is more an effective cure for impaction through giving an enema, and the second is a herbal vermifuge. Pelagonius' remedy for worms, or 'lice in the intestines', is to drench with juice of coriander, mustard, panax root, honey and oil, and to sprinkle the horse's barley with salt water (*Ars Vet.* VII.118). Various vermifuges were used in ancient veterinary medicine, and many potions intended for other ailments contained vermifuges such as wormwood, southernwood and common garlic, so the well-cared-for horse in Roman times must have been on a fairly constant regime of doses and drenches containing plants which, along with other ingredients, offered a level of protection against parasites.

Other general treatments given by grooms would be hoped-for cures for coughs. The most common cures in potion or pill form recommended by Pelagonius (ibid., V) included various fats liquefied in oil, honey, grease, wines and water, all providing a medium in which to mix herbs, the most common of which were pellitory, myrrh, horehound and squill. Pellitory can induce salivation and is used as a local irritant, and horehound is still used today against coughs. Squill, a kind of onion, is recognized as an expectorant. Along with the practical remedies, various incantations and superstitious scratchings of the owner's name on the horse's hooves were common.

Poisonous bites must have been quite a worry to farmers in Italy and other Mediterranean areas. According to Virgil, snakes bred in long-accumulated dung and lived in cracks in the walls (*Georgics* III.416–17). Other poisonous bites came from the shrewmouse and spiders. Pelagonius (*Ars Vet*. XX) gives a variety of 'cures' for these, together with the imperative to recite the religious words, implying that he had little faith in the remedies. Amulets were also hung round the horse's neck. From the scant attention paid to each form of poisoning it can be taken that viper, spider and shrewmouse bites were not fatal (I remember being concerned over possible snake bite when I first lived in America, and being reassured by the vet that fatality would be unlikely if the horse was kept calm). Most deaths from viper bite occur through asphyxia, not because of the venom. Cobra-like snakes, which are of the family elapidae, must have caused the military far more problems in places such as Egypt. Snakes do breed in heated dung heaps, so Virgil was not fantasizing; they also live in the crevices in walls, as I can attest from my own experience.

Good management included giving each stabled horse a daily grooming. Arrian (*Cyn.* 10), who was a superb horsemaster, recommended massaging the legs and body as it strengthened the legs and rendered the skin supple, removing impurities and imparting lustre to the coat. In total accord with modern practice, Columella says a good daily grooming is very therapeutic and often better than a feed.

Good horsemastership also included ensuring that horses did not fall ill as a result of easily avoidable excesses. All the classical authors who comment on it, including Columella, Varro and Pelagonius, affirm that most ailments are caused by cold, fatigue, drinking when overheated or immediately after violent work, or working hard after a long period of idleness. Rest is recommended as a cure, along with a soothing drench of oil mixed with wine. For a chill, applications of hot oil over the loins is suggested, accompanied by bathing the head and spine with tepid fat or ointment. Pelagonius (*Ars Vet.* IV.43) recommends that repair to a damaged shoulder, which could well result from violent work after a period of idleness, should be undertaken by letting blood from veins in the middle of the leg, mixing the blood with incense dust and plugging the wound with horse dung. Blood would again be let the next day, and from the third to the sixth day oil and leek juice in drench form administered. Finally the horse should be induced to walk gently and if at all possible swum in a pond. It has taken until the twentieth century and some modern research to recognize the therapeutic effects of swimming on horses with various forms of lameness, amongst which shoulder lamenesses are the most difficult to cure (see Ch. 3).

Nutrition

For favoured equines, nutrition in Roman days was very good. For the poor overworked mill mules, donkeys and broken-down hack and chariot horses, it was very poor. All the veterinary and farmers' manuals are full of recipes for nutrition, and they do not change very much over the four centuries from Varro to Vegetius.

Many areas of Italy offer good pasture land for stock raising. The main grassland areas were Apulia, Calabria, Umbria, Lucania and Bruttium. Sicily also had large *latifundia*. The main agricultural product in other areas, in particular Umbria, Picenum and Etruria, was grain. The most common grains grown were various types of wheat, particularly in Campania, and barley. Oats were considered a type of degenerate barley (White 1970) and were not often found in the mixed grain rations for horses. The varieties of wheat and barley grown differed very much from those we are used to today, and in the main had a far higher nutritional content than modern strains. The three main wheat strains were Einkorn (*Triticum monococcum*), with a protein count of 17.5 per cent dry weight; Emmer (*Triticum dicoccum*), 20 per cent protein; and Spelt (*Triticum spelta*), 19 per cent protein. Modern bread wheat (*Triticum aestivum*) has an 8–9 per cent protein content (Reynolds 1979). The three main groups of barley were *Hordeum distichum*, *hexastichum* and *glabrum* or bearded barley. Columella much preferred *hexastichum*, also known as horse barley, for animal feed as opposed to wheat (White 1970). With a similar high protein content ancient strains of barley would be on a par with the wheats. Modern barley has approximately 11 per cent protein content, as do oats and maize.

Ancient grains would have given much better nutrition than the modern feedstuffs and consequently a smaller quantity could be fed and still achieve good results. The fact that the Roman army allowed only 3.5 lb (1.5 kg) of grain (known as 'short feed' or 'hard feed') for a cavalry mount per day is one indication of the higher nutritional value. When considering any feeding ration, ancient or modern, the protein content is very important, but it is equally important to understand the total digestible nutrients (TDN) obtained from specific feeds. Animals need a certain level of nutrition for both maintenance of body weight and energy for performance, but all the protein contained in a given feed is not absorbed into the animal's system. Therefore it can be seen that a large amount of feed with a low protein content would not be as efficient as smaller amounts of high quality feed with a high protein content. The digestible nutrients in a feed are about half the protein content. In that respect ancient feeds of high quality gave more nutrition for less outlay.

The other basic component of the equine diet when grazing is short or non-existent is hay. In the areas lacking adequate supplies of fodder the Romans resorted to a wide range of tree leaves to supplement 'long food'. Cato (*de Agri Cult.*) recommends that cattle, which term included equines, be fed clover, vetch, fenugreek, beans and bitter vetch, plus elm, poplar, oak and fig leaves. To these Virgil adds willow and broom (*Georgics* II.436–7). I find horses are very partial to poplar and willow and they will strip any accessible tree. In the New Forest ponies that browse fare better than those that only graze. They supplement the meagre Forest diet, which is particularly sparse in winter, with tips of broom which grows there profusely.

The hay and green fodder mentioned most often and favourably in Roman literature is what we know as lucerne or alfalfa. The Romans called it *medica* as it originally came from Media where the Nisaean horses were raised and were renowned for their large size. Being fed such highly nutritious 'long feed', for lucerne has an extremely high protein content, enabled them to reach their genetic potential. Good grass hays have a protein content ranging from 7 to 10 per cent, whereas lucerne cut at the optimum time has almost double that (Hyland 1980, p. 115). Lucerne can be cut from four to six times a year, provided it is well irrigated, so that one *iugera* (⅝ acre or ¼ hectare) could keep three horses well fed, and according to Varro each sowing lasted up to ten years. It also has the advantage of feeding the land, by putting nitrogen back into the soil in the same way as clovers do. This was also true of other green manure crops such as lupins (White 1970).

Modern horsefeeds usually consist of what is called a 'mixed ration' or a 'coarse mix', including oats, barley, maize, minerals and linseed cake. Occasionally, particularly when heavy horses worked the land, beans were used. A Roman coarse mix recommended by Pelagonius (*Ars Vet.*, II.24) and others, and measured in *modii* and *sextarii* of 22 and 1.25

Roman pounds respectively (16 and 0.9 lb; 7 and 0.4 kg), consisted of 3 *modii* barley, 6 *sextarii* horse beans, 6 *sextarii* wheat, 8 *sextarii* each of chick peas and kidney beans, 4 *sextarii* vetch, and 3 *sextarii* greek hay (fenugreek), plus an optional but very nutritious addition of a pint of separated sparrow egg yolks and also whole sparrow eggs. Why particularly sparrow eggs is not explained, but Pelagonius often recommends the eggs of various birds, usually normal chicken eggs. The vetch and hay must have been chopped up or chaffed. Chaff is often added to feed if a horse is liable to bolt his grain and thereby risk getting colic. It was recommended to soak the amount to be used the night before, a very necessary instruction as whole barley and wheat would be hard to digest unless either ground or softened. The various legumes would be coarsely ground.

This example was of an expensive ration used by Cappadocian racehorse breeders. By modern standards it is a very heating feed because of the addition of peas and beans, and would only be suitable for a horse in hard work needing both a high protein and a high starch content in the feed. Pelagonius, however, recommends it for a horse suffering from emaciation, and advises keeping the horse stabled for 30 days in a warm environment, followed by a further 21 days' stable care if he does not improve. Naturally the Romans did not link too high a feeding and stabling without exercise with azoturia (see p. 226). Recognizing that not all horseowners could afford such high feeding he offers an alternative for 'poor but hardworking people' (*Ars Vet.* II.25), and advises giving parched wheat mixed with honey water on the same scale as the army rations, which as we saw was 3.5 lb (1.5 kg) a day, and to continue this for 20 days, or more if necessary.

Another food considered especially good for debilitated horses was cooked sweet lupins, but Pelagonius warns against colic resulting from the horse ingesting unripe lupins (ibid., II.28). Lupins are currently making a comeback in British fodder crops, though it remains to be seen if the ultra-conservative British horseowner will use them. Sweet chestnuts were also considered nutritious and were given toasted and mixed with barley (ibid., II.29). Sweet chestnuts are still used as animal fodder in the Florac region of France.

After the debilitated horse had been returned to health he was put on to an ordinary maintenance diet of horse beans (our broad bean) and barley. The *Codex Theodosianus* (15.10.2) shows the extent to which animal feed relied on beans: in AD 381 Gratian and his Co-Emperor informed Valerianus, Prefect of the City, that the people of Campania could not be allotted any racehorses from the pool held in Rome until they had supplied each faction with 2,000 *modii* of beans each. This identifies one of Campania's main crops and also the huge numbers of horses kept at Rome to need such a vast amount of beans. It was presumably only a part of the yearly consumption, levied from one district, not to mention barley, hay and all the other feeds comprising the Roman coarse mix fed to hard-working racehorses. The rest of the text makes clear that this was an annual payment.

Farrago was a popular and nutritious fodder crop consisting of emmer wheat sown with other cereals and legumes, cut green and fed long. There were three main types: barley with vetch and other leguminous plants; emmer winnowings sown with various vetches; and *ocinum* consisting of broad beans, common and bitter vetch (White 1970). At the beginning of spring horses were purged by being fed *ocinum* for ten days (Varro, *de Re Rust.*). Nineteenth-century grooms in a hunting stable used to purge or physic horses when brought up from grass at the beginning of the hunting season, and the *ocinum* purge at the beginning of spring, which was also the beginning of the campaigning season for the military, served the same purpose. Green fodder is highly laxative, especially when fed to horses that have wintered on dried hay or lean pickings, and it is advisable to introduce them gradually to lush grazing. After the green purge Varro recommends feeding barley in gradually increasing amounts for five days, then to feed the same amount for the following ten days. After that the horse was fit to begin moderate exercise. In lean-cropping years and in poorer districts the stores of fodder and grain must have been severely restricted, suggesting that horses went into spring in a rather debilitated state after being kept on pitifully inadequate maintenance rations during the non-working winter months. Consequently they needed feeding up before they had enough strength to sustain a work load. The precious hoard of barley from the previous year's crop would have been doled out only to working horses.

The level and quality of feeding has a direct bearing on the adult size of any animal. It has a far greater impact on domestic animals than on those that fend for themselves in the wild, as man regulates the feeding pattern. In the horse it is important that the in-foal and lactating broodmare be fed well, and both Virgil and Varro imply that this was done. Varro gives a guide to feeding the youngster by introducing it to barley flour and bran at five months of age. This is the time when the mare's milk supply normally decreases He also says to add 'anything they fancy', which implies offering a wide range of foodstuffs which would result in a more balanced diet. Varro says the foal is not weaned until it is two years old. That can only be in the case of the Noble Horse breeding in alternate years, as when a mare foals again she will not permit a yearling to suckle with another youngster at foot. She may or may not tolerate even its company, depending on her individual temperament. In any case, any milk she gave to a yearling would be very low in value and of minimal quantity, until immediately before the next foal and the beginning of another spell of lactation.

Balanced nutrition from an early age will allow the growing animal to prosper. Any prolonged periods of inadequate, lean feeding will show in tell-tale hoof rings, as will any cases of overfeeding which have caused laminitis. From the various 'ration recipes' it is obvious that the hard feeds had a high protein, high starch content. Protein is needed for muscle and tissue repair, while starch provides energy. Racehorses in particular expended a tremendous amount of energy and were subjected to very hard use. They would utilize fully the high feeding prescribed. Military horses, with their basic 3.5 lb ration of hard feed, did not fare so well, but slow travel at the speed an army marches would not burn up nearly as much energy as the stresses of the racetrack. Also I imagine that the army ration was only a basic minimum that an animal could be expected to survive on and still be operational. Logic suggests that when more generous rations were readily available the military horse benefited from them.

We know from the many descriptions of esteemed breeds that one of the characteristics the Romans admired in a horse was large size. It has always been thought that all the horses of the ancient world were small, pony-sized at best. Finds of various skeletons, and long bones from which the overall size can be deduced, have proved otherwise. It would not take more than a few generations to upgrade horse size and establish a new upper limit in height. And 14 to 15 hand (142–152 cm) animals can seem a reasonable size as body mass is also a determining factor. A weedy 14.2 hand runt appears a much smaller horse than one of the same height which has good bone and muscle development and is also in good flesh. For Europeans in particular the idea is prevalent that anything less than 16 hands (163 cm) is small, yet to a rancher in America a 15 hand animal is more than adequate, so mental conditioning can often label a horse large or small. The high protein feeds which privileged animals received in the Roman era certainly boosted their size. To support this theory, evidence in Britain shows that between 1710 and 1785 stock offered for sale at Smithfield Meat Market in London doubled in weight due to better farming methods and nutrition (Trevelyan 1967, p. 393). The Romans had a very wide Empire from which to draw not only their racing and cavalry horses, but also the harvests with which to feed them. In his tour around the Mediterranean the unknown author of the *Expositio Totius Mundi* was fond of listing the main export products of each country, and horses and corn feature in many: Pannonia, Spain, Mauretania, Numidia, Africa, Sicily, Cyrenaica. Many of the areas we know as desert were still fertile in the Roman era as desiccation did not become such a massive problem until the fourth century. The Romans in

Africa had extensive irrigation works that made the desert fertile. We know today how rapidly desiccation can overtake fertile land, with parts of southern Africa losing half a mile a year to encroaching sand. North Africa was of course Rome's grain basket from which both horse and man fed.

Early handling and training

The only complete training manual we have from the ancient world is that written by the Greek Xenophon. Snatches of an even earlier Greek work by Simon, to whom Xenophon refers, are extant, but there is no specific work in Latin on the art of horsemanship. In AD 136 Arrian, a general in the Roman army and sometime Governor of Bithynia, was commissioned by the Emperor Hadrian to write a *Tactical Treatise* on army manoeuvres. Part Two of his work deals with cavalry exercises, but only the results of training are discussed, although from that much can be inferred. We have to go back mainly to the poets and the gentleman farmers for a few glimpses of what was expected of a young horse. In the main the Romans, admiring much that was Greek, and also having such a strong Greek presence in the southern half of Italy, absorbed Greek methods in regard to horses, riding and racing. Much of equine management, handling and riding is common sense combined with a feel for the animal you are working with. These factors alone make it a following for the few, but in the ancient world the average peasant would be much more at ease with animals than today's countryman, whose closeness to horsepower is usually with his motorized vehicle. The knight and senator class would of course be brought up with riding as just one of the things boys were taught to do, much as today's boys ride bicycles.

At this stage I only wish to cover a few general points in horse training, as specific areas such as cavalry, racing and hunting are dealt with elsewhere.

It was important to know a horse's age before putting it under the stresses of training and work. Naturally a large proportion of animals would be known to the stud manager who had colts broken before selling them, but with the dealers, of which, as we know from Pelagonius (*Ars Vet.* I.9), there were many, it would be as well for the purchaser to be able to tell a horse's approximate age, as I imagine Roman dealers were no more honest than some modern traders. Maybe Roman dealers too altered a horse's apparent age by the dishonest practice of 'bishopping': filing the teeth and so changing the depth of the cups to resemble those of a young horse (Hayes 1968, p. 519).

Horses, like humans, have two sets of teeth. A young horse sheds its first full set of teeth by the time it is five years old, but this shedding occurs over quite a long period. It is possible to age a horse accurately by the state of eruption of its permanent teeth. Accuracy diminishes after the horse has what is termed a 'full mouth'. It is worth quoting Pelagonius on this:

> At two and a half the middle teeth in the upper jaw erupt. At four years of age the teeth called canine erupt. In his sixth year [i.e. as a five year old] the first change occurs. At seven all the teeth fill up. Nor after seven can the age be verified unless the man is very experienced, which we may learn by further reading. At ten the top and bottom teeth become prominent, and at twelve black spots in the middle of the teeth appear. (*Ars Vet*. Int.1.)

Varro agrees with Pelagonius until the horse reaches seven years of age, then he says, 'you cannot tell the age after that until the teeth become prominent and the eyebrows grey with hollows under them. Then it is sixteen years old.'

The veterinary practitioner and the gentleman farmer are both reasonably accurate. The shape of the cups in the teeth are one means of telling a mature horse's age until he is seven years of age. At seven he develops what is termed a 'hook' on each outside incisor in the upper jaw. This is smooth by the time he is nine. In other words between seven and eleven it is difficult to age a horse accurately. The teeth begin to become more prominent as the horse ages. At nine he develops a groove on the same outside incisor and this progresses down the length of the tooth so that by the time he is 15 it has reached half way. At 20 it starts to go into reverse, disappearing by the time he is 30 (Hayes 1968, p. 519). Ageing is represented by greying over the eyes and deepening of the occipital depressions, although this varies in some horses, but Varro was quite accurate.

The age at which a horse entered into his allotted work varied. Pelagonius (*Ars Vet*. I) says that education of a racehorse starts as a three year old, but that domestic horses can be used at two years old. However, the racehorse did not appear as a competitor until he was five. Varro recommends handling the foal while young and accustoming it to the chink of bits rattling in the stable. At three years of age, as soon as it is handleable, by which he means the ground work has been done, a young lad should lie across its back a few times. The next step is for the youngster to sit astride the colt. This is still the same practice followed today. Varro disagrees with breakers who start a colt at 18 months, saying that by three it is mostly grown and has had time to muscle up.

Virgil is very explicit and refers only to cavalry and racehorses, saying that they must be trained to watch the panoply and noise of war, or hear the squeal of chariot wheels and the jangle of harness (*Georgics* III.182–4). Training should be taken a step at a time, trying a rope bit in the horse's mouth at weaning (which for Virgil is two years of age) while he is still unsure of his strength. At three he can be ridden and taught correct paces and posture in the training ring (ibid., III.182–3). Virgil mentions the training ring twice (ibid., III.116,191) and this is of special interest in a later military context. The method Virgil advises shows empathy with the young horse, first trying a soft bit in his mouth so as not to bruise it or to scare him by the use of normal bitting, which is clearly described in later lines on horseracing at Elis, where the horse is sweating and his mouth is flecked with bloody foam (ibid., III.202–3). This indicates a degree of very harsh handling with the reins. Virgil recommends that a young horse in early training be kept underfed, or he will not obey whip and curb, putting up resistances and refusing to be broken. Mistakenly some people still believe this, and although with some horses it does undoubtedly work to keep them on a lower ration until they are amenable, in normal practice it creates more problems than it cures. However, the Romans, and other peoples of the era, were not noted for their kindness to animals, in fact generally the reverse. The very fact that the training involved 'the lash and the cruel curb' is indicative of suppression rather than persuasion. It would seem that the horse beginning work was given some leeway, a little time to learn; but once introduced to the full training and later the full work regime he was expected to submit with no argument at all, and if he did not he heard and felt about it to his cost. In war and racing, stallions were used as well as mares so more resistances could be expected – from the stallions by their very nature, and from the mares when in oestrus. Virgil implies this use of stallions by his statement that the most effective way to reinforce their strength is to 'bar them off from the passion and blinding goads of lust' (ibid., III.209–10). Geldings, unless a rig or if the vet has done a bad job, are not very lustful.

However, geldings were used in other spheres by the Romans. Varro says: 'Nor does the man who wants to turn out horses for carrying proceed in the same way as he who wants them for military service. For just as we need them high spirited for camps so we prefer to have them quiet on the road. Castration effects this' (*de Re Rust.*). This confirms that stallions were used in the army as a general rule. No doubt if one became too obstreperous it was castrated to make it more amenable to discipline, but the lash, the curb and the muzzles used, plus a heavy work load, would have sorted out most stallion aggression. Columella recommended that an unruly stallion be quietened by putting it to turning a mill. (Such treatment does straighten out a horse's mind. On several occasions I have given recalcitrant animals, stallions among them, very hard work, including a 60 mile fast race over demanding Dartmoor terrain for one stallion who spent too much time on his hind legs. It had the desired effect and he was far more amenable afterwards.)

A 'green' or just broken colt offered for sale was expected to be sold under warranty. This was very similar in content to today's certificate of soundness in wind and limb and suitability for the work the animal is intended for. The Roman warranty was a legal document with the requirements shown in the Manilian actions which governed the sale of slaves. Horses came under the same category as slaves. In addition to a warranty similar to our modern one, the Roman deed of sale also had a clause indemnifying the purchaser against any damage the animal may have done. Both Varro and Pelagonius mention this warranty, showing its continued importance down the centuries. It covered all classes of equine.

3
Veterinary medicine

In spite of the enormous loss of classical manuscripts in all fields, a considerable amount of literature on the subject of veterinary practice in the Roman period has come down to us. For the most part treatment was empirical, based on the experience of various practitioners by trial and error, and changing little throughout the course of several hundred years. Lacking the specific scientific knowledge and modern drugs that today's horses, and other animals, can benefit from, Roman animals were treated in what we would consider a rather hit or miss manner, with a vast range of medicaments being utilized, some of which were no doubt efficacious, others definitely harmful, and a whole collection which did no harm but probably did little good either. In some of the 'recipes' for unguents, plasters and potions, it is possible to extrapolate the active ingredients. Treatments were given using varying amounts of medicinal herbs, many caustic preparations such as pitches and resins, and a few metallic substances obtained from lead, zinc, copper and iron. Some we can recognize in preparations used within living memory in our own veterinary pharmacopoeia before the advent of modern drugs, and some are still current.

There was still a residue of the very ancient Assyrian 'dung pharmacopoeia' (Mann 1984), where the dung of various animals was recommended – powdered and added to potions and unguents, or moist in the form of plasters and poultices; practices one would think were guaranteed to add to the bacteria already present in a wound, or to start a dangerous reaction where none existed before. The fact that this very unhygienic practice continued for so long can possibly be attributed to the fact that the drying process killed off most if not all harmful bacteria, and secondly that when combined with one of sometimes a dozen or more other ingredients the antiseptic quality of many of these counteracted the dung impurities.

Though of very ancient origin, the 'dung pharmacopoeia' nevertheless persisted into the twentieth century in farming areas where old folk remedies were still used. My near neighbour, a heavy horse man from a long line of such horsemen, tells me it was common practice to apply a hot, fresh, cowpat to horses' skinned legs and other wounds if the prescribed veterinary treatment took too long. He assures me that there were no ill effects! A piece of advice backed with a scientific rationale was offered recently by the veterinary adviser to the Endurance Horse and Pony Society of Great Britain. Jim Kerr, MRCVS, recommended the addition of dried droppings from a healthy donor horse to the feed of a yearling who had a bacteria imbalance of the gut. Also recommended to correct the same problem was the administration of fresh droppings from the donor horse via rectum or naso-gastric avenue.

As a last resort, if all the Roman potions and plasters failed, sympathetic magic was employed. Favoured by many of the era's veterinary practitioners, this was held in disrepute by Publius Vegetius, who although not a veterinary practitioner wrote a treatise on veterinary matters in the last half of the fourth century AD. He in turn was following the bald statement of his main source, Chiron, a Greek *hippiatrik* or horse doctor, that such superstitious practices revealed the officiating veterinary as '*minus intelligentes . . . idiotae et minus scientes*' (Chiron, *Mulomed*. III.4; Walker 1973).

The Roman veterinary practitioner fell into one of several categories. The *mulomedici* was the name given to the state-owned slaves who cared for the animals of the *Cursus Publicus*; the *veterinarius* was the man in what we would term private practice who catered to the needs of the wealthier strata of society, and the needs of the state-owned court, ceremonial and circus horses. The *veterinarii* in the army were *immunes* and attended to the many animals necessary to the smooth running of the army: *ballistae* mules, pack mules, ponies, horses, troopers' and officers' mounts, as well as other beasts such as sacrificial animals, draught oxen, and in some eastern provinces dromedaries for troopers and baggage. Most veterinary medicine, however, was slanted towards the care of equines.

Many treatments which fall into the veterinary sphere today would be carried out at the farm or stud by the grooms. Columella, writing in the mid first century AD on farming practice, lists cures for skin eruptions such as mange, for parasites such as worms and lice, and for harness galls, emaciation and general sprains and strains occasioned by animals pulling excessive loads. If Varro's advice were followed (see Ch. 2), grooms would have been expected to note and record cures for the more common diseases, among them colic and founder. Here Varro comments:

In general what causes most diseases will be found to be sickness induced by heat or by chills, or again, by too much work, or the opposite extreme lack of exercise, or by giving food or drink immediately after exercise. The symptoms are: in case of a fever which is the result of overwork an open mouth, rapid and moist breath, and a hot body; the treatment when this is the case is as follows: the animal is bathed all over with water and thoroughly rubbed with a mixture of tepid oil and wine, its strength is kept up by good feeding, and some wrapping is thrown over it to prevent it from taking cold. If it is thirsty lukewarm water is given. If nothing is gained by this method of treatment the animal is bled – preferably from the head. (*de Re Rust.*)

Varro is describing a classic case of what is widely known as founder, and this is one of the few cases where the symptoms are described in *almost* twentieth-century fashion. Founder can be caused by any of the four mentioned conditions, or by bad management. In most cases laminitis follows: the hooves are found to be hot, the horny outer sheath preventing normal dissipation of heat. Because of the pain involved the horse will not move voluntarily, thereby causing congestion in the vascular system within the hooves. The ancient treatment accords well with many common-sense remedies today, though now if any bleeding is to be done it is from the further extremity of the toe (Hayes 1968, p. 208) to relieve pressure within the hoof. The bleeding from the head is a frequent recommendation in ancient veterinary medicine, the head being considered the seat of many ailments and therefore the area to be relieved by bleeding. Fever, heightened breathing and a hot body are found in severe cases of founder, and we would still blanket against a chill today. Any water offered after excessive work should be tepid, as excessively cold water given to an overheated horse causes internal contractions, too rapid a lowering of internal body temperature, and colic to add to the founder. The bathing with water helps to reduce fever – it is common practice to sponge endurance horses with cold water at rest points to help reduce external body heat and thus heart and respiration rates, though care must of course be taken to avoid chill in cold or windy conditions. Today, feeding would be monitored very carefully in a case of founder.

Founder and colic must have been two very prevalent disorders, easily avoidable but very damaging to the health of all strata of equines, especially those employed in the circus, on the *Cursus Publicus* where there were laws against overriding and overdriving animals, and in the army, where excessively hot and sometimes very humid conditions, particularly in the eastern provinces, must have occasioned such illness when cavalry had to travel at speed regardless of danger to animals, which was a lesser consideration on many occasions. Every *strator*, farm labourer and trooper must have been expected to be able to cope with any such incidents.

In practice the four sections of Roman society that would need the services of a qualified veterinary practitioner were the circus, where literally hundreds of horses were employed in the main cities with magnificent facilities provided, and a considerable number in the smaller but still important towns that boasted a circus or hippodrome; the *Cursus Publicus*, with its many stations, some large with a heavy concentration of animals, some smaller with a relatively smaller nucleus of four-footed personnel; the army, with its thousands of animals per legion; and finally the civilian section, where the services of a private *veterinarius* would be restricted to the wealthier classes. For the animals on the farm, as already stated, the landowner's husbandmen would be expected to cope, and for the wretched animals sentenced to work in the city's bakery mills and other such lowly occupations, as they were usually at their lowest ebb when they fulfilled such functions the cost of treating them would often outweigh the little value left in their carcasses. Pack animals owned by merchants would receive treatment from their handlers, and owing to the peripatetic nature of their work would only be of value if they stayed healthy and sound in wind and limb, an off-work animal being dead money as far as a merchant was concerned.

One veterinary treatise that has come down to us is the 1892 Leipzig edition by Maximilian Ihm of Pelagonius' *Ars Veterinaria*. Pelagonius came from Salonae (modern Solin in Yugoslavia, on the coastline of the Adriatic opposite Picenum in Italy). There is an area of Greece known in ancient times as Pelagonii, so possibly Pelagonius the *veterinarius* studied there, particularly as Greece was known to produce good horse doctors. Pelagonius compiled his *Ars Veterinaria* in the last half of the fourth century AD, and was known to Publius Vegetius, who criticized his near-contemporary for inadequate treatment of the subject matter, although the same could also be said to a lesser degree of his own work. Both offer similar herbal and what we call homoeopathic cures. Indeed there are some surprising points of similarity between the modern homoeopathic treatment of horses and some of the practices recommended by Pelagonius. True scientific knowledge of veterinary practice was lacking in the Romans, but, as with some of the points on breeding brought out in Chapter 2, there must have been a knowledge that such-and-such worked even if the reason for it escaped them.

Scribonius Largus, practising human medicine in the first half century AD, noted that it was beneficial to a patient to drink his own blood (*Compostitiones*; Mann 1984). Pelagonius frequently recommends that a horse be bled, and most bleeding must have had an extremely debilitating effect on the poor animals. The puncture site for bleeding depended on which part of the horse was considered to control the malfunctioning part of his anatomy. The blood drawn off was then mixed with other ingredients and either ingested by the animals as a potion, or smeared over its body as an unguent. In homoeopathic veterinary practice today it is recommended that a nosode should be made from the infected blood of a horse suffering from equine infectious anaemia (MacLeod 1977; p. 115). The resulting medication can be used both to heal and to protect against the disease. Infected matter is also employed in other nosodes, an example being in equine viral rhino-pneumonitis, a disease of the upper respiratory tract. In this case the nosode is used as an oral vaccine (ibid., p. 117). Pelagonius often recommends that purulent matter is scraped off a suppurating wound, mixed with a medication, and given orally. Again we see here an early, if crude, method of oral vaccination, lacking the modern methods of distillation, but nevertheless under less hygienic conditions probably performing a somewhat similar therapeutic action.

Though nowhere in his treatise does Pelagonius say in what area of veterinary practice he operated, throughout his book there are a considerable number of references to circus horses, injuries occasioned by blows from wheels and axles, charioteers, bony excrescences caused by blows to limbs, scarification of eyes, inflammation of eyes, and abraded hooves. There are also cures for a host of diseases caused by keeping horses in close proximity to each other, although there seems to be no realization that infectious diseases can be transmitted by such proximity. From these many references it is quite clear that Pelagonius was a veterinary practitioner for one of the circus factions. In which city we are not told, but to have a major veterinary practitioner attached it certainly must have been one of the larger centres of racing, such as Rome, Antioch, Constantinople, or maybe in one of the many provinces that boasted monumental circus facilities.

The chapters dealing with a host of diseases and injuries throw light on how the veterinarians tried to cope with ailing animals. They also show what afflictions were most common, by the plethora of cures for some and the dismissal of others with a brief mention. More importantly they indicated what stresses, injuries, uses and abuses circus horses were subjected to. A far clearer picture of a racehorse's life can be culled from the jigsaw of ailments and cures than from all the inscriptions by victorious charioteers extolling their ability to drive teams of *quadrigae* and *bigae* to fortune and acclaim and recording it in stone. The pertinent circus ailments are dealt with in Chapter 15 below.

Most of the advice on horse nutrition and general care given by Pelagonius is a mirror of earlier writers such as Columella, on whom he frequently draws for some of his cures, either admitting their provenance or copying them so completely that it is obvious who his source was, even though Columella pre-dated him by some three centuries. Scattered throughout the work are cures recommended by other veterinary practitioners, and some cures advised by doctors who treated humans. They range from Mago of Carthage to Apsyrtus, veterinary surgeon at the court of Constantine the Great – a time span of many hundreds of years.

When we get to the specific ailments some of the descriptions of symptoms are confusing, many seeming to duplicate other diseases, others almost the same with maybe one symptom different. Many are wrongly diagnosed; others are ailments we would recognize today. There is a thread of common sense running through some of the cures; others are quite plainly more damaging than helpful; and in many cases, particularly the cure for tetanus, it is obvious from the plethora of remedies that nothing was really known and all were a shot in the dark with not much hope of efficacy. Even today tetanus is a disease that causes a high percentage of fatalities among horses who have not been vaccinated against it, and are therefore exposed to the bacillus that causes it, mostly through puncture wounds. In the circus and particularly the army at war there must have been numerous occasions when wounds, especially of the puncture type, were open to the tetanus bacillus.

Occasionally Pelagonius digresses from his concern with the ailments of the track horses and gives advice to private clients who have written to him, so it was clear that he had a private practice in addition to his state retainer. From the manner in which the text is arranged, and allowing for corruption throughout the centuries and repeated editions down the years, the material is set out in a rather random way with some attempt to group the ailments into recognizable sections. During his daily round of the horses he must have dictated to his attendant scribe how such-and-such a horse was to be treated, and then moved on to a horse with a completely different sickness or injury, commenting on that, so that until one has gone through a considerable portion of the work it appears somewhat confusing. One can almost hear him saying, 'Note this down for such-and-such a horse', and occasionally backtracking with 'Oh! I forgot, and this too to the treatment I ordered for so-and-so'. In one section devoted to cures for 'injured leg joints or joints of the neck' (*Ars Vet.* XV), the advice is given for the former but nowhere for the latter. The subsequent section on 'cures for nasal polyps' (ibid., XVI) continues the cures for the 'hoof joints', and eventually gets around to the nasal polyps, and very much further along gives advice for the injured neck. It is also quite usual throughout the text to find most of a prescription tallied, the text then pursuing a different line only to return entirely out of context with an addition to a previous recipe. It takes time, and a considerable amount of common sense and experience with horses and their day-to-day ailments, to get to grips with Pelagonius.

From the text it is apparent that many of the ailments were those we would associate with keeping horses in large groups, rather than in individual stables. Many ailments are infectious, some contagious, some parasitic. The most common among these are strangles, colds, coughs, mange, internal parasites and various fevers, all of which are transmittable in close proximity either from viruses, infections or in the case of external parasites by touching, and internal parasites by ingesting fodder fouled with fecal matter bearing the eggs or larvae of parasites. This highlights the Roman lack of knowledge about contagion. For instance, the ailment known as strangles is an extremely invasive condition when horses are kept *en masse*. It is caused by the *Streptococcus equi* bacillus, is highly contagious, occasionally fatal, and extremely debilitating. In the ancient world it undoubtedly would have caused many fatalities. It is also known, incorrectly, as Shipping Fever, from the fact that animals transported in large groups seem to contract it more readily, probably because one infected animal leaves a residue of purulent matter from a nasal discharge or pus from a burst abscess on the transit container, or because horses incubating the disease show no visual signs and are thus not isolated. It attacks young horses, usually under the age of six years, but can affect older animals. It also confers immunity once the animal recovers from it. It is mentioned in Chapter V of Pelagonius under the heading 'Cures and medicines for head ailments', lumped together with colds, painful ears, lice in the ears, cut tongue, painful teeth and nosebleed. Where the majority of the ailments and cures in this chapter appear once, or at most twice, tumour in the jaw, parotitis and swollen glands appear *seven times*, an indication of how prevalent strangles must have been. Pelagonius also states that throat discharge is thick. Today we recognize that the main signs of strangles are raised temperature, a horse off its feed, and a clear nasal discharge, later turning thick and opaque. A hard lump appears in the submaxillary space under the jaw, and to accommodate this the head is held stiffly out. Inflammation of the parotid gland is also sometimes due to strangles. When the hard abscess ripens and bursts thick yellow matter erupts from under the jaw.

Because of the contagious nature of the disease a considerable number of animals must have been affected in the three main areas where equines were used – the circus, *Cursus Publicus* and army – particularly as the bulk of these would have been conscripted or bought or donated as the 'offertory of horses' (*Codex Theo.*, 7.23.1), in their young, valuable and susceptible years. The disease must have been a constant worry to stable personnel who had to contend, at the least, with animals rendered useless while the disease ran its course and the animals recovered. Horses in all three occupations were prime targets for spreading the disease because of the close proximity in which they were kept, and by the nature of their work. The *Cursus Publicus* animals were extremely peripatetic. It is known that racehorses sometimes travelled to 'away meets'. The army too would carry contagion with it, for even if sick animals were left at base to recuperate, those incubating the disease would be sure to keep it with the legions. All three sections also constantly received fresh loads of animals, many young ones among them.

Treatment today consists of isolation, keeping the animal under hygienic conditions and administering modern drugs. All implements such as grooming gear, horse's harness, and handlers' clothing are kept separate from other animals' gear for fear of passing the disease on. Pelagonius' only remedy is to recommend hot plasters, in which the main ingredients are resin (the variety is not indicated) and hot grease, and the lancing of the mature abcess which must then be kept clean and covered with a pad soaked in oil and vinegar. Vinegar would have antiseptic qualities. Sprinkling the healing wound with ground pomegranate rind, an astringent with a content of gallotannic acid, would promote healing.

Pelagonius does not recommend the isolation of infected animals. In fact the only time he does so is in his section on 'Dropsy and gastric gas' (*Ars Vet.* XIII), where he recommends using a hot ash and lye salve on the navel or stomach, followed by a drench of oil, wine, panax root and gall nut (ibid., XIII.213). The subsequent separation of the horse from the others was no doubt as a safety precaution should he thrash about and cause injury to either himself or the other horses. It also suggests that circus horses were kept in groups, not individually stabled, at least at the training stables if not at the track stables reserved for individuals due to race. Pelagonius describes the symptoms of gastric gas as 'swollen stomach, neck rigid and often stretched out, and the internal swelling bursts as the horse passes dung' (ibid., XIII.210). What he is imperfectly describing is gastric impaction accompanied by tympany. It is commonly known as 'stomach staggers' because in the ailment's progression the horse may stagger about, hence the recommendation by Pelagonius to separate it from others (ibid., XIII.213). Modern treatment via stomach tube to give relief from the impaction is followed by a purgative. The colic drench given by Pelagonius would induce relief, and passing dung, or as he puts it (not understanding the true nature of the ailment), the bursting of the 'internal swelling', also gives relief. One of the main causes of intestinal impaction is the feeding of bulky and dry goods, especially after hard work and to a greedy horse. Gastric tympany can be caused by ingestion of too new feeds (with their higher moisture content) or mouldy feed. In the Roman era, although there were large granaries supplied with air vents, it must have been extremely difficult to keep all feeds in prime condition, particularly in the quantities recommended by Publius Vegetius, Pelagonius and others.

There are many types of lamenesses, which of all ailments are the most common reasons for unsoundness in the horse. Among the hardest to pinpoint and also very slow to repair are lamenesses connected with the shoulder. Cavalry and circus horses who were subjected to wrenching movements would be particularly susceptible. However, due to the design of harnessing, traction animals would not have been as prone to shoulder injury as they were in later ages when all the brunt was brought to bear via the shoulder collar. Neck and spine injuries, on the other hand, would have been common because of the neck yoke.

Pelagonius deals with shoulder wounds and injuries in Chapter IV of his work. For open wounds he recommends a nosode made from the horse's own blood and dung which would today be considered unhygienic. Drenching with oil and leek juice for six days as recommended would largely be wasted – leeks, as members of the onion family, have certain antiseptic qualities and would have been better used in place of the dung as an onion poultice for drawing inflammation! The diet was reduced to hay only and when work was re-started after six days it was slow, and where possible the animal was swum. These are sensible precautions (*Ars Vet.* IV.43).

Bleeding was recommended because the Romans thought that by reducing the amount of heated blood in the damaged area they were removing the cause. They failed to recognize that inflammation was a symptom, not a cause, and that circulating blood carried impurities away, thus reducing infection. The poultices recommended would have been therapeutic when drawing the pain out, but some of the ingredients – soda (natron), liquid pitch (tar), and sulphur – were rather drastic, equating with a modern mild blister, although the added wine and oil would mollify the action. Massage and fomentations are still employed today.

In writing of fevers (ibid., III), Pelagonius is not as specific as Varro who admittedly is only describing founder (see Ch. 2). He lumps all the possible signs of fever together and leaves it up to the poor groom to sort it out (ibid., III.33). No doubt a very experienced groom coped well enough. However, one very interesting passage (ibid., III.34) shows that some people were centuries before their time in using the pulse to determine illness, especially fevers. Unfortunately Pelagonius, from his eminent position as a *veterinarius* of note, scotched the idea, saying: 'Those who think that by touching the ear, or vein, or artery in the side under the shoulder may discern if the horse has fever are ignorant of the true reason because it cannot be told by the appearance of the veins.'

Horses' pulse rates rise when they are in pain or have any fever or other illness. Even without any other sign, an elevated pulse rate is indicative that the horse is in trouble. One method of taking the heart rate is to locate any of the great number of pulse points and count the beats, exactly what Pelagonius' 'ignorant' person was doing. The use of the pulse in aiding diagnosis was not accepted until over a thousand years after Pelagonius' time.

The debilitating practice of bleeding was the favoured 'cure all' treatment for fevers (ibid., III.37), combined with a variety of potions. Until the advent of modern veterinary drugs most stables had standard drenches (potions) for colic, coughs, as tonics, and so on, in the medicine cupboard. Of these the most common would be colic drenches. From the great number of Pelagonius' colic remedies it would seem as if stable management was often sub-standard, as colic can usually be avoided. Because of the frequency of colic grooms sometimes panicked, or had no faith in the potions, and backed up their drenches with a fair number of 'mumbo jumbo' incantations.

Dysuria, strangury and ischuria, where the horse finds it difficult or even impossible to urinate, are recognized as very serious conditions (ibid., VIII). The diagnoses for the urinary problems are interwoven with the symptoms for azoturia (see Ch. 15 below). This is not surprising, as azoturia is a condition about which the veterinary profession is still gaining further knowledge. Some cures offered for urinary problems are sensible, such as administering a diuretic, although the method of pouring it up the horse's nose is not. Today a stomach tube can be used, but it is dangerous unless the practitioner is very skilled. Fomentation over the loins would help reduce tension and relax muscles and encourage the horse to stale. The efficacy of a live fly irritating the penis is somewhat doubtful: it would be more likely to drive the horse frantic with kicking at his belly, but maybe the secondary action would trigger the required response! One inference that can be drawn from this chapter is that, as it emerges from the book that Pelagonius worked at a racetrack, most horses in work were stallions, for there is no suggestion of how to make a mare urinate. From the type of work Roman horses did – the long hours they were in harness or on the march in cavalry, and the excesses they endured at the track – it would be fair to suggest that most urinary problems were linked with azoturia rather than dysuria or strangury, though some of the symptoms are similar.

One chapter is devoted to various cures for a condition which, literally translated, reads 'Bloody swelling of the ankles' (ibid., XI). This is a rather vague diagnosis for a number of disorders. However, reading between the lines and considering the remedies offered, the conditions to be treated would today be classed as windgalls, various hyatides (blisters), and ruptured and/or bowed tendons. The recommended cure for the majority is firing (ibid., XI.193). Up until about the 1960s firing was a common treatment for a bowed or ruptured tendon. It drew blood to the damaged tissues and hastened the healing process. Windgalls, or 'bloody swellings of the ankles [fetlocks]', are puffy joints. If no heat is present the swelling is harmless. If heat is present it would be classed as an unsoundness and almost certainly be accompanied by a slight lameness (unless all four fetlocks were affected, in which case the horse would not appear lame but rather would show some discomfort on moving). The Romans interpreted heat in tissues as too much blood in the localized area, as discussed above. Pelagonius recommended that a new swelling be dressed with a caustic plaster which would draw the impurities to the area, peel away unwanted excrescences, and promote healing of deep tissues. If the blemish was of long standing he recommends firing. But he also advises that the condition may be checked by making the horse work on unyielding ground and in a staccato rhythm, such as a pack or traction mule would exhibit (ibid., XI.196). Windgalls, unless they are hardened, do respond to work. The swelling disappears after a short time in action, as the blood supply to the extremities disburses the swelling. However, at rest the swelling returns. The remedy still used today for reducing puffiness around joints brought on by extensive work was well known to Pelagonius and other practitioners. He advises standing the horse in cold water or a running stream (ibid., XVI.263). Today this is called tubbing or hosing. The caustic poultices mentioned above, and which Pelagonius mentions on many other occasions throughout the treatise, are what we term blisters. (Under veterinary supervision 15 years ago I had to blister a horse to reduce capped hocks. It was a drastic treatment, very uncomfortable for the horse, but it worked in some degree.)

These conditions and the considerable space given to them tell us that Roman equines were subjected to really hard work, much of which must have been excessive as windgalls are the result of considerable wear and tear which does not necessarily cause lameness. Ruptured tendons are the result of grossly overstressing already tired limbs and/or sudden violent wrenches, and they cause extreme lameness.

All respiratory disorders are gathered in the chapter on 'Broken wind' (ibid., XII), but it is clear that symptoms were not always correctly linked to the disease the horse suffered. Laboured and stertorious breathing was recognized as serious. Broken wind, or permanent respiratory problems, is caused by many factors, the most common being mouldy feed, or working an unfit horse to excess when he already has a cough. Cardiac malfunction was not recognized, because laboured breathing with drawn-up flanks, which is one of the symptoms, is also indicative of broken wind. Other symptoms, including unsteady gait and congestion in the eyes, taken with the respiratory defect point to cardiac malfunction, as indicated by Hayes (1968, pp. 70–1)

Eye ailments were frequent and apart from those specifically relating to the circus (see Ch. 15) the most common seem to have been conjunctivitis, keratitis, cataract and white spot (*Ars Vet.* XXX). So many treatments were offered that it seems they were not much use, and most were tried with little hope of success other than a palliative remedy while nature did the real healing. Flies would have transmitted and greatly exacerbated keratitis and white spot. The latter is a disease common to cattle in the New Forest today, and although it can occur in horses it is now rare. A horse with cataract would have been incurable, unless the Romans had a remedy forgotten in later centuries. Clearly, vision impairment was a major threat to a horse's health and serviceability in Roman times.

There are many facets of Roman equine medicine, but the above touches in some small measure on the disorders most common and those most likely to affect the usefulness of the equine population. The bases of some remedies still hold good today. Other ailments with a relevance to a specific sphere of horse activity are contained in the appropriate chapters below, such as those dealing with military and racing matters, where some of the common ailments mentioned briefly in this chapter are discussed in greater detail.

Part Two

THE ROMAN CAVALRY HORSE

Introduction

We are indebted to a number of poets and gentleman farmers for recounting many aspects of civilian equestrian life, but it is to historians we owe the most for the military details. Many historians, frequently of senatorial class and writing in their later years, would have seen military service in their youth. Some, like Ammianus Marcellinus, were active career men. He was present at the scenes he so vividly describes, and the equestrian content of his narrative is often very revealing.

For the most part, however, information on horses is confined to isolated comments. Occasionally the writer gives us a more detailed paragraph on some aspect of either the Roman or the enemy's cavalry. Details cover a wide spectrum: weapons, armour of rider and sometimes horse; cavalry duties; horse descriptions; terrain; climate; water or the lack of it; grain and fodder; horse selection; the scorched earth policy. The list of relevant facts that affect or can be linked to cavalry and troopers is extensive – far more so than would at first appear. Yet to a horsemaster each isolated reference means something. For example, high temperature and scarcity of water suggests to me loss of body fluid, trace elements and salts, lightheadedness, and eventual motor dysfunction for both man and horse. To an army, especially a mounted army, it could be more of a killer than enemy weapons. A horse's weight is over 60 per cent fluid content. Deplete it extensively, by more than 10 per cent, and death follows if the trend is not reversed; result – end of operational cavalry unit.

By carefully garnering a multitude of references it has been possible to gain an idea of life on the hoof for a Roman cavalryman and his horse. Archaeological evidence has offered other clues as to what the cavalry horse wore for tack and armour. Roman forts both legionary and cavalry have yielded evidence that attests to some form of stabling and certain facilities for training cavalry mounts. Literary evidence in the form of *papyri* gives a little personal information about horse recruitment and trooper duties. Laws reflect the supply system, and its abuses, as well as human recruitment. Occasionally where a point is not clear or seems unbelievable, or at best stretching the imagination, ethnography comes to the rescue, sometimes only tenuously. This occurs, for instance, with regard to the Numidian cavalry's method of riding, guiding the horse by a tap with a stick on the neck and no bridle for restraint, at most having a withe around his neck. Watch any pack equine being driven on foot in Tunisia today. A tap, albeit on his rump, gives the clue, and he does not even have a halter on his head should he bolt. The two seem unconnected but the link is there – to these people it is the normal way to guide an equine, be it horse or ass.

Military writers give us rules for the cavalry to abide by and ideals to aim for in the execution of manoeuvres. Common sense allied to a knowledge of how the horse interprets orders, as well as how he reacts to certain stimuli, both favourable and alarming, fill the gaps left by the lack of specific literature on the subject.

As the power of Rome grew, and with it the size of her armies, an increasingly significant role in the military sphere was played by equines, either the horse carrying the trooper or the hardy mule his baggage. Eventually the cavalry became a large part of the forces and an even larger drain on financial, reproductive and agricultural resources. Cavalry needs had tentacles fingering their way into many non-equine areas.

We shall never know exactly how every aspect of the equine side of the Roman army worked. Because equines of all types were a part of everyday life a knowledge of them was assumed in their masters, and therefore there was little need to record such mundane facts. Flavius Vegetius Renatus produced a detailed manual for the infantry of his day. He gives a few pointers to cavalry practices but he treats the subject inadequately, affirming that as cavalry had already been brought to perfection no more need be said (*Ep. Rei Mil.*). Even were we fortunate enough to possess a detailed horsemanship manual from any era of Rome's long history, it still would not cover the subject. Horses are notorious in that the exception usually proves the rule. Broad outlines for management, training and operation were no doubt laid down, troopers adhering as closely as possible to ideals and standards expected of them and their horses. However, their equine partners had foibles of their own that would have made the machine-like uniformity of the infantry extremely hard to maintain, if not impossible without intensive training. Even then it could easily be disrupted. Down the ages good horsemen have always been observant and inventive. This has resulted in improvements in equipment; in techniques for handling horses; and in nutrition and care. Each horse was an individual and for the trooper's safety had to be respected as such while still being moulded into acceptable behaviour, the principles of which are still the same today.

A horse is generally an amenable and malleable tool, but one that needs special care and understanding. The cavalry horse and his humble cousin the baggage mule carried out the major functions of Roman equines.

4
Psychology and physiology of the Roman battle charger

In any logical discussion about horses and their use in warfare several things must be considered, particularly the mental and physical responses elicited from individual animals and from groups both large and small.

By nature the horse is not aggressive *to other species*. He is a herbivore and as such has no need of aggression as a prime characteristic, unlike carnivores. Although not as docile as some domesticated species he possesses several qualities that have made him useful to man, especially those nations bent on far-flung conquests who used him as a means to further their dominance over other peoples.

As a species he is reasonably intelligent. Some breeds are more intelligent than others; some individuals are very bright and at the other end of the scale some are incredibly stupid. Horses have a certain amount of reasoning power. They are capable of learning and, more important, are usually amenable to so doing. Several things have a direct bearing on this: their early experiences with man; the amount of patience the trainer employs when teaching them, coupled with the right degree of firmness; their level of intelligence; their innate temperament – a facet which is not linked to intelligence.

On the physical side their size, speed, weight-carrying ability and durability make them an attractive tool for the military. The ability to forage on the move also makes them reasonably self-sufficient under some military conditions, although not under others.

On the debit side several characteristics reduce the horse's military attractiveness. As a grazing animal he relies on speed to outstrip predators, and so he will flee rather than stand up to an enemy. His attitude can change when he is kept solely with others of the same species. In a herd, without fences or space restrictions, most arguments which result in fights are usually attributable to two factors: stallion dominance over younger or weaker colts which are driven off; or mare supremacy where one older female rules the rest. The stallion usually chivvies the herd while the dominant mare leads it.

When man intervenes and either stables, corrals, pickets or otherwise restricts movement by herd containment, animals that in natural surroundings obeyed the normal 'pecking' order can exhibit undesirable traits. Biting, chasing and kicking matches ensue. These often have all the aspects of a bar-room brawl, escalating as attacked animals, with no avenue of escape, retaliate in self-defence, and other animals are also provoked. For the military especially this can be very costly in maimed or temporarily injured horses. It also has the side effect that it *could* put a cavalryman relying on his charger to cooperate and carry him directly to the enemy in danger. Aggressiveness by one animal to another when being ridden side by side can result in the more timid animal hanging back. Also neither animal listens wholeheartedly to the rider, balancing rider orders against the subversive intimidation/domination by-play going on amongst themselves. However, once committed to a charge or other action this by-play ceases.

The size of the horse does not have as great a bearing on its ability to carry weight as would at first appear, but its conformation does, and this also affects its durability. Speed is not a major requirement for a warhorse. Any *ala* would travel at a conservative speed except when harrying or in a sudden charge. Then even the slowest animal would have mustered sufficient energy for a short burst. The more compact the animal the greater its load-bearing capacity, and the short stocky breeds that still retain enough refinement to give a smooth ride and achieve sufficient speed are far more suited to the arena of war than overlarge, lumbering, excessively heavy-fleshed animals. The latter are expensive to feed, utilize too much energy propelling their own bulk around, are prone to leg and joint ailments, and also give a rough and unseating ride.

At the other end of the scale ponies would also be unsuitable. At this point it must be explained that ponies are not small horses. They belong to a different sub-species that can interbreed, the resulting crosses having a mix of characteristics. Both species evolved from the same sources but diverged and acquired slightly different traits. Pony and horse gaits differ, the former frequently being more stilted. For a cavalryman riding with or without benefit of a saddle a pony's gait would be very tiring, with an upthrust that would hinder seat security. Without a saddle at all it would take too much of the trooper's attention merely to stay aboard. In the centuries of continuing Roman conquest many of the enemy tribes known for their horsemanship did ride ponies, but these were men brought up from childhood to ride 'by the seat of their pants'. It could be argued that these same tribes then provided large numbers of cavalrymen and mounts to the Roman forces and so would have been satisfied with ponies. Undoubtedly, and from some bone evidence, this was so, but as time rolled on the *alae*, although originally raised in specific locations, lost their ethnic content and riders of different nations were drafted in. It is too much to expect that all enlisted cavalrymen were natural horsemen (the majority of the approximately two million people who 'ride' in Britain are passengers aboard a docile animal that follows the tail in front of him). As cavalry became an increasingly important arm of the Roman forces more troopers had to learn from scratch. For this a horse's gaits would have been far more suitable than a pony's.

Though classified as 'large' or 'huge' by various Roman and Greek writers (see Chapter 1), the Thracian, Parthian, Cappadocian, Hunnish and Thessalian breeds would not be so considered today. They would now fall into the category of medium sized. Many military marches would have resembled the endurance rides now run in many countries, where in the main the horses used range from 14.3 to 15.2 hh (150–157 cm) (see Hyland 1988, part 3). From the published results of bone finds dating from the Roman era, we see that among the cannon bones, which determine the animal's approximate height, there are several that indicate a similar height for the Roman horse, tending to the lower range. The Pasyryk burials show horses of 14.3 hh (150 cm) and over (Rudenko 1970, pp. 56–7). The Krefeld Gellup finds from the Batavian battlefield of AD 69 contained the remains of 31 horses (Nobis 1973, p. 251). There were two isolated burials in which the horses measured 117 cm and 126.5 cm. The animals from the other graves ranged from 138 cm to 154 cm. There are approximately 10 cm to a hand (4 inches), the unit used to measure horses in Britain and most English-speaking nations. Thus 150 cm is exactly 14.3 hands, the height of Katchina, the horse which has been the main equine research partner for this book. Therefore, apart from two small ponies of approximately 11.2 and 12.2 hh (117 and 127 cm), the animals, from the smallest of approximately 13.2 hh to the largest at just a hair's breadth under 15.1 hh, were of sufficient size to operate efficiently and with smoother gaits than the small ponies. Newstead in Scotland (Curle 1911, p. 371) also yielded the remains of 14 to 15 hand horses. Roman Corbridge yielded cannon bone evidence of horses between 14.2 hh and 15 hh amongst other pony remains (Meek & Gray 1911, p. 226; Prof. J. Mann, pers. comm.). The Roman town of Colchester in Essex has also produced evidence of 15 hand mounts (Loch 1986, p. 63).

To get a good idea of the height of the Roman horses that were classified as 'large', some modern breeds that approximate in height are the Arabian (universal distribution), the Quarter Horse, Morgan and Appaloosa (found mainly in the USA but with a growing presence in most European countries, New Zealand and Australia); some of the larger British native ponies such as Fell, Dale, Highland, Connemara and New Forest, the latter ranging from 13 hh to 14.2 hh; the Camargue

(France), and the Haflinger (Austria). As discussed earlier, height is only one aspect of size, the other being body mass. From descriptions of the Roman 'ideal horse' it was obvious that an animal of robust appearance was preferred.

Where it proved feasible, when recruiting large bodies of cavalry, particularly in the Early Empire, mounts would accompany the men rather than be issued to them. Later, when the cavalry grew, Rome's military experts realized that a strong remount industry was vital to keep the men mounted, as losses through a variety of factors were inevitable. The natural progression was to become selective over the cavalry horse – bred, purchased, or levied – and the *Codex Theodosianus* (6.31.1) stipulates that horses shall 'meet certain requirements as to shape, stature, and age'. Unfortunately we are not told exactly what these requirements were, but common sense dictates that the animals drafted would have been adequate to superior. In the following regulation (ibid., 6.31.1.1) it is clear that the stablemasters were not above taking a bribe for accepting sub-standard horses, indeed to such an extent that it had to be legislated against.

A horse of robust, but withal breedy, appearance would be far easier to sit, particularly as the Roman military saddle had no stirrups, and large numbers of tribal cavalry undoubtedly rode either bareback or on a saddle cloth rather than on the more expensive saddle. Narrow horses are very difficult and very uncomfortable to ride without benefit of a proper saddle, and the small evidence for the Roman military saddle does not indicate that the structure of the frame or 'tree' had reached an advanced stage to suit all types of backs. Pads underneath a saddle can only ameliorate minor discrepancies in fit. A broad-backed horse with the required 'double chine' is more comfortable to ride, and it is much easier to achieve good balance on such a back. The compact, well to moderately fleshed animal usually has a good food conversion ratio with a slower metabolism than the leaner types. This would be highly favourable to a large body of cavalry that had to forage on the march, as such animals would maintain body flesh more easily and would need correspondingly less time to graze. On the debit side, the heavier-fleshed horse is usually not such an enduring animal as the lean, racy type of equine, and as will be shown below the type of animals used by Rome were partly responsible for a protracted campaign in Africa where the enemy were mounted on the leaner Libyan horses.

Whether heavy-fleshed with short muscle fibres, or lean with long-fibred muscles that make for greater endurance, any horse will be debilitated by continued campaigning without adequate forage and grain, or by excessive use without adequate rest. Subjected to continuous travel a horse will eventually become 'leg weary' and perform less efficiently. If not rested he will finally become unserviceable, as lamenesses will occur more frequently. Throughout Caesar's *de Bello Gallico* there are constant references to troops going out on forage parties. Cavalry naturally operated best in the late spring to late autumn months, and again from Caesar it is clear that winter sometimes put a halt to manoeuvres because of lack of forage growth. When the Belgae began stirring up trouble, Caesar enrolled two new legions under Quintus Pedius. Caesar himself had to stay in Hither Gaul, not travelling to the war zone until the spring grass had grown sufficiently to give adequate grazing for his cavalry (ibid., II.2). Caesar frequently differentiates between forage and corn. Grass in spring and summer, and hay in winter, is not adequate for a hard-working horse, and grain has to be fed to keep the animal healthy and allow him to maintain flesh and vigour.

The above covers some aspects of the pertinent mental and physical requirements of a cavalry horse. Many tasks faced the Roman 'wranglers' and quartermasters. The troopers and foot soldiers could be given orders and knew the dire punishments which disobedience incurred. If necessary they could march and fight on reduced rations and could carry a sufficient supply for an extended march in their packs. The cavalry horse eventually learnt to obey, but he could not carry sufficient fodder and corn to remain at top efficiency level, and the daily permitted ration was meagre even for a horse at rest – a bare subsistence ration for any but the really good 'doer'.

The Roman wrangler's job was to select the horse with the right conformation, and then induce those animals to perform well in a totally alien environment.

5
Supply of equines to the Roman army

The supply of equines to the Roman army falls into two categories:

(1) Traction and baggage mules, and packhorses and ponies.
(2) Chargers for the various levels in the hierarchy: high-ranking officers; legionary cavalry; cavalry *alae*; *cohortes equitatae*; and possibly a special requirement for speedy horses for scouts.

Stock for hauling or carrying equipment varied according to country of origin. The eastern and Mediterranean sectors were supplied with mules and larger donkeys such as the Arcadian and Reatine ass. In the more northerly climates indigenous ponies would have been used as pack animals and draught horses for traction, although the Column shows that Trajan operated a mule corps for his *ballistae* even in the cold Danube region. Oxen must have played a part, but that does not concern this book.

As humble beasts of burden the mule and donkey did not attract much interest from writers, except the gentleman farmers such as Varro and Columella, to whom they represented a source of considerable income, or the humorous authors such as Apuleius and Martial. Consequently specific information on mules and pack animals in general is sparse.

We know from Pelagonius that horse dealers abounded as he talks of the dealers from Sicily and other areas (*Ars Vet.* I.6), the breeders of Galicia (ibid., I.5) and Cappadocia (ibid., II.24), and of the Tuscans who love Asturian horses (ibid., II.27), indicating that there was lively trade in equines across provincial frontiers as well as close to home. Caesar tells us of the Celts importing draught horses (*de Bello Gall.* IV.4), and more specifically, in 170 BC, 20 stallions were exported from Italy to Transalpine Gaul (Ridgeway 1905).

In an era where transport was either by animal or water, wherever there were horses and donkeys there were also their hybrid offspring. In Italy, Reate, Apulia and Brundisium had large herds of mules whose main purpose in life was to transport goods. Mules are larger than donkeys and stronger in a size-to-weight ratio than horses. The general practice of stock-raising from the ones or twos of the small farmer (Juvenal, *Sat.* VIII, referring to horses) to the herds of mules bred by Varro would have resulted in a seasonal crop of valuable foals. Columella affirms that prices for mules were as high as those paid for 'Noble' stock intended for track or civic use. This made mule breeding an attractive prospect on the large estates as well as on the smallholdings. Later, when all but privileged classes were forbidden to own a horse (*Codex Theo.* 9.30.1.2.3), breeding must have been concentrated into large *latifundia* owned by the rich senatorial class – a move sure to make the plebs as dissatisfied with the Roman government as most are with today's politicians.

The army must have been a ready market and one of the biggest buyers of stock, and we can safely assume that mule breeding and purchase or procurement by levy, tax or appropriation paralleled that of horses as they were required in increasing numbers by the expanding army. When the Roman world was confined to Italy, and the country was still largely agricultural with a relatively small army, purchase from breeders would probably supply sufficient animals, the regular income acting as a spur to keep breeders producing foals. Later, when the landworker deserted his *iugera* or was called up into the army, other arrangements would have come into force. Large estate owners such as Varro could provide quantities of baggage stock. When the *Cursus Publicus* also had to be supplied Imperial estates must have bred a large proportion of mules as well as horses. Being a humble beast, with not very spectacular duties when compared to the *éclat* of a charger or chariot horse, his worth was not extolled but taken for granted.

Mules and donkeys do not do well in miserable wet and cold conditions. Neither do horses and ponies, but the latter are much better adapted to withstanding the northern type of climate. Ponies can carry a greater burden in size-to-weight ratio than a horse (one has only to participate in a present-day cattle drift or colt hunt on the New Forest to appreciate this, as ponies of 13.2 hh and 14 hh carry 14 stone (90 kg) and more all day long). Many riders consider their 15.2 hh horse overburdened with such a weight, which is ridiculous. Europe has many breeds of weight-carrying pony that would have supplied the legions in place of mules.

The supply of cavalry horses opens up a wide area of discussion. Many factors governed it, and at certain stages in the Empire's growth different aspects can be seen. It was not merely a question of getting enough animals for troopers to ride. From a host of small references regarding horses a picture can be pieced together. The duties a horse had to perform dictated the requirements in type, temperament, intelligence, conformation, age, training required, and care bestowed. The wide span of Empire also influenced the types or breeds used according to the *origones* of cavalry units in the Early Empire, and the subsequent availability of remounts in any given locality. The means of acquiring mounts varied. Much information from the Later Empire is contained in the *Codex Theodosianus*, and the most useful documentation to colour this is that of the *Cohors XX Palmyrenorum* stationed at Dura Europos in AD 251 (Fink 1971, no. 83). This describes horses, ages, colours, markings, brands, prices, and even in one case country of origin. What comes out of the document most strongly is that there was no standardization other than the requirement of passing the *probatio* or what we would today term 'trial period', which included a veterinary examination for soundness. The *Codex Theodosianus* makes it clear that this was a requirement (6.31.1), and in the following addition to the same law (ibid., 6.31.1.1) it is equally clear that bribes were offered to the stablemasters to let sub-standard animals pass inspection. Ammianus Marcellinus indicates the penalty for this offence (*Res Gest.* 29.3) when he tells of a *strator* or riding master on assignment in Sardinia exchanging adequate mounts for inferior ones. Valentinian ordered him to be stoned to death. This story also highlights the continued good standing of Sardinia as a breeding ground. Although these and other references pertaining to cavalry are from the Later Empire it is likely that a similar practice had previously applied and only became codified under Theodosius.

In Rome's republican days the equestrian class provided their own warhorses. Under Servius Tullius the cost of providing mounts for the *eques* was borne by the state, who granted 10,000 *asses* per century for the purchase of horses, and 2,000 *asses* per year for their feed and maintenance. This fodder grant was levied on rich widows (Livy, I.43). At that time, with the emerging state, the numbers of horses needed were not great, and the Italian allies, or *socii*, provided most. Several regions of Italy were noted for producing good horses – Apulia, Campania, the islands of Sardinia and Sicily, Liguria and Tuscany. Of these Campania was noted for producing the finest cavalry chargers. In Sybaris horses were raised in huge numbers, 5,000 being used in one religious procession alone according to Timaeus, while Aristotle asserts that at the Battle of Sagra chargers who had also been taught to dance broke off their military duties at the sound of flutes played by the enemy to distract them and started dancing instead (Frederiksen 1968). This is not entirely far-fetched, as horses definitely learn to move to music and perform accordingly in quadrilles and dressage tests, matching chords and steps in their performance.

Levies on Italian allies provided the bulk of cavalry mounts in the conflict between Rome and Gaul in 225–224 BC. The Celts mustered

50,000 foot and 20,000 cavalry and chariots. In answer, Rome could call on the conveniently rounded figures of 700,000 foot and 70,000 horse (Polybius, *Hist.* II.23–4). One suspects here a little of Herodotus' tendency to enlarge numbers. The Campanians, Iapygians and Messapians, Samnites, Lucanians, Marsi, Frentani, Marrucine and Bestani provided most, especially the first three. Horsebreeding must have been a major money earner for stud owners, and Italy bursting at the seams with equines at all stages of growth, as the horses provided were only those of sufficient age and so youngstock must have far outstripped them in number. With the exception of earlier Greek imports, which by then had been absorbed into Italian stock, the days of major outside cavalry influences were still to come. However, the input of Celtic stock from the battle of Telamon alone must have given Rome a boost to her immediate needs for replenishment and a limited gene pool of outside blood (although, as we have seen, the trend was for the Celts to import Italian stock for upgrading). According to Polybius, the Celtic dead numbered 40,000 with 10,000 captured. This meant, allowing for dead and maimed animals, a very large number of riderless horses running loose, many of which would have been mares.

Hannibal and his vastly superior cavalry was the real catalyst for introducing superior stock. His Numidian, Libyan, Spanish and Celtic horse inflicted repeated defeats on the Romans. Not only did their styles of fighting on horseback show to advantage but the stock introduced into Italy and Spain was to have a lasting effect. Although his initial number of horse that succeeded in crossing the Alps only numbered 6,000, during his long sojourn in Italy replenishments came in. He picked up Italian mounts at every battle, as well as requisitioning them; witness the 4,000 head his troops rounded up in Apulia and Sallentine territory and subsequently broke in (Livy, XXIV.20). Stock movements between Carthage and New Carthage in Spain were frequent. Scipio Africanus was quick to take advantage of Numidian cavalry when he turned the tables on Hannibal at Zama in 202 BC. African and Spanish bloodstock figure largely as both racing and cavalry horses, and in the Empire large numbers of both types were produced on Imperial estates.

Numidian cavalry is specifically mentioned in 125 BC fighting under Fulvius Flaccus against the Saluvii (Ridgeway 1905), and again in Caesar's *de Bello Gallico* (II.10). Caesar made extensive use of cavalry in the Gallic Wars in the mid 50s BC and both the human and equine elements of his cavalry must have presented a very cosmopolitan appearance. In addition to his own Roman chargers he levied units from several pro-Roman Gallic tribes, notably the Aedui, and purchased a large contingent of remounts from Italy and Spain (ibid., VII.55) which reneging Aedui appropriated and distributed amongst opposing Gauls.

While considering German mounts inferior and ill-favoured to look at, Caesar esteemed their endurance, high standard of training and speed (ibid., IV.2, 4). Initially Caesar suffered a setback when 800 Germans charged, causing chaos in the 5,000 Roman horse. They then dismounted and fought on foot, stabbing at the Roman horses' bellies, while their own mounts obediently stayed ground-tied and available. Caesar turned the tables in a counter-engagement when the Germans did not follow up their advantage. Later he sent into Germany for cavalry to use against Vercingetorix (ibid., VII.65), but instead of the German mounts he substituted those of his own officers and legionary cavalry which he appropriated. As his own personal troop of cavalry he employed 500 Germans.

Sixty years later in the wars of Germanicus against Arminius in AD 16, the toll in horseflesh was high. The German chieftain made the troopers' mounts his first target, and though Italy and Spain, along with Gaul, provided remounts, the steady drain totally depleted Gaul of serviceable stock (Tacitus, *Ann.*, I.65, 69, 81). Clearly by this time Rome relied heavily on Gaul and Spain for a large percentage of cavalry horses.

In the east, Syria, a Roman province since 63 BC, supplied a steady stream of mounts for the Jewish Wars conducted by Vespasian and his son Titus. As well as Antiochus' Syrian cavalry, Soeamus of Emesa, Agrippa and the Arabian King Malchus sent contingents of horse (Josephus, *Ant. J.*, III.64–8). Josephus mentions these several times and is always careful to state whether they were mounted archers or cavalry, the latter implying that some were of the type best known in the east – heavy armed cataphracts. This also suggests that two types of horse would be used. The heavier, taller animal would be either full-blooded Nisaean stock, of which there was plenty available as the breed had entered several countries well before the Roman era, or partbred stock – in other words, local breeds upgraded for weight-carrying with Nisaean blood, the progeny of which would in time have become new breeds in their own right. The archers would have been mounted on lighter-framed, speedier stock of Oriental blood, similar to today's Arabian.

Rome would also have had plenty of time since annexing Syria to equip herself with Oriental weight-carrying stock. Josephus mentions mailed cavalry several times, specifically at Jotapata (ibid., III.254) where the 'bravest cavalry' are described as 'protected by armour from head to foot and with lances couched'. These were cataphracts armed with the *contus*. Nowhere does Josephus refer to armoured horses in conjunction with mailed or armoured riders, but does use the term 'caparisoned' horses (ibid., V.348–52). Having taken great care to be explicit about the men, had the horses carried mail protection it is probable that he would have been equally specific. It is also quite clear that the normal cavalry were only equipped with helmet and cuirass similar to the infantry (ibid., III.93–7). Josephus (ibid., I.101) also contradicts Strabo (*Geog.* 16.4.26), who says that Nabatea had no horses, when he states that Aretas the Arab, King of Nabatea, provided 10,000 cavalry for his war with Antiochus XII just before Syria became a Roman province. Josephus' word must be taken over that of Strabo as he was the 'man on the spot', and would hardly have been so concerned with accuracy of description and then have been so far out in his calculations over the King of Arabia.

Cavalry units that had sufficed earlier were now being augmented by regular cavalry *alae* of *quingenaria* (500) and *milliaria* (1000) strength. These were being drawn from many sources – allies, client kings, and peoples conquered and subsequently attached to Rome. From the time of Augustus onwards, as cavalry increased so too did the ethnic content of the auxiliary *alae*, fighting after their own methods and using native weapons. Complementing their national type of warfare were mounts indigenous to their native country. As described in Chapter 1 there were a great number of distinct breeds in existence. Some had acquired certain similarities through proximity of locations and crossbreeding. Others with more potent genes retained distinctive traits. At this time, when many of the *alae* were compulsorily drafted *en bloc*, their own country provided their mounts as part of the costs borne by annexed or client peoples. Inevitably as time passed the *alae* and *cohortes equitatae* mounts needed replacing, and the breed content of units would become diffused by inclusion of new mounts from the area in which the cavalry units operated. Cavalry raised as an ethnic unit could expect to see service in many places. For example, horses from Thrace were sent to Britain, Germany, Raetia, both Pannonias, Syria, Egypt and Mauretania Caesariensis (Cheesman 1914). From the variety of postings it is obvious that no concern was felt about how the horses would adapt to different climates, which at times were the complete opposite to that of their native country. Transfer from a hot to a colder zone would not have such a disastrous effect as change from cold to hot. It is only in recent years that research has shown the deleterious effects of loss of body salts and trace elements through excessive sweating. Merely drinking quantities of water is insufficient for rehydration. Modern solutions of electrolytes are necessary for rapid rehydration to allow fluids to be absorbed through the gut wall.

It is known that the army had large ranches (*saltus*) for stock-raising. Common sense dictates that horses no longer fit for military service would, where possible, be retired to stud, particularly the mares. A horse lamed through injury would still have years left to produce valuable offspring. A stallion tested in battle would be useful in imparting certain characteristics of courage, or at least his suitability in war would be proven. Throughout the Empire production of sufficient stock must have been a constant burden and all sources must have been tapped. There were many means open to the military by which they could acquire cavalry mounts. Some would allow the requisitioning or purchasing officers to demand certain standards, others would not. The most obvious methods would include:

(1) National contingents that brought their own horses with them.
(2) Requisition from large landowners.
(3) Levies on provinces.
(4) Tribute from client kingdoms.
(5) Taxes where the whole or the part value of a beast was levied on individuals.
(6) Public services.
(7) Outright purchase from breeders and/or dealers.
(8) Imperial/army stud farms.
(9) Capture of enemy horses.

Cheesman, in his book on the *auxilia* (1914), has a useful list which although it relates to the period around AD 70 gives a very good idea of which provinces were the most prominent in equestrianism. Those which stand out by virtue of large numbers are as follows:

	Cavalry	Coh. Equitatae
Lugdunensis	13,000	375
Belgica (Gaul)	3,500	1,750
Narbonensis	1,000	–
Tarraconensis (Spain)	6,000	1,250
Thrace	4,500	875
Pannonia	4,000	250
Syria	2,000	1,075
Africa	2,000	250
Britain	1,500	375
Palestine	1,000	250
Moesia	1,000	250

In addition many countries provided enough cavalry for one *ala*; others sufficient to flesh out the mounted part of one or more *cohortes equitatae*. Some of the above nations had a very long history of horsemanship. The Gauls were noted as mounted warriors. Rome suffered under their horses' hooves as early as 378 BC, but had eventually turned the wealth of Gallic horseflesh to their advantage, using it as a main source of supply. Pannonia (what is now western Hungary and northern Yugoslavia) provided a sizeable contingent. Hungary has been famous for horsemanship for centuries. Early in the Empire the Iazyges Sarmatians had settled in the Hungarian plains (Sulimirski 1970, pp. 133–4). It is only to be expected that the Sarmatians had a very strong influence on the Pannonians in equestrian matters. Much later the Sarmatians, whose nomadic life centred around the horse, provided huge numbers for the Roman army. They fought against Trajan in his Dacian Wars, and were later recruited into the Roman army by Marcus Aurelius. Heavy tribute of 8,000 mounted troops was demanded, 5,500 of which were sent to Britain and stationed at Ribchester.

Thrace was a horse-orientated nation, their whole culture centring around the animal. The horse appears constantly in Thracian art and religion (Fol and Marazov 1977), and the main literary descriptions of it as 'huge' (Homer, *Iliad*) and 'easy keepers and excellent performers' (Gratius Faliscus, *Cyn.*) suggest that the Thracian horse was eminently suitable for war. The ugly neck and curving spine to which Gratius objected (ibid.) would not impede normal cavalry duties, and from many depictions in Thracian art it is obvious that the breed was a weight carrier, as many are shown with a fully mailed rider. Spain had been supplying droves of horses for centuries, as had Africa, while in the east Syria and Palestine were heir to the idea that wealth equated with numbers of horses owned. Strabo tells us of the huge herds owned by the Seleucids (*Geog.* 16.2.10). Clearly the diverse characteristics of the dozens of breeds produced by so many countries affected the type of warfare that could be conducted aboard them. As we have seen, the *Codex Theodosianus* (6.31.1) states: 'certain requirements as to shape, stature, and age must be observed'. This law was enacted four times between AD 365 and 373, showing that although the army had its guidelines they were obviously flouted on many occasions. Nevertheless there was a standard that stablemasters strove to achieve in their selection of mounts.

Staying with the theme of selection, the other extremely important requirements would have been soundness, temperament and intelligence. Soundness would be covered by the *probatio* examination. Intelligence would reveal itself once the animal was put into training and would no doubt determine whether it became a top trooper's mount, a not-so-talented equine member of an *ala*, or a member of the *cohors equitata* where quality of animal – which is not only measured by visual standards – was not so high. However, temperament would be the real key to the horse's suitability. Until an animal was put into training, including experiencing mock situations, his true temperament might not reveal itself. If, as was most likely, the horse had been destined as a cavalry mount from foalhood he would have spent the first two or three years running relatively free and been sold as soon as he reached riding age. Once grouped in a concentrated mass, temperament very quickly decides what place the animal secures for itself in the pecking order. The bully or the constantly picked on horse would not be the ideal cavalry mount, the former needing a few manners rammed into it, the latter much confidence.

Varro says horses destined for camps should be high spirited (*de Re Rust.*). Virgil (*Georgics* III.72–85), when discussing breeding stock, especially that intended for war, lists many of the qualities essential in a charger: 'how the animal from birth picks his feet up high; . . . is the first to venture on to the highroad; to ford a menacing river; cross bridges; does not shy easily; has a proud carriage; gets excited at the sound of battle and is impatient to engage.' He also says that bays and roans are the soundest and white or dun horses the worst. As we have seen, bays and roans have black points and hard hooves and are frequently freer of leg and hoof troubles than white (grey) horses, whose hooves are often weaker. Some greys are also prone to melanoma. Duns, if the true dun with black points and hooves is meant, are very tough animals, but the palomino shades which Virgil may be referring to often have light-coloured hooves.

Temperament would also govern the animal's progress in training. The sluggish animal that needed constant prodding would be a danger to a rider demanding instant responses. The bad-tempered, excitable idiot was even worse. Such horses are very difficult to control and can be almost unridable when in company or moving fast, as speed excites a horse more than anything else. This must trace back to the grazing animal's use of speed to escape danger. Any restraint may anger such a horse who retaliates with unsocial acts – rearing, bucking or bolting being the most common (a most uncomfortable position to be in and very dangerous). Aulus Atticus was killed at Mons Graupius when his horse bolted into the enemy ranks (Tacitus, *Agr.*, 37). The mettlesome horse described by Tacitus was probably unnerved by the clangour of battle and panicked. Undoubtedly more cavalrymen lost their lives as a result of panicking mounts charging into enemy ranks than has probably been estimated. Bits of increasing severity, many of which have been found, attempted to control such horses. They did not always have the desired effect but would have been a last resort before giving the animal a dishonourable discharge and relegating him to the baggage train, stud or shambles.

Intelligence in a horse is not directly linked to temperament though the two characteristics work together. The ideal cavalry horse had to be smart, but not too smart. Arabians are sometimes too clever and individualistic, more suited to the type of Oriental warfare where each man was an entity, rather than a member of a close-order pack. The Oriental archers and the Numidians relied on a superb rapport that enabled them to ride their animals with little head restraint, leaving both hands free. They also rode in a looser formation. A more phlegmatic animal is better suited to close-order action. These are usually from a heavier breed with a calmer disposition, but the fact that they are calm does not mean they are less intelligent. It takes much greater skill to ride a volatile animal which, with tactful training, can be a very valuable cavalry mount. Phlegmatic types can withstand a few blunders by insensitive riders and trainers and still be useful. As pointed out before, using a comparison with today's riders we can assume plenty of hamfisted, heavy-seated riders in Roman days.

Choosing animals with the right mix of temperament and intelligence must have been one of the hardest of the stablemasters' tasks. One characteristic desirable in a cavalry charger and highly undesirable in a mount for a civilian was aggression, albeit manageable aggression. Varro is very explicit on this, as we have seen: 'For just as we need them high spirited for camps so we prefer to have them quiet on the road. Castration effects this' (*de Re Rust.*). This raises the very important question of the sex of cavalry mounts. It need not be thought that stallions would have been unsuitable because of the potential nuisance value of disruptive behaviour, and that in consequence males would be castrated. Certainly castration was used by certain tribes, and the geographer Strabo (*Geog.* 7.4.8) comments on the Sarmatians and Scythians having the *peculiarity* of gelding to make horses easy to manage. Ammianus Marcellinus, several centuries later (*Res Gest.* 17.12), also comments on this practice of the Sarmatians and Quadi, saying it was to prevent the stallions bolting at the sight of mares, or betraying their presence in an ambush by neighing. Some stallions are sometimes extremely noisy, others as quiet as any other horse. (My own stallion Nizzolan whuffles politely and quietly with his mares, others almost roar, the neigh is so loud.) From all this, however, it is very clear that gelding was not the norm for the army in Roman times. There is also sufficient evidence from carvings that stallions were used, as the full complement of equipment may be seen!

The use of muzzles also implies that stallions were used. Horses of both sexes and geldings may bite, and in mares and geldings it usually denotes bad temper and lack of sufficient training. It is a habit very easy to break, and needs early correction by a swift rap on the offending muzzle. But with stallions it is not so easy. Some stallions never bite, others do so occasionally. Others are a great nuisance, constantly nipping and mouthing at anything within range. Unchecked this can easily turn to savagery. Most stallions can be taught manners, others never can. With such horses in training it would save a lot of damage to other horses and frustration to their riders if they wore muzzles; the riders would not want to spend too much time on curing one individual of this obnoxious habit. In certain battle circumstances it could even be advantageous, as a warhorse will use both teeth and feet (fore and hind) against the enemy if so encouraged. It is natural for stallions to use their teeth. Some do so when covering mares, gripping them at the base of the neck or withers. Watch colts playing: uncut ones will constantly nip each other's flanks. Later, as mature animals, it is done seriously. Herodotus (*Hist.* V.110) tells of Artybius, a Persian cavalry commander, who had a horse trained to use teeth and feet. Medieval destriers also acted in this manner. Unruly stallions will also employ such a measure against their riders, a dangerous trait (a top trainer told me of a champion show stallion that dragged his rider off by savaging her leg and breaking it in 17 places), but one that could be used to advantage against the enemy.

The argument that stallions would be too disruptive does not in fact carry much force. Provided common sense is used, and we know the Romans had plenty, it should not be a problem. Danger under saddle would be very easy to avoid by following a few straightforward rules. Do not put a gelding between a stallion and a mare, as to do so means certain attack. Avoid riding a stallion alongside a mare in oestrus, though in a well-mannered stallion even this should not cause a problem: most entries adequately ridden are quite safe to ride in this situation, although a few are not. In the stable, common-sense precautions would have been used. The sectioning off which according to the limited archaeological evidence was apparently used would have made it possible to put stallions in one section, mares and/or geldings in others. I have kept stallions, geldings and mares in close proximity for decades and have never had any problems. Stallions treated like any other equine, provided sensible precautions are taken, blend in very well. In battle, with the turmoil of action their minds would be on the furore around them, not the sex of the horse alongside. The few that refused to behave would have been gelded very quickly. But it is probable that castrating a horse would not have been resorted to unless essential because of wound infections, particularly in hot countries with a fly problem. Horses were too valuable a commodity to risk unnecessarily. The other method of castration, by ligature and atrophy, would be very drawn out. The final argument for the considerable use of stallions, particularly in the east, is the dislike men of Oriental blood have for riding mares. Today in eastern countries it is still the norm to leave males entire. Stallions are worked together in harness in Tunisia.

Before leaving the subject I would also suggest that more males than females were used as chargers. One stallion can serve many mares so relatively few would be needed at stud. Mares produced the replacements for cavalry and unless barren would be more likely to be kept in the breeding herds. The records of *Cohors XX Palmyrenorum* of AD 251 show that out of the 13 horses described, eight were male (presumably stallions in the east), three female, and two not stated. Of the 31 found at Krefeld Gellep, however, around half were male, half female. As the Krefeld Gellep horses were being used in the Batavian revolt of AD 69 every available animal was probably drafted for military use regardless of breeding potential.

The last physical consideration in selecting a horse would have been its age. Although the *Codex Theodosianus* tells us that animals had to meet certain requirements as regards age, it does not state what those requirements were. We saw in Chapter 2 that Pelagonius says that horses, other than racehorses, can be broken at two years of age (*Ars Vet.* I); Columella agrees; Varro recommends leaving breaking until three because horses are more muscled up by then (*de Re Rust.*), and Virgil (*Georgics* III.191) concurs with him. The modern method is normally to break a youngster in at three but not to work it until it is four. I prefer to back it at two, defer any other training until three, and work it at four. If an animal is worked hard too young its period of usefulness is shortened, as it will not stay sound for long. The military must have had to balance the long-term need of not being constantly forced to replace unsound horses with current needs, which may frequently have dictated that immediate numbers overrode long-term use. Evidence from military sites from a very wide geographical and time spread gives a rough guide to the ages of animals used. As we have seen, the ancients aged a horse whose actual date of birth was unknown by its teeth. They could, with a fair degree of accuracy, age a horse up to seven years of age, after which they called it *aequatus*, or what we would term 'aged'. The same method is used today but we can be more accurate up to eight years of age.

The excavations at Hod Hill in Dorset show buildings reliably supposed to have been stables because of the traces of manure and the horses' teeth which were found. Horses shed their teeth from around two and a half years of age until they are five, when all permanent teeth have erupted. From the Hod Hill evidence it is clear that young horses were being used. At the Batavian battlefield at Krefeld Gellep the majority of the animals found were seven years of age or under (Nobis 1973, p. 251), the largest group being between four and five years old. This argues for the preferred age of chargers being in the age group that had achieved physical maturity but had not seen the excessive wear and tear of hard usage. In the records of the *Cohors XX Palmyrenorum* stationed at Dura Europos there is a list of horses with their descriptions dated to AD 51 (Fink 1971, no. 83, p. 341). Of the 13 horses actually described the ages of nine of them are shown (the records of the others are in part blank because of the age of the papyrus). Four horses are shown as four years old on purchase, four as seven or more (i.e. *aequatus*, rather than the exact age), and one as a two year old. It is significant that the two year old was purchased in AD 245 and was still sound and on the rolls seven years later. It may well have been a 'long' two years old (i.e. nearly three) when purchased and approaching riding age. One other interesting point about the teeth of the horses is the comment on the Commagenian horse of Abedsalmes' son. This had a marking (*prorostratum*) that Fink said he could not understand. He says it is not clear how a horse's muzzle would protrude enough to be a distinguishing mark. I think it could well be an extreme case of the condition we know as 'parrot mouth', in which the top teeth protrude over the lower, making it difficult for the horse to eat. Today such a horse would not get a veterinary certificate of soundness, and most breed societies would not accept a stallion with this defect. The only other explanation would be a very pronounced Roman nose (convex head), but that would start further up the facial plane. In Spain a horse with a Roman nose was known as 'ram headed', and as the Spanish influence was so strong in the Roman equestrian sphere I think the term 'ram headed' would have been used in this case if that was what was meant.

This document brings us to another phase in the selection of horses: supply, other than by national *en bloc* drafting. It names 19 men, six of whom have lost their horses for one reason or another – a very high percentage in such a small number. Of the 13 horses that are described six are branded, some are specifically referred to as unbranded, and for others there is no comment. The descriptions point to purchase or requisition from a wide variety of sources, as the branded horses were not all branded in the same manner, two carrying brands on right thigh and shoulder; one on right thigh and left shoulder; one on only the right shoulder; and one with just the left thigh branded. One is branded on the left side, but the actual place is undecipherable.

The *Codex Theodosianus* has several laws relating to the supply of horses to the army. Sometimes instead of the horses their equivalent value in gold was exacted. The rates fluctuated between 15 and 23 *solidi* per horse, and the stablemasters received from nothing up to two *solidi* for each animal they passed. This led to pressure to pass unsuitable animals and thus corruption, and it may be of interest to tabulate the actual amounts and the years in which the laws were passed. These exactions were mostly on provincials and dioceses that had to supply a certain number of horses for army use (see Table 1).

Table 1. Laws relating to the supply of horses (*Codex Theodosianus*)

7.22.2.1 AD 326	Constantine to Octavianus, Gov. of Lucania and Bruttium	Sons of veteran cavalrymen can go straight into cavalry if they have a horse.
7.22.2.2	" "	If any son of a veteran shall have two horses, or a horse and a slave, he shall serve the rank of patrol, which rank is conferred upon others only after service, and he shall have two subsistence allowances.
6.31.1 AD 365, 368, 370, 373	Valentinian and Valens to Zozimus, Gov. of New Epirus	Only 1 *solidus* to the stablemasters; horses offered to be of certain standards.
11.17.1 AD 367	Valentinian and Valens to Alexandrinus, Count of Privy Purse	23 *solidi* per horse to be exacted of *coloni* and other persons subjected to this tax. Cash to be paid rather than horses.

7.23.1 AD 369	Valentinian, Valens and Gratian to Probus, Praetorian Prefect	Cost of letters patent conferring honorary status:
		  for a Count 3 horses
		  for a Governor 2 horses

7.23.1.1	" "	These horses to be levied every five years
11.17.3 AD 399 and 401	Arcadius and Honorius to Praetorian Prefects and Count of Sacred Imperial Largesses	Command that military horses be commuted into money payments. 2 *solidi* allowed to stablemasters. Annual levy. At request of Gaudentius, Count of Africa, 7 *solidi* allowed each soldier for each horse.

11.17.2 AD 401	Same emperors to Pompeianus, Proc. of Africa	20 *solidi* per horse to be exacted from provincials and 7 for each soldier.
11.1.29 AD 401	Same emperors to provincials of Proconsular Province of Africa (including Numidia, Byzacium, Tripolitania)	A reduction from 20 *solidi* to: 18 for horses from Numidia 15 for horses from Byzacium and Tripolitania. Nothing to be paid to stablemasters for approval.

This short list of laws illustrates that in the Late Empire part of the supply of horses came via tribute or taxes. A small number came from recruits providing their own mounts, and an even larger number through outright purchase by the army, who had the bulk sum gathered from the provinces when the taxes had been commuted into money payments. From the earlier law of Constantine it is clear that in his time the animals themselves were provided, and from the wording of the other laws this seems to have been the regular method. It was replaced by commutation when perhaps the need for large numbers of replacements was unnecessary, but it could just as easily be reversed. The levy on honorary personnel occurring at five-yearly intervals shows that a horse was considered a very valuable animal. It also gave time for homebred offspring to mature. That there was an interim period where, although money was preferred, horses could still be provided, albeit in defiance of the general rule which later became law, is shown by *The Abinnaeus Archive* (Bell et al. 1962, pap. 13). Flavius Abinnaeus, a cavalry officer, had already had more than 30 years service before he was given command of an *ala* at Dionysias in the Arsinoite Nome of Egypt in AD 342. One of his duties was the collection of taxes. When he sent a batch of horses to the *exactor*, Plutammon, he received an irate reply which complained of receiving beasts instead of cash.

The sum of 23 *solidi* per horse was very high indeed when it was based on 72 *solidi* to the Roman pound. That is approximately 4 oz (105 g) of gold per horse. This does not tie in well with the 125 *denarii* paid for each horse in AD 251 as shown in the records of the *Cohors* XX *Palmyrenorum*. Massive inflation would account for some of the discrepancy, but it would appear that the government had a tidy sum left over and was fleecing the taxpayer. The 125 *denarii* per horse would suggest that the army set a fixed sum when purchasing horses, and the breeder would be forced to accept that amount. I doubt very much if when the army requisitioning people came round a breeder would be able to haggle in time-honoured horsetrading fashion. The 7 *solidi* allowed in the Later Empire suggests that a horse was expected to last approximately three years on active duty, given that the law of AD 401 fixing 20 *solidi* per horse (*Codex Theo.*, 11.17.2) and the laws of 399 and 401, where Gaudentius asked for 7 *solidi* per soldier for each horse, both covered the Province of Africa. Unless of course the difference between the amount the soldier was allowed and that gathered in tax was government profit!

6
Cavalry logistics

Providing, operating and maintaining a cavalry force would have presented the High Command with an enormous logistical task. Add to that the procurement and maintenance of baggage and *ballistae* mules and the problem doubled. Armies were accompanied by a vast catalogue of supplies. Not many commanders would have taken Hannibal's risky move of dispensing with a baggage train on the premise that if he was successful, supplies would be forthcoming, and if he was defeated he would not need them (Polybius, *Hist.* III.79) The problem can be roughly divided into two sections: (1) base facilities and provisions; (2) provisions on campaign manoeuvres.

According to Vegetius (*Ep. Rei. Mil.*), the Camp Prefect was in overall charge of arms, horses, clothing, provisions, vehicles, battle horses, wood and fodder. He was also expected to see that the horses were exercised. Under him came the centurions, the people who did the actual work.

Fodder

The most obvious need for cavalry mounts and baggage mules is fodder. Equines can do without hard feed (grain) but they cannot do without grass or hay. In work, however, grain is necessary to maintain health. Therefore the prime requirement is sufficient grazing in summer and enough palatable hay in winter. Spoiled and/or musty hay is dangerous. Secondly, a sufficient store of grain must be laid down to last from one harvest to the next. Historians so far have not shown much appreciation of the huge task presented by maintaining the army's horses and mules. In addition there would be animals for sacrifice, and some cattle for meat, as well as chickens and possibly pigs. To present a reasoned argument it is necessary to be more specific about numbers of animals. Even the small contingent attached to a *cohors equitata* would present considerable provision problems, with 120-plus animals eating their heads off. One approach is to show the animals needed in a given area. Hadrian's Diploma of AD 122 lists a large number of units in Britain, comprising:

4 legions
12 *alae quingenariae*
1 *alae milliaria*
4 *coh. equitatae milliariae*
14 *coh. equitatae quingenariae*

Dr Brian Dobson has put forward the suggestion that the number of mules needed per legion was 1,000 (pers. comm.). Vegetius says that two mules per vehicle were required to draw the complement of 55 *ballistae* per legion – roughly 10 per cent of the total. I would suggest that the heavier type of draught pony was used in Britain in place of most or all of the mules. Mules and donkeys do not do so well in the British climate, but ponies are inured to it. Caesar mentioned that the Gauls bred a heavy type of draught animal in his day (*de Bello Gall.* IV.2). By Hadrian's time, with the constant crossings over to Britain, many of these would have found their way to our shores as the army became aware of their value. Today we see their descendants in the heavier, taller British native ponies such as Fell, Dale, and further north the Garron and Highland. Fell ponies were extensively used – possibly from Roman times – to pack lead out from the lead mines around the Durham area, which is rich in Roman sites and close to Hadrian's Wall. Added to the baggage and traction beasts would be the mounts of the different units stationed in Britain. At a very rough computation, not taking into account variations which could arise for any number of reasons, the animals needed would be as shown in Table 2.

The 10 per cent remount pool for cavalry horses and baggage beasts would account for average wear and tear, horses lost in battle or ambush, run off or temporarily incapacitated, and so on. It would not allow sufficient replacements in the case of a viral epidemic, which could well hamstring a unit, or if an unusually large number were lost in an engagement. It would also not allow a sufficient animal replacement quota to keep the whole animal corps up to strength. That would have to be done by breeding and levy on a regular basis, and conscription where a heavy influx was suddenly needed. The figures given in the *Codex Theodosianus* (8.5.34), in a law passed by Valentinian, Valens and Gratian in AD 377 concerning replacements for the public post horses, allow an annual maximum replacement of 25 per cent, which meant that a post horse could be expected to last four years on average. A post horse's life could be shortened by having many indifferent riders. A

Table 2. Number of equines required by units in Britain

Animals for the four legions
Baggage and draught ponies (or mules)	4,000
Mounts for the legionary cavalry at 120 per legion	480
Officers' horses with remounts (legate, tribunes, Camp Prefect, centurions, etc.)	252
Horses for others entitled (e.g. scouts), say 25 per legion	100
	4,832
Remounts and baggage replacements at 10%	480
TOTAL FOR LEGIONS	5,312

Animals for the mounted units
Horses
12 *alae quingenariae* with 560 horses per *ala* (incl. *decurion* and *duplicarius* remounts)	6,720
1 *ala milliaria* with 1,120 horses (incl. remounts as above)	1,120
14 *coh. equitatae quingenariae* with 132 per unit (incl. officers' remounts)	1,848
4 *coh. equitatae milliariae* with 264 per unit (including officers' remounts)	1,056
	10,744
Remounts at 10%	1,074
	11,818

Baggage ponies/mules
12 *alae quingenariae* with 64 animals	768
1 *ala milliaria* with 128 animals	128
14 *coh. equitatae quingenariae* with 16 animals	224
4 *coh. equitatae milliariae* with 32 animals	128
	1,248
Replacements at 10%	125
	1,373
Total for mounted units	13,191
Grand total	18,503

cavalry horse with possibly only one rider who was in tune with him might last longer, but the turnover would still be high. Horses in the ancient world did not have the benefit of the variety of drugs and medicines that keep equines healthy today, in particular modern vermifuges and anti-bacterial treatments. In peaceful times, when many troops would be fairly sedentary, fewer animals for haulage of gear would be needed, but the cavalry would have to be kept up to scratch, although the animals' working life would probably be longer and fewer remounts would be needed.

Polybius, in his chapter on the Roman military system, gives rations for cavalry horses based on the system of several horses per man then in use (*Hist.* VI.39). Worked out per animal, it equated roughly to 3.5 lb (1.5 kg) dry weight of barley per day per horse, as we have seen. Rations remained fairly constant down the centuries. A sixth-century papyrus from Oxyrhynchus (no. 2046) also attests to a similar weight (Walker 1973). This would provide sufficient calories for a small horse, such as bone evidence has shown the Romans used, while it was in very moderate work, remembering that the protein content of ancient grains was higher than that of modern strains. There are no actual poundage rates laid down for hay for each animal, but many literary references attest to contracts for hay and deductions for hay made from cavalry pay. Many examples of these appear in R. O. Fink's *Roman Military Records on Papyrus* (1971). Historians, particularly Caesar in his *de Bello Gallica*, refer to cavalry going on foraging expeditions as well as receiving supplies of corn. Caesar (ibid., II.2) and Ammianus Marcellinus (*Res Gest.* 30.3) both refer to lack of grazing as a reason for delaying the start of a campaigning season. At the very least a horse or mule would need 10 lb (4.5 kg) of hay per day for late autumn and winter consumption. Time needed on good grazing would be a minimum of four hours a day for the exceptionally easy keeper, correspondingly more for those with normal metabolisms, and even longer for the poor doer. Poorer quality land would necessitate animals grazing for longer periods. For a force stationed at a permanent base, provision would be made for storing the annual grain harvest and a certain amount of hay. By a law of AD 362 given by the Emperor Julian to Secundus, his Praetorian Prefect (*Codex Theo.*, 7.4.8), no fodder was to be issued to animals before 1 August. In the east, where Julian spent most of his short reign, the grazing would have largely dried up by that time. In the west many Roman provinces would still have had ample grazing, although the spring flush would have started later. Vegetius tells us that when the men were in camp, the horses were pastured outside with four horsemen on guard each night from each century (plus four infantry). Cavalry also furnished the guard at night and the outpost guard by day. Guards were relieved every morning and night because of fatigue to both men and horses. Vegetius does not mention a day guard of pastured herds, but that must be taken as read if they were not on manoeuvres or other mounted duties by day. Baggage animals no doubt came under the same system. They are the silent and invisible part of the army and largely neglected by historians, but obviously they needed adequate care and protection too.

There are repeated laws in the *Codex Theodosianus* concerning grazing and the abuses the military perpetrated by grazing animals on privately owned and public pastures (*Codex Theo.*, 7.7.3.1.4.5 and 7.7.3.4.1.5). As the laws span several decades, it seems that either penalties were not imposed, or that the soldiers refused to pay with impunity, probably terrorizing the poor owners into keeping silent. *Decurions* (civil) were obliged to find sufficient pasture land for military animals. Public lands equated with the English common, which are for the use of residents with grazing rights, not for any passer-by to depasture stock (even today in the New Forest grazing rights accompany certain properties, and when that property is sold the incoming owner automatically has those rights transferred to him).

There are several inscriptions referring to *prata* (meadowland) specifically set aside for the military, and on these the cavalry and baggage beasts would be grazed. Whether the land was managed well enough to set aside a part for hay is another matter, and would depend on a variety of factors – adequate fencing and/or containment of grazing animals so that they did not ruin a growing crop of hay before it was harvested. One method nowadays is to allow animals to graze the early first flush in the spring, then to lay the fields up for hay, and after the first and if desired the second crop of hay has been taken, turn the animals back on to it to graze for the rest of the season. This depends to a great extent on fertilizing and of course on control of the amount of stock. Where military animals were depastured it would mean heavy stocking, and unless the *pratae* were extremely large taking hay might not be possible. In managed grazing the pastures are rotated to allow grazed-down fields to regrow. The other alternative with less fertile but more extensive lands is to allow free range, where the stock will not graze so intensively and therefore the rotation is not so necessary. This method would not permit a hay crop to be taken, whereas the first would. Examples of these *pratae* are found near Santander, in the Burgos area of Spain, where there was an Imperial boundary stone dividing the grazing land of the *Legion IV Macedonica* from the territory of Juliobriga (*ILS*, 2454); from Segisanio (*ILS*, 2455); from Dalmatia near the legionary fortress at Burnum, where a boundary stone was set up between the *prata* of the legion and the boundaries of some land belonging to Flavius Marcus (*ILS*, 5968); and another site in Spain where a stone divides the grazing land of the IVth cohort of Gauls from the city of Bidienienses (*ILS*, 5969).

As far as facilities at base are concerned, a little arithmetic will give the figure for, say, an *ala quingenaria*. Food consumption per day, at 10 lb (4.5 kg) of hay per beast would be 6,860 lb (3,100 kg) of hay, and 3.5 lb (1.5 kg) of grain per animal would be 2,401 lb (1,000 kg) of grain. This is fractionally over three tons of hay per day and about one ton of grain per

Men's and officers' mounts	560
10% remounts available	56
Baggage beasts	64
10% replacements	6
Total	686

day. But the example we have used is for by no means the largest concentration of animals in the military sphere in Britain. And it ignores that forgotten component of stabled horse care – bedding. Bedding provides two functions. It absorbs urine which would otherwise make any but stone floors a morass; and where stone floors are used it is necessary as a cushioning layer for the horse to rest on or his legs suffer. When lying down on stone a horse may get capped hocks and other unsightly blemishes, as well as be prone to chills.

With regard to the growth of grass for hay and grazing, this obviously varies geographically according to warmth and precipitation, but the basic growth and nutrition outline for Britain and much of Europe is shown in Table 3. If hay is needed, large areas have to be set aside from grazing at least by the beginning of May for a June/July cut. Such areas can be grazed thereafter or left for a second August cut. Therefore at the very least the four winter months would be on gathered feed; a further two months on supplementary rations. This would work out at the equivalent of 22 weeks of the year where animals depended on stored rations.

Table 3. Seasonal growth and value of grass

Season	Dates	Growth	Nutritional value
Winter	Early November to end February	Minimal to none	Very poor
Early spring	March to mid April	Little	Insufficient
Mid spring to early summer	Mid April to end June	Rapid	Maximum
Mid summer to early autumn	July, August, September	Reasonable	Reasonable
Late autumn	October	Minimal	Insufficient

Hay occupied considerably more storage space than in modern times. Today baling machines compress it down to a fraction of its loose dimensions. Ricks needed careful construction, and from Ammianus Marcellinus we know that hay was stored to a considerable height and in great quantities in the east. He tells the story of a rick at Batnae in Osroene collapsing and smothering 50 grooms who were collecting fodder (*Res Gest.* 23.2). Conditions in the east favour outside storage. In the west, ricks had to be well thatched to preserve them during winter rains, and a percentage would be lost to mould.

I would suggest that obtaining the mere subsistence ration for all the animals needed by the army occupied a far greater amount of time, energy and ingenuity on the quartermasters' part than has been previously considered, and indeed probably formed the most important non-military task of legionaries and auxiliaries stationed at any one location. In the case of a fortress for a whole legion with an area of roughly 50–60 acres (20–25 ha), *horrea* could house the massive amount of grain, and a proportion of hay could also be kept in the area under military control around the fortress. Acquiring such a vast amount would mean denuding pasture lands for miles around. The Emperor developed his own estates with farms and stock-breeding establishments (*saltus*), appropriating large tracts of land to do so. He was the largest landowner in the Empire. Fodder and grain would also be requisitioned from local farmers, and in times of special need further supplies would have been purchased. The *annona* kept the Emperor's army supplied with cereals in the frontier provinces. Not only would the acreage needed to produce sufficient hay be extensive, but so would the manpower to cut, cure and cart it, and in addition to local populations there would be army personnel and their servants to carry out these tasks. In a law of AD 396 from Arcadius and Honorius to Hilarius, the Praetorian Prefect, the *Codex Theodosianus* makes it clear that the 'provincials' were bound to supply the hay, but not to deliver it (7.4.23), and equally that the military could not refuse provisions levied as tax (ibid., 7.4.21). The soldiers were obliged to collect their own fodder up to 20 miles distant from the camp (ibid., 7.4.7 and 9). Presumably if requirements were excessive and local sources depleted, cartage had to be mutually arranged between military and civilians.

Today one acre (0.4 ha) can be expected to produce an average hay crop of one and half tons (1.5 tonnes), but ancient crop yields were not nearly so high, as farming was not so intensive and fertilizers did not give the massive growth boost obtained through modern chemicals. Modern grain yields are as high as 2.75 to 3 tons per acre for wheat, with approximately one-quarter of a ton less for barley, but this profusion is due to artificial fertilizers. In the 1950s and 1960s 1.25 tons was an average wheat yield (D. H. Deptford, pers. comm.). In Celtic times in Britain the yield of wheat was 0.6 to 1.0 ton per acre (1.5–2.5 tonnes per hectare) (Reynolds 1979), so much more land was needed to produce adequate crops. In other areas of the Roman world where different strains of grain were grown, as for instance Einkorn in Asia Minor, the yield would be comparable. Certain provinces, notably Africa and Egypt, were considered Rome's grain basket. Pliny the Elder and others refer to the grain yield being a hundredfold and more in the most fertile areas. The Celtic grain yields in Britain were the highest known until modern farming methods came into use. From a strain redeveloped for experimental use in Britain and shown in the Old Fulling Mill Museum, Durham University, I counted 64 grains to one head. This does not allow for any that had fallen off through accident, so maybe Pliny was not stretching the truth as far as usual. This high yield may have made Britain an attractive proposition for the Romans. If Britain had the farming techniques to produce a good grain yield, it must be assumed that hay making was also done proficiently. Fertilizers were mainly animal dung and green manures, of which there were rarely sufficient, but there would be a relatively high amount available near a legionary and cavalry garrison with its concentration of animals.

Although barley is mentioned by Polybius as a standard horse ration, he does not mention the other standard Roman horse feed – beans – which were grown in great quantities and fed to stock. All the ancient recipes for a mixed feed contain a high proportion of beans and they can be grown easily. Britain grew a variety, a related strain of which is also grown today for animal fodder. It is very high in protein. That it formed a high proportion of horse feed is shown by the *Codex Theodosianus* in respect to levies on towns in Campania, who were obliged to supply beans in massive quantities to the Roman racing factions (15.10.2). It is hardly to be expected that such a ready source of high protein nourishment would be ignored by the army for its stock. I also suggest that the Polybian figures were merely subsistence rations. When horses needed extra grain, in times of continued high energy expenditure, if they did not receive necessary supplements they would become debilitated and be a liability in action. In Asia Minor, Italy and certain other provinces the use of medick (lucerne/alfalfa) could cut down the poundage required, as considerably less of this needs to be fed for adequate results. However, it did not grow well in many parts of the western Roman Empire.

Stables

An equally important facet of stock management is 'where to put them'. Not much seems to be known with certainty about the stabling arrangements for horses within permanent Roman camps. A variety of buildings have been excavated which are *thought* to have been stables. There seems to have been no standard design for these, and in only a few instances is there certain evidence that horses were stabled there: grain particles and dung and urine stains on the floors. With the great number of horses attached at any one time to a cavalry unit it is very doubtful if all animals were kept within the fort. There would just not be enough space for cavalry, officers, remounts and baggage stock.

In Britain some of the sites with buildings that are reliably recorded as stables are Brough on Noe (manure, teeth and a wide drainage channel); Hod Hill, Dorset (urine and muck stains on the chalk); The Lunt, Warwickshire (stabling recognized adjacent to the *gyrus* entrance). In all these there are few internal partitions. The Hod Hill building has only 11 in a run of 197 ft (60 metres) (Holder 1980). Evidence as to how the horses were stabled consists usually of very slim traces. A long run of buildings with a wide rear channel and compressed footing at the wall suggests that horses were tied to the walls with the channel intended to provide drainage for urine. The teeth, if the positioning of where they were found were exactly plotted, would indicate the stabling arrangement, as young horses frequently shed teeth into the feed bucket or manger at around four or five years of age. The 11 partitions suggest that a modicum of safety was adhered to, as should an argument start between two horses it has a knock-on effect. With the partitioning any fights would at least be confined to a few, and attendants could soon restore order by disciplining the offending horses. Roman stables in Germany, Dormagen and Krefeld show drainage sumps and fodder and grain spillage. More reliable information could be gained if the specific location and density of such spillages were plotted in order to give a clue as to where the animals were tied, as horses are messy eaters, often scattering grain about. They also pass a certain amount of grain in dung. At Dormagen the stalls measure 11 ft 6 in. square (3.5 × 3.5 m) which is roughly the size of a modern loose box. It would just be possible to tether three amiable animals to one wall. As with all hierarchies it would be almost certain that the officers' horses received preferential treatment, particularly those of the highest-ranking men such as the *praefectus*. His charger would rate a box all to himself.

As we have seen, certain precautions would need to be taken when stabling animals together. Geldings are notably the most amenable, though not necessarily. Mares can become quite aggressive, or the opposite – frenziedly stupid if separated from their particular female companion. Stallions need a little more caution, for although some can quite happily be accommodated together – with only a partition between them if necessary – others require separate individual accommodation.

Separating the sexes would be vital, although geldings can go with mares, and some stallions tolerate geldings provided no mare is near. The arrangement of stabling and its occupants therefore could not go by the book, as the rest of the camp organization would. Horses' individual characteristics would have to be taken into consideration. It would be up to the cavalrymen and grooms to sort out the problems and ensure amenable behaviour in the horse lines (see Ch. 5). It is worth mentioning that all the horses kept at the Spanish Riding School in Vienna today are stallions, and the stabling arrangements consist of stalls for most, with a few having the luxury of individual looseboxes. The performance of these horses is superb and no friction is evident between stallions.

Vegetius specifically mentions horses at pasture (see p. 90 above), and for practical purposes the bulk of the camp's animals would be kept outside the walls, adequately herded by sufficient mounted men. Although herd animals, horses are not as docile as bovines and should one break away it cannot readily be turned back into the herd. In peaceful occupation grazing herds would be moved about during appropriate seasons, and in winter corralled with long feed brought to them. To minimize feed requirements, unless all animals were on constant active service, I would suggest that they did not always receive full grain rations, the long fodder being increased if possible, and that the animals' condition tended to go up and down according to season, work and level of feeding. I would also suggest that a sufficient number were kept stabled within the fort to provide a ready contingent of mounts. These would be kept in rather better condition than the stock herded outside.

The sheer amount of dung and soiled bedding that would have to be removed each day would also preclude all animals being kept within the fort. Hygiene would be difficult enough with only a moderate number kept inside. When in current use or awaiting manoeuvres, stock would be kept close to the fort. Such a number of animals would destroy grazing right down to the root system if they stayed too long on any one parcel of land and feed would have to be brought to them whatever the season. Water too would present a problem. A horse can consume five gallons a day in normal circumstances and in hot weather considerably more. In addition, fed grain and hay a horse drinks far more than a horse which is only grazing, because of the high water content in fresh grass. Grazing grounds must either have had clean water within easy reach, or the herds would have been driven to it at least twice a day. A dehydrated horse cannot work. The outside stock could not have been kept in top condition in much of the European part of the Roman Empire. Animals can withstand cold, but they cannot tolerate incessant rain, as various skin and hoof conditions render them unsuitable for service. Weight also falls off horses subjected to constantly wet conditions. This argues again for a certain contingent to be kept at the ready in stables.

On campaigns

In campaigning times, the picture would change considerably. The animals would have to live off the land and rely on frequent foraging expeditions to provide their grain. There must have been periods of plenty and even more periods of scarcity for cavalry mounts, when troopers would have become concerned over their own horse's welfare. The baggage trains would only have been able to provide at best a minimal amount of hard feed. The Roman cavalry horse had to be adaptable, not a fussy feeder, and his digestion able to cope with a constantly changing level of nutrition. Highly strung and overbred animals are usually unable to do this. Writing of a marching camp, Polybius specifically refers to tethered horses, and men detailed to keep a watch over them to stop fights breaking out or animals getting entangled in their tethers (*Hist*. VI.33). In his time cavalry numbers were not great, and as the numbers of squadrons increased picketing would probably have given way to herding with a very strong guard, and when absolutely necessary each trooper would have stayed with his horse at all times.

When armies were in winter quarters waiting for the campaigning season to begin, those in charge of the stock would have been very concerned to have their animals coming into spring in as good a shape as possible. Nature's way is to pile fat on in the good seasons in order to see an animal through the winter. Army requirements preclude this and indeed reverse it. Stock would have finished the campaigning season in need of rest and high nutrition, and it must have taxed those concerned with caring for the animals to ensure that they ended the winter with a surplus of condition to sustain future campaigning. That the cavalry increased rather than diminished in numbers says much for the organizational ability of Roman officers detailed to see that all stock was adequately maintained and fit.

Other requirements

Other than the basic requirements of animal food and lodging, there are many other requirements for specific supplies. Harness for horses and pack animals would require a tremendous amount of leather. Meat did not figure prominently in a legionary's diet in the Early Empire, so the

Trieres

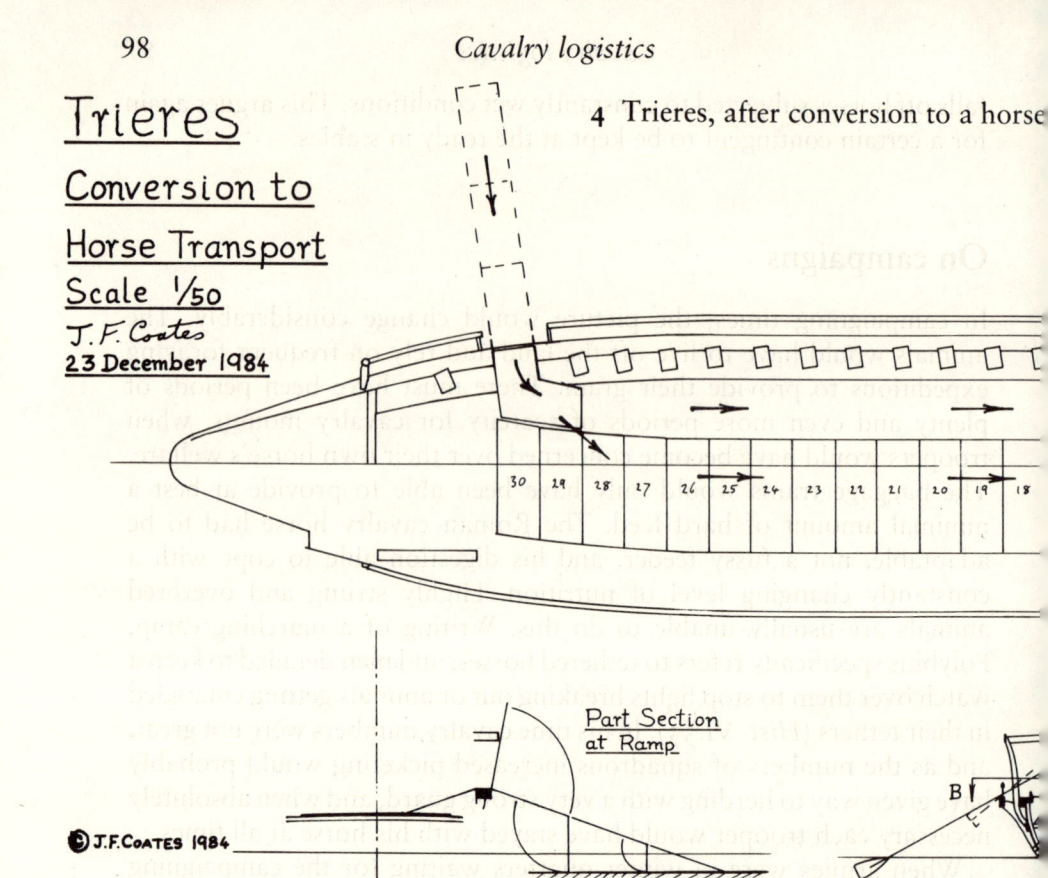

Conversion to

Horse Transport

Scale 1/50

J. F. Coates
23 December 1984

4 Trieres, after conversion to a horse

Part Section at Ramp

© J.F. COATES 1984

number of skins available for tanning would not be high. Much of the harness no doubt came from *fabricae* that specialized in military equipment. We know of several that specialized in certain items from Diocletian's reign. He established about a dozen, some in the east, others in the west (Williams 1985). In addition to the arsenals producing armour and weapons, other factories produced articles for military use. Some must have produced saddlery and harness on a production-line basis, but other equipment had to be made to measure. Each base with a cavalry contingent of any size would require a saddler (and possibly a tanner) to produce items from scratch (saddlers make all items of harness, not just saddles). He would be one of the legionaries known as an *immunes* and given relief from fatigues so his special craft could be utilized. He would also be expected to alter and repair existing tack, as bridles and haunch and breast harness in particular would be liable to regular breakage. In action reins would often be severed. (There is no record of rein chains, as used by medieval knights and some modern Californian reinsmen, but the many similarities with Roman horseman-

er. The same principle was used by the Romans

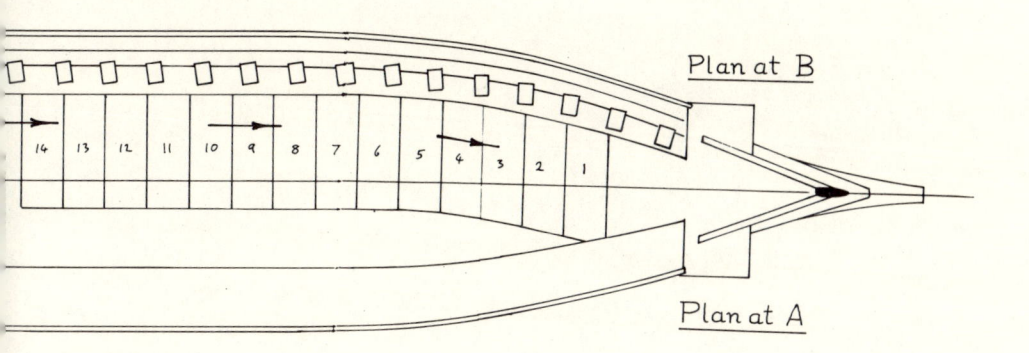

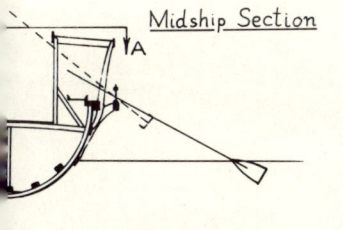

Plan at B

Plan at A

Midship Section

ship which appear in Western methods today leave room for speculation on this point: any chains found in Roman sites might not have been recognized as reins.) A sufficient quantity of hides would be a regular part of provisions so that repairs could be effected. Fresh hides from sacrificial and meat animals would not be wasted, but tanned on site for later use.

A *veterinarius* and assistants were needed to treat sick animals and to perform any minor surgery, such as stitching up wounds or castrating any unruly stallion that proved too obnoxious to be useful. The task of the *veterinarius* would also include hoof trimming, although this could easily be learnt by most troopers. In addition to knowing how to treat the animals the *veterinarius* also needed to know much about herbs, unguents, caustics, and so on, including what was readily available on or near the site for preparation, and what had to be ordered through army administration.

A periodic, rather than day-to-day, need would be to provide transports for shipping horses, and equipping them with sufficient fodder and water to maintain the animals on board for the *maximum* time that a journey could take. Journey length in Roman times was not predictable and vessels got blown off course, as happened to Caesar at Ruspina when he was waiting for his cavalry transports to arrive (*de Bello Afr.* I.2, 11.3).

7
The horse's education

After the army acquired a green horse the next step would be to train the animal for cavalry duties as a trooper's mount. There are no surviving manuals that give us categoric proof that any one method was used in schooling Roman chargers. Occasional comments by classical writers inform us about aspects they found noteworthy enough to include in their histories or poetry. Most information comes from the cavalry section of Arrian's *Tactica* written in AD 136. Flavius Vegetius Renatus, writing in the latter half of the fourth century AD, also gives us a little information.

Much Roman expertise was inherited from the Greeks and we have Xenophon's book *On Horsemanship*, a text which is required reading for those sitting for British Horse Society examinations today. It is clear from Arrian that although there was knowledge of how the Greeks (and others) operated their cavalry (*Tact.* 16–19), the Romans used a different approach. Arrian is quite explicit about the manoeuvres that formed the base of Roman cavalry expertise (ibid., 35–44).

Arrian's *Tactica* describes the 'acme of perfection' achieved by cavalry on display before the Emperor. Under battle conditions certain movements would not be meticulously executed, nor would the horses behave in the rigid framework laid down for these exercises. Their purpose would be to satisfy the Emperor, or any other general for whom they were performed, that the mounted divisions were well trained, fit, and mentally and physically competent. They were the showpiece of the Roman cavalry. Today, horses are entered in shows that exhibit the degree of training the horse has reached. Jumping a working hunter course only superficially resembles the real thing in the hunting field with its often treacherous going and tricky fences. Cutting cattle in an arena is not the same as working cattle on a fenceless range amongst bush.

The *Tactica* gives us the result of horse and rider training, and from that a good trainer can deduce how the result was achieved. It was definitely more than just a question of 'the cavalry fought at such and such a battle', or the 'cavalry went in pursuit', as has so often been portrayed. Training could make or mar a troop of cavalry. A disobedient horse could cost a rider his life. Attention to detail and a constant eye to the fitness of mount and man was very important. Vegetius makes this quite clear (*Ep. Rei Mil.*) when he informs us that at least three times a month there were 20 mile (30 km) exercise details, in which the horses practised the moves likely to be encountered in warfare – pursuing, retreating, reforming, and charging again, in effect covering far more than the 10 miles out and back of the linear route. Riding over mixed terrain would teach the horse surefootedness, build muscle, quicken responses, strengthen tendons and joints, and give the rider an eye for country. No wonder that Fronto, writing to Lucius Verus in the mid second century, was horrified at the laxness of the Syrian cavalry at Antioch. Although the spectacle definitely had its funny side, particularly the clumsy mounting, it augured badly for the state of the troopers' readiness. It must be borne in mind that the Syrians were the butt of Roman criticism, much as the Irish often get tagged with the epithets 'stupid' or 'fighting'.

> The army you took over was demoralized by luxury and immorality and prolonged idleness. The soldiers at Antioch were wont to spend their time applauding actors and were more often found in the nearest tavern garden than in the ranks. Horses shaggy from neglect, but every hair plucked from their riders, a rare sight was a soldier with arm or leg hairy. Withal the men were better clothed than armed, so much so that Pontius Laelianus, a man of character and a disciplinarian of the old school, in some cases ripped up their cuirasses with his finger tips; he found horses saddled with cushions, and by his orders the little pommels on them were slit open and the down plucked from the saddles of the cavalry as from geese. Few of the soldiers could vault upon their steeds, the rest scrambled clumsily up by dint of heel or knee or ham; not many could make their spears hurtle, most tossed them like toy lances without verve and vigour. Gambling was rife in camp, sleep night-long, or if a watch was kept, it was over the wine cups. (Fronto, *Epistulae*, letter to Lucius Verus XIX)

Fascinating details emerge throughout the literature that link Roman equestrian usage in many fields to that of American Western riding, or more specifically Californian stock-seat riding. This is not as strange a connection as it may seem. The Californian style of Western riding originally reached the USA via South America and Spain with the Conquistadores and their successors. Many clues hint that it stretches even further back from sixteenth-century Spain to Rome. There are similarities in curb bitting and neck reining, with the need to ride one-handed and leave the right hand free for a weapon (or a rope); the Roman military saddle appears to be a prototype Western saddle; the hackamore or bosal is a refinement of the *psalion,* and the mechanical hackamore is very similar in action. The modern Western parade horses decked out in silvered bridles, breastplates and saddles heavy with metalled lozenges or discs resemble the Roman *phalerae;* the heavy-fringed parade blankets over the loin area echo the Roman type of saddle covering; and that very 'modern' American invention, the 'Easyboot', was being used, albeit in a cruder form, 2,000 years ago by Roman vets and muleteers, known to them as a *solea ferrea* or *spartea* according to whether they were made of metal or rush. A rancher frequently starts training his colts in a round pen with high sides; a Roman *gyrus* is so constructed but on a much larger scale. Even on the racetrack there are similarities: American starting stalls, left-hand turns, construction of racing surfaces for harness horses, even the sulky is similar to the lightweight Roman chariots. I think the *connecting* link was Spain with its long enforced occupation by Roman forces, and its subsequent Romanization where large *latifundia* belonging to wealthy landowners or part of the Imperial estates were used, among other things, for raising both military and track horses. These links facilitate the understanding of the type of horsemanship used by the Roman cavalry; indeed, that used by any weapon-wielding horseman. Modern well-schooled Western horses are ridden with one hand, usually in a curb bit, and should obey the slightest signal from the legs and weight, and similar manoeuvres to those executed by Arrian's top decurions would all be seen in the Western showring.

In essence, horse training is a blend of much common sense, some talent on the part of both the trainer and the horse, and a degree of empathy between them. Arrian explains the differences between Greek and Roman cavalry manoeuvres, but the Greek influence was strong in the training of cavalry horses. Campania had long been famed as an area that provided Italy with its early top-class cavalry, and although by Hannibal's time outside influences in the form of Numidian, Spanish and Celtic horses and riders had appeared, the traditions that the Greeks brought into Campania left a legacy. After all, 2,500 years later we still follow much of Xenophon's advice for training a young horse, so to the Romans it must have been current practice. A horse's mind does not adapt to modern thinking. Modern equipment is only an improvement on ancient saddlery – kinder to the horse, more comfortable and offering greater security to the rider. Although the Romans were not noted for their kindness to animals, the intelligent horseman must have realized he got nowhere with brutality. Under work conditions the severe bitting and *psalions* in use meant that the schooled horse would have suffered a great degree of discomfort and pain with a heavy-handed rider. Nothing changes! Today many poor riders think they are proficient and insist on overbitting their animals. It is painful to the horse, and often dangerous to the rider.

Understanding the psychological aspects of training will prevent arguments between horse and rider later on, and convincing the very young horse that he must knuckle under is no bad thing. It makes it easier for the three year old as 'he starts to pace the ring and step harmoniously, and learns to move at a limber stride and begins to look like a worker' (Virgil, *Georgics* III.191–3). From Xenophon we learn that it was the groom's job to teach the horse decent manners and to allow himself to be led and handled, before he went on to the professional trainer (Xenophon, II.5).

Basically the army nagsman had to start his work with green, maybe rather unruly, animals of two or more usually three to four years old. In the duty roster of the *Cohors XX Palmyrenorum*, (Fink 1971, no. 1, p. 18) the cavalrymen's duties are noted. One in particular, Aurel Amaeus Magdei, stands out because he is detailed to inspect horses. He is the only one with this duty, which implies a special ability. Although high-ranking officers would need to sign the chit confirming that the horse had passed the *probatio*, it is hardly to be expected that the actual nuts and bolts of choice and training lay with them. A more feasible method would be for the more gifted and athletic trooper, who was also an observant, knowledgeable and *natural* horseman, to be given this duty, in much the same way as rough-riders are on a ranch.

The Romans had special riding grounds for exercising their cavalry. They also had indoor arenas for schooling at a few main depots. Virgil tells us that the Lapithae were celebrated horsemen who invented both the bridle and the training ring and taught the cavalrymen the arts of *haute école* (*Georgics* III.115–17). This is a most interesting passage, as Thessalians were noted from antiquity as top horsemen. Alexander the Great's horse, Bucephalus, was of Thessalian breeding and his elite Companion Cavalry were also mounted on Thessalian chargers (Hyland 1988, p. 24). The remains of what is thought to have been a *gyrus*, or outdoor training ring, have been excavated and rebuilt at the Lunt, Baginton, Warwickshire. It is round with a box-like entrance, similar to an American rodeo chute but large enough to contain several animals in the box. The sides have been reconstructed to a level high enough so that horses could not see over the barriers while working. The area itself, though rounded, is at least as large as a modern dressage arena, and thus able to cope with a considerable number of animals working as a ride for instructional purposes. Comparative dimensions are as follows:

Roman Lunt *gyrus*	1,024 m²	1,225 sq. yd
Normal-sized dressage arena	800 m²	955 sq. yd
Grand Prix level dressage arena	1,200 m²	1,435 sq. yd

The *gyrus* also resembles, except in its larger size, the American round pen used for breaking. A fence of any type surrounding a training ring has a psychological effect on a horse, especially one in the early stages of discipline. The high sides of a Roman *gyrus* or a modern breaking pen keep the animal's attention on the job and away from disruptive outside influences. The implied restraint afforded by containment tends to diffuse even the most 'ornery bronc'. The round shape affords the animal no '*querencia*' in which to hole up in a corner, but is an aid to continuous forward movement. For early lessons with fairly green horses such rings must have been invaluable, as quite a few of the cavalrymen would also have been beginners, at least prior to promotion to a mounted unit, and would have started on older, more staid animals. Sarcastic wit has always been part of a cavalry riding instructor's armament and Roman beginners must also have withered under verbal scorn as they floundered to stay aboard, let alone become proficient. One special advantage that the Lunt *gyrus* possesses is its siting on top of a steep hill. This would have afforded an ideal training area for riding up and down hills, and riding without stirrups it would have taken considerable skill to negotiate the hill nimbly, keep the horse under control, and still act in a defensive or offensive manner as orders dictated.

As with any military department there would have been guidelines for training cavalry mounts. Common sense dictates that all mounts, whatever their provenance, would go through the system after being drafted. Naturally some would take longer to be processed than others as there would always be some horses that needed longer to learn, including those cunning beasts that defied discipline. Reducing them to a barley ration would be a very palatable punishment!

There are many representations, mostly on tombstones, of horses being driven on long reins with the reins run through the two horns of the saddle and thence to the bit. Long reining is used in the early stages of breaking. The main difference today is that we run the reins either through rings on the surcingle or, once the horse has learnt to carry a saddle, through the stirrups. It does not stretch the imagination to expect a Roman trainer to use a girth or surcingle and run the reins along the horse's sides during early training, rather than direct to its mouth. The purpose of long reining is to teach the horse to go forward straight at a flick of the rein or whip; to give to the bit; to turn smoothly; and to get used to the reins on the sides and learn what pressure there means. Later the rider's legs substitute for rein pressure. The horse initially learns without the unbalancing encumberment of a rider on his back. It also teaches him discipline, as should he be recalcitrant it is very easy to swing him around very sharply on either rein.

Training any horse well takes time. It cannot be achieved in the time taken for a soldier's basic training unless the animal is both exceptionally amenable and bright. Hurried training confuses an animal who regresses in proficiency. In an army horse this could be dangerous, costing human lives. Although the horse is a herd animal and therefore basically does what its fellows are doing, it must also be willing and able to respond to individual orders from its rider without argument. The sheer cost of replacing an animal that takes several years to come to maturity before it is of use would dictate that it received adequate and unhurried initial training. I am often asked how long it takes to train a horse, or rather (if the owner were honest) how quickly I can do the job. My answer is that it normally takes four to six weeks before the horse is able to do the simplest tasks and be reasonably safe under saddle *provided* it is an amenable animal. At that stage it is still awkward, unformed in its paces, and lacking all refinements. A further six weeks will see it polished enough to perform in very easy riding horse classes where nothing much is asked but to behave well and give a smooth performance among other horses at the same level of training. To bring a horse to the stage that Arrian describes in his cavalry *tactica* would take skilled and intensive training over many months. All cavalry horses must have been expected to receive such a grounding to be of value to the military. The majority would not have excelled themselves, but they had to be reasonably proficient. Doubtless there were crack divisions with superb riders and exceptional horses that would not have been risked as readily as horses that were slightly less able but still useful. We get some idea of this from Hadrian's *adlocutio* to the troops at Lambaesis, where he compliments cavalrymen of the *Ala I Pannoniorum* and of the VI *Commageniorum Coh. Eq.*, saying that the latter performed well in spite of not having such quality animals and equipment – the point being that the *ala* riders were better mounted than the men of the *cohors equitata* (CIL, VIII.2532, 18042; ILS, 2487, 9133–5).

The round pen would have made horses supple, which would have been vital in the exercises described by Arrian. It would also have been easier on a constantly arcing track to teach a horse to take the correct lead at the canter. When a horse is cantering, one foreleg comes further forward on each stride than the other. If the horse is travelling on the left rein, that is counterclockwise, it should lead with the inside foreleg (when the first leg to strike off will be the offside hindleg, a point difficult to appreciate visually). When travelling on the right rein the horse leads with the right leg. The Cantabrian gallop would have necessitated use of the right lead, and the javelin exercises described in *Tactica* (36–9) would at different phases have required both left and right leads. A horse must know these, as turning at speed on the incorrect lead could under certain circumstances bring him down. It would also make riding in the Roman military saddle extremely uncomfortable, especially on turns, so much so that on a rough-gaited horse it would be difficult to stay aboard. Add to this the unbalancing effect of armour and a full-weight shield on one side and it will be appreciated how important smoothness of gait becomes.

One other advantage of the high-sided arena, or in winter the solid walls of those *basilica exercitatoria* that were enclosed, rather than merely roofed over, would have been to teach a horse to turn very rapidly to either the left or the right from a full gallop. This is very difficult to do in an open area. The movement is known in modern Western 'reining' competitions as a rollback, and consists of galloping to a given point (usually a marker at the end of the arena), checking but not completely stopping, turning in the horse's own length, to the left or to the right, and galloping back to the starting point. Again correct leads are vital or spills could occur. This move would be one practised in a charge and a rapid retreat. Xenophon entitles this move the 'career' (VII.14–18), but we have no information as to what the Romans called it though a similar move was a component of the Gallic *toloutegon* (Arrian, *Tact.* 43). If originally taught outside an arena the tendency is for the horse to overshoot the mark, or to ignore the rider's signals for a tight turn and go clumsily wide of the mark. In a closed arena the horse can be pushed hard and fast to the wall or fence and in self-defence learns to turn. (This is how Western reining horses are started on their fast turns, and I have used the same principle when working cattle to teach Nizzolan to come off the fence fast and smoothly.) Initially the horse is reluctant to go up against the solid object, but quickly learns that a rapid turn extricates him. A slowthinking or torpid type of animal is not suited to this move. Obedience to the bit is essential, as is the positioning of the animal with his hocks well under him in the turn. If he is not collected he sprawls, slows, and could strain joints and tendons. In every area of training, if it was skimped it meant cost and danger to the military. In the Gallic *toloutegon*, where the rapid turn over the hocks is employed followed by retreat, if the horse resisted and ploughed straight on it would be right into the enemy's midst or on to the point of a killing lance.

As with all grazing animals that rely on a speedy escape route, horses see not only to the front but to the side and partially to the rear as well. Their natural inclination is to run from danger, which they normally construe as anything that looks strange, moves suddenly, smells obnoxious, or sounds threatening. Part of a cavalry horse's training would be to accustom him to these things.

Horses see things well from a great distance but not so well if it is right in front of their nose. Hence the posture a horse takes when approaching a jump. A smart trooper could learn much from observing his horse's ears. Ears pricked straight ahead and head raised means that something has caught his attention in the distance. Ears held pricked to the left or right means that he has seen or heard something laterally and is thinking of shying away from the direction his ears are pointing. Things that flap, flutter and hiss are a threat, so standards and dragon banners need getting used to. Snakes, however, do not seem to worry most horses (my worst experience when a rattler was in the path was that my mare Magnet stopped, but not in panic, and when I had dismounted, armed myself with a stick to throw at it, and remounted to do so, she moved on with no fuss). However, in the east particularly, snakebite was a problem and Pelagonius' concern was well warranted, even if his remedies were useless (*Ars Vet.* XX; and see Ch. 2 above).

The horse sees objects in a different way to humans. Hence he may well shy at something that seems perfectly ordinary to us. Sometimes this is genuine apprehension, sometimes just naughtiness which can become a vice if allowed to go unchecked. However, the myth of a fallen man causing enormous alarm to a horse is not true. To the horse it is just another object on the ground which may elicit an initial shy. In battle, if it were accompanied by the smell of corruption and/or blood that is a different matter and could well alarm the horse. Horses would have to be taught to cope with such incidents, and the obvious common-sense remedy would be to use the products of the shambles to defuse their apprehension.

The clangour of arms, drum beat and trumpet calls take some time for the horse to become accustomed to. Virgil recommends getting the colt used to such noises at an early age (*Georgics* III.182–3). In general horses can become reassured about noise much more quickly than about other alarming occurrences.

Some horses show more fear of smells than anything else. This is usually followed by panic and flight, or by such obstinacy that it seems as if their hooves are rooted in the ground. There is a saying that a horse can smell if a rider is frightened, and this is true. The explanation is that the odour which a frightened human emits, though not picked up by another human, is smelt by a horse. Fear in a rider, if it is of something ahead, transmits itself to the horse who in turn becomes fearful. If the rider's fear is of the horse's actions, the mean animal usually obliges with an unsocial act. When Perseus of Macedonia fought the Romans, his horses found the Roman elephants so noxious that the Macedonian had dummy elephants constructed and smeared with unguent. His horses were paraded back and forth before them until they lost their fear (Dio, XX).

In the Civil Wars both Caesar and Pompey sent to Italy for elephants so their own horses could become used to them (Dio, XLIII.3.5–4.1).

All young horses would have been taught to cross water hazards. Horses swim naturally but some are extremely loath to enter water. They can refuse to cross by exhibiting either rigid stubbornness or unseating violence. Vegetius recommends swimming as part of horse and rider training, and Tacitus describes the Batavians' cavalry force whose speciality was to swim wide rivers while retaining full control of their mounts (*Hist.* 4.12). Horses were also taught to jump over walls, presumably low ones, and over trenches (Arrian, *Tact.* 44). The former is easier for both horse and rider as walls are clearly visible from a distance and the horse can gauge take off and degree of spring. Trenches and ditches, particularly when approached blind (i.e. without a prior look) as they would be in a pursuit, tend to make a horse prop, look, and then leap up and over in an uncomfortable deer-leap. Without stirrups this would be extremely unseating, especially if it happened from speed, and could send the trooper over the horse's head.

Arrian describes fully accoutred men leaping on to galloping horses (*Tact.* 43). Today trick riders have special saddles with high pommels and rear handgrips to facilitate this. The grips are in a very similar position to those of the cantle horns on a Roman military saddle, and the Roman saddle had two pommels set laterally instead of the modern central single pommel. The exercise needed extreme agility, precision and sheer strength to leap while heavily burdened with armour, not to mention weapons and shield getting in the way. I cannot imagine any but the very best would do this well. Most would resemble the Syrian cavalry at Antioch about which Fronto complained, scrambling up every which way, at least until well into their training. The horse would have needed to be honest, not shying away, and very strong, as 230 lb (105 kg) or more hitting him hard amidships would have given him a severe jolt in the back. Occasional sore backs, and lamenesses stemming from back injury, must have resulted. Modern trick riders are lighter and barely touch down in most movements before they are swinging off again. Also their horses are specially trained purely for trick riding.

Speed work up and down hills would be necessary as it does take time for a horse to know how to cope with hills to best advantage. The weight on his back would also tend to unbalance him to a great degree. Ill-balanced animals can injure themselves descending a steep slope at speed, whereas a sensible animal learns to regulate his speed and limb coordination without much help from the rider. A trooper on such a horse had his hands free to use weapons when in pursuit; for a member of a mounted archer unit a really steady animal allowed better aim and loosing of arrow. As well as natural hazards horses would be subjected to manmade traps – lilies, caltrops, ambuscades or softened ground that could bring an animal down. An astute rider on a very intelligent and well-trained horse *may* have advance warning of some of these. Certain horses sense rather than see, hear or smell an ambuscade, although they are inclined to be the suspicious ones that also scare easily. A horse used to being ridden fast across every type of terrain does have an awareness of irregular depressions and changes in the appearance of the surface, and a canny beast will go warily. Artificially softened ground will always catch a horse unawares, though natural boggy going will send alarm signals to some horses, usually those, like British native ponies, raised roaming free over vast tracts of land. In a mass charge natural animal caution is overridden by the urgency of action.

Once having become used to the various noises of camp and battle, frightening objects, rough going, swimming and so on, Arrian's advanced stage of training could be started. The two major things a horse would have to contend with would be continuous bombardment and hand-to-hand fighting. In the *testudo* formation (*Tact.* 36) he would have to learn to stand his ground while an opponent attacked. This is very unnerving, even in close order with other horses. The mere approach of another horse at a gallop, let alone the impact of javelin on shield, needed a rider calm enough to stand and hold his horse in place. The rider's legs clamping on the horse's sides are the most effective means of holding a scared but *well-trained* horse in place. The pressure of the rider's legs can mean dozens of different things to schooled horses, according to how they are used and where they are placed on the horse's anatomy (the average horse used for riding is not normally so well schooled). The individual horses placed in front as targets would try to wheel back to the relative safety of numbers in the *testudo*, unless the riders could hold them steady. Hand-to-hand combat is also very unnerving for the horse, who sees a *spatha* cutting down as a threat to him, not just to his rider.

8
Rider training

Rider training depended a great deal on a cavalryman's nationality. If he was a Roman citizen belonging to either the senatorial or equestrian class his riding career started early. Children from rich families could expect to have their own ponies (Pliny, *Epist.* 4.2). Dio frequently refers to the Troy games which were first mentioned as occurring under Sulla but are supposed to date back to the mythical days of Aeneas. Suetonius also mentions them several times (*Caes.* 39). He describes them as a sham cavalry fight between two groups of boys, one younger than the other. How young we are not told, but quite small boys took part as Nero 'earned loud applause' when very young (ibid., *Nero* 7). Suetonius' tales are chronological, and the text then goes on to relate Nero's adoption by Claudius at age 11. The Troy games were dangerous and tumbles and limb fractures were not uncommon. Two youngsters – Gaius Asprenus and Aeserninus Pollio – took a toss and each broke a leg (ibid., *Aug.* 43).

Virgil gives more information (*Aeneid* V.545–600). He was referring to the landing of Aeneas in Italy, but Augustus encouraged the annual ceremony. According to Virgil, the boys rode horses rather than ponies, mostly of Sicilian breeding, with the exception of the troop leaders, one of whom rode a Thessalian. The first manoeuvre was a circle around the spectators, and then on command the file formed three squadrons, splitting the numbers by filing to left and right. They next wheeled to face each other, dipped lances and charged, each group weaving in and out of the opposing line – rather like pole bending in a gymkhana today. This was followed by a sham skirmish, with one group fleeing and then turning to take an attacking position. Later similar manoeuvres can be seen in part in Arrian's *tactica* moves. He uses the circle in the Cantabrian gallop, and the charging with lances, and the wheeling to face an enemy is similar but not as complicated as the *toloutegon*. With such a grounding in horsemanship, the youths of equestrian families went straight into their military careers as junior cavalry officers (Suetonius, *Aug.* 38). Vegetius stated that the *decurio* of a *turma* should set an example by being a better rider and more adept with weapons than his subordinates (*Ep. Rei Mil.*).

The annual Troy game ceremony and a youth spent hunting would give a youngster a good grounding in equitation, encouraging him to develop a very firm seat and the ability to handle a horse under pressure. In the hunting field today horses and riders learn to cope with all types of going and fences, often in a hurly-burly that resembles an old-time cavalry charge. In difficult country riders really do learn to ride 'by the seat of their pants', and horses learn to find that fifth leg over tricky obstacles.

When cavalry was raised in large numbers from tribal levies, the men arrived already trained as horsemen, albeit after their native fashion, and initially they operated as an ethnic unit. We know from Arrian's *Cynegetica* (Ch. 24) that, in Numidia, children rode almost as soon as they could walk and by the age of eight could successfully hunt onagers, riding their horses bareback, guiding them with a whip, and when the onager was tired out lassoing it and leading it away. In a similar way, riding from early childhood, Sarmatian nomads and later the Huns and Alans were all but born in the saddle. Ammianus Marcellinus graphically describes the Huns (*Res Gest.* 31.3). We get a distinct picture of grimy, smelly riders and uncouth horses welded together. He comments on the loss of dignity if a boy had to walk, and the intensity of their training as warriors. He also attributes the Persian skill in fighting to riding and mounted warrior training. Though this depicts Rome's enemies, it applies equally to several nations who provided her with mounted auxiliaries. Other peoples of Asia Minor – Syrians, Armenians, Medes, and so on – had learnt from the Persians. In the great days of Achaemenid rule a premium was put on teaching young Persian nobles, the *kardakes*, to ride, shoot and tell the truth. Later Strabo tells us that Armenia followed suit, as they 'originally got their zeal for horsemanship and archery from the Medes' (*Geog.* 11.13.9).

Many of the auxiliary *alae* were already adept at riding and fighting after their native fashion before they were drafted into Roman forces. Later, as a unit retained its name but lost its ethnic content, it relied on its strength being kept up by individual or small-batch recruitment. The need then arose to train cavalrymen to ride. Some had to be taught from scratch, and this Vegetius makes clear when he states that troopers first tried mounting from either side on wooden horses without accoutrements, and later did it armed (*de Re Mil.*). By stages they progressed to the real thing, and at the finish were expected to be able to mount armoured, armed, and with sword drawn if necessary while the horses were moving. Arrian shows that this was not new in his day (*Tact.* 43), as he describes the same manoeuvre, but done spectacularly in the Hippika Gymnasia.

Sons of cavalrymen had an advantage over other recruits, particularly if they owned their own horses, because they could go straight into the cavalry (*Codex Theo.*, 7.22.2.1). As boys normally followed their fathers into the forces they would have had the opportunity in their teenage years to learn as much as their father could teach them of cavalry ways, manoeuvres, and of the handling of a variety of horses specially trained to cavalry tactics. It must have been a tremendous advantage for such a lad, and it would also add greatly to his safety in combat if he were a natural rider. The *Codex Theodosianus* also makes it clear by inference that the normal route for an aspiring cavalryman of the Later Empire was up through the ranks of foot and then through promotion into the cavalry (ibid.). It also suggests that the remount pool might well be in excess of 10 per cent if, as the regulation also states, a lad was expected to provide two horses for his use. The earlier system, which had relied on ethnic units, gradually broke down as the ethnic content became diluted.

Most riders can be divided into roughly four grades:

(1) Those who, however they strive, will never make horsemen.
(2) Those who can just about pass muster but are bad or indifferent horsemen.
(3) The adequate horseman who can operate efficiently.
(4) The brilliant horseman who is at one with his horse.

Any cavalryman who fell into the latter group would have performed the advanced exercises Arrian describes. The adequate riders would have been proficient enough to be team members, and the rest were best ignored. The unfortunates who belonged in the first category probably spent the rest of their military careers footslogging.

The tyro Roman cavalryman had to learn to ride a variety of horses. His own mount may have been lost in battle and the replacement entirely different in size, width of back, gait, mouth sensitivity and temperament to his previous mount. He would not have much time, if any, to acquire a rapport with his new partner, but he would be expected to perform adequately the moment he put a leg across its back. Normal riding is difficult enough to master. Good riders spend years perfecting techniques, and in effect never stop learning. The Roman cavalryman had first to learn to ride, and then to learn to ride encumbered with the weight of armour and weapons. The way the weight was distributed, with a very heavy battle shield on the left side, also made the burden lopsided. When he was wielding weapons, his body movements further affected the balance and a very different picture evolved. The cavalryman had to become so much a part of his horse that all his movements aboard it were performed instinctively. His horse had to be able to respond immediately.

Learning the fundamentals of riding is the same in any era. For those readers who are not riders, a brief résumé of basic riding tuition will show what had to be accomplished. This will help towards understanding just what was required, and how difficult it could be. It was not merely a matter of putting a man on a horse, and 'hey presto' we have a cavalryman!

Most riders approach their first riding lessons with one of two main emotions. They either consider that the horse is a dumb beast, that all horses are the same, and that riding is a pushover, or, more likely, they mount for the first time with some trepidation. The tyro is soon disabused of the idea that he is aboard a dumb beast, as said beast tends to make a complete fool of the overconfident. The second category, according to whether his first mount is amenable or a bit unkind, can find himself taken care of by the horse, aboard a mulish brute that refuses to move unless coerced, or a helpless passenger on a horse whose main interest is in severing connections.

Presumably cavalrymen of all ages were trained in what is known as 'a ride'. Here the mounts tend to follow the tail in front, and any individual movement away from the group is often resisted. The first thing to get used to is the movement of the horse underneath one and the rudiments of starting, guiding, turning and stopping the horse. At the walk this is not too bad, but even so does not always progress that smoothly. After getting the feel of the initial gait, the next step is to try trotting. This is the pace that causes most alarm. The tyro is still unsure of himself and the horse knows it. In the Roman era there were no stirrups to help security, and at that stage of experience the rider would not be able to use the protruding horns of the saddle as intended. He may have grabbed at them to stay aboard and got berated by the instructor. Indeed, it is probable that a saddle was not even used at the early teaching stage. Many British instructors with a cavalry background felt that bareback riding was the finest way to teach a firm seat. The natural inclination for a rider when first trotting is to let the horse drop back to a walk. There is usually total rider uncoordination at this stage, and he cannot use his legs to push the horse on because if he moves them he loses his balance and falls off. He usually carries his hands high, thus throwing himself off balance, and in consequence will make a grab for the reins and jab the horse in the mouth. The chain reaction, especially with a severely bitted horse, is resistance, head throwing, and possibly a bloody nose for the rider. With his arms flailing to retain balance, the considerable weight of the upper torso is deflected and at this stage it is quite common for the rider and horse to part company.

Several sessions later the rider would have learned to coordinate his and his horse's movements, and to relax enough not to grab constantly for the reins or saddle every time the horse changed pace. The next thing would be to use the legs independently of the hands and body, and at the same time maintain a deep seat instead of bouncing on top of the horse's back. There is of course the strong possibility that some horses would have been what is termed in America 'gaited', having a four-beat syncopated movement or even a lateral pace. This would be somewhat easier to sit to than the trot, especially the former, as four-beat gaits such as those sometimes termed rack or slow-gait are very comfortable. The Spaniards provided a large number of cavalry and mounts, and according to Pliny the Elder the Asturian horse was gaited.

Once trot is learnt satisfactorily, the horse is asked to canter. It is clear that all the exercises Arrian describes were executed at canter, hand gallop, or gallop. Even very bold lads often show trepidation when a horse first canters as, although the speed may be minimal, it feels as if the horse is running away. The normal way for a beginner to get a horse to canter is from a faster and faster trot, which is very unseating. The actual moment the horse breaks into canter he is already moving fairly fast and so the gait change comes as a lurch, and back the tyro goes to grabbing at anything convenient to stay aboard.

This paints a rather comic picture and one that may be thought to be exaggerated, but I can assure readers that it is really very common. It would have been no different in Roman days, except that the recruit would not have been able to opt out. Common sense dictates that retired cavalry mounts were used to teach incoming recruits. Flounderings by tyros on horses in current war use would have taught horses to evade orders. They would have become untrustworthy. And dangerous in battle. A horse will often cheat on a rider, as event and showjumping riders frequently find to their cost when their horse tries to evade a fence at the last moment.

I would think that at any base camp which had a regular draft of troops coming in, or in the Later Empire when levies of troops were promoted to the cavalry, they first went through some sort of parade-ground drill under the riding master. It is a point ancient historians have not enlightened us on, but again common sense suggests it was so. Cavalrymen had to start learning somewhere. There are very, very few natural riders, and even they take time before they realize they have an affinity with all horses. Once the initial stages of mastering basics, gaining a modicum of mastery over the horse, and improving co-ordination have been passed the rest of the training proceeds more smoothly and at a faster pace. The recruit would be expected to be able to execute circles, turns, fast starts and stops, both in a group and solo. Once he had mastered that he would start over again clad in armour, and progress by stages to *carrying* his shield and weapons, and later to using them on the horse. It would all take time, and the investment in both horse and rider training made the cavalryman a valuable commodity not to be lightly risked in wasteful encounters. This would have become one of the reasons that Roman cavalry were accorded duties that did not cost too heavily, if such cost could be avoided.

The Roman cavalryman had to reach a level of expertise never demanded of modern riders. He may have lacked the finesse of today's top experts, but he had to be a fighting machine working in concert with an animal responsive to his slightest movement. Horses are put off balance very easily and lose smoothness of performance when a rider is not in concert with them. The wearing of heavy armour, and manipulating weapons and shield, is very unbalancing to the man, and by extension to the horse. Peter Connolly, the historian who reconstructed a Roman military saddle, has also used his considerable talents to produce arms and armour of authentic weight. In May of 1988, tests were conducted to see how it all felt when put together with a well-trained horse. The horse was my gelding, Katchina, who is obedient, but gets very excited at continuous speed work. The practical application taught me a considerable number of things pertaining to the horse's movements, the saddle, and the armour and shield in particular. I have outlined the weight carried and the added military performance possible using the military saddle in Chapter 10. Here I think it relevant to describe the effects which the equipment had on riding, starting with the rider's clothing. Some of the points made will be speculative, but if maximum efficiency was to be obtained they are common sense.

Before donning the armour I started riding the horse in ordinary jodhpurs, and found the material fibres slipped on the shiny saddle leather. I then put on leather chaps with a rough suede finish. This afforded considerably more security. I no longer felt insecure when the horse did rapid turns at the gallop, although I envisaged that with the top-heavy and unbalancing effect of armour and shield I might 'go out of the side door'. Obviously the Roman cavalryman's leather *bracae* had a duty other than merely clothing him. They added to his security in the saddle.

I had previously practised with the horse and the shield to accustom him to its presence and to accustom myself to its weight. I found the 12 lb (5.5 kg) tired my arm very quickly, so later I asked a friend to ride the horse carrying the shield, but he confirmed my opinion that it was not just my lack of muscle, but the shield was a drag on the left arm. The Roman soldier would have had to accustom himself over a period of time to riding with the shield. For Hippika Gymnasia manoeuvres, special parade armour and lightweight shields were used (Arrian, *Tact.* 34). The horse did not mind me passing the shield over his neck and manipulating it every way I could manage – he did not flinch. Other horses might take considerably more time to become accustomed to this. Mike Bishop of Newcastle University had asked me if it was possible to hold the reins in the same hand as the shield. It is, but one loses a lot of subtlety in control – hence one of the reasons for the rather savage bitting used for instant response by Roman cavalrymen. Katchina, being trained to Western saddle and a member of the British team at Aachen's International Western Championships, was used to being neck reined, where the rider holds the reins in one hand, as all cavalrymen must learn to do, and turns the horse by laying the rein on his neck. The method of holding the reins is different if one is to operate the shield and the reins at the same time. Contact control is maintained but the directional use of the left rein is lost, and has to be substituted for by pressure of the shield on the left side of the horse's neck, allied of course with the leg pressures for turns – although in the heat of an engagement I doubt if a cavalryman was too troubled by the niceties of correct leg pressure! Katchina very quickly learnt that the pressure of the shield meant a turn. Naturally the harder I pressed and the quicker the pace the more rapid the turn, until we were able to execute a complete about face (180 degrees) from a gallop to the right, that is using the shield to turn the horse – Arrian's *toloutegon* manoeuvre (*Tact.* 43), although I must admit I could not manipulate the shield as Arrian describes. But it does prove the point that the horse had to be well trained to do such a move. In this case the rider's ability to deal with the weight of shield was lacking (in other words, the horse performed better than the rider!).

Throughout the trial sessions the horse became more and more excited by all the galloping about (my historian spectators did not appreciate that a horse can verge on the uncontrollable if this is carried to excess). It was at this point that the real advisability of leather *bracae* came in. Burdened and unbalanced with a 30 lb (13.5 kg) cuirass and a 12 lb (5.5 kg) shield carried to the left, at one point I almost did 'come out of the side door' to the left, but the leather chaps enabled me to shift back and grip. With slippery garments I do not think this would have been possible. The horse's gaits were getting shorter and bouncier as he became more excited, whereas when calm the stride is smoother and longer. The choppier gait is harder to sit. In action a cavalryman must have had all this and an even more heightened feeling of activity underneath him. He had to have an extremely secure seat and instant responses to stay aboard and fight at the same time.

Wearing the cuirass was revealing. Peter Connolly had said that it had to fit loosely to allow the wearer freedom of movement. I would raise the question of how loose. At walk and trot it was fine, but at canter, with every stride the horse took it banged on my shoulders, particularly so on my shield-bearing side. Two days later I had the painful reminder of deep bruising of the bone and had to use painkillers for a few days. However hard a man trained, his flesh and bone would not be conditioned to the continued pounding of heavy metal. I would suggest that underneath his cuirass he wore a tunic that was padded at the shoulders where the brunt of the banging was felt, or alternatively he wore an overall garment rather like a Mongolian *kalat* or medieval gambeson that absorbed the impact of body armour. Such garments would not survive in their entirety. If isolated shoulder pads were used their function might not be understood by archaeologists. A point worth noting here in favour of a padded or quilted gambeson is that in medieval days not only did it absorb impact, but it helped prevent links of mail being driven into a wound, with the possible development of gangrene.

When using the shield with an ungloved hand on the grip, the back of my hand was pressed hard against the inside rim of the shield boss, causing bruising. At the first time of using this was not apparent, but on subsequent occasions when the bruising, though not yet visible, had occurred, I found it painful and impossible to manage the shield without some form of padding between the back of my hand and the rim. Because of the lack of flesh and the many small bones in the hand protection was needed. I would suggest that either there was padding around the rim (which has subsequently rotted), or the rider wore some protective padding in the form of a fingerless mitten on his left hand, leaving the fingers free to manipulate reins and shield. I tried with a pad and glove. I found the glove restricted my finger movements as the space inside the boss was rather small. Although my hands are long they are not as large as those of a beefy-fingered man. When cataphract armour, complete with articulated gauntlets, was used the metal itself would have afforded protection. The Emperor Julian writing to Constantius in the fourth century AD gives a very detailed description of the cavalryman's armour (Lindsay 1958): 'one does not see anything of the body left bare, since even the hands are protected by the chainmail made so as to follow the fingers in their movements'. This mail had to be stitched to cloth which would provide some padding against boss pressure.

These experiments with Katchina helped me appreciate to a greater degree what it must have really been like to operate burdened with all the cavalryman's paraphernalia. Finally I was asked to ride the horse with a *hasta* (not having a heavyweight *contus*) in both hands, leaving the horse without means of hand guidance. He partially obeyed directional pressure but tended to drift to the centre of the arena. I then tied the outside rein to my leg so that I could twitch him over if he drifted. I am not suggesting cavalrymen did this as it is dangerous. But I would like to propose that in a charging mass of *contiarii* holding the *contus* in both hands, the steadier, heavier-bodied horses were placed on the flanks to hold the mass intact, and that possibly their riders did not assume the two-handed method of holding the weapon until all the horses were committed to the charge. Once a body of horse is galloping straight they will keep formation for some distance.

We know that cavalry training was expected to be thorough, and the finished article when parading was expected to cut a real dash before the Emperor. Arrian outlines many of the exercises in his *Tactica* and Hadrian was effusive with praise when the troops at Lambaesis performed superbly in a demonstration. He gave well-earned commendations both to the *Ala I Pannoniorum* and the *Cohors VI Commagenorum*.

At major cavalry installations we know that the *alae* were provided with suitable training grounds (Davies 1968). The *cohortes equitatae* also had training arenas, although they rode on a smaller area as Hadrian makes clear in his address to the cavalry of the *Cohors VI Commagenorum* at Lambaesis in Numidia in July, AD 128 (*ILS*, 2487, 9133–5).

Parade grounds where the cavalry performed these exercises have been discovered in Britain. Two examples are Hardknott Castle, with an area of 540 × 300 ft (165 × 90 m), and Pudding Pie Hill near Maryport, at 285 × 279 ft (87 × 85 m) (Davies 1968, p. 77). Arrian tells us that the cavalry chose a level space and dug up the soil until it was fine and soft (*Tact.* 34). This would give a surface very similar to the arenas so vital for training horses to any reasonable degree in climates where the soil either bakes hard or is a constant pudding of mud. Either condition is hard on the horses – hard ground injures joints and is concussive; puddingy ground pulls on tendons and causes severe strains, not only in the legs but possibly in the back as well. The sizes given above permit a considerable number of crack cavalry to perform brilliant manoeuvres at speed, while the more individualistic performances requiring only a few men taking rapid turns would have concentrated in a smaller area in front of the tribunal. The Household Cavalry frequently give displays of precision riding in the larger arenas used by international shows such as Olympia, Wembley and Birmingham in England. The ground space is not nearly as generous as those quoted above.

Basilicae exercitatoriae, or riding halls, were erected for winter use and covered with tiles, shingles, reeds or thatch, in other words whatever was available locally (Vegetius, *Ep. Rei Mil.*). The large open halls described by Vegetius which were constructed in the same manner for the infantry must mean that the sides of some were left open to the elements.

Remains of several *basilicae excercitatoriae* have been found in Britain with the following dimensions (Davies 1968):

Inchtuthil, a late-first-century structure	140 × 70 ft	43 × 21 m
Chester, early second century	250 × 80 ft	76 × 24 m
Newstead, from later second century	160 × 50 ft	49 × 15 m
Haltonchesters, Severan (late first century)	160 × 30 ft	49 × 9 m
Brecon, probably first century	147 × 40 ft	45 × 12 m

A modern outdoor arena is usually based on the requirements for lower-level dressage competitions, which use an area of 40 × 20 metres. The more advanced competitions require 60 × 20 metres. Comparing the modern requirements with the Roman sizes it is clear that there was adequate length in all the Roman ones for several horses to operate together. A modern indoor arena used for dressage and showjumping competitions will range in size from 180 to 200 ft (55–60 m) or more in length and be from 80 to 100 ft (25–30 m) wide. Privately owned indoor arenas are frequently much smaller. Roman sizes tended to be narrower than the modern arenas used for public shows, though some approached the required length and in some cases exceeded it. Some are far too narrow for any but basic exercise and practice of the simplest manoeuvres. However, the Chester *basilica* permitted a full range of exercises to be performed and several horses could work together at controlled speed.

In the previous chapter I mentioned many similarities between Roman equestrianism and the modern style of Western riding, practised mostly in the USA. Another very interesting parallel is the size of the area used for the American Quarter Horse Association 'reining' patterns and that of most of the above *basilicae excercitatoriae*. Reining patterns are designed to test a horse's ability to perform intricate patterns at speed, such as fast starts, rapid turns to left and right, figures of eight, circles, pivots, quarter and half turns and spins, and straight line galloping. The area allowed for these patterns is 150 × 50 ft (45 × 15 m) and the horse is penalized if he goes outside the designated area.

As we have seen, many of the horse's moves are also very similar to those described by Arrian: the modern rollback is the *toloutegon* in Arrian's *Tactica*; circling at fast canter or gallop is Arrian's Cantabrian gallop; a fast start from the halt is the charge from a standstill. For an attack against the tortoise formation as described by Arrian (*Tact.* 36), the horse needed to be controlled, instantly responsive and very well balanced. Fidgeting and anticipating the launch into gallop is penalized today, and could have been unseating for a cavalryman, whose aim would suffer in addition. The other moves in a 'reining' pattern such as spins, pivots, quarter turns and half turns show the absolute control a rider has over his horse. A spin is one of the most difficult moves to execute. The horse does 360 degree turns on the spot almost faster than the eye can see. In a battle, a horse could be hemmed in while his rider spun him, trying desperately to counter attacks from all angles. It would need a rider with nerves of steel, and a horse with total obedience and ultimate skill to extricate themselves from such a dire position. In a pivot the horse turns either 90 or 180 degrees. In battle such a move would be used to avoid injury delivered by a downward thrust of the enemy sword. It would need split-second timing, and immediate response from the horse. If successful it placed the rider in a very good position to deliver a counterthrust to the opponent's side while he was still delivering a now useless attack. The quarter and half turns are similar to a pivot except the horse raises his forehand, turning over his hocks. This gives a cavalryman the added advantage of thrusting more powerfully from the height of a half-rearing horse, which would have been taught to raise itself higher than is permitted today in competition. It also has the added bonus of deflecting any frontal attack, giving the attacker nothing to aim at.

The fluency needed for *tactica* manoeuvres and modern 'reining' competitions is not so very different. Both represent the acme of ability of horse and rider. For the Roman cavalry it was the difference between life or horrible and probably fatal injury.

9
Hazards and health

Owing to the nature of their work cavalry horses and mules were exposed to more health risks than equines in other spheres, and though veterinary practice has been dealt with in a wider context (Ch. 3), the military sphere brought special hazards that the civilian veterinary surgeon would not often encounter in his private practice. Such risks fell into four categories:

(1) Lameness.
(2) Injury.
(3) Endemic illnesses.
(4) Day-to-day ailments.

Forts had their hospital blocks set aside for the treatment of the men. Specially trained medical personnel administered to their needs. The area set aside for veterinary care was usually near the hospital block (Davies 1970). Qualified veterinarians were appointed and *pecuarii*, assistants to the veterinarians, tended the animals. The smooth running of a cavalry *ala* depended as much on the health of the horses as of their riders. Although horses might pass their veterinary inspection prior to being accepted as cavalry mounts, it would not be until they had been subjected to rigorous training and subsequent regular manoeuvres and the occasional bouts of intensive and prolonged activity that any weaknesses would show up.

Lameness

By far the most common cause of attrition amongst horses is lameness. Most lamenesses are caused by working an unfit animal; overstressing a fit horse past its endurance; or by sudden wrenches to ligaments, tendons, and joints and muscles. Frequently a young horse throws a splint (a bony excrescence on the splint bone) and the animal is out of work until the splint hardens, which can take anything from one to six weeks. Some splints are thrown without laming the horse. Less serious lamenesses such as stone bruising, cuts to the sole of the hoof, sore hooves from constant wear, corns, thrush, and fever, and greasy and cracked heels, although temporarily incapacitating, can be treated and would not keep the animal out of use for any great length of time, provided the condition was dealt with promptly. On his journey through Italy before the Battle of Lake Trasimene in 217 BC, Hannibal's cavalry were impeded when many of the horses went lame as a result of constant tramping through muddy marshes (Polybius, *Hist.* II.79). Such lameness can be merely soreness through continual wet and resultant skin cracking, or painful inflammation, swelling and subsequent scabs and loss of leg hair. In extreme cases such sores can extend to the belly. At best the horse is uncomfortable, at worst hopping lame. Winter campaigns would have produced a fair crop of such lamenesses and been costly to the cavalry.

Shoeing was only in its infancy during the Roman era, and it is through the Celts that farriery made its major development. There is archaeological evidence of pre-Roman Celtic shoes, but the practice was not widespread until after AD 400 (Butler 1974, pp. 16–17). Shoes and nails have been found in Gaul on sites occupied between 50 BC and AD 50 and in Britain for Roman sites of all periods (Manning 1976, p. 31 and Fig. 20, nos. 90–6). The earliest shoes had wavy rims with punched holes, and the nails used were the fiddle-headed type with round shanks. The wavy outline was unavoidable because the metal was softer than that used today, and the act of punching holes caused the rim to bulge. The successor to the early Celtic horseshoe was closer to the plain type used today with a firm rim and square holes. A partial shoe has been found at Vindolanda, which from its narrow shape could be a mule shoe or the hind shoe of a horse. It measures aproximately 5 inches (12.5 cm) from heel to toe, with a 1¼–1½ in. (3–4 cm) web, rolled over calkins at the heel, and a square nail hole in the outer edge. This would be large enough for a 15 hand (152 cm) horse, and would cover approximately two-thirds of the underside of the hoof. The modern equivalent would have a narrower web. A similar shoe was found in the Roman gravel layers on the Thames foreshore. It has been securely dated from the strata to the first to second century AD (Hickman 1977, p. 23). Though the more advanced type is attested, the wavy rim continued to be used, presumably depending on quality of metal available. Iron horseshoes have also been found at the late third–fourth century villa at Brislington (Brannigan 1977, p. 77).

For the greater part of the Roman era most horses and most mules went unshod. Veterinarians attended to hoof trimming for a small fee, noted in Diocletian's *Edict on Prices* (Leake 1826). They probably also attended to any other bad hoof condition. Corns would have been cut out and the horn left to repair itself before the animal returned to work. The forms of hoof protection known to the Romans, in addition to early farriery, were the *solea spartea* and the *solea ferrae*, which we call the hipposandal. The former was of tough sparta grass (or any suitable rushy material). The latter could be either completely metal, or a leather foot with metal sole, and was fixed on by means of leather or fibre thonging with a band around the coronet. These sandals could be used for the horse with a hoof ailment that merely needed relief from pressure on the ground; as a means of keeping a dressing in place; for an ailment or lameness that needed the hoof raised; or for slow traction animals that had to use the hard surface of roads when pulling vehicles. Where the practice of farriery was well known in the Empire, common sense dictates that muleteers and teamsters would have availed themselves of the benefits. Hipposandals have been found with ice crampons on the soles, rather like calkins or anti-slip ice studs on modern horseshoes. Some also had the undersides grooved, rather like modern fullering, but giving more traction. Today's equivalent of the hipposandal is the 'easyboot'. I have not found these suitable for any but slow work, and definitely a hindrance in mud as they get sucked off however tightly they are fixed. Hipposandals had the same drawbacks. For any speed work they are far too clumsy, and regular use would have caused friction from the bindings. The weight and awkward shape would alter the horse's action and cause self-inflicted injuries when the horse's legs interfered with each other. However, it is certain that they were used in a limited way as regular shoes, since the skeleton of a horse with hipposandals on all four hooves has been found on a site on Rome's Persian frontier (Sparkes 1976, p. 4). They were common in Roman Britain (Manning 1985, pp. 63–6, Fig. 16). The variety and number of retrieved hipposandals implies that proper shoeing was rare, as otherwise there would have been very little use for the hipposandal other than medical.

Abraded hooves would have been a very common reason for temporary lameness in times when horses had to travel long, hard and fast. The hot dry regions of some of the Roman provinces were conducive to hooves becoming very hard and wear resistant. In wet climates with boggy underfoot conditions hooves can become very soft and break down quickly, with the sole liable to injury and the outer horn splitting and chipping, and the laminae often separating, permitting foreign particles to work their way in between. On the whole the cavalry in the eastern sector would have been able to cope much better with extended marches, although excessive, continuous movement would not give the hoof time to grow and keep pace with the wear. It grows about a quarter to half an inch (5–10 mm) a month depending on the individual horse and the state of its nutrition. When I trained and campaigned horses for endurance work in dry conditions in the USA with few roads, I found they only needed shoes in stony regions. In England, the same horses needed shoeing as soon as they had to work in the softer climate.

It is significant that shoeing as we know it developed among the Celts and came into use through Rome's contacts with Celtic peoples. From the finds in Britain alone it is evident that some horses were shod, presumably the few that had excessive duties, were owned by the wealthy, or had very poor hooves but valuable other qualities. For the most part when travelling along Roman roads the cavalry would have had the sense to use the softer going alongside the built-up road. Their practice of riding flank was not only to protect the centre of the column but to preserve the horses' hooves.

Pelagonius (*Ars Vet.* XV–XVI) gives many recipes for curing abraded hooves, abscesses, and so on. Some reflect recent practice, especially before modern drugs came into common use. He recommended various poultices, among them bran and mustard; and applications of pitch (up to recent times Stockholm tar was a regular stable standby); but his recipe for curing rotting feet, by which he must mean thrush, is alarming. He recommends applying liquid dog dung mixed with sharp vinegar to the hooves (ibid., XVI,240), assuring the horse's owner that he will be surprised!! Maybe the vinegar's antiseptic qualities destroyed the bacteria in the dung?

Injury

Many of the ingredients used in veterinary medicine were ancient, well-tried homoeopathic remedies and also used in treating humans. Iron rust and verdigris were used by doctors to dry and cleanse wounds (Davies 1970, p. 93). Amongst the recipes of Pelagonius, these figure many times and are used for the same reasons. Davies quotes Celsus' use of other products that can also be found in the veterinary medicine chest such as turpentine (terebinth), figs, pitch, lard, oil, honey and eggs. Bacteria do not live in honey. Pelagonius uses a wide range of birds' eggs, and many herbs were also used. It is therefore not surprising that the two hospitals – human and veterinary – were placed adjacent to each other and that there was such a close affinity in some of the treatments.

Cavalry horses suffered a number of severe injuries. The worst were puncture wounds because of the complications of possible tetanus. Very little can be done for a horse suffering from tetanus if he has not received an anti-tetanus injection. It was recognized as a serious complaint and

Pelagonius, quoting Apsyrtus, admits to not understanding its cause (*Ars Vet.* XVII,267). He describes it fairly accurately and gives cures from several veterinary sources. Apart from various useless potions and unctions the main treatments were drastic – sweating it out and cauterizing – with not much hope of success. Some horses do recover if the attack is slight, but the majority do not (Russell Lyon MRCVS, pers. comm.). The injuries likely to introduce the tetanus bacteria would have been caused by staking in pits, caltrops piercing the hooves, and the upwards stabbing of infantry crawling about amongst barded horses and thrusting upwards at their bellies. Ammianus Marcellinus describes this as one of the German tactics at the battle of Strasbourg in AD 357, where the horses were an easier target than the mailed riders. Arrows would have been one of the main causes of puncture wounds, twisting as they entered, tearing flesh and burying themselves deep. The prime target in a horse's anatomy must have been the Achilles tendon, which incorporates all the tendons and muscles attaching to the calcaneus, a bone in the hock. Once this was severed the horse was useless. Slash wounds, though more alarming, are not so dangerous provided they do not sever any vital artery, muscle or tendon. I have seen some really terrible wounds heal very well, given time.

Celsus, on the treatment of wounds in humans, stipulates cleanliness (*de Medicina*, V.26.21–4). He advises stitches for a wound easily drawn together, and *fibulae* for large gaping wounds not easily stitched. Much the same process applies to horses, except where wounds are so close to a leg joint that no stitching is possible. Here nature takes its course provided the wound is kept free of dirt, although too much washing induces growth of proudflesh. The main drawback with a horse is that as a wound heals and starts to itch he will try to lick or bite at it. Nowadays this is prevented by a cradle around his neck when he has wounds that can be reached by bending the neck. For wounds reached by turning the head to the flank, or by raising a hind leg towards the mouth, tying the horse short enough to prevent access would have had to suffice. For extracting arrow heads or other small missiles embedded in flesh Celsus gives clear instructions (ibid., VII.5.1–5). Naturally, because of the horse's body mass, extraction by pulling right through would rarely be possible except through the neck. Anything passing through the upper fleshy part of a limb would destroy so much muscle and tendon tissue that the horse's usefulness would cease. Enlarging the wound, as Celsus advises for a man when it is not possible to draw the arrow through, would be necessary – there must have been some horrific scars on veteran horses.

The main problem in dealing with this type of wound would be in restraining the horse. Without sedatives most horses in pain are very difficult to treat. However, when a horse that utterly relies on his own special human gets hurt, *sometimes* the effect is to make him very trusting and very docile in their care. Others fight at every step of the way. There are several methods of overcoming this, all of which must have been known to the Romans. We do know that they had stocks for containing horses – similar to breeding crushes used at many Thoroughbred studs today. Inside these the horse was restrained and safer to handle. However, when a *veterinarius* had to get close to the horse to attend to a wound, stocks would not be suitable, and, in a military field camp, not available. Twitching, the most common age-old practice, is a method of distracting the horse's attention from localized pain. It consists of pressure on the nose which releases morphine-like substances into the horse's body. Most horses are safe to handle when twitched, although a few are dangerous. Casting the horse, that is, getting it to the ground, is another method of immobilization. Provided someone sits on its head, or the legs are lashed together at the fetlocks, it cannot rise. I would suggest that this method, if the wound was not too traumatic, was used when twitching or rope restraint failed. (Casting a horse is also a sovereign cure for an animal that refuses all attempts to be broken to man's will. I have used it occasionally and somehow it deflates even the most aggressive animal and shows him who is boss. It may not be scientific, causing raised eyebrows in some quarters, but it is painless for the horse, and very, very demoralizing. I would suggest it had a place in the no-nonsense Roman horsebreaker's yard.)

Skirmishes, harryings, ambushes and occasional retreats leave the rider no choice but to take the most direct line over often very rough ground with concealed hazards. Hurtling into these at speed would be the main cause of tendon rupture, joint stress or fracture, or shoulder dislocation. Hadrian, in his address to his troops at Lambaesis in AD 128, stresses this, praising the cavalry and at the same time instructing them that 'the cavalryman should ride out from cover and use caution in pursuit. For unless he sees where he is going and is able to check his horse whenever he wants to, he will surely be exposed to pitfalls' (*ILS*, 9133–5). Ruptured tendons take months to repair.

Just from this small sample of hazards it can be seen that a cavalry horse would have to be a very sound, well-trained, nimble, obedient and intelligent beast. Injuries are chance happenings, but a horse with recurring lamenesses would have been a liability and would have been discarded. In my own sport of endurance riding much the same stresses are put on the limbs that a cavalry horse would have been subjected to. Nearly all endurance horses which fail do so because of recurring lameness of some sort. A small number fail for other reasons, and a cavalry horse, particularly one operating in heat, would encounter similar problems. Greater numbers would have suffered because pace and location were dictated by events, not choice. Dehydration, loss of body salts, and azoturia (a condition where the horse completely seizes up due to the build-up of lactic acid; see p. 226) would have plagued cavalry horses, especially those operating in Africa and Asia Minor.

Pompey, in his war against Mithridates in 66 BC, lost troops to thirst and heat. When he finally reached the River Cambyses the water was so cold that it proved injurious to the men who drank great quantities (Dio, XXXVII.3–56). Presumably the men colicked. There is no mention of the animals also suffering, but they would have been in even worse straits as pound for pound they needed more fluid than the men. Hot horses colic very easily if allowed to gorge quantities of icy water. In the Parthian campaigns water was a constant problem. Dio comments on the Parthians' discovery of a way to procure drinking water (ibid., XL.15.1–6). I can only think this must have been the bushman's trick of trapping moisture from the sand by slow distillation, if it is the open, waterless plain that is implied in the passage. Any large cache of water would be smelt by the animals long before it was sighted. Extreme measures against thirst are described by Lucan (*Pharsalia* 93–4). He says that when they were under siege the Pompeians killed horses, desperately trying to draw milk from slaughtered mares. No doubt Lucan was taking extreme author's licence as cavalry mares would not have been lactating, but it does show how desperate they were for water, and that animals used too much of the precious reserves. The problem was a perpetual one, as more than two centuries later the Emperor Severus was hampered by lack of water and almost lost a number of men due to dehydration after crossing the Euphrates in his AD 195 campaign against the Osroeni (Dio, LXXV.2.1–2).

When cavalry units were transferred by sea and journeyed in horse transports, it took some time for the horses to find their land legs again, Dio is specific about this when he says that when Caesar had landed in Africa and was out on a grain-collecting patrol, Pompey's men 'drove his cavalry which had not yet recovered its strength after the sea voyage, back upon the infantry with the aid of the Numidians ... and killed many soldiers'. Sea travel where the horses were expected to be operational on landing must have caused much concern to generals, as horses do suffer. They cannot be sick like other animals. I took two horses from Harwich to Hamburg and had a very rough 24-hour North Sea crossing; the horses took four days to bounce back to full vigour. With the small boats used in ancient days sea journeys must have been horrendous for horses.

Endemic illnesses

Large masses of equines are always subject to endemic and contagious illnesses which run rife through the horse lines. In ancient days not enough was appreciated about contagion, and the need not only for isolation of the animal itself, but for the prevention of other horses coming into contact with any article of clothing or equipment his handler had worn or used. The east in particular must have had a number of very unpleasant diseases.

Before the 1914–18 war, when many countries still had appreciable cavalry forces and horses were shipped about in huge numbers, there were a considerable number of very contagious diseases. Equine infectious anaemia, glanders, farcy, epizootic lymphangitis, and ulcerative lymphangitis are a few. They had a high mortality rate. Surra, an intermittent fever due to a trypanosome, a parasite in the blood, is usually fatal and transmittable by biting flies. Dourine, horse venereal disease, is a disease slow to diagnose in its early stages. It has a high mortality rate in mares, and an almost total fatality count in stallions, and it can be confused with other diseases such as surra or glanders (Hayes 1968, pp. 220–62).

There must have been a high toll in both horses and mules due to the rapid spread of infection through proximity or insect bites, and through lack of drugs and ignorance in diagnosis and about the dangers of contagion. The diseases mentioned above are all ones that would have been found within the confines of the Roman Empire.

Day-to-day ailments

For day-to-day ailments such as colics, minor cuts, abrasions, and saddle or harness galls, the trooper or groom in charge of the animal would have been responsible. He would have been expected through good management to prevent most of these happening. When unavoidable instances occurred he would have reported it to the *veterinarius* and probably treated it himself under supervision. All the ancient authors writing on horse care stress cleanliness of stable and horse, and Polybius even gives a reason for Hannibal's success at the Trebbia as the fact that his horses had been groomed and fed prior to battle, whereas the Romans' horses went hungry and ungroomed (*Hist.* III.72). The careless cavalryman that allowed a gall or minor cut to go unattended could well find that it cost him dear in an engagement if his horse went lame, or colicked violently at the onset of hard work if fed mouldy grain earlier in the day. The often praised spit and polish of the legions must have been even more vital in the horse lines.

10
Military equipment: the horse's tack

The saddle

For much of antiquity the horse's harnessing was very rudimentary, comprising, at the best, bitting of more rather than less savagery operated by headstall and reins, and a loose covering over the horse's back to afford the rider some protection against sweat and dirt, and the irritation and skin abrasions which friction and salty sweat could cause to the rider's legs. Painful discomfort lessened efficiency. The saddlecloth would have afforded almost no security: at best this would be minimal if the material were absorbent enough to soak up slippery sweat, thus reducing the very real likelihood of rider and mount parting company. Even the advent of saddle pads which could offer a modicum of support by providing a meagre depression for the rider's seat only took security a small stage further. With the rider thus inhibited, the realization of the cavalry's full potential was impossible.

To ride bareback, or almost so, at full gallop in a straight line is relatively easy for a *good* horseman. Such a horseman would also be able to cope with turns, circles, levades, rears, horses striking with forefeet, and so on, if such movements were dictated by the rider and at moderate speed. The picture changes once that same rider is armed and armoured. The extra weight of armour, particularly that carried by the torso, has a very unseating and unbalancing effect on a rider whose upper body movement is energetic, as would be the case when employing weapons whose use would be dictated by need, not by rider choice. To be of any use the fighter must be able to deliver swinging cuts of *spatha*, and launch a spear, *hasta*, javelin, arrow, and so on without having to worry about unbalancing himself or his mount. As a long-time professional horse-woman and instructor, I have found that more falls and near falls are occasioned by the rider who, in danger of losing his balance, inadvertently uses excess upper body movement in a vain attempt to stay aboard. The movement is counterproductive, the solid mass of the rider's torso and his grabbing arms causing the fall rather than any action of the horse itself.

Battle dictates the need for quick turns, levades, sudden stops, and equally sudden spurts, quarter and half turns. The rider loses the benefit of choosing the tempo and thus cannot brace himself against sudden unseating movements. Without a firm saddle offering definite support in all phases of movement by both horse and rider, the effective use of the horse was greatly reduced, particularly so in 'shock troop' engagements. The riders lacked the security of seat to act as a heavy thrusting force. Lack of a retaining and firmly constructed saddle reduced the power that a rider bracing himself against such a saddle could harness to deliver maximum poundage into his thrust, whether of hand-held weapon or launched missile. Too violent a movement would detach both weapon and rider from the horse's back.

Many individual monuments and sculptures of cavalrymen, usually funerary dedications showing the trooper mounted on his charger, and often in the act of despatching a fallen enemy with a lance, show what until fairly recently has been supposed to be a stuffed saddle pad, or at best a non-rigid tree saddle. Similar representations appear on Trajan's Column and the Arch of Orange, among others.

The turning point for understanding the Roman military saddle came in 1967 when finds from Valkenburg and Vechten were listed and published by Dr W. Groenman-van Waateringe. His assessment was taken immeasurably further by the understanding of these finds shown by Peter Connolly, who through study and practical ability was able to interpret and translate the archaeological finds into a reconstruction of the actual saddle. Using the measurements obtained from the find of the leather saddle-housing and component parts, a ridable piece of equipment was constructed (Connolly 1987, pp. 7–27).

This saddle was fitted on to a horse of mine approximating in height to the skeletons found at various sites such as Krefeld Gellep and Newstead. From my own studies Katchina also appears to mirror closely the type of horse favoured by the Romans. He is a 14.3 hh (150 cm) horse of good conformation with a moderate wither, good shoulder, well-set-on neck with moderate crest (being a gelding he has less crest than a stallion), good broad back, ample barrel, and substantial hindquarters, having what the Romans admired – a double chine: the muscles of the hindquarters rise on either side of the spine when the horse is in good condition. His bone structure is that of a well-bred horse with good clean legs, and his temperament on most occasions exhibits the eagerness allied with tractability that would have been so vital for profitable cavalry performance. As I mentioned in Chapter 8, however, he does evince excitement when repeatedly put through fast paces, which with the encumbrance of armour and shield took some handling. He has had a thorough education in both what is known as the English style of horsemanship and, *far more importantly* when it comes to understanding the style of Roman horsemanship as discussed by Arrian in his *Tactica*, a deep grounding in the intricacies of Western or stock-seat horsemanship as practised by Californian reinsmen, a point expounded in Chapter 8. With Katchina it has been possible to take Peter Connolly's saddle one stage further and put it to the test of *practicality*.

From the reconstructed saddle several points become apparent:

(1) That it had to be used in conjunction with a sufficiently thick pad underneath.
(2) That the edges of the tree or framework formed a hard ridge under the inner thigh of the rider. This is an oddity which needs to be checked by further finds, if by lucky chance any should come to light. Were all saddles constructed in this way? Or did some enterprising Roman saddler improve on the basic construction to taper the edges so that no bruising ridge interfered with the rider's performance? Any such tapering would have to be done carefully so as to retain the strength of the tree, but saddle comfort is an important factor in getting the maximum performance out of the rider. Or, as Stephen Bartle suggested, was there a saddle cloth over the saddle to absorb hard ridge pressure? Carved reliefs show this, and I would accept it as quite possible under non-warfare conditions, such as a parade when colourful trappings would enhance the horse's appearance and gratify the trooper proud of his and his mount's turnout. However, in warfare or under marching conditions it would be a nuisance and a danger as the moving substance between rider and saddle would decrease seat security.
(3) The front and rear breeching straps fulfilled to *some extent* the purpose we understand for them today. This is enlarged on below.
(4) The construction of the saddle with its four horns gave such an increased possible effectiveness, depending on the expertise of the rider, to the use of Roman cavalry, that its introduction into the Roman military sphere must totally have changed cavalry capabilities.

To date, it is not known who actually introduced the idea of a rigid tree saddle to the Romans, but early prototypes dating from the fifth–fourth century BC were found in the Pazyryk burials in the Altai Mountains of Asia. The Pazyryk people, as shown by grave goods, had trade links with Persia and also had horses of considerable size, as did the Persians of that era. The saddles found in the Pazyryk burials showed that they were constructed of two cushions with rigid bow arches to the front and rear of each cushion. The cushions were stitched to a felt underpad. Stuffed to maximum capacity they would be reasonably rigid. The addition of wooden spacers both held the cushions apart and prevented them splaying out, thus turning the cushions into a true saddle that stayed clear of the horse's withers (Rudenko 1970, p. 133). The introduction of the spacers must have been found necessary, as a pad pressing down on a horse's withers will eventually cause abrasion and suppuration and the condition known as fistulous withers. This renders the horse temporarily unusable. The arches on the Pazyryk saddles could well be one stage towards the development of the subsequent Roman saddle with its horns. Or it could stem from the Celts, as shown by the Gundestrup cauldron with its cavalrymen seated in a horned saddle. Whatever its provenance, a rigid-tree saddle was a major step forward in using cavalry to maximum efficiency.

In hard use its merits become even clearer. The seat is somewhat shorter from pommel to cantle than that of a modern saddle. With a normal English saddle one should be able to have a clear hand's width between the back of the rider's buttocks and the cantle of the saddle. With the Roman tree this is not possible, there being scant space between the rider's buttocks and the rear horns. The fit of rider to saddle is such that the rider's pelvis is close to the front arch of the saddle and his upper thighs are partially covered by the two angled and projecting horns. The rider's position in the saddle is therefore one of reasonable security, the front horns acting as a locking-in device that also helps to counteract the natural tendency of some less able riders to bounce upwards with the thrust of the horse's movement. The rear pommels, particularly if the metal stiffeners of wider construction are used (Bishop 1988, p. 93), would afford a strengthening of the cantle area, and also a rigid substance against which the rider could brace himself when delivering a thrust. This bracing movement would add considerably to the poundage behind such a thrust. Larger rear stiffeners would also indicate that in the Roman military saddle lay the seeds of the later medieval jousting saddle, where the very high cantle area gave both added poundage to thrust, more rider security, and some protection to the rider's kidney area. The rear pommels also acted to prevent a rider being butted out of the saddle too easily.

For uphill work, the rear horns and rigid raised cantle would restrain the rider's natural tendency to slip backwards. The front horns would assist in keeping the rider in a safe and secure position while negotiating a downhill slope at speed. Without such a saddle, these actions would have been considerably more difficult. Onasander considered that cavalry could not operate successfully in hills. From my experience of riding bareback up a very steep hill, having repeatedly to pull myself forward by my stallion's mane, it is clear that under such conditions a mounted trooper with the added weight of weapons, shield and other gear, not to mention his own bulk, would have scant chance of staying on.

When doing lateral work from the horse's back the value of the rigid horns becomes even more apparent. They enable very sharp, rapid turns to be executed during which the front horns lock the rider in very effectively. When using a weapon, as for instance if the *spatha* is employed from the right over the horse's neck and delivered in a downwards cut to the left of the animal's shoulder, the natural tendency would be for the weight of the torso and weapon arm, plus the poundage of thrust, to disrupt the rider's equilibrium. By locking the right thigh hard under the right horn the rider can maintain his seat, if not with ease, with a greater sense of security than when riding on a soft pad or bareback. The same principle would apply with the left hand wielding a shield, when the left thigh and horn would be similarly used. In an overhand throw, at the moment of loosing any missile the front horns can be used as a brace against which to rise in the saddle and put that little bit of extra height and poundage behind the launch of the weapon. Rapid transitions from full speed to a halt are also possible while still staying firmly on board.

Although all my initial experimental cavalry riding was carried out with the smaller-horned Roman saddle, Peter Connolly later constructed another saddle from further evidence. Similar in concept to the first saddle, it has far more pronounced horns that sweep back from the pommel and forward from the cantle to lock the rider in with even greater security. Indeed, a cavalryman receiving a shocking blow would be very hard to dislodge, and a wounded trooper would also be able to remain mounted until he could retire and be assisted to dismount for medical care. On the debit side, should a horse be killed underneath a trooper it would be very difficult for him to extricate himself with alacrity. In addition, should the rider start to fall from the horse there would be a great likelihood of his mail catching on a horn and thus panicking the horse, who might be frightened into dragging the rider.

When I first saw the reconstructed saddle the modern equivalent that immediately sprang to my mind was an American cutting horse saddle. This is designed to lock the rider in with a high cantle and very high, and sometimes angled as in the Roman saddle, front swells. The seat is also correspondingly shorter than other Western and all English saddles. The speed with which a cattle-cutting horse moves under the rider makes such a saddle necessary when working cattle.

Saddle accessories

The Roman saddle is always shown with breast and haunch straps. The girth is rarely glimpsed, as it is usually covered by an over-saddle cloth or the rider's legs.

Today we rarely use breeching straps around a saddle horse's hindquarters. Very occasionally, if the horse is mutton withered, a crupper is fitted around the dock of the tail and attached to the rear of the saddle to prevent it slipping up the horse's neck in hill work. The haunch straps attached to the Roman saddle served much the same purpose, but because of the angle at which they were attached to the saddle they did not give as efficient control as today's methods. The Roman method means that with some horses the straps could ride up above the point of the horse's buttock and become ineffective.

The breast harness helped prevent the saddle from slipping back. The Roman model is similar to a modern hunting breastplate. More horses send their saddles back than send them forwards, and only horses with an exceptionally good saddle position can operate in steep hill country without breast collars. Because the Roman saddle had not achieved the quality of design and fit that today's vast selection of saddles offers, the breeching and breast straps were not only customary but necessary.

No girths have survived that have been recognized as such, but there are a variety of extant girth buckles (Bishop 1988, p. 128) and all are approximately 1¼ inches (3 cm) wide. From the archaeological remains it is not possible to tell if there were one or more girth straps or buckles used on each end of the girth, but they are of such a scant width that I doubt if a Roman trooper would trust his safety to just one buckle. Western girth buckles, which are very similar in *design* to the Roman buckles, are up to 3½ inches (9 cm) wide, and only one such buckle is used with a many-stranded webbing girth. English buckles are much closer to the Roman *size*, measuring from 1¼ to 1½ inches (3.25–3.75 cm) across. Two such buckles are used on each girth, which range in width from 2¾ to 3½ inches (7–8.5 cm), and may be of leather, canvas or similar fabric, cotton or nylon webbing. A wide girth spreads the girth pressure over a greater area, offers more security, and is definitely more comfortable to the horse. A very thin girth, such as is indicated by the width of the Roman buckles, would be liable to dig uncomfortably into the flesh and would chafe more easily than a wider one. A narrow girth puts greater localized pressure on the framework of the saddle. I would envisage that either two girths were used, each with a single buckle at each end, or one similar to an English girth which has two buckles at each end.

The original Roman saddle constructed by Peter Connolly is on a carved wood frame with the leather cover closely fitted over the tree. Such a saddle had to be used with a thick pad underneath to protect the horse's back against friction and pressure. Modern Western saddles, which reflect the Roman pattern, are used with a separate blanket or pad. English saddles have integral padding in the panels, so a saddle pad is not essential. However, any pressure irregularities in the saddle construction can be minimized by a sufficiently thick pad, and as mentioned previously the pressure caused by the hard edge of the tree would be diffused by sufficient thickness between saddle and horse. The natural fibres of the padding allow sweat absorption and help keep the back dry and sound. Localized pressure, when unrelieved for many hours at a time, can cause what are termed 'pressure bumps', which are oedematous. If ignored and the saddlery not altered, these bumps can become calloused and result in permanently thickened skin which constantly flakes, causing tenderness for the horse. The hair also grows through white in areas badly affected.

Decoration of equipment

Roman military horses had their tack adorned with various types of *phalerae*. These came in a great variety of designs and some were of atropaeic significance, but their use was basically decorative. The larger *phalerae*, fitted at critical points on breast and haunch harness, also served to join different sections of leather, but this could easily have been better done in a more conservative manner. Michael Bishop's work on cavalry equipment (1988) depicts an extensive range of many types of *phalerae*.

Some of the cavalry funerary monuments show the horse tacked up in very colourful saddlery, and if we accept this as an accurate representation a military horse in full panoply must have presented a glittering and colourful sight, with glinting *phalerae* and the rainbow-hued, fringed saddle cloths fluttering over the paintbox colourings of the saddle leatherwork. Horses today, with the exception of parade or circus horses, are far more conservatively equipped.

Bitting, hackamores and muzzles

The bit

Both Roman and modern bits fall into two categories: the curb and the snaffle. The term 'curb bit' is often loosely used to refer to any severe bit, but to a horseman 'curb' *always* implies that a curb rein conveys the

Military equipment: the horse's tack

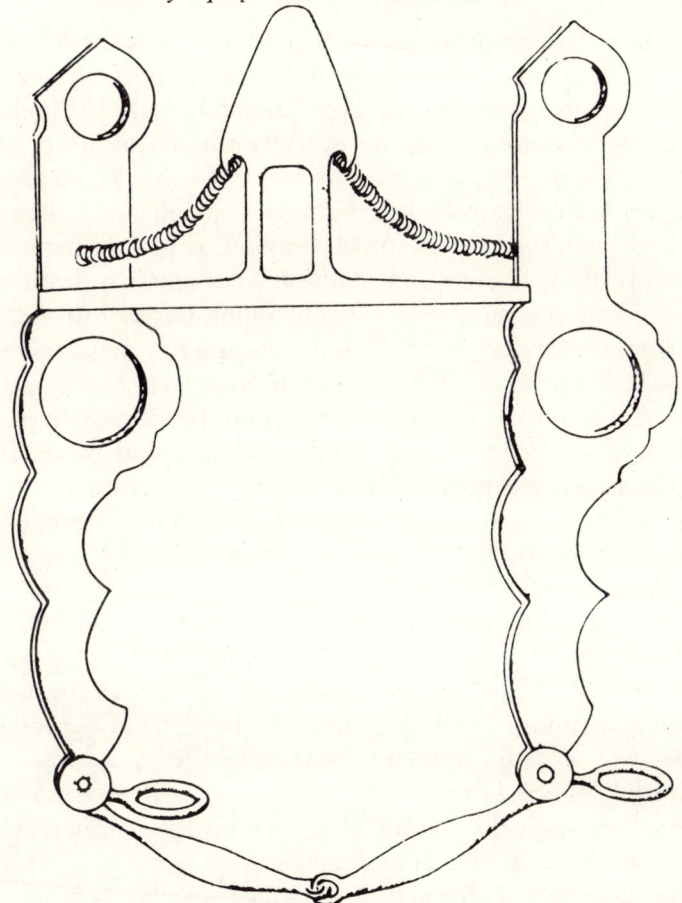

5 A Santa Barbara spade bit, a Western curb that closely resembles the Roman bit

message to the horse via the extended cheek or shank below the mouthpiece, and that the bit is used in conjunction with a chain or strap lying in the chin groove. A snaffle, on the other hand, is nearly always a bit where direct contact with the mouth is achieved, and where there is no extended branch either above or below the bit. Each bit shows a wide variety of mouthpieces, especially in the curb category.

Some Roman curbs have mouthpieces that resemble those used by horsemen practising the Western style of horsemanship at an advanced level. This type of bit is so severe that used roughly it can cause extreme discomfort and pain to the horse. It should never be used by a novice. Western curbs which most resemble the Roman high-ported bits are the mouthpiece of a Santa Barbara spade and various cutting horse and roping bits. The action of the port is such that when the curb rein is operated the port, or in the case of the Santa Barbara and the Newstead Roman curb the spoon-shaped central part, will hit the roof of the horse's mouth unless he holds his head in the correct position: neck bent at the poll and the frontal plane of the face almost vertical – the ideal sculptural representation of quality Roman horses. The higher the port or spoon the more severe the pressure on the inside of the mouth. Externally, severity is governed by length of shank. The height of the metal part of the bit above the mouthpiece, coupled with the action of the curbchain, determines how much pressure is put on the sensitive poll area between the horse's ears. Without a curbchain or leather curbstrap severity is minimized and much controlling power lost. Other Roman curbs have either straight or jointed mouthpieces, frequently with round discs or little square plates fixed to the mouthpiece. These would bite into the tongue of the horse if he fought against control. Coupled with the curb action, and the pressure over the poll, the control exerted would be savage if used to full power. Of the two types, the jointed curbs are more severe than the straight mouthpieces as not only does normal curb action operate, but the jointed mouthpiece compresses the tongue and lips in a squeezing action like the snaffle.

All Roman curbs were meant to be used with a single rein which was held in one hand. The direct pull on the mouth coupled with the curb action offered by the English type of curb bit with four reins, such as a Pelham or a double bridle, was not possible. The horse had to be more responsive and better trained to operate in a Roman curb, as are highly schooled Western horses today. If he did not respond he could be punished through the mouth in a very savage manner, which is not possible with the milder English curbs.

Peter Connolly has made a facsimile of the Newstead curb bit reconstructed to exact dimensions. I was able to study it in great detail, use it on Katchina, and borrow a horse's skull from my veterinary surgeon to have it photographed in use from all angles, including a very important shot from the hollow between the lower jaw bones. This shows the exact placement of the spoon at rest, and how it rotated and gouged the roof of the mouth in action. The cheekpieces also rotate from vertical to horizontal, thus exerting great pressure over the sensitive poll area.

As a cavalryman would be holding a four-foot (1.2 m) shield in his rein hand, he would need to hold the reins considerably higher than is normal today in order to give his upper torso and head adequate coverage. This position would, when pressure was exerted via the reins, cause the heavy metal bar between the bit shanks to bump the horse hard on the lower jaw, while the other components of the bit acted as described above. Once pressure was released the lower half of the bit dropped down and the spoon and cheekpieces returned to vertical, thus relieving the horse of the punishing effects of the bit.

Many other bits of similar design but even greater severity were in use, particularly some of Thracian design, but I think this is the first time that such an ancient design of bit, albeit reconstructed, has actually been used on a modern horse. I *assure* my readers that I did not use it with the severity that was originally intended to be employed. I could, however, readily understand how effective it was. Coupled with the horned saddle such bitting made use of cavalry an extremely effective military medium.

The other category of bit – the snaffle – is considered to be a milder type than the curb. This is true, provided the rider handles the reins and the control sympathetically. Most snaffles today have what we term smooth mouthpieces. Many Celtic snaffles also had such mouthpieces, but a number of variations on the snaffle have been found dating to the Roman era. The Newstead straight-bar twisted snaffle with rigid under-chin metal loop is one type. It is not a subtle bit. It relies on the multiple ridges of the twist to exert pressure on the tongue, and also on the corners of the mouth as the ridges continue along its entire length. Hence the horse receives multiple pressure/power points when a direct pull is exerted. Another type of Roman (Celtic) snaffle is that from Caerleon. This too has several pressure points in the mouthpiece, which if one does not understand the principles of bitting appear as decorations only. There are other jointed snaffles fitted with discs similar to those described in the jointed curbs. Some have a refinement to add to the sharp discs in the form of sharp spurs fitted to the discs. Others have everything piled on to one bit; sharp discs, pointed squares and sharp spurs, all separately fitted and with just enough room between each attachment to allow the tongue to be pinched as well as cut by the various contraptions. Some bits had spikes fitted to the branches so that external pressure was applied to the sensitive outer lip area when the reins were pulled. Roman techniques undoubtedly left nothing to chance. Should training and coercion fail, force would definitely be employed.

The size of Roman bits shows that the animals were smaller in the muzzle than the horses and ponies we ride today. Even allowing for the fact that Romans rode on average smaller horses than we do, there is still a great discrepancy. In the archaeological literature, illustrations with an accurate scale show the largest bit measuring only slightly over 4 inches (10 cm). By today's standards that would indicate a medium-sized pony, between 13 and 13.2 hh (132–137 cm). The average pony bit for a large pony of 13.2 to 14.2 hh (137–147 cm) is approximately 4½ inches (11.5 cm) wide. The range of English curbs for a horse is from 5 to 5½ inches (12.5–14 cm), and for snaffles 5 and 6 inches (12.5–15.25 cm), with the average being 5½ inches (14 cm). Western curbs are usually approximately 4½–5 inches (11.5–12.5 cm) wide. It is difficult to find bigger ones; in America at an all Quarter Horse show most of the curbs on sale were 4½–4¾ inches (11.5–12 cm) wide. The well-bred, fine-headed American Quarter Horse has a very small muzzle in relation to the rest of his bulk.

Today we pay very great attention to the comfortable fit of a bit. It should lie snugly in the corners of the mouth and not pinch the mouth when the reins are pulled, which it would do if the mouthpiece were too small. Too wide a mouthpiece, on the other hand, prevents the bit from operating correctly, but is not such a serious misfit as a bit that is too narrow. With the evidence of such cruel bits being stock equipment for the Roman military rider, I doubt very much if any attention was paid to whether a bit pinched the corners of the mouth, so the narrowness may not necessarily mean that horses' muzzles were that much smaller than those of similar-sized horses today. However, the fitting of the bit would not allow for a great discrepancy in size, and it must be remembered that there was a great deal of eastern Asiatic blood in the Roman horse, and the percentage increased as the cavalry was enlarged in size. Eastern horses of the hot-blooded type are finer boned and therefore finer headed than the more cold-blooded northern horses of the same height. The best example of eastern influence is the Arabian head. My Arabian stallion Nizzolan has a small muzzle, and when perfectly bitted he takes a 4⅞ inch (12.4 cm) bit. Katchina, representing the more cold-blooded northern type, needs a 5½ inch (14 cm) bit. Nizzolan is 15 hh (152 cm) and Katchina is 14.3 hh (150 cm). Granicus, Nizzolan's son, is 7 inches (18 cm) taller than Katchina but takes the same size bit. Thus although some idea of the height of a Roman cavalry horse can be gained by bit size, not too much should be read from this one measurement, particularly when we take into account that whereas today we avoid pinching the horse's mouth the Romans actively sought to do so with some of their spiked bits.

The Roman hackamore

In addition to normal snaffle bitting and the wide range of curb bits, the Romans also used a metal hackamore to enforce a very rigid control over warhorses who needed that extra check. Called a *psalion* from its scissor-like action, it was a very vicious piece of equipment, especially with a heavy-handed rider. The following description shows just how powerful the combination of curb bit plus iron *psalion* was, and how it was a very foolhardy horse that fought the restraint imposed.

After lengthy discussions, the experienced Western horseman Jim Chapman and I worked out the actual mechanics of hackamore operation with the help of various photographs of Roman hackamores, a line drawing of the horse of Flavius Bassus showing hackamore and curb bit used in conjunction (Bishop 1988, p. 69), and a similar line drawing of a snaffle and a hackamore (Taylor 1975, p. 112). I also have a fairly extensive range of Western curb bits, thankfully not of Roman severity, but with the same operating principle as used in Roman days. A metal hackamore of the Roman style was made and used in conjunction with a variety of these bits, and we were able to gauge the effectiveness of each one. Some were more severe than others. The link between hackamore and bit was effected by a small connecting leather strap from the *psalion* ring to the upper ring on the curb bit. The headstall was also attached to this ring. The Roman hackamore was designed to be used in conjunction with a bit whereas the modern metal hackamore is used by itself, but combines the Roman hackamore principle and the principle of the curb bit without the mouthpiece.

As outlined above, the curb bit operates by leverage applied by the rider via the rein attached to the cheeks or shanks of the curb bit. To be effective it has to be used in conjunction with either a curb chain or curb strap, and the control exerted is multi-faceted. The bit shanks act as a lever which when pulled cause the mouthpiece to rotate in the horse's mouth, and the higher the port the sooner it comes into contact with the roof of the mouth. Another factor governing severity is the length of both the shank of the bit and the branch above the mouthpiece. The longer these are, the more severe the action. As the bit comes into play, so too does the curb chain in the horse's chin groove, and at the same time the leverage applied via the branch above the mouthpiece puts pressure on the sensitive poll area. The well-schooled horse blessed with a rider with light hands will respond to the first pressure by lowering his head and yielding to the bit. That horse is both happy and comfortable. However, a horse trying to resist restraint will open his mouth, in which case a major part of the bit's power is lost, whether the bit is a snaffle or a curb. The high-ported curbs cause considerably more discomfort in these circumstances with the port hitting the roof of the mouth. A horse who circumvents bit action is today frequently fitted with a drop noseband which prevents him from opening his mouth. In Roman times the *psalion* fulfilled this function but it was extremely severe. The varying degrees of severity were governed mainly by the length of the cheekpiece. As with the branches of the curb, the longer the *psalion* cheekpiece the more severe it was.

If the horse tried to resist the restraint of the bit by opening his mouth, the rigid nature of the all-metal *psalion* would prevent this, and the more he resisted the more it would hurt. The noseband would put pressure on the broad nasal bone, and the under-jaw metal part dug in close to where the lower jaw meets the bulge of the mandible. Each *psalion* would have had to be individually made for a particular horse, or alternatively chosen from a wide stock in which many sizes and types were available.

Because of the differing length of horses' heads and the width of their lower jaws, the vicelike action would not act to maximum power if badly fitted. The area in between the jaw bones is sensitive, and the lower jaw bone is relatively thin so that enough pressure can actually break or crush it. In effect the bit action coupled with that of the *psalion* held the horse's head in a tremendous vice.

Psalia vary in thickness and width of the metal over the nose. Basically the wider a piece of equipment is, be it width of bit, noseband, breast or haunch harness, the wider the area any pressure is diffused over. The narrower the more painful, so the wider nosebands on *psalia* would be milder. Some *psalia* have a central disc or integrated lozenge in the middle of the noseband. Where these are large enough, pressure could be sufficiently diffused to press in against the very sensitive area just above the nostrils without impairing air intake; just another reminder of who was in control above. The combined action of bit and *psalion* would render a horse very obedient to the rider's restraining hand. Some animals, no matter what force is applied, still fight restraint and in that case damage to the jaw could result, or the more likely result would be that the horse would erupt into uncontrollable motion. The most common vices engendered by pain in the mouth are constant head tossing, followed by serious rearing. A horse rearing against restraint is virtually uncontrollable, and this vice is considered to be one of the most dangerous by most horsemen, the author included. In these circumstances, without the military saddle it would be virtually impossible for a trooper to stay mounted. With such a saddle, the trooper would have enough security to relax his hold on the reins while the horse regained his equilibrium. Once the pain caused by the bit and hackamore action ceased, unless the animal was what is termed a confirmed rearer, he would come down voluntarily. Otherwise he could well go over backwards, or come down only to bolt.

The hackamore must have been a valuable tool for the trooper, provided he used it with discretion. No doubt it saved many a débâcle when without it some horses would have bolted. But it probably also caused untold misery to warhorses ridden by insensitive riders.

Muzzles were necessary to stop vicious horses savaging either other horses or riders. Xenophon recommends that unless the horse is bridled he wear a muzzle at all times when being handled (IV.3). Savage horses had to wear a muzzle in conjunction with a bit, and this device is shown admirably in a sketch by Annabel Lawson (Lawson 1978, p. 144). The fitting has the effect of acting in the same way as a modern Kineton noseband, which stops the horse opening his mouth against bit restraint. It has been suggested, because of the muzzle shape with the attached rings for securing the headstall, and the indentation to receive the bit, that the Roman *psalia* were also fitted this way but without the continuous strip of metal that formed the device into a muzzle.

This is correct for some of the *psalia*. There are two such pieces of equipment at Vindolanda. One is a bright metal *psalion* and the only place it could possibly have fitted on the horse's head is over the nose and in the chin groove where the curb chain in a modern bridle fits. It is too small to fit any higher up the jaw. The other, partial *psalion*, which has enough metalwork left in good order for the whole to be envisaged, has a much larger piece to fit under the lower jaw. If it was fitted in the same way as the first, the horse could open his mouth, thus avoiding some of the bit action, before he felt the iron bar under his jaw bite. To connect without opening his mouth the *psalion* would have to be worn several inches up the head. This would still give reasonably good nasal control.

I have had another Roman hackamore made to scale but enlarged in size to fit Katchina's larger head. It is copied from the *psalion* in the British Museum. It has been tried in two ways. When tried in the same way as the Vindolanda *psalia* it is non-operative, as what should be the chin groove section is far too large and is not in contact with the horse, nor could be however wide he opened his mouth. Closer study of both the way muzzles were fitted and the Flavius Bassus *psalion* shows that the key link is that in the muzzle the bit fitted *over* the metal of the nosepiece, and in the Flavius Bassus example the bit fitted *under* it. Used like the Flavius Bassus *psalion*, the British Museum hackamore is extremely effective, and would stop a charging tank! I would never allow other than a superbly gifted rider with light hands to use it, and I have been very careful in applying it. Scarcely a touch is needed for it to register.

Therefore I would suggest that there were just as many variations in *psalion* design and application as there are today in the ranges of bitting and nosebands used for correcting an undesirable trait in the horse. 'Gadget' nosebands are all designed for maximum control on horses who need something more than a plain bit. They are particularly useful on horses who negate bit action by opening their mouths and pulling at the same time. The Roman hackamores were also used for basically the same reason. Knowing how pragmatic the Romans were I would suggest that they improvised and used equipment to their best advantage, as do today's thinking riders. With some minor manipulations some equipment can be used in ways not normally expected.

It may be of value to note that the American word 'hackamore' is a corruption of the Spanish word *jaquima*, and we have seen how much of Roman equestrianism was apparently introduced to the USA via Spain. The *jaquima* is very similar to the bosal used on Western horses. It is not a drop noseband, although the word implies that the equipment is intended to be used over the horse's nose. It also acts on the soft sides of the lower jaw a few inches above the mouth, and via the heel knot under the jaw.

11
Military equipment: the horse's armour

The chamfron

The chamfron was used to protect the horse's head from injury and was made of either leather or metal. It is known to have been used at the annual Troy games (Garbsch 1978, p. 69). The two examples available for study from Newstead and Vindolanda are leather of double thickness, tooled on the outside layer. Many leathers were available to the Romans and the inside underlayer would most probably have been of soft goatskin, or other comparable skin, to avoid chafing the skin of the horse's face which is particularly thin and sensitive around the eyes and nostrils. The outer, thicker layer, to offer protection, must have been made of cattlehide and treated by the process known as 'cuir-bouilli': tanned and subjected to hot immersion for a considerable time to toughen the skins. While still moist the leather is then moulded, and when dried the finished article is extremely tough and resistant to cutting weapons. The Newstead chamfron, when reassembled measured 22½ inches (57 cm) long and 20 ¾ inches (53 cm) across, with eyeholes of 3 ¾ inches (9.5 cm) diameter, taking the photographic guide of three to one. Other measurements are only approximate because the leather is of course fragile and cannot be stretched or smoothed for accurate measuring. The Vindolanda example is a recent find, but by courtesy of the Trustees of Vindolanda I have been allowed to mention it prior to publication and, in conjunction with Peter Connolly who has constructed a facsimile from the trace pattern, I have been able to measure accurately the vital points in the chamfron's construction and try it on several horses.

The measurements from the Vindolanda example are given in Table 4 with the approximate measurements of the Newstead example alongside. From this it is clear that there are only very slight discrepancies, even allowing for the Newstead one not being stretched exactly to its original proportions. It was only on trying the Vindolanda facsimile on several

Table 4. Measurements of the Vindolanda and Newstead chamfrons

Vindolanda			Newstead	
inches	cm		inches	cm
21½	54.6	length	22¼	56.5
21	53.3	width (cheek-to-cheek)	20¾	52.7
4⅛	10.5	eyeholes (diameter)	3¾	9.5
3⅜	8.6	between eyeholes	3¾	9.5
3	7.6	top of eye to base of ear	2¾	7.0
8⅜	21.3	bottom of eye to nasal bone	9	22.9

horses that the importance of certain measurements became apparent. The measurements needing the most accuracy are of course the size of the eyeholes and the distance between them covering the nasal bone. If they are not perfectly fitted to each horse the sensitive outer lid-lining of the eye on each side would be badly chafed and also impair vision, as well as driving the horse mad. The next most important measurement is top of eye to base of ear. This has to be tailor made to each individual. A horse is particularly sensitive about the ears and some cannot abide theirs being handled or touched. The ear coverings probably remained rigid and were possibly further reinforced from the inside, as that would offer the best protection against a frontal cut. (In the British cavalry at one time it was thought best to crop chargers' ears under veterinary supervision at home, rather than risk having them cropped in battle without benefit of veterinary attention. This cropping practice was followed throughout Europe as a fashion fad.) The measurement from bottom of eye to nasal area is also important, but not as vital as the other measurements as more freedom is permissible here. However, if it came too low down over the nostrils intake and exhalation of air would be impeded. Particularly in a hot climate this would be crucial, as a horse regulates his overall body temperature in part by his ability to get rid of heat via exhalation. Too high up the nasal area and the nostrils would be vulnerable to cuts. An indentation between cheek coverings and the widest part of the nasal winging allowed the horse's bit to operate.

The four horses I tried the chamfron on were in the range of 14.3 to 15.1 hh (150–155 cm). The shortest and stockiest, Katchina, has a moderately large head and the chamfron was far too small in every respect. It almost fitted the 15 hh (152 cm) Nizzolan, but because he is a stallion and an Arabian the width between his eyes is just that much more, the discrepancy amounting to half an inch. Wearing it would have resulted in a bad chafe. It was next tried on a Quarter Horse of 15 hands and with a narrower head than the Arabian, and it almost fitted. The one it fitted best was the tallest of the lot, a 15.1 purebred Arabian mare with

1 Long-reining: Longinus Biarta, son of Bisa (Thracian) Bessus = from Thrace, an eques of the *Ala Sulpiciana*, 46 years of age; from the Rhineland.

2 Method of holding the reins in the same hand as the shield. Note the limited finger play possible on the reins.

3 The quarter turn in modern Western riding: the horse, with hocks underneath, turns to the right. In battle such a position would enable the rider to avoid a direct blow and put him in place for a downwards thrust. If necessary the continuation of the spin would be a complete avoidance tactic.

4 Vonatorix, a member of the *Ala Longiniana*, in a typical pose. His stallion's conformation is more refined than that of Flavius Bassus' horse (see front cover) and in better proportion. Note the simple bridle compared to Flavius Bassus' curb and *psalion*.

5 The small horned Roman saddle with breast and haunch breeching. Katchina's mane hides some of the breastcollar.

6 Close up of the rider's position in the small horned saddle.

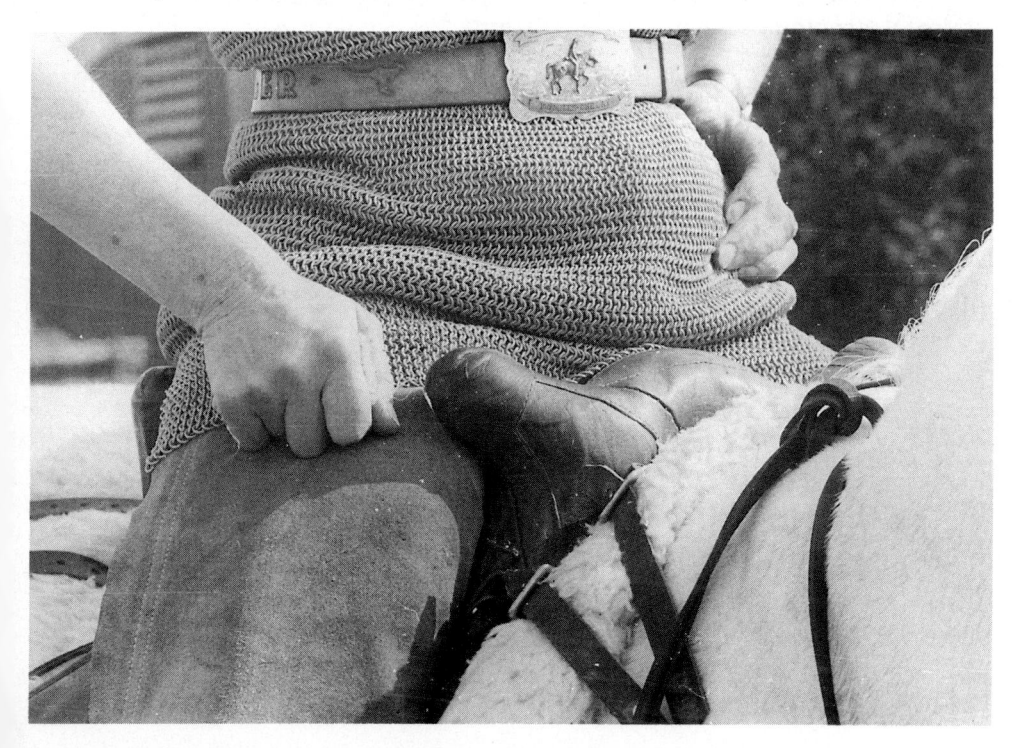

7 Katchina at the canter on the right lead. Note the position of the rider with heels down, which is essential for maintaining a deep seat in action. To have the toe down, other than at a halt or when reaching down, is an artistic convention.

8 Close up of the rider's position in the large horned saddle. Note how the horns wrap around the rider's thighs and seat.

9 A modern Western bit with a moderate port, 5½ in. (14 cm) shanks below the bit, 2¾ in. (7 cm) above the bit. This is considered quite severe by today's standards.

10 Facsimile made by Peter Connolly of the Newstead curb bit.

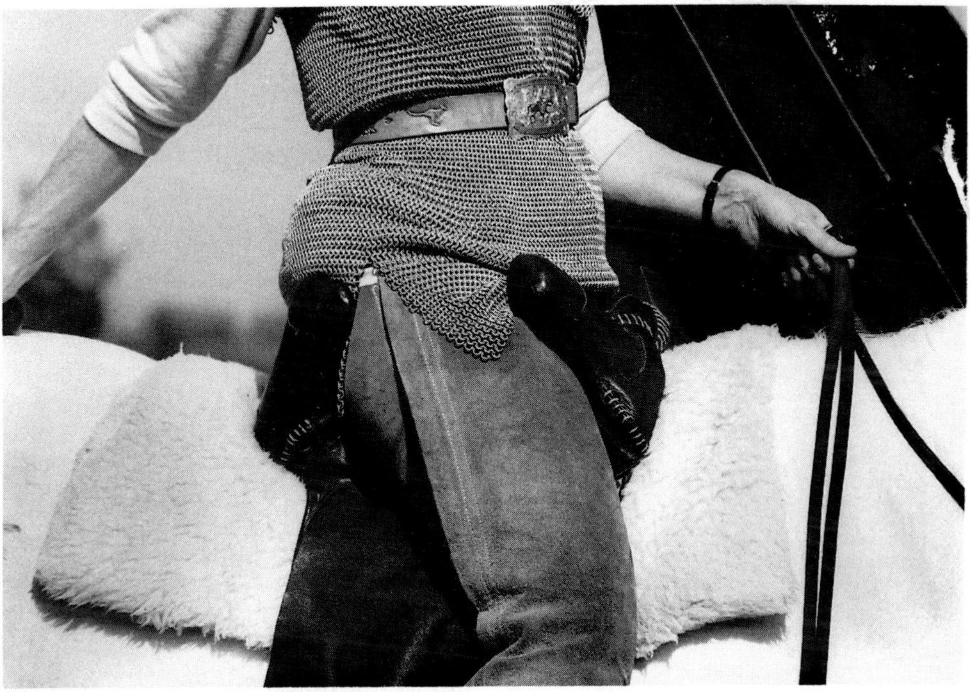

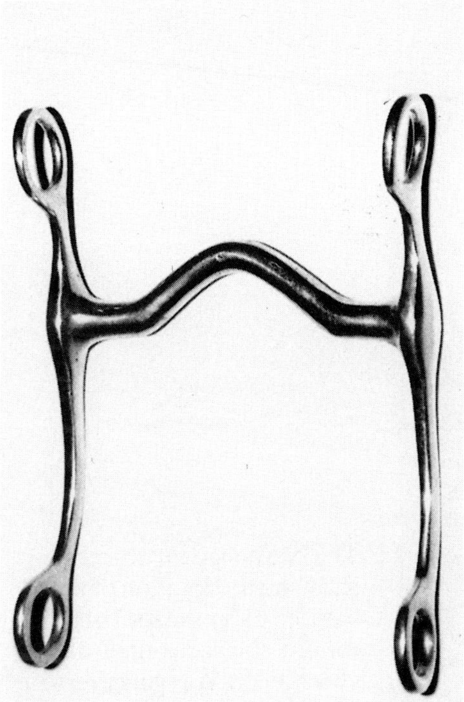

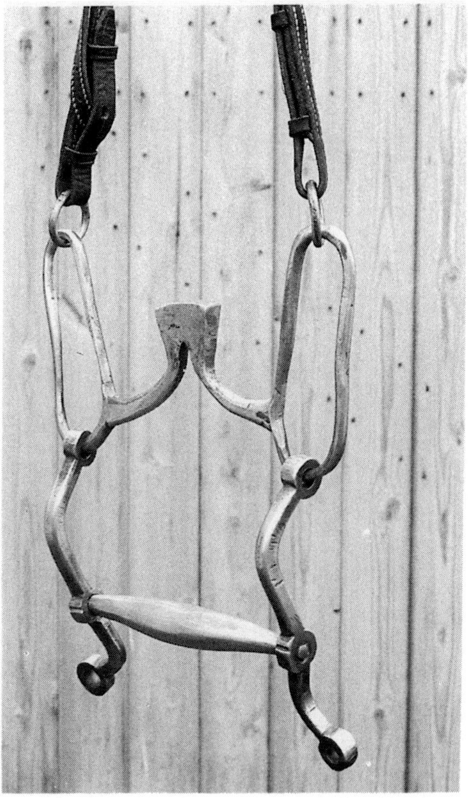

11 Horse's skull with the Newstead bit in place vertically, showing the position of the 'spoon' in the mouth at rest.

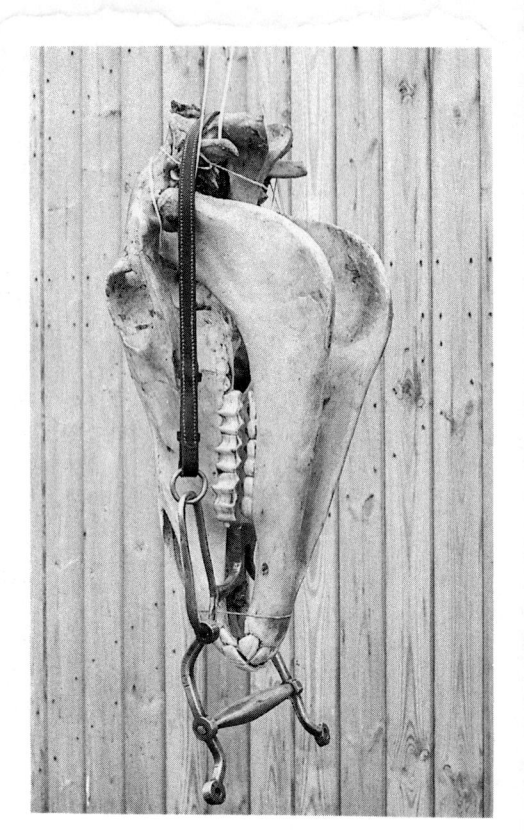

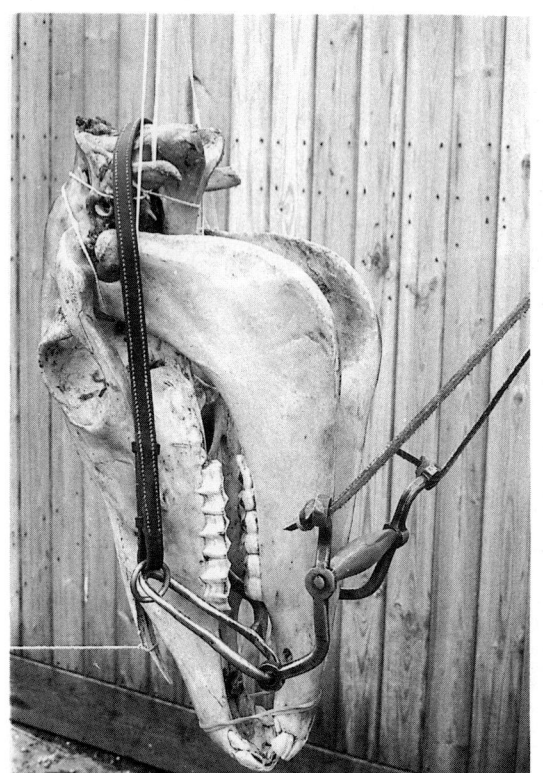

12 The Newstead bit in action, showing the rotation of the 'spoon' to hit the roof of the mouth, the horizontal cheekpieces applying pressure over the poll, and the crush bar in heavy contact with the lower jaw.

13 The Newstead bit in Katchina's mouth, with no pressure being applied. Note the horse's ears are pricked up and his eye is happy.

14 The Newstead bit with pressure being applied, moving the cheekpieces to the horizontal. The horse's mouth is wide open, and his discomfort is shown by the unhappy ears and eyes. Here, pressure is being applied gently with no sudden, punishing jerk. In action, sharp usage would be extremely painful.

15 Katchina's modern Western bit and drop noseband illustrate the action of the *psalion*, to keep the mouth closed and to aid control. The difference in Roman times was that the bits were very severe, and, whereas leather yields, the metal *psalion* caused cuts and bruises.

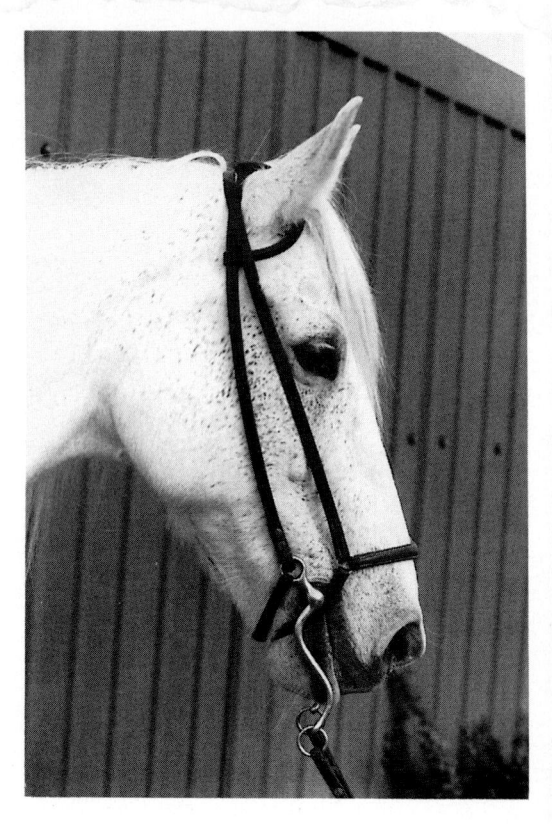

16 Snaffle bridle and headpiece showing the working principle of a *psalion* used above the bit as shown by the Flavius Bassus sculpture (see front cover). It is comfortable only as long as the horse keeps its mouth shut.

17 A metal parade chamfron.

18 Facsimile of the Vindolanda chamfron in place.

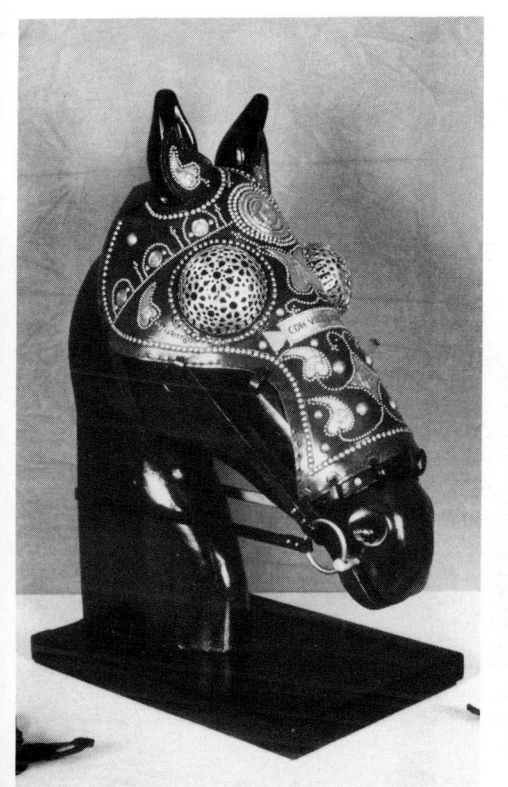

19 Leather chamfron in place on Katchina.

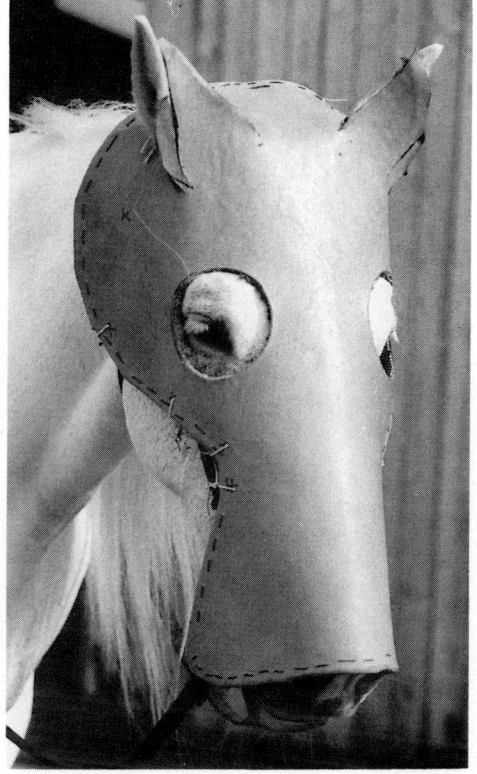

20 Roman cavalrymen in Britain riding down four Britons. The plaque commemorates the building of a section of the Antonine Wall by the Second Legion, Bridgeness, Scotland.

21 The battle of Pydna, 168 BC, on the monument of Aemilius Paullus at Delphi.

22 Detail of horses ready for battle from the base of the column of Antoninus Pius.

23 The Lyon Circus mosaic, showing quadrigae, carceres and white lines for both starting and finishing.

24 The wreck of a chariot in full movement, the rearing pair panicking, the near pair crashing to their knees, and the pole and yoke upended in the air. On the right is a charioteer tipped out on the floor behind the wheels.

25 Mosaic depicting the racehorses Adorandus and Crinitus, who bear the Sorothi brand. Note their light conformation.

26 Four racing stallions – the huge muscular jaw is a stallion characteristic. The leg wraps are for support, and the bound tails minimize rein fouling (as well as for fashion). The overall physique is much heavier and more powerful than those in Figure 25, suggesting that these were bred for sprinting and Adorandus and Crinitus for longer distances.

27 A pastoral scene of mares with foals and youngstock.

28 Hare hunting with hounds, showing the riders bareback.

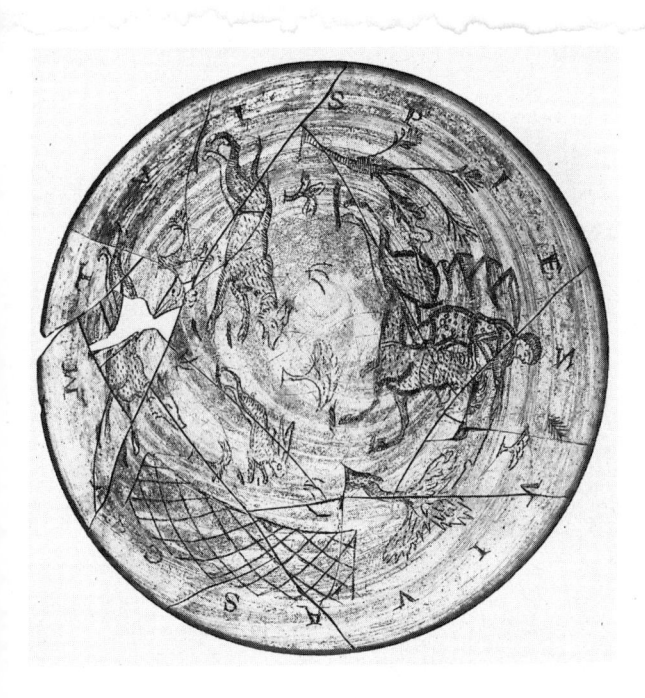

29 An engraved glass bowl showing a hunting scene.

30 Travelling.

31 A hunting scene.

a slightly narrower space between the eyes, and just about a short enough space from top of eye to base of ear. The fitting is quite simple, going from the position of the slits in the trace pattern. It merely fixes to the horse's ordinary headstall and other slits attach to other parts of the bridle. The mare needed considerable pacifying before she would allow it to be put over her face. The trying-on process was very informative, as it proved that there were either considerable stocks of different sized chamfrons to hand so that the correctly fitting one could be selected, or that each was tailored to a specific animal. I would suggest the latter as there are so many facial variations, and they depend on the horse's type, breed and sex. Height of horse is almost no indication, and nor is the possibility that troop horses were drawn from a standard type in a given area.

Using the Vindolanda facsimile as a pattern I made a chamfron to fit Katchina, enlarging all its measurements while keeping the proportions the same. I then attached it to an ordinary snaffle bridle. The bottom of the chamfron came far below where it has been assumed it was laced to the noseband, and as the *proportions* were adhered to this raises a question. How far did the chamfron come down over the nose? The illustration of the reconstructed chamfron on a model of a horse's head, which I have been given permission by Dr Robin Birley from Vindolanda to use, shows it ending rather higher than the one I used on Katchina. However, the Vindolanda horse-head model is excessively long and when I tried the Vindolanda pattern facsimile on the Arabian mare mentioned above it fitted much as the one fitted on Katchina, coming down lower on her nasal area. This way it afforded protection to the delicate muzzle area. The curved lower side pieces allowed for the bit to be operated, and there was also provision for ample air intake and exhalation. Medieval chamfrons (other than what are known as half-chamfrons) came low over the nostrils.

Katchina did not object to wearing the chamfron. He was puzzled at first and moved hesitantly, but then acted in a normal fashion and worked the same as usual. He has always accepted strange circumstances well, and other horses, witness the mare, would not have accepted it so readily. When fitted a very important aspect became clear. Not only would the chamfron protect the horse's head but it would also scare the enemy's horses and cause them to balk and refuse to go forward. A horse tries to whirl away from whatever object scares him. This would cause a deal of havoc in enemy ranks, particularly if they were not similarly equipped. Obviously horses would eventually get used to seeing other horses wearing such contraptions, but for the first time (and maybe several times) viewing it would unnerve *some* horses. It would only take a few to cause chaos. Horses would not reason that behind the mask there was just another horse. There are many instances in the histories of horses being scared by the sound, smell or sight of elephants. Very insignificant things can trigger off a shying session, and many horsemen are left wondering what caused it!

Although chamfrons found so far have all been decorated parade harness, I would suggest that the protection afforded and the fright value would not have been ignored by the practical Romans, who would surely have used it for more than parades and games. In battle, plain rather than decorated chamfrons woud presumably be used.

Eye guards

The eyeholes of the chamfrons afforded space for fitting further protection in the shape of eye guards, resembling large tea strainers with a pierced surface to allow light to penetrate, like a mesh. This would have affected the horse's vision quite considerably, and in any close assault the framework could have been easily penetrated, although one supposes that during such proximity amongst fighting troopers piercing an eye guard would be the least of the men's concerns.

The peytral

The peytral protected the horse's chest and guarded him against a direct thrust into a very vital area. Those constructed to come around the point of shoulder also afforded some protection against slash attacks. They have been found made both from cattlehide, toughened by the same process that would have been used for the chamfrons, and also from bronze. Examples of the latter have been found in Campania and date to around the fourth century BC. Some extremely elaborate parade examples must have been very weighty and therefore not intended for practical use.

Body armour

Well before the Romans were experimenting with barding their horses, other races, notably the Armenians, Parthians and Seleucids, were protecting their heavy cavalry mounts with armour housings. Plutarch describes them in his histories of Lucullus and Crassus (*Lives*, vol. II, pp.26, 62), and Dio mentions Antiochus at Magnesia in 190 BC (XIX).

J. W. Eadie (1967, pp. 161–73) traces the development of Roman mailed cavalry and mentions the two types of armoured horses: the

Military equipment: the horse's armour

cataphractarii and the *clibinarii*. The first term has been used by some writers to cover both types of equipment but there was a difference, as discussed below. The cataphract was an armoured man aboard a horse that was also usually armoured, but not necessariliy so. Tacitus makes this very clear when describing the Roxolani Sarmatians of the first century AD, who were clad in armour of iron plating or toughened leather while their horses were not (*Hist.* 1.79). Arrian (*Tact.* 4) describes cataphracts of the mid second century AD as wearing a chamfron and scale housings (Rostovtzeff et al. 1936, p. 445). Ammianus Marcellinus describes the Persian method of totally encasing the man's body in metal scale armour, with a helmet in which the only place a weapon could lodge were eye or nose holes (*Res Gest.* 25.1). He also describes the horse's leather housings (ibid., 24.6). From the manner in which he frequently seems awed by the Persian way of arming man and horse it is clear that such totally encasing equipment was not widespread in his day in the Roman army. He was writing of campaigns in which he had actually taken part in the 350s and 360s, and his writing is very matter of fact with apparently no author's licence taken. The Parthian and later Persian method of total encasement was what is known as the *clibinarius*. The literal meaning is 'oven man', and considering the temperatures they operated in, both inside their armour and on the Parthian plains in summer, the term is very apt. That there was a distinct difference in meaning is shown by the *Life* of Alexander Severus, where both types of heavy armoured cavalry are named (*SHA*, 56.5). Cataphract and *clibinarii* units are attested in literature and both types of unit are attested in the *Notitia Dignitatum* (Eadie 1967, pp. 169, 171).

In the *Notitia* the 'insignia' of the Master of the Offices includes the products of the *fabricae* (armaments factories) that were under his control. These included the jointed armour used to protect the arms and legs of heavily armoured Roman cavalry, and two types of body armour – one probably intended to represent a shirt of scale armour; the other a solid breast and back plate. It is possible that the *clibinarii* were equipped with the latter, which besides being uncomfortably hot for the wearer, perhaps recalled the appearance of the terracotta ovens from which they derived their name (Mark Hassell, pers. comm.).

Heliodorus (*Aethiopica*, 9.15) gives a detailed description of a cataphract's horse: 'The horse is armoured like its rider. On its legs are strapped estivals [greaves] and its head is completely covered by a chamfron. From its back to its belly on either side hangs a housing of iron mail which both protects it, and by its looseness does not hinder its course' (quoted in Rostovtzeff et al. 1936, p. 445). Examples of these bardings dating to the third century AD were recovered from Dura Europos in 1932 and tally with Heliodorus' description. There were three housings, two of which were more or less complete. Both resembled present day horseblankets in shape, with metal scales stitched to the fabric and a hole cut out for the saddle. Housing One, made of bronze scales, was approximately 4 ft long by 5 ft 5 in. wide (122 × 169 cm). The hole for the saddle was 15 inches long by 27 inches wide (37 × 68 cm). This housing was devoid of breast protection. Housing Two was of iron scales and larger than the bronze example. The body piece was 4 ft 10 in. (148 cm) long and in addition had breast coverings 12 in. (30 cm) long on each side. It was apparently 3 ft 7 in. wide (110 cm). The saddle hole was 24 in. long by 15 in. wide (61 × 38 cm). Both housings had a tail guard attached to protect the dock.

A modern horseblanket is measured from the crossover pieces at the chest to the rump, and of course they come in various sizes. I use a 68 in. (173 cm) long one on a 15.2 hh (157 cm) horse, and a 62 in. (157 cm) model that fits a 14.2 to 15 hh (147–152 cm) horse of robust build. The body pieces (minus the chest extensions) are both 48 in. (123 cm). In the 68 in. blanket the chest extensions are designed to overlap for a few inches, thus taking up some of the chest extension. The depth of each side in these blankets is 32 in. (81 cm) (× 2 for total width). This accords well with Housing One at 65 in. (169 cm), but Housing Two is only 43 in. (110 cm) wide and would not give much lateral protection (which leads me to wonder whether this measurement has been correctly reported). Going from the sizes of the Dura Europos finds and the modern equivalents above the horses were of considerable size, and this suggests a general improvement in breeding. Mail housings would have to fit reasonably well. If too small they would constrict movement and not afford sufficient protection. If too loose they would bounce about and chafe. The length of the saddle hole in Housing One accords well with the size of the Roman military saddle, approximating to Peter Connolly's reconstruction, and the depth of the hole allows for sufficient room for the panels to be fitted to the horse's body. The size of the hole in Housing Two is perplexing. The length of 24 in. (61 cm) gives a very long tree room, and the width of 15 in. (38 cm) is not enough room for the whole saddle to sit comfortably, as the housing would come partway up the saddle panels. Modern saddles come in sizes which are measured from pommel to cantle and can vary enormously, but no saddle would measure 24 inches. The horse's conformation in its back region would not be able to carry such a tree, so part of the 24-in. length must have been either error when cutting out the housing, or implies that the saddle had pliable extensions to the rigid tree that took up the excess. Western saddles have something like this, as do modern military saddles with extended trees that fit either side of the spine, but not on it.

The Dura report includes a picture of a horse wearing Housing One and Rostovtzeff (1936, p. 448) comments that the housing, 'although for length it goes well upon a short modern horse, sits so loosely, particularly in the forepart, as to presuppose in the horse for which it was intended a much greater comparative development of barrel, shoulders, breast, and neck'. The horse pictured is what we would term a 'weed', ewe necked, skinny haunched, and with no substance about it at all. The Roman ideal which the army *stratores* accepted for cavalry duty would have needed better and sturdier conformation than such an animal.

In addition to the housings, fragments were found which, it has been suggested, could have been the crinet or neck covering. Laces attached to the housings would have permitted secure fixing of a crinet and, in the example where no chest protection was afforded, a peytral also. Heliodorus does not mention the crinet, but he does mention the estivals (greaves) or leg coverings which were strapped to its legs. He does not say where they were fitted. The housings reached to the forearms in the front and the gaskin in the back, but actually left the lower forearm and lower gaskin area uncovered. If the upper limb was protected at all it could only have been the forearm, as the shape and articulation of the upper hindleg from the stifle down to the hock would make it almost impossible to fit anything without a severe chafe and eventual lameness. The horse would resent the discomfort and violently refuse to tolerate it. It is possible, however, to protect the lower limbs. Today this is done with a variety of boots and bandages for exercise and when travelling in a box. However, effective protection would have presented immense problems to the Romans, as any weighty material such as armour around the slender and almost fleshless cannon bones would have needed integral padding and a very secure form of buckling on.

From the literary evidence and its confirmation by archaeological finds it is clear that the armour of both man and horse developed in stages from the earliest Republican days, when horses wore chamfrons and peytrals, to the Later Roman Empire, when nine units of *clibinarii* were attested in the *Notitia Dignitatum* (Eadie 1967, p. 171). The major step forward was made by Hadrian with the forming of the *Ala I Gallorum et Pannoniorum Catafractorum* (CIL, XI.5632). Arrian, writing his *Tactica* at the behest of Hadrian in AD 136, says that: 'Cavalry may or may not be provided with armour. In the cataphracts both horse and man are protected, the horse with chamfron and scale housings, the rider with body armour of mail, canvas or horn, with thigh guards. The other kind of cavalry has no protective armour' (*Tact.* 4).

Only thirty-five years later the Column of Marcus Aurelius depicts mailed cavalrymen riding unarmoured horses. The intervening reign of Antoninus Pius was an era of relative peace, so armoured housings for Roman horses would not have received extensive field trials. If one accepts Arrian's descriptions as proof that cataphracts did bard their horses in his day, why were future representations only of unprotected animals? Units still went by the name of 'cataphract'. Had the Romans found such armour to have more disadvantages than advantages and so discontinued for the most part their experiment, keeping the rider mailed but not the horse? Later in the same passage of the *Tactica* other cavalry that wore some armour – iron helmets, plaited breastplate and small greaves – are mentioned. There is no mention of their horses being armoured. There is evidence for cataphract units from inscriptions of the late third and fourth centuries AD. On the funerary *stelae* of members of *Equites Catafractarii Pictavenses* and *Equites Catafractarii Ambianses*, although the riders wear some armour, the horses do not (Eadie 1967, p. 168). From Arrian's description of second-century barded horses and later sculptural and inscriptional evidence of cataphracts using unbarded animals, it would seem that 'cataphract' was rather a loose term. Unless a description is specifically given, as Arrian is careful to do when he says he is going to be precise in his explanations and make terms of nomenclature and practice abundantly clear (*Tact.* 1–2), it would seem that the term 'cataphract' went into common usage and could be applied to either partially mailed or totally mailed riders on unbarded animals, or to the mailed man and mailed horse together, the latter being interchangeable with *clibinarius*. That is, a cataphract *could* be equipped like a *clibinarius*, and a *clibinarius* was *always* completely equipped, the term having a more rigid meaning. Limited pictorial evidence does not prove conclusively that no horse was barded in the Roman sphere at that time. It is hardly likely that Hadrian's innovation would have had such a short lifespan, and been discarded only to be reintroduced as the full-blown *clibinarius* of the third century, as shown by the Dura Europos find. Limited use of cataphract units offered a continuing thread to link the periods.

Barding had definite advantages, even if it also had serious drawbacks. It offered some protection against cutting and thrusting weapons, and against almost spent arrows. The metal links could turn a blade, forcing it to glissade off, or at best deliver a more glancing blow; a javelin, spear, *contus*, and the like might also be deflected. However, if the thrust were powerful enough or the force in flight not spent, the scales could be driven into the animal's flesh causing a nasty wound at best, and possibly a fatal wound with death immediately or occurring later as a result of gangrene. An arrow, particularly from the Parthian type of bow which has greater poundage than a stave bow, would lodge deep into the armour, or carry some of it into the horse's flesh. According to Dio (XXXVI,5.1–2), these Parthian arrows were especially vicious, carrying double barbs designed to break off inside the victim's flesh. The Topkapi

Museum in Istanbul has a collection of wicked-looking Turkish arrows very similar to Dio's description. One of the Dura Europos housings has a hole in it caused by a *ballista* missile (Rostovtzeff et al. 1936, p. 439).

The obvious disadvantage of barding would be to restrict the mobility of the animal, even though the housings moved freely around the horse. The cataphract whose horse was not mail clad would be far better able to operate under all conditions for two very important reasons. His horse's speed would not be reduced by weight of armour, and the horse would be able to regulate his body temperature more efficiently.

The matter of sheer weight needs some consideration. It has been assumed that a horse of the height the Romans were thought to be using would not be able to carry the burden of a mailed man without undue difficulty. Add the extra weight of the horse's own armour and it may seem that he would be at a very serious disadvantage. This is not necessarily so. A progressively heavier animal would be needed for the different grades of cavalry. Scouts would need a racily built, speedy mount; *sagittarii* (horsed archers) a similar type; and troopers equipped with cuirass, helmet and shield a reasonably substantial animal, as would the type of cataphract where the man is mailed and his horse is either unprotected or only partially protected by chamfron and peytral. The fully armed warrior would need the best type of weight carrier. The sizes of the housings from Dura Europos suggest that the animals used had a fairly wide height range, from about 14.2 to 15.2 hh (147–157 cm), with a reasonably stocky build. The stocky animal is a far better weight carrier than his leggier and taller cousin. In some of my own field trials using reconstructed Roman equipment of authentic weight, I rode Katchina who is 14.3 hh (150 cm), of substantial conformation weighing around 900 lb (405 kg), but withal well bred without the clumsy conformation shown by some very slow stocky animals that go under the general term of cob. I measure 5 ft 9 in. (175 cm) tall and weigh approximately 145 lb (65.7 kg), and Table 5 shows the various items that made up the total package.

The horse was not in a fit condition, in that he was not in current training, but he worked in the same fashion as he does when carrying a normal weight of rider and English saddle, which is an approximate total weight of 165 lb (75 kg). Katchina was not distressed. This same horse, when younger and very fit, took part in a competition over rough going of 75 miles (120 km) at an average speed of 9.5 m.p.h. (15 k.p.h.; the average rider out for a hack travels at 4–5 m.p.h. (6–8 k.p.h.)), carrying normal weight and earning full marks for condition. In the USA, on a 100 mile (160 km) ride which I joined, a 14.2 hh Arabian was among the top award winners in the heavyweight division, carrying a rider of 6 ft 4 in. (193 cm) and a heavy Western saddle that totalled well over

Table 5. Weight carried by a Roman cavalry horse

Items carried	lb	kg
Roman military saddle with breast and haunch straps	13	5.89
Heavy duty pad underneath saddle	5	2.27
Leather girth	1	0.45
Hackamore, bridle, bit	3	1.36
Shield	12	5.44
Arms: *spatha, pilum, hasta*, all of which were underweight	4	1.81
Mail shirt	30	13.59
Leather belt to keep shirt in place	1	0.45
Helmet (approximate weight as advised)	3	1.36
Clothing: to include leather trousers (I used leather chaps at 4 lb/1.8 kg,) boots, at 3 lb/1.4 kg, and approx. 6 lb/2.7 kg for tunic, underwear, socks, and Arrian's thigh guards	13	5.89
Total	85	38.51
Rider*	145	65.68
	230	104.19

* A Roman cavalryman, unless a 'beanpole', would weigh considerably more than me, taking into account that male muscling is definitely heavier and so men weigh more than women, size for size.

240 lb (108 kg), the guideline for the upper limit in the heavyweight division. The Florida heat we encountered in that ride would have been close to the temperatures met on the Parthian plains, where cataphracts and *clibinarii* were the norm. One more example that is very pertinent and really puts the weight-carrying capacity of medium-sized horses into perspective are the details given to me by a farrier who shod my horses many years ago. The incident he related shows a link between cavalry marches and today's distance-riding competitions which are based on pre-war cavalry endurance tests; these tests must have closely resembled many of the putzches made by ancient cavalry on rapid manoeuvres with time against them.

Harold Parr, AFCL, was a member of the 14/20th King's Hussars regiment in the early 1930s. When stationed in Egypt, War Office orders came for an endurance march. Each troop took three days to do a 90-mile (145-km) trek across the shifting sands from Cairo to Wadi le Trunie. They then took a 24-hour break before the real test began: the return 90-mile trip in 12 hours, starting at 4 a.m. and arriving back at the Pyramids at 4 p.m. Each horse carried over 300 lb (136 kg) and proceeded at walk, trot and canter for five-minute periods, repeated throughout the ride. There was no attrition due to sound animal management (Hyland 1974, p. 16). Taking this as a very good example of the weight-carrying ability of good sound horses, the armoured horse would not be unduly stressed by the weight alone.

The cataphract and *clibinarius* horse had a far more serious disability to contend with, one which in my opinion was the real reason why large-scale use of these units did not take off. Quite simply the reason was *heat*. Many of Rome's battles and marches were carried out in very hot, arid territories. A heavy horse operating in heat suffers stress far more easily than a lighter-framed animal. It sweats more and loses more vital fluids than the lighter animal (see p. 63 above). It also finds difficulty regulating its body temperature. Quick reduction of body heat is essential to prevent accumulated stress. Respiration and heart rate rocket up to danger levels. Wearing head and body armour would compound this by obstructing any natural ability to recover which the horse possessed. While body temperature, particularly the deep core of heat in a very solidly built and fleshed animal, remains high, respiration and heart rates will not show any appreciable recovery levels. Horses that could not achieve a good recovery would quickly become a hindrance rather than an asset, and attrition through heat stress and loss of fluid, body salts and trace elements would be very costly. These facts have been proven by practical experience with endurance horses of both the lighter and heavier types.

It may be argued that Parthians, and others, who used armoured cavalry were equally affected. They had two advantages not always available to the Romans. We know that in battle they had ample replacements in the form of 'whole droves of horses, so that they can use different ones at different times' (Dio, XI.15.1–6). This implies that the Romans were not so well equipped with spares. Though the Parthian empire was huge it was not so varied or spread out as its Roman counterpart, so that animals would be better acclimatized to the conditions. Horses take considerable time to get used to working in heat, but the reverse is not so. Stress in cold conditions is rare, as body heat disperses rapidly.

We also know that Parthia, Media, Armenia and Persia raised horses in vast numbers and acquired tribute horses on the same scale. The great Achaemenid kings owned vast breeding herds of Nisaean horses of up to 150,000 animals. Herodotus tells us that Tritantaechmen, a Persian satrap of Assyria, had 16,000 mares and 800 stallions, and *in addition* he owned warhorses (*Hist.* I.193). Even allowing for undoubted exaggeration, this firmly places the horse as a major product of Parthia/Persia throughout the centuries, and therefore a more expendable commodity.

It is also highly improbable that such gifted horsebreeders would breed animals not able to cope with the area's climatic rigours. Although some of Rome's horse supplies came from Asia Minor and would be acclimatized to that region, many cavalry units came from as far afield as Gaul and Pannonia, which have climates vastly different from that of Asia Minor.

Another possible reason for limiting the expansion of totally armoured horse units would have been cost. To achieve the rigid standard required for specialized work such as *clibinarius* horses executed entailed a very strict breeding programme, culling any not up to the mark, and allowing suitable animals that extra year or two to reach full maturity. Young horses, particularly the heavier sort, frequently look mature when in fact they are anything but. Loading them with an excessive burden and expecting them to operate so laden would result in breakdowns from sources such as stress, and joint, muscle and tendon lamenesses.

It is very significant that of nine units of *clibinarii* attested in the *Notitia Dignitatum* (Eadie 1967, p. 171) only two operated in the west. Horses acclimatized to or raised in the east would be better suited to these units. Those in the west would often have to contend with muddy, holding conditions. Such a contingent would not be much use if it literally got stuck in the mud; they would have been sitting ducks. The consequence of lack of mobility was shown in AD 312 at Turin where the *clibinarii* of Maxentius were wiped out by the more mobile cavalry of Constantine (ibid., p. 171).

Continued use of armoured units proved they had their uses. Their drawbacks meant that they did not supplant the more mobile horses who worked under less stress and would have been a better economic investment, lasting longer because of better health and fewer injuries due to their manoeuvrability. They would also have cost less to raise because they would have been able to undertake their duties at a somewhat earlier age than the ironclads.

12
Practicalities

The cost of supply of equines

In the early days of Republican Rome cavalry did not represent a very costly investment for the army. *Equites* were obliged to supply their own mounts and the total number of operational cavalry was small. Later when Rome expanded, drawing in other nations, these provided the bulk of her auxiliary cavalry. Replacements were levied as the need arose during campaigns, as is clear from Caesar's *de Bello Gallico* (I.15), and from Tacitus (*Ann*. II.1–4) we learn that Germanicus exhausted the supply of horses from Gaul.

Initially cash investment in horseflesh was not very high. Levies of tribal cavalry implied that the horse came with the man free of charge, but subsequent restocking of animals, especially away from tribal levy locations, needed hard cash to seal the deal, and maintain cavalry-horse strength. There are instances of this throughout the classical writings. Caesar, who provides some of the best examples when it comes to detailed use of cavalry, tells us that he had purchased a great number of horses in Spain and Italy (*de Bello Gall*. VII.55). Sallust also mentions the Italian horses brought into Africa in the Jugurthine Wars of 112–106 BC (*Bellum J*.).

After levying and recruiting cavalrymen with their own horses, and spending time moulding them into some semblance of a Roman military unit, the army was occasionally hard hit by mass desertions. Again from Sallust we learn that two Thracian cavalry units deserted to Jugurtha, lured by African gold. Some foreign auxiliaries may not have had any qualms over loyalties to Rome, and Jugurtha was on a lucky streak.

As cavalry expanded cost began to be one of the problems. We know that it was policy to purchase horses for military use during the third century from the records of the *Cohors XX Palmyrenorum* stationed at Dura Europos. The normal price for a horse seems to have been 125 *denarii*, that paid in AD 208 for a four-year-old, blaze-faced chestnut for cavalryman Julius Bassus (Fink 1971, no. 99, p. 403). Forty years later the same price applied to the majority of horses in the list of men and mounts written in AD 251, but including horses purchased over a period from AD 245 to 251 (ibid., no. 83, p. 341). Clearly the army did not believe in paying more than necessary or keeping in pace with inflation, to the detriment of the poor sellers. It also suggests a standard price regardless of the individual qualities the horses may have had, although there were exceptions at lower prices: namely, the bay horse of Aurelius Abumarius (ibid) at a final price of 100 *denarii*, and another payment of 100 *denarii* to an auxiliary for purchase of a horse (ibid., no. 75, p. 218).

By Constantine's time taxes were payable in horses for certain classes who in AD 219 attracted high taxation (*Codex Theo.*, 6.35.1.1). Palatines assigned to state services and those who worked on the governor's staff did not have to pay this tax (ibid., 6.35.2). The system changed very shortly after Constantine, as we learn from the Abinnaeus archive (Bell et al. 1962). In AD 342 or thereabouts (Abinnaeus held his command from 342 to 351), the tax collector, Plutammon, is grumbling about receiving horses instead of cash as tax payments. Obviously there was an interim period before it became a fixed rule that cash had to be paid. In AD 367 Valentinian and Valens issued a law demanding that 23 *solidi* should be paid for each horse previously levied as tax (*Codex Theo.*, 11.17.1). The law stating that horses offered had to meet certain requirements was also repeatedly issued. The dates of this law enacted under Valentinian and Valens and sent to Zosimus, Governor of Epirus, were AD 365, 368, 370 and 373 (*Codex Theo.*, 6.31.1). In AD 399 and 401 Arcadius and Honorius were demanding that horses levied on the Diocese of Africa should thenceforwards be commuted to a money payment (ibid., 11.17.3). Clearly over the centuries methods of acquiring animals changed. Hard cash was always involved to some extent, but in the Later Empire the system seemed to depend on individual areas, some producing horses, some cash, as the dates of the laws appear to demonstrate.

Several reasons could be put forward for preferring cash to animals. The most obvious is that demand fluctuated according to natural attrition (horses becoming too old or unfit for service) and the demands of military activity, which would vary according to the prevalent situation in different dioceses. There was also corruption running rife throughout many government departments in the Later Empire. Commutation was an effort to curtail this, presumably to stop inferior animals being accepted as taxes and proving useless for the cavalry afterwards (ibid., 11.17.1). During relative peace, the number of replacements needed would be fewer than in periods of hostilities, when massive numbers would be required. The administration would have called on cash reserves to purchase the required numbers, but there must have been many occasions when cash reserves were inadequate. The first resort would have been to exact additional levies to meet demand. But however much was demanded, young colts and fillies took time to mature, and there was also a limit to how much could be squeezed out of overtaxed provincials in the form of either animals or cash. To fulfil possible needs a strong breeding programme was vital, not only in the large *latifundia* owned by rich senators and the state, but in the smaller landholdings belonging to those who had the right to own a horse. During peace, when taxes were still levied but demand for remounts fell off, breeders would have been doubly penalized. Unwanted animals needed maintenance or they would be sold to dealers in a buyer's market, and at the same time breeders would have to pay taxes in cash. If they decided to keep their surplus stock, rather than let a dealer profit from it, it would put pressure on their land and labour resources, as a given acreage can only feed a finite number of animals. Today a breeder faced with a falling market puts fewer mares in foal while he waits for the market to improve. It must have been a nightmare situation for the breeder in Roman days, as he would be expected to keep up a supply even if the prospect of immediate sale was slim. The practicalities of supply changed constantly throughout the long centuries of Roman power.

Cavalry duties

Once supply was sorted out, and the green horses and equally green youngsters taught to work together as teams, young cavalrymen would be expected to operate in a wide variety of roles. The two main divisions of cavalry were the *alae* and the *cohortes equitatae*. The units were mainly of *quingenaria* strength but a few were of *milliaria* status. They would have been taught to act primarily as a fighting unit according to the expertise of the rider, and the quality, intelligence and cooperation of the mounts. The *alae*, as we learn from Hadrian in his address to the troops at Lambaesis in AD 128, were better mounted, equipped and paid than the mounted section of the *cohortes equitatae* (*ILS*, 9133–5). The earliest reference to a *cohors equitata* is to the *Cohors Ubiorum Peditum et Equitum* dating from the reign of Augustus (Davies 1971; *ILS*, 2690). The Ubii were a German tribe noted for their skill in horsemanship.

Vegetius says that an aspiring cavalryman had to measure six Roman feet (5 ft 10 in. or 178 cm) with an absolute minimum of five feet ten inches (5 ft 8 in. or 173 cm). Shorter men who wished to enter the cavalry did it by the hard route, working their way up through the infantry before being permitted to join the 120-strong mounted section of a *cohors equitata*. Vegetius comments on this, saying 'that the cavalry have a regard for the infantry because promotion to cavalry is through the infantry ranks, notwithstanding the natural antipathy existing between the two corps' (*Ep. Rei Mil.*). Cavalry have always been considered the superior units in armies from earliest times down to the last world war when Poland, Russia and Germany used mounted cavalry. Vegetius also says that in accepting recruits overall suitability is more important than merely fulfilling the physical requirements. With their usual common-sense approach to most matters, Roman recruiting officers would surely have assigned men who showed a real aptitude for horsemanship, or indeed were already accomplished riders, to the *alae*. It would have been wasteful to make them serve first as footsloggers. In the Later Empire rules were relaxed so that sons of cavalrymen, or rich lads with a horse or two of their own, were accepted straight into the cavalry (*Codex Theo.*, 7.22.2.1–2). Vegetius wrote in the 370s AD about rules governing practice before and during his time, and the laws of Constantine oted above dated to AD 326. Clearly material possessions or social standing brought preferential treatment, and it made sense to utilize already partially trained personnel. Service in cavalry units was preferred, as it paid better and had a higher social standing.

The *alae*, ranking above the *cohortes equitatae*, were the front line cavalrymen. Their minimum strength was 500, as opposed to the maximum strength of a *cohors equitata* at 240. Superior weapons, horses and training better equipped them to act as prime fighters. The part-mounted *cohortes equitatae* would join them when required, and on them devolved many of the less glamorous but necessary jobs. However, when needed members of an *ala* also would perform duties of a less military nature. The archives tracing the career of Flavius Abinnaeus, *Prefectus* of the *Ala Quinta Praelectorum* at Dionysias in the Arsinoite Nome of Egypt in the 340s AD, make it clear that the *ala*'s members acted as a military police squad, conducting territorial surveillance, carrying out general policing and administration, overseeing collection of the *annona* and the tax in horses (when it should have been cash), and even supervising the gathering of natron fertilizer. Providing military escorts, which gave them a chance to use at least a percentage of cavalry training, must have been a welcome change. Mundane duties were hardly what a youngster entering the cavalry arm aspired to! However, one other duty, that of providing nets to trap marauding gazelles, may have been a bit more popular if it also gave them a chance to do some hunting on the side.

A duty roster of the *Coh. I Hispanorum Veterana Quingenaria Equitata* dating to either AD 100 or 105 highlights several duties of cavalrymen in a *cohors equitata* (Fink 1971, no. 63). These were stationed at Stobis in Macedonia and then posted to Dacia. At the time of this particular duty roster, they were not on active duty but their time was taken up in the general running of a military garrison. The only fatality recorded was caused by bandit attack. Presumably a detachment out on some far-ranging collection duty was surprised and one man was lost. The area in general might have been subdued but sporadic outbursts still had to be guarded against, and the chance of acquiring fresh horses must have been tempting to bandit groups. A few cavalrymen were sent to other places, one even being sent to the Moesian naval depot. For the most part they were kept busy as guards for grain-collecting detachments; accompanying newly levied batches of horses back to camp; collecting clothing for the camp stores from outside the province; or acquiring cattle. For the latter task, it would be interesting to know if the cattle were merely levied and driven in by the locals, or whether the cavalrymen acted as gauchos themselves. Working cattle brings out the best (or worst) in a horse, as bovines are incredibly stupid and constantly make a break for the bushes, generally dawdle, or go off at a tangent for no reason. It can be fun to work them, and sometimes infuriating, but it must have given the younger cavalrymen a welcome break from boring guard duties and taught horse and rider a lot about harrying techniques. That the area was anything but truly pacified is shown by the need for a 24-strong detachment allocated to protecting crops. Of these, 22 were cavalry and 2 infantry *sesquiplicarii*, who must surely have been mounted for the job or remained useless. Corn on Danubian rivercraft was guarded by a cavalry detachment, who would no doubt act as escort on the way back to camp for any corn unloaded. Other cavalryman were out scouting. Some were at the garrison at Prioboridava, others seconded to Buridava. The variety of duties shows that cavalrymen away from frontline action were kept extremely busy with the everyday running of a garrison. It also meant that their horses were kept fit and alert. As the district is mountainous we can assume that a considerable remount reserve was needed, as rocky going is very abrasive on the hooves.

Over a century later, in AD 219 and 222, the working rosters of the *Cohors XX Palmyrenorum*, a *milliaria* unit stationed at Dura Europos, showed duties of the cohort's mounted men (Fink 1971, no. 1, p. 18). Some are detailed *ad leones*. There was an amphitheatre at Dura Europos, so maybe they were helping out on a lion hunt to supply that, or even the ever-open maw of Rome's Colosseum, as lions were shipped in quantities to the capital. It is also known that the Mesopotamian area was infested with trouble-making lions, so maybe they were doing a service to the community, such as a modern foxhound pack will occasionally do if foxes are decimating poultry. At any rate, it was a duty not without risk and needing courageous men and horses. In Column 38 of the roster an

Aurel(ius) Amaeus Magdei is detailed to inspect horses. Could he have been the unit's 'wrangler' or 'rough rider', or a man with expert knowledge trusted to choose the right mounts for the unit? He is the only one listed as having this duty. A good rider with a background of horsemanship since childhood would be just as well qualified in some respects, and more in others, as a veterinary surgeon.

A considerable number of cavalry acted as scouts, a total of 16 from these two rosters, and a total of 30 acted as couriers carrying despatches, etc., between different towns that had detachments stationed in them. A 20-man party was detailed *ambula* which Fink suggests meant they were out on a training exercise, or alternatively on guard duty at the Bazaar at Dura. Twenty mounted men seems rather a large force for the latter, so a training exercise would be more likely, and although it is a small number from a 240-strong contingent, many of the others were occupied elsewhere. Some were seconded to Appadana, Beccufrayn and Chafer Avira, towns within the Dura Europos sphere. The pay chests were carried on dromedaries and these were guarded by a detachment of horse and foot from the cohort, as was the rather peculiar Syrian Priest-Emperor Elagabalus. When not fighting, the *cohortes equitatae* had a very varied life, and the Dura losses from the same cohort 30 years later shows that the *cohortes equitatae* also had a role to play as fighting cavalry (Fink 1971, no. 83, p. 341). Of the 19 horses described, 6 had been lost. Also the fact that many of the 19 horses had been acquired near the date of the papyrus illustrates a rather precarious situation. The difficulty of acquiring suitable remounts is shown by the fact that a third of the riders in the list were still awaiting new horses.

In times of relative peace many soldiers and cavalrymen could expect to spend most of their time fairly close to their base, going out on regular patrols to ensure the peace and on military manoeuvres to keep up to scratch. In troubled times, when reinforcements were necessary in a war zone or a recently conquered area, postings could be expected, and the experience of *Cohors I Hispanorum Veterana Quingenaria Equitata* shows that long-range travel was part of the cavalryman's job. The unit's name implies that it was originally raised in Spain and had travelled far from its home territory. However, by Trajan's day nationally named *alae* had lost much of their ethnic composition, and the Spanish ones particularly had a mixed nationality content (Holder 1980).

Distance capabilities

Good management must have been paramount and a cavalryman's maxim in the Roman *alae* the same as for cavalry down the ages: 'horses first, men second'. Travel in the horse divisions would have been regulated by the speed of hoof growth and the condition of the hooves: in dry climates they wear better, in wet they abrade, soften, split and generally break down easily. Relief measures of temporary hoof coverings would get a horse over the worst if he were forced to travel excessive distances, and troopers would have learnt how to fashion leather on the spot in cases of urgency. The American Indian used the same principle for temporary hoof coverings. Cavalry travelling by themselves could move faster than mixed units, and in such circumstances it would have been quite possible, provided it was not over excessively stony ground, to average 30–40 miles (50–65 km) a day without overtaxing the animals, given adequate feeding, a moderate pace and the occasional day's rest. Some weight loss would be encountered initially until the animals hardened off. (When living in a sandy soiled region of North Carolina, USA, I prepared two horses for 100 mile rides by undergoing several months of high mileage work, topped off with three competitions at 40, 40 and 20 miles on successive days. Both horses did well. All work was done without shoes. Average speed in the competitions themselves was 6–7 m.p.h. (9.5–11 k.p.h.), inclusive of rest periods, so the pace was brisk but not too taxing.)

Excessive and continuous speed without sufficient rest would run the flesh off even the fittest horses. It was the sight of unusual shields and skinny horses that alerted Hasdrubal at Sena that the Consul Livius had received reinforcements from the Consul Nero in 207 BC when the tide was turning against the Barcids. Nero had covered over 300 miles (480 km) in a seven-day forced march from Canusium to succour Livius, and in spite of fatigue his 6,000 foot and 1,000 cavalry helped turn the Metaurus into a Roman victory. Afterwards he turned about and returned to Canusium in six days, before Hannibal realized that the Roman camp was below strength (Livy, XXVII.45–50).

Postings

Up to Flavian times many of the auxiliary cavalry units were raised as a national contingent and posted abroad, and for the most part retained their ethnic content with only a few non-nationals recruited (Holder 1980). This must also have been reflected in the equine recruitment, so that units could still be identified according to men's nationality and to a lesser extent by breed of horse. Naturally, in wartime, both human and equine replacements would have been levied on the spot and the ethnic content of many units weakened. As large numbers of cavalry were raised in Gaul, Spain, Pannonia and Thrace these units would have changed the most, and even though there were attempts to maintain ethnic content distances involved in a rapidly expanding empire made this virtually impossible. After the civil wars of AD 69 and 70 many cavalrymen were recruited to serve in their home territories. Many auxiliary units were stationed in the frontier provinces, and in peacetime a top priority would be to patrol the limes. It was only natural that men wanted to serve in their own or adjacent districts.

Occasionally units were still transferred long distances from home, as happened with the Petulantes and Celts under the future Emperor Julian. In AD 360 Constantius had ordered them to the east where the Parthians were massing aggressively. To avoid mutiny, Julian allowed their families to accompany them, using vehicles of the public post (Ammianus Marcellinus, *Res Gest.* 20.4). This was considered a great concession. In the east the usual pattern had been for cavalry units to be raised in the area and stay there with very few long-range postings. However, they were shifted about within the eastern bloc, so that the Phrygian, Bosporan, Syrian and Iturean units remained mostly ethnic with a few individual 'foreigners' (Holder 1980). Bridleless Mauretanian cavalry are shown on Trajan's Column fighting on the Roman side in the Dacian Wars. Their commander, Lucius Quietus, must have found their tactics of feint, draw off, and run and regroup totally at odds with normal Roman methods, but the fact that African units were used shows that they had their disconcerting uses. Numidians, Africans, Mauretanians and Libyans had a long history of being used in the Roman west ever since Hannibal's day.

Deployment on marches

Vegetius recommends that well-mounted men should reconnoitre the way ahead and if possible do so by night. Cavalry were to be deployed as a protective wall around the rest of the marching column with detachments in front, behind and on both flanks. The order of march was infantry, baggage animals, officers' horses, army servants and baggage and *ballista* vehicles. The cream of the infantry and top cavalry were to bring up the rear to guard against any surprise attacks (*Ep. Rei Mil.*). The fact that officers' horses were protected implies that a considerable number of remounts were considered necessary for each officer. Presumably spare horses for the *alae* and *cohortes equitatae* were also herded in the centre, or alternatively led in small strings of a manageable two to four by a mounted trooper. The latter would be preferable in difficult territory, as a surprise attack could result in many valuable horses simply scattering and so falling to the attackers.

Moving from the textbook example to a real example from the Jewish Wars, Josephus provides a very clear illustration of how the orders were put into practice, but with modifications, when he records the order of Vespasian's army on its march into Galilee (*Bell. J.* III.115–26). Cavalry figure prominently as security men, and also at the tail end of the column of march, to protect the rear. The auxiliaries were the archers and mounted contingents several thousand strong supplied by the local kings Agrippa, Soaemus and Aretas. Josephus' list is as follows:

(1) Auxiliary light-armed troops and archers sent in advance, to repel any sudden incursions and to explore woodland for ambuscades.
(2) Heavy-armed Roman soldiers – auxiliary infantry and cavalry.
(3) A legionary detachment of ten per century carrying their own kit and tools for marking out the camp.
(4) Pioneers to straighten the road, level rough ground, cut down woods.
(5) Vespasian's personal equipage and that of his lieutenants with a strong mounted escort to protect them. He himself rode behind with the pick of the infantry and cavalry and his guard of lancers.
(6) Cavalry units of the legions, 120 per legion.
(7) Mules carrying siege towers and other machines.
(8) Legates, prefects of cohorts, and tribunes, with an escort of picked troops.
(9) Ensigns surrounding the eagle (*aquila*) which precedes every legion.
(10) Trumpeters.
(11) The solid column of legionaries marching six abreast accompanied by a senior centurion.
(12) Servants attached to each legion conducting mules and beasts of burden carrying the soldiers' kit.
(13) Auxiliary units.
(14) For security, a rearguard of light and heavy infantry and a considerable body of cavalry.

Combat tactics

In combat, terrain dictated how well the cavalry could operate. Open plains were the obvious choice for a cavalry manoeuvre; wooded ground was a death trap and negated the cavalry's usefulness. It is the latter type of terrain that has given rise to the belief that some cavalry, notably the *cohortes equitatae*, rode to the scene of battle, dismounted and fought on foot. Admittedly they did so in the early days of recruitment into the Roman army but later only on rare occasions when the woods impeded forward movement while mounted. It is often far quicker to dismount and proceed on foot in thick brush or with low-hanging branches, as I find in endurance riding where routes cover all different types of terrain. Bent double over a horse's neck a trooper would hardly be in a position either to defend himself or to keep a wary eye out for the enemy. Tacitus is quite clear when he describes Roman troopers pursuing Britons at Mons Graupius. Troopers dismounted where the thickets were dense, and led their horses, and when the thickets thinned out they remounted and gave chase (*Agr.* 37). The idea that cavalry regularly dismounted to fight is surely disproven by the question of what the horses were expected to do while the troopers were fighting! They would hardly wait around, and all the soldiers would be needed to fight, not act as horse-holders. In addition dismounting, except in difficult terrain, put a trooper at a disadvantage. The classic example is the Battle of Cannae. The Romans had already sustained massive losses, largely due to Hannibal's cavalry. The Consul Lucius Aemilius Paullus, earlier injured by a sling-shot, became too weak to control his charger, so he and his cavalry dismounted. This elicited the cryptic comment from Hannibal that Paullus might just as well have delivered his men up to him in chains (Livy, XXII.49). No sane trooper ever dismounted to fight unless exceptional circumstances forced him to. A mounted man can always inspire fear in a man on foot, a fact well illustrated by mounted police deployed in crowd control today, and they are not wielding swords or javelins! The average non-horseman is extremely wary of any equine, even without just cause.

At Mons Graupius, Tacitus quite honestly tells us that Agricola used auxiliaries as cannon fodder, with 8,000 infantry forming a strong centre, and 3,000 cavalry on the flanks. The legions were stationed out of harm's way in front of the camp rampart, because 'victory would be vastly more glorious if it cost no Roman blood'. They could go to the auxiliaries' aid if need be (*Agr.* 35)! Caesar had the same attitude. Throughout his books on the Gallic Wars he mentions numerous occasions when cavalry were used prior to sending in the infantry, or in shock tactics. Almost every Gallic tribe that resisted Rome felt at some time the force of Caesar's cavalry, largely levied from Gallic tribes allied to him. A few examples come from his war against the Belgae (*de Bello Gall.* II.10–11, 19), where cavalry were to the fore, fighting, pursuing and slaughtering. The harrying must have been terrifying, as once a horse is excited by the chase he can become extremely aggressive towards the person or animal he is chasing, particularly if he is a stallion. The victims would not only have had weapons scything into them, but horses grabbing them with their teeth. As an example of this, a horse working cattle will often reach out and bite a recalcitrant cow, and left undisciplined could well savage it. Or when chased by a vicious dog the horse trained for cattle does not merely return the compliment but does so with intent (one horse I had, while impeccably behaved in normal circumstances, would not tolerate being chased and would plant an accurate blow on a savaging dog; he was also very adept at working cattle, which as far as the horse is concerned is very akin to harrying).

Josephus is far more explicit than the normal dry military comment that usually only tells us that the cavalry harried and slew beaten foes. His tale shows just how superb a rider could be and the exceedingly high degree of training of – and rapport between – man and horse. At Mount Olivet, when the Jews attacked the Romans, several incidents stood out. One of the most remarkable involved a trooper named Pedanius who was from one of the cohorts. Chasing the fleeing Jews down into a ravine he urged his horse to a flat-out gallop, drew level, and leaning out and down at a perilous angle from his horse snatched up one of the fleeing foe, a sturdily built youth in full armour, grasping him by the ankle. Using tremendous muscular strength he kept hold of him and, as Josephus says, 'came with his prize to Caesar' (*Bell. J.* VI.161–3). This confirms several points. It would be almost impossible to remain mounted, however good a horseman one was, unless a saddle were in use because the weight of an armoured man would drag the rider off the horse's back. The saddle's front horns would have been put to very good use as a locking device as the trooper leant down and grasped the weighty prize. It also shows the degree of physical fitness and coordination reached by the cavalry, that one-handed a trooper could carry out such an act, while at the same time manoeuvring and controlling his horse with his other hand. More importantly it indicates that the *cohortes equitatae* had achieved a very high standard indeed. It is hardly the type of feat of which low-grade cavalry would be capable, even allowing that Pedanius may have been an exceptional rider.

Equine responses in battle situations

In actual battle conditions where cavalry charged, hurled javelins, and then fought hand-to-hand it might be expected that horses would flinch. There would of course be some horses more timid than others, but the order of action would serve to get the animals well fired up. Once committed to a charge, speed would excite the horses who would in effect be racing their fellows. The horse would not realize that javelins discharged by the opposing side came from a still reasonably distant enemy. Horses do not generally associate missiles with the *distant* man who launched them, unless these come in such quick succession as to pose a continuing threat (close-order launches are different). Once engaged the excitement, plus any natural aggression the horse possesses, would tend to override the immediate possibility of fear. Watch any two horses fighting – not necessarily stallions. They will bite and kick each other regardless of pain until one overpowers the other and drives it off. These bickerings can be over any number of things, but usually over territorial encroachment – over a bucket of food, a 'two's company, three's a crowd' attitude, or just the fact that a newcomer is resented – and the fights can be quite damaging and quite relentless. A similar attitude would be encountered in battle and the trained trooper would capitalize on it, and at the same time minimize damage to himself and his horse.

The fact that the same horses went again and again into battle suggests that the horses were anything but docile. In fact Varro confirms this, as we have seen, when he says: 'for just as we need them high spirited [I would substitute the word courageous] for camps so we prefer to have them quiet on the road. Castration effects this' (*de Re Rust.*). This implies that stallion aggression was valued, although certain mares can also be very sharp. One other fact helps to explain why a horse would go into battle willingly. Arrian is careful to explain in two places in his *Tactica* that training weapons are without iron tips (*Tact.* 34, 40). This was to avoid injury, particularly to the horse, during the annual *alae* ceremony. In the movement known as the 'Cantabrian gallop' explicit instructions are given not to throw the spear at the horse (*Tact.* 40). If in repeated training sessions a horse is used to weapons being wielded and javelins and spears thrown that never touch him, he will have no fear of such weapons. Horses in general do not like having things whirled around their heads, and flinch as something goes hurtling past their ears or if someone nearby aims something at them. I have trained horses to become used to a lariat: some never seem to mind it, others are at first very scared of a rope whirling overhead and snaking past them, or of it being worked close by, and assume they will be hurt. Repeated sessions defuse the horse's fears, and so it must have been with all weapons training for the cavalry. The horse in his first battle would be confident that he would not be hurt. Some, the best from cavalry point of view, would be so excited that when wounded immediate realization would not intrude. Once the turmoil of battle had ceased, adrenalin had ceased to flow and pain to be felt, the horse would not link a previous occurrence with current pain. This is not because the horse is stupid, but because he does not link two separated actions together. Should a blow be inflicted in cold blood with no excitement to mask the pain the horse is very aware of cause and effect (which is why punishment for wrongdoing must take place immediately the horse disobeys or acts in an uncivil manner; punish at a later time, even a few minutes later, and the horse does not link wrong-doing and punishment). If a battle between a man and a horse over a matter of discipline gets out of hand, it will not be resolved by increasing the amount of punishment because the animal that fights discipline to any great extent usually has a volatile temper and is fighting back not against the pain inflicted but in sheer anger as to who is going to win. Understanding the psychology of the horse was one reason a horse would continue to be useful in cavalry service. Timid or cowardly animals would be weeded out as liabilities.

Loss of nerve must have been an ever-present problem, particularly amongst the riders. Much can be done to prevent a horse losing his nerve, as outlined above. However, if a rider lost his nerve, his fear would transmit itself directly to the horse and a formerly confident, obedient horse, which was also a useful weapon, could become a real danger to the rest of the unit. A frightened rider will make a horse panic, which then infects the others in close proximity. No horse will perform courageous acts if his rider is nervous. He balks and becomes sour, and finally loses his own confidence. On the other hand, a horse with a temporary attack of nerves can quite often be cajoled and coerced by a strong and confident rider. One of the most difficult feats in horse training is getting the nervous horse to have confidence first in his rider and then in himself. It is a bond that is shattered when the rider loses courage.

Caesar gives an instance of cavalry's loss of nerve in the Illerda campaign during his Civil Wars against Pompey. Pompey's commander Afranius was claiming victory. Later, when Caesar's cavalry was boosted by Gallic reinforcements, the roles were reversed. Caesar's cavalry made successful razzias on Afranius' foraging parties (*de Bello Civ.* 1.55) and later harried Afranius' troops on the march to the Ebro, outmanoeuvred them at every turn, wiped out four cohorts of Afranius' men and generally demoralized the enemy (ibid., 1.70). With continued harrassment and picking off the rear of Afranius' troops they thoroughly frightened them with the result that, although Afranius' cavalry was very large, it had to be put in the centre of the column for protection because the troops had completely lost their nerve in the earlier skirmishes against Caesar's cavalry (ibid., 1.79). With his usual massive self-confidence Caesar does not admit to any such occasional lapse bedevilling his own cavalry *alae*!

13
External influences

As Rome evolved into the major military force in the western hemisphere, she drew into her orbit diverse peoples. Unlike other warrior nations instead of grinding them out of existence she made them her own. Rather than merely reject or subject what was alien, she frequently had the good sense to adopt anything that would further her aims, whether in the civilian or military sphere. This was especially so in her treatment of cavalry.

In early Republican days before the legions were sent abroad, cavalry was a minor part of the Roman forces. Horses belonged to the wealthy, whether for sport or war. Their owners became known as the equestrian class, which indicated the possession of sufficient means to own a horse.

From earliest times Etruria had a strong equestrian society. This is attested to in literature, art, pottery, figurines, and archaeological finds of horses' tack – bits and fragments of harness, as well as sections of chariots (Frederiksen 1968). Many of the tomb paintings of either chariot or riding horses show certain characteristics that were still present in representations of Italian (particularly the Gonzagan) horses of medieval times, indicating that type fixation had a long continuity. In contradiction to many later sculptural representations, the man to horse proportions in Etruscan depictions are closer to today's expectations of size. Allowing for the smaller stature of humans in those days it suggests that the horses driven or ridden in war and sport were of reasonable size. Being told horses were 'small' or 'large' is meaningless unless we have some idea of measurements (see Chapter 5, where this is enlarged upon). The Etruscans, and later horsemen, neither drove nor rode under-sized equines.

Etruscan riders are also shown using a *balanced* seat which enabled them to move with the horse and achieve greater seat security than that afforded by the ridiculous loin slouch affected by later Roman riders – if we are to believe that sculptors were depicting reality and not merely a fashionable convention. This slouching position would only have been tenable on a placid animal using gaits similar to Pliny's Asturian horse from Spain (*Nat. Hist.* VIII). (In the modern American show ring some riders of four- and five-gaited horses sometimes ride in this inefficient way.) The size of horse and the riding methods portrayed for the Etruscans would have been suitable in both war and sport; although they maintained a cavalry force the prime use of equines was in the field of racing and hunting.

Campania, on the other hand, was famed very early on for her cavalry, and long before Rome had extended her influence over Italy, Greeks had put their mark on horsemanship in Magna Graecia. One of the needs of the incoming Greek aristocracy was an ideal location for raising and keeping stock (Frederiksen 1968). I would go even further and say it would be the prime requisite. Breeders today seek land that offers good grazing and is well watered. Leaving the largely poor soil of mainland Greece the mounted aristocracy would seek to occupy better land as well as an area that offered suitable stretches for easy cavalry manoeuvres. Campania offered both, and in the process the Campanian cavalry absorbed much of Greek horsemanship, the benefits of which were felt right into the first two centuries AD when cavalry units were greatly increased. Sicily, too, with a large Greek population, was famous for both cavalry and racehorses. It had ample means for producing top-class stock that would reach optimum size, as the soil was extremely fertile and produced grain in abundance. In later years Sicily was also a favoured location for the large *latifundia* where stock was raised on a massive scale.

The Greeks already had several superior types of cavalry horse (Ch. 1) and the infusion of new blood in indigenous Latin stock would have had a beneficial effect in many instances. To upgrade existing stock outside blood must be introduced, whether a different bloodline of the same breed, or a totally new breed being crossed on to one that needs improvement. Greece had had centuries of trials proving performance on the racetrack and the battlefield. The legacy of both the Persians and Macedonians had resulted in superior horses infusing blood into the earlier and smaller Greek horses. In later Roman times the horses of both Thessaly and Thrace were noted for their size and usefulness in war. As well as the new blood the Greeks also introduced lucerne (alfalfa) which they had initially obtained from the Medes. As the protein content of lucerne is at least 16 per cent compared to a maximum of 8 per cent in other grazing crops, and it gives multiple croppings instead of the usual two cuts of hay and can withstand drought, it was a significant import, greatly affecting the Italian agrarian economy and improving stock nutrition. For feeding large concentrations of cavalry mounts it must have proved a boon.

Campanian cavalry had had an impact on battles for centuries. They not only fought in their own defence, as when Cumaean cavalry under the tyrant Aristodemus crushed the Etruscan cavalry in 524 BC (Dionysius, *Rom. Ant.*, VII.3.11), but down the ages hired themselves out as mounted mercenaries. Most notably this was in the pay of Sicily, first under the Athenians and later under the Carthaginians when they were mounted on Sicilian-bred animals (ibid., XIII.44.1). Hired at different times, and occasionally by one or the other at the same time, they formed a crack force in Sicily for 150 years. Capua was said to be able to mobilize up to 4,000 horse and 30,000 infantry (Frederiksen 1968). For the times, this was a very high ratio of horse to foot. In the Hannibalic Wars Campanian cavalry tried to hold out against Hannibal, first at Trasimene and later in their own Capuan homelands. Lucilius (*Car. Rel.* 506–8) records the fire and mettle of Campanian chargers, but notes that their stamina was inferior to that of Spanish horses. In this we can see a sideways reference to the tough Numidian/Libyan horses imported into Spain by the Carthaginians of Hamilcar, Hasdrubal and Hannibal. These Numidian horses and their lithe riders were to become well known to the Romans as a very telling part of Hannibal's forces.

In 390 BC Rome had a foretaste of Celtic invaders, augmented by large numbers of cavalry when they looted the city itself, the prime aim being plunder of the increasingly wealthy capital. From then on Celtic cavalry was to play a growing part in Roman history.

Rock paintings have been found in France and Celtiberian Spain depicting a wide variety of equines from the pre-Celtic era. These include pony types, large heavy draught animals, and oriental-looking specimens. They include smaller species resembling Exmoor ponies and a semblance of the larger breeds represented today by the heavier Fell pony and the lighter-boned New Forest. (Note that this is not a suggestion of breed provenance; they only resemble these breeds. The New Forest in particular, and in the form we know it today, is a mix of many breeds turned loose on the Forest in Victorian days in order to upgrade local stock, with not altogether happy results.) In Spain the oriental type of horse is depicted, attesting to a very early traffic in horses, via the North African mainland, of breeds already developed in Asia Minor.

Later, as the Celtic nation fragmented and dispersed into the Danube territory, Spain, France and Italy, the horses they rode would initially be individuals brought from their original area and then crossed on to what they found in their new territories, enabling stock to develop some size and a variety of breed characteristics. The small, swift British ponies, isolated in an island, would not have had many (if any) foreign outcrosses for a considerable time, assuming that earlier incoming Celts had added to indigenous stock by their own importations. It is hardly to be thought that an equestrian people such as the Celts arrived in Britain without at least a nucleus of their four-footed war partners, albeit maybe only the better specimens owned by nobles and chiefs. Horsebreeding formed an important part of Celtic culture, reflected in religious beliefs centred around Epona, the patroness of horses. Celtic cavalry frequently cost Rome dear, but later repaid in extravagant measure for any earlier depredations with the large numbers of auxiliary cavalrymen coming from the Celtic tribes of Gaul. Line breeding and incest breeding in equines will sometimes produce superior specimens, but more often has an adverse effect. Continued use of the same lines over many generations will eventually result in smaller animals whose temperaments will also have suffered, inheriting rather more of the vices than the virtues and so making them unsuitable for cavalry. As the Celts were larger than the average Latin, it is only to be expected that to produce their chargers, strong infusions of blood from the heavier type of animal would have been introduced into their broodmare bands. Caesar tells us that the 'Gauls delight in the draught horses they import at great expense' (*de Bello Gall.* IV.4). In 170 BC, 20 Italian stallions had been purchased by brothers of Cincibulus, a Gallic chieftain, and used for upgrading stock (Ch. 1).

The Punic Wars brought other superb cavalry nations to the costly attention of the Romans, and in accordance with her repeated practice Rome eventually brought these horsemen into her own armies, using their particular breeds of horse and their riders' fighting skills. It was centuries before Rome admitted that there was a need for a larger cavalry force than her early legions and allies provided. Hannibal was the one to give her her most expensive and continuous lesson in cavalry tactics; he was particularly strong in cavalry, combining the best of his own Carthaginian horsemen with the Numidian, Libyan-Phoenician, Spanish and Celtic cavalry. The numbers of cavalry he brought to his invasion of Italy represented a far greater ratio of horse to infantry than anything the Romans, other than possibly the Campanians, had ever used. Polybius and Livy both give specific numbers of horse mustered by the Carthaginian, and it is due to the continued presence of the Carthaginians in Spain that much of the foundation stock was developed which later supplied the Roman cavalry with a steady stream of remounts. Early in his preparations Hannibal planned ahead, leaving Hasdrubal in Spain to guard against attack by Roman forces who might be spurred to seek revenge over the Saguntum dispute. Wisely he had sent Spaniards to Africa and various Africans to Spain to cement loyalty, as Polybius euphemistically calls the insurance against treachery (*Hist.* III.33). Amongst these troops 1,200 Spanish cavalry were sent to Africa and a total of 1,950 African, mainly Numidian, horse to Spain. The small

Spanish contingent of 300 (presumably disaffected) Illergetes, from Romanized Spain north of the Ebro, were no doubt mounted on the now indigenous stock of the previously mentioned oriental type of horse. Carthaginian presence in Spain and their use of Numidians and Libyans as cavalry had introduced a steady reciprocal flow of horses between Africa and Spain, so the influences were manifold – equine, human, the systems of horse care, and also methods of fighting and weaponry used by the peoples involved in the human half of cavalry.

When he finally left Cartagena (New Carthage) in 218 BC, Hannibal had a very strong force of 90,000 infantry and 12,000 cavalry. It took him five months to arrive in Italy and *en route* he left 10,000 foot and 1,000 horse under his brother Hanno to guard his back in Roman Spain, and allowed a similar number of Spaniards to return home to ensure a willingness on their part to answer the Carthaginian call to arms. The number of battle-hardened veterans that reached the Rhône had diminished to 50,000 foot and 9,000 cavalry. Thousands were lost in crossing the Alps so that the numbers that arrived in Italy were reduced to 20,000 infantry and 6,000 horse (ibid., III.38). These were augmented as promised by the Celts in the Po valley.

Foremost of the cavalry were the Numidians, riding in their natural style without a bridle and guiding their horses by taps of a stick on their necks and a withe around their necks. This style of riding relies on superb training and rapport between horse and rider, where the horse obeys the rider's weight displacement and body movements for guidance. Pliny, with his usual mix of fact and fantasy, says that these mounted javelin-men guide their horses by swaying with the body, and the horses are said to pick up the javelins and pass them back to the riders (*Nat. Hist.* VIII). Considerable pressure can be applied to the horse's windpipe via the neck rope, or Numidian withe, but such control is obeyed very much at the whim of the horse and so complete rapport and trust is essential between man and horse. (Although bridleless riding is still practised today, I have only come across two horses in which I would have utter confidence under all circumstances. Both are of Arabian breeding –Strathdon, a mare owned by well-known Scottish horse-woman Shuna Mardon, and my own stallion Nizzolan – both have given demonstrations of bridleless riding.) The unusual control methods are highlighted by the number of ancient writers who comment on the Numidians' methods, and also by the very savage bits that were used to control horses in almost all other contemporary mounted divisions, with possibly the exception of some Celts using milder types of snaffle.

While Hannibal's massed bridled and heavy cavalry, mostly Spaniards, took the brunt of a head-on charge, the Numidians on their smaller, nimbler horses and using their charge and disperse tactics fought on the flanks, being most effective at Ticinus where they swamped the Roman's Gallic cavalry, taking a heavy toll with their harrying, relying on their short daggers once javelins were spent. With an eye to the main chance, the Celts in the Roman pay then deserted to Hannibal, boosting his cavalry to over 10,000. At Trebia the Numidians were again the most useful of Hannibal's cavalry. Employed on the flanks of the army they used their favourite hit, run and re-form, recharge and harry techniques, terrifying the Romans. At Trasimene, when the trap was sprung, Hannibal's cavalry pursued the cornered Romans, driving them down into the waters of the lake where they were killed or drowned. At Cannae, the worst disaster of the Hannibalic Wars, the Romans mustered 86,000 against the Carthaginians' 50,000. Yet again, in spite of greater numbers, the Romans suffered a crushing defeat, mainly as a result of the superior numbers and effectiveness of Carthaginian cavalry. The Roman horse totalled just over 6,000 to the Carthaginians' 10,000 mixed Spanish, Celtic and Numidian squadrons (Polybius, *Hist.* III,113–14). The Carthaginian methods were as usual flexible: contingents of Spanish and Celtic horse met the Romans head-on, dismounting and fighting on foot, while the Numidians who fought on the Carthaginian right kept the opposing Roman cavalry so occupied with hit, run and re-form tactics that they were of no use to the main body. Hasdrubal, meanwhile, had annihilated the squadrons of Roman cavalry at the River Aufidius and returned to help the Numidians out. Seeing him with his heavy cavalry about to charge, the Roman cavalry turned and fled, to be harried and cut down by the Numidians, leaving Hasdrubal free to give aid to the African troops in the thick of the fighting. At Cannae, 70,000 Romans died and 10,000 were taken prisoner. Of the more than 6,000 cavalry a mere 370 survived. The Carthaginian dead totalled 5,500 infantry and a mere 200 horsemen (ibid., III.116–17).

Clearly the Numidians were the most feared of Hannibal's cavalry. They rode swift, nimble and obedient horses. The Romans could not come to grips with them, and in harrying they were merciless, tearing the fleeing Romans from their horses' backs (ibid., III.116). Unlike the heavy cavalry they were also used in scouting and skirmish manoeuvres, as well as generally disrupting Roman foragers and water carriers outside the protection of their camps.

Eventually the tide turned against Hannibal. Reinforcements of men, horses and elephants from Carthage and Spain ceased. In 210 BC harsh Carthaginian rule in southern Spain, combined with misplaced confidence that their stronghold of New Carthage would never suffer serious assault from subjected Spaniards, prompted the astute Roman general, Publius Scipio, to make a lightning strike. The speed of his march – 325 miles (520 km) in seven days – has been questioned as being impossible to achieve, but it is under 50 miles (80 km) a day and perfectly feasible. (Note that although the figure of 325 is given in Livy, in Polybius it is over 500 miles. However, checking on a map shows that the Livy figure is by far the more accurate.) With the encumbrance of a slow baggage train such speed would be impossible, but a rapid strike force would carry rations and live off the land. Even so, 50 miles a day is tough on men and horse. No doubt some animals fell out lame or seized up with azoturia, but for most, who would have been mainly Celtiberian stock with inbred oriental toughness, it would not have been unduly debilitating. The main concern would have been foot and hoof soreness. The men's feet is not the concern of this book; and we have seen how hooves of the oriental type of horse and of horses raised and used in rocky dry terrain have superior quality horn. Spanish horses had long been coveted by other peoples and had been improved by Libyan and Syrian imports long before the Punic importations (Loch 1986).

Scipio's successes at New Carthage, including the very important acquisition of Masinissa, King of Numidia, who had come over to his side in 206 BC, was followed by victory over Hasdrubal, Hannibal's brother, a spell in Rome, and transfer to Africa to carry the war to its conclusion on Carthaginian soil. Recruiting certain cavalry for African service had proved difficult. The Sicilians, noted horsemen and breeders, were reluctant to answer Scipio's call, so he adopted a novel solution, enrolling 300 top-class infantry on the Italian mainland and crossing to Sicily where he not only forced the young Sicilian nobles to train them as effective cavalry but to supply them with arms and horses (Livy, XXIX.1). This small batch of men in themselves could not have had much effect, but the key would be the quality of the Sicilian stock, noted by Oppian as good hill horses and therefore tough. Already first-class infantry, these men with their new training and four-footed equipment were well suited to form the class with which Scipio officered Masinissa's cavalry (Polybius, *Hist.* XV.4). Such a costly and humiliating experience would have served warning on Sicilians not to be so tardy about volunteering in future.

In the Punic War now being fought in Africa, Scipio engineered and won several victories, not least his first blow outside Utica. By night he fired the Carthaginian camp where thousands of men, horses and mules perished (ibid., XIV.5). Hannibal, once more on Carthaginian soil, was having difficulty raising enough men and horses for cavalry and recruited a body of 2,000 horse from Tychaeus, a Numidian prince (ibid., XV.3). With these reinforcements he marched from his base at Hadrumetum (Sousse) to Zama. Masinissa, having regained his own kingdom and annexed that of Syphax, a Numidian prince in Carthaginian pay, brought a force 10,000 strong to Scipio. When the forces engaged,

Hannibal's elephants caused havoc on both sides, crashing into their own cavalry. The Italian horse of Laelius and the Numidian horse of Masinissa charged successfully, pursuing and effectively neutralizing the Carthaginians' main strength of cavalry. Eventually returning to the infantry battle, they were able to carry out a decisive charge into the rear of the Carthaginians, ensuring Scipio's victory (ibid., XV.12–13).

The Romans had good reason to fear Numidian cavalry. Careful never to get trapped in a mêlée where horses could not manoeuvre, its hit and run tactics minimized fatalities so that any return charge came in strength. Scipio used it very effectively against its former paymaster, and thereafter it became a regular part of the Roman forces, the horses more than the Numidians themselves. Valued for their endurance they and their descendants were found in many Romanized areas. In Gaul in 125 BC, a Numidian cavalry force serving under the general, Fulvius Flaccus, saved the day for Rome in the fighting against the Saluvii, who were mounted on horses whose descendants we know as Camargue ponies. The ensuing occupation of the area around Arles resulted in infusions of Libyan/Numidian blood into the indigenous stock (Ridgeway 1905). Later, in the first century AD, horses of the Libyan type were in service at Newstead (Curle 1911, p. 368). The Romans had quickly adopted the world's toughest breed, using it in war and later, in more settled times, for sport.

At that time parts of Africa were extremely fertile. According to Strabo the area between the Gaetulians and the Mediterranean had vast herds of horses and the kings there raised 100,000 foals a year (*Geog.* 17.3.19). Quite clearly the agrarian economy, in what became Roman North Africa, was largely centred around horsebreeding. The resources must have been heavily taxed during the Punic Wars by exports to Hannibal in Italy, Hasdrubal in Spain, and by the continuous battle casualties, not to mention the sheer old age of many chargers throughout the protracted wars. It says much for Numidian horse management that fertility of stock was kept high, for all that Aelian denigrates the care which Numidians gave their horses, while praising their ability to endure fatigue: 'They neither rub them down, roll them, clean their hooves, comb manes, plait forelocks, nor wash them when tired, but when dismounted turn them loose to graze. The Libyans themselves are slim and dirty like the horses which they ride' (*de Nat. An.* III.2). Even if it were laziness that prompted such treatment, turning a horse loose to graze immediately after a tough ride is the best treatment he can have and often prevents muscle and limb ailments. Additionally it is well known that a slim horse is a better breeder than an obese animal, and also endures fatigue and is less likely to get azoturia than his chubby cousin. During the Punic Wars some Gallic, Spanish and Italian horses were drafted, looted or confiscated, or accompanied tribal contingents. Livy tells of the 4,000 Apulian horses rounded up for breaking in by Carthaginian cavalrymen, but they must have provided only a fraction of the needs for a 16-year campaign. Rounding up whole herds non-selectively would deplete the countryside of breeding stock for further reproduction and also deny the locals a useful weapon to use against their oppressors.

Many eastern nations in periodic conflict with Rome had large tracts of flat plain ideally suited to massed cavalry such as the Parthians and her neighbours used. To be of maximum use cavalry has to deployed in strength, and although a horse can operate well in mountainous districts as far as straightforward travel goes, or on a scouting task, military cohesion and vital speed would be lost. Fodder supply would also be of much greater importance to a mainly mounted force. The Medean plain was noted for its lush grazing; Armenia had high fertility in lowland regions; Syria was noted for its wealth of horses. The Parthians were on record as being summer fighters (Dio, XL.15.1–6). The table on p. 92 shows at what times there is any nutrition in the grass. The limited use of cavalry would afford more fodder to fewer animals. Where whole armies were mounted, and the armoured stock of cataphracts and *clibinarii* used more energy per animal, available grazing resources would certainly dictate the campaign season. In the east, other than in heavily watered or irrigated areas, grazing burns off earlier but also has an earlier spring flush and a longer period of autumn growth. In Armenia, western Iran, Parthia and Bactria, bitter winter cold would also preclude using cavalry to any great extent. Fodder would be minimal, and horses do not function efficiently in ice or snow. Hooves have no traction on ice, and snow forms balls in the hoof making safe travel impossible. Incidences of lameness would be so high as to render the animals a liability. The eventual general use of horseshoes not only prevented hoof abrasions but afforded grip via calkins that could be fitted to the rear of the shoe, thus extending the horse's serviceability in distance and season.

War in Asia Minor produced two main divisions of mounted warriors, both formidable, both with built-in problems: horsed archers armed with a recurved bow and mounted on swift, nimble horses, and cataphracts and *clibinarii* (see p. 149). Horsed archers, the *sagittarii*, with riders of mainly Asiatic blood were quite easily incorporated into Roman auxiliary forces. Syria in particular produced them, as it also produced large numbers of horses. Cataphracts and *clibinarii* were slow to appeal to the Romans. It took several centuries and repeated contact with the Parthians before Hadrian included cataphract divisions in the Roman cavalry. The introduction of *clibinarii* took even longer, appearing in the Later Roman Empire when it was fractured into eastern and western halves.

Roman introduction to heavy mailed cavalry came not long after the Battle of Zama in 202 BC. The Syrian Seleucids already had a history of heavy armed cavalry dating back to Seleucis Nicator in 356–281 BC. His royal stud held over 30,000 mares, stood 300 stallions and employed colt breakers and instructors in heavy-armed warfare (Strabo, *Geog.* 15.2.1). His descendant, Antiochus III, held most of Asia Minor extending from the eastern capital Seleucia on the Tigris to Iran, Parthia and Bactria, and to the western capital, Antioch, was added Palestine. Bent on expansion, Antiochus launched an expedition towards Thrace. Along the coast of Asia Minor several Greek cities resisted, sending a plea for help to Rome.

Riding a crest of success after victories at Zama and over Philip IV of Macedon, Roman forces marched against Antiochus, coming to grips with him at Magnesia in 190 BC. The Roman forces were led by Lucius, whose brother Scipio Africanus served under him, probably taking the role of second in command because of ill health. Apart from chariots and elephants, Antiochus' army was almost entirely mounted, consisting of horsed archers and heavy mailed cavalry. From the start, events favoured the Romans who, anticipating the chariots' massed charge, counter-charged, panicking the chariot horses who wheeled and crashed into their own elephants. Rain and a following heavy mist made bowstrings wet and obscured the Syrian archers' vision, neutralizing them while the Roman foot hacked their way forwards. The only effective part of Antiochus' army was the mailed cavalry which routed the Romans opposing them, harrying them back to their camp. The garrison chief, Lepidus, only turned his fleeing countrymen by killing those leading the rout, and then stiffening them with his own men succeeded in checking Antiochus' cavalry. Meanwhile the Roman camp was being freely pillaged by Zeuxis, leaving Antiochus' own camp an easy target for Scipio to capture (Dio, XIX). Thus the first major engagement with mailed cavalry hardly left a strong enough impression for the Romans to entertain adopting such a weapon.

Mailed cavalry from Asia Minor was to be encountered on many occasions in the next hundred years, but never with sufficient success to impress the Romans. Dio Cassius gives accounts of both Lucullus' and Pompey's engagements. Lucius Lucullus had mixed success. In 68 BC the Armenian cavalry cost his Roman horse dear, but when the legionaries assisted the horse, Mithridate's Armenians turned and feigned flight, shooting as they went and costing Lucullus so many men that he withdrew into Mesopotamia, turning his forces against Nisibis (Dio, XXXVI.5.1–2).

Pompey, on the other hand, also fighting against Mithridates two years later, had better fortune. On a constantly moving front he varied his tactics according to need. When Mithridates used his cavalry in repeated sorties to dislodge Pompey from his chosen site, Pompey answered by seeking cover in wooded ground where Armenians could not operate, then taunted them by an open challenge, and, drawing them into a trap, killed many. Mithridates fled. Pompey in pursuit launched a night attack when cavalry could not operate, but again failed to take Mithridates who had headed for the River Cyrnus. Here Pompey employed Carthaginian tactics, using his cavalry to dissipate the river's force (Caesar was also fond of this ploy) so that pack animals could cross in greater safety. Any swept downstream could be salvaged by the infantry crossing below. As a side venture, he subdued the Albanians, here using his cavalry in much the way Hannibal employed his Numidians. He lured the Albanians on at which the Romans feigned flight, but then closed in on the Albanians' wings and rear. Mithridates, still pursued by Pompey, found that his former Armenian ally, Tigranes, had put a price on his head. Eventually his own son, Pharnaces, revolted against him, murdered him and submitted to Rome, receiving back the kingdom of the Bosphorus as reward (Dio, XXXVI.47.2–3, 49.1–6; XXXVII.3.4–5, 4.1–4).

It is only from Plutarch's life of Crassus that we learn that the Armenian heavy cavalry were also covered in mail, or as he puts it 'armed at all points'. Strabo is more enlightening, telling us that the Medes taught the Armenians horsemanship and archery (*Geog.* 11.13.9), that the Armenians sent a huge annual levy of foals (i.e. weaned colts and fillies) to the Persian king, and that not only Medes and Armenians armoured their horses but also Albanians (ibid., 11.14.9) and Syrians (ibid., 16.2.10).

However, it was the Parthians who eventually taught the Romans really to respect such cavalry. From Plutarch, we learn just how effective both the archers and the heavy mailed cavalry were. From his description of the run-up to the Battle of Carrhae in 53 BC, the deployment of Roman forces, and his behaviour afterwards, Crassus comes out as a quite execrable character – arrogant, stupid, mean and gullible. Spurred by desire to match Pompey and Caesar, he launched his seven legions and 8,000 horse, half heavy, half light, in an unprovoked march against Orodes, the Parthian King. Preparations were negligible, winter training having been ignored, the offer of 16,000 Armenian heavy cavalry arrogantly turned down, and the eventual solid mass deployment of Roman forces already travel-weary from a forced march stupid in the extreme. The Surena, the Parthian general and next in rank to Orodes himself, headed the Parthian force, half the number of Crassus' but nearly all mounted. Initiating a charge with the heavy *contus*, the Parthians surged forward, only to halt and feign dispersal at sight of the massed Romans, but then wheeled and surrounded them. Their mounted archers sent a devastating hail of arrows into the Roman 'sardine' formation. Both Dio and Plutarch confirm the strength of the Parthian arrows. A longbow of the type used at Crecy needs a pull of anywhere from 90 to 120 lb (40–55 kg) to take it to full stretch. The recurved Asiatic bow, though shorter, delivers an arrow with greater penetrating power when loosed. Coupled with double-barbed heads such poundage would have penetrated any but the most effective armour, even piercing mail, and often taking the links with the head into the wound. In the Middle Ages many knights died from gangrene as a result; the Mongols answered the problem by wearing close-woven and very strong silk shirts, which meant that arrow heads could be extracted more easily with the twist of the silk that had wrapped itself around barb and shaft as the missile penetrated.

Crassus' son, coming to his father's aid with mixed infantry and cavalry, at first thought he had the Parthians on the run when they used their usual deceptive turn and flee tactics. But turning, the Parthians made a stand, heavy cavalry in a solid line, archers galloping in a circle around the Romans and stirring up the dust to blind their adversaries, shooting inwards as they went. With the infantry pinned down Crassus, in desperation, headed a cavalry charge, but Gallic light horse with lightweight javelins were no match for mailed cuirassiers armed with heavy lances which were driven in powerfully enough to transfix two men at a time. What losses the Parthians sustained were dealt them by Gauls desperately pulling the enemy off their horses – leaving them unable to rise because of their armour – or spiking the horses in their unprotected bellies. Pain-maddened, they threw their riders, trampling them underfoot. Most of the Gallic horses, unprotected, were despatched by thrusts of the Parthian pikes. Carrhae, the most devastating blow suffered by Rome since Cannae, was a triumph for mailed cavalry and light-horsed archers.

In 36 BC Anthony, another glory seeker, led a vast expedition against the Parthians, mustering 60,000 foot, 10,000 Gallic and Spanish horse, plus 30,000 auxiliaries, many of them cavalry. In addition he was joined by 6,000 horse and 7,000 foot from Artavasdes, King of Armenia. The whole campaign was a series of disasters for Anthony. Even his supposed victories were hollow. Early on in Media, he was separated from and then lost his irreplaceable siege engines, along with the 10,000 men guarding them, when the Parthians attacked. Artavasdes then apparently pulled 16,000 horse out and returned to Armenia (these figures are given for Artavasdes by Plutarch although they do not add up). But in the major engagement at Phraata in Media, the Parthians held firm against the Roman cavalry although their horses panicked at the infantry charge, fleeing uncontrollably; Anthony, harrying with foot and horse, secured a mere 30 prisoners and killed only 80. Winter was approaching and Anthony hoped the Parthians would cease operations during the cold as was their normal custom, but his hopes were dashed. Foraging was impossible because of the danger of attack, and with hunger facing men and horses he retreated, fighting 18 separate engagements. Although Plutarch says the engagements were successful, they read more like a desperate retreat in which the Parthians harried unmercifully, pushing the Roman foot at the speed of the cavalry, until 27 days later they reached the River Araxes which constituted the Median/Armenian border. There the Parthians let them cross, no doubt content to have them out of their territory, and in such poor shape plunder would have been unproductive. Plutarch blames Artavasdes for Anthony's disaster in which he lost over 24,000 men to battle and disease, saying that the 16,000 Armenian horse equipped in the same manner as the Parthian horse would have ensured Roman victory by harrying the Parthians after the Roman infantry had beaten them. As it was, the Parthians returned again and again to sting the Roman rear and force them to turn and fight at bay (Plutarch, *Lives*).

The oriental manner of fighting was proving to the Romans that it took more than the solid mass of legionaries to secure a victory. Julius Caesar had shown great use of Gallic cavalry in repeated pursuits of beaten enemies in his Gallic Wars, and clever use of cavalry in his Civil Wars against Pompey. In the eastern sector casualties would have been slight in an enemy that never stood to withstand a charge; that had man and horse protected; whose archers were both nimble and fleet and just as dangerous retreating as advancing. Both arms of the cavalry could return largely undamaged at a later time, for Vegetius, Strabo and Oppian all tell us that Parthian horses were swift. In their own territories they would already be acclimatized and possess greater endurance than the Gallic and Spanish mounts who accompanied Anthony and who had already been pushed 1,000 miles (1,600 km) to Armenia, and then, without sufficient respite, onwards over the River Araxes to Phraata, only to face an even tougher return journey: hungry, debilitated and being harried all the way. No wonder that afterwards Rome tried to minimize casualties by adopting the methods of her enemies to some extent. It is significant that the fully armoured man and horse combination was used more extensively in the east where conditions permitted better mobility, than in the west where conditions underfoot were often diabolical. The *sagittarii* too were largely of eastern origin.

The eastern horsemen had a great advantage over mounted Romans. Their heritage was the horse. When the Parthian, King Phraates IV, died early in the reign of Tiberius, his son Vonones, who had been held in Rome since he was a child, was sent back to succeed his father. The

Parthians took an instant dislike to Vonones, whose habits were alien to those expected of a Parthian prince. 'He rarely hunted and had little interest in horses' (Tacitus, *Ann.* I.81). Old Persian nobility expected their young men, the *kardakes*, to excel at riding, shooting and telling the truth. Their inheritors, the Parthians, obviously were expected to do likewise.

Over the centuries many peoples influenced the burgeoning power of Rome, and as we have seen a few made their mark as horsemen, providing cavalry units to match the marching legions. Others, such as the Parthians, kept Rome constantly occupied on foreign fronts and had great influence on the way cavalry was used or equipped, particularly in the Later Empire.

One nation had a very chequered history of contact with Rome. The Sarmatians, those superlative horsemen of the frozen steppes, rode into Rome's sphere in the mid 70s BC when we hear of a punitive expedition being sent against them after they made incursions into Roman territory north of the Danube (Sulimirski 1970, pp. 133–4). As with all nomads the horse was an inseparable part of their culture, used for transport, clothing, meat, drink, and even as companions in the after life, occasional quality specimens being buried with the richer nobles.

The early Sarmatians were horsed archers. By the time they came into contact with Rome their main weapons were the long sword of up to 52 inches (130 cm) and the heavy iron-headed lance. The horses' equipment included protective armour, though not the impossible-to-fit head to hoof mail of Trajan's Column. Both men and horses wore corselets (ibid., p. 127), by which I understand that the horses wore peytrals. Eye guards (Chesters) and a chamfron (Vindolanda) have been found on Hadrian's Wall, where there was a heavy Sarmatian cavalry presence after Marcus Aurelius sent them to Britain in AD 175 to make sure they did not renege on the recent peace treaty. Between that first mention in the mid 70s BC and the time Marcus Aurelius used Britain much as Siberia is used for modern Russian dissidents, the Sarmatians appear frequently in Roman literature. The two tribes most mentioned are the Roxolani and the Iazyges. When Roman historians recount Sarmatian exploits they are usually referring to the Iazygian peoples. The Roxolani, under pressure from the Aorsi, another Sarmatian tribe, in turn pushed the Iazyges into the fringes of Roman territory. Throughout the first half of the first century AD the Iazyges made repeated attempts, often with the Dacians, to cross the Danube. Finding their way south blocked they moved westwards, settling in the Hungarian plains around AD 20. There they based themselves for the next 400 years (ibid., pp. 171–3). They were always a force to be reckoned with, especially as cavalry whose main tactic was to break the van of any opposing force by a thunderous massed charge, horses impelled by herd instinct allied with the excitement of speed, riders armed with heavy lance. In keeping with their normal cavalry tactics, if a heavy charge was successful it would be followed by merciless harrying.

According to Tacitus, Sarmatians hired themselves out as mercenaries, often fighting on both sides. In AD 35 when Tiberius, for reasons of foreign diplomacy, was appointing various royal hostages to Armenian and Parthian thrones, Sarmatians fought both for the Roman appointee to the Parthian crown, Tiridates III, and for his opponent, Orodes. In typical headstrong fashion they would not wait for battle orders and fight in the Parthian way, but employed their national tactic of massed charge followed by hand-to-hand fighting (*Ann.* VI.34).

The Iazyges continued to have very mixed relations with Rome, at one time treating with them and fighting as auxiliaries on the Roman side while respecting the Roman frontiers of Pannonia; at others, ranged in opposition. In the German tribal wars of AD 50, they supported Vannius of the Suebi against Vibilius of the Hermundurii, but again their lack of discipline helped in their defeat. Claudius, knowing the tribes' fickle nature, had given instructions that the losers in the battle were to be protected and the winners intimidated in order to protect Roman borders from possible incursions (ibid., XII.26).

In AD 68 the Roxolani went marauding into Moesia, bent on plunder, with a 9,000-strong mounted force. Caught unawares by *Legion III Gallica*, they were worsted in battle, being heavily laden with booty and unable to use their horses' speed to escape because of the slippery conditions underfoot (ibid., *Hist.* 1.79). Tacitus gives a good description of the Sarmatian nobles' equipment: iron-plated or toughened-leather body armour, which was proof against blows, but so cumbersome that once unhorsed the man could not easily regain his feet. When he did he floundered in the deep, soft snow. Because of the thawing ground they could not deliver their accustomed and very effective massed charge, and their enormous two-handed swords and heavy lances were of no avail. Tacitus makes no mention of horse armour, from which we can infer that only the nobles were armour clad.

During the Dacian Wars, Sarmatians fought on both sides. The Roxolani fought against Domitian and the Iazyges with him in the campaign of AD 85–8. The Roxolani again invaded Roman Moesia in AD 85–6, and between Dacian campaigns the Iazyges followed suit by a raid into that province in AD 92. After the Dacian Wars, the Roxolani were paid to stay away from Roman borders, but when Hadrian stopped the subsidy in AD 117, Rome not only had trouble with the Roxolani attacking Dacia from the east, but with the Iazyges who took their opportunity to attack it from the west. Hadrian repulsed both, renewing the subsidy to the Roxolani and concluding a peace treaty with them that lasted until AD 260, and another treaty with the Iazyges that held for 50 years until the Marcommanian Wars of Marcus Aurelius (Sulimirski 1970, pp. 168, 174).

From AD 166 to 175 there were repeated engagements with the Iazyges and the Marcomanni, and Dio graphically describes one encounter on the frozen Danube. The Iazygian horses, who had been trained to operate on ice (the Mongols could also operate on ice, their ponies being shod with felt), charged the Romans, others riding round to take them on the flank. The Romans retaliated by forming a shield 'tortoise', jerking Iazyges off their horses as they rode up, grabbing bridles, spears, even knocking horses down on the ice (Dio, LXXII.7.1–5). Peace was concluded in AD 175, the price to the Iazyges being 8,000 cavalrymen and mounts, of which 5,500 were sent to Britain where Ribchester (Bremetennacum) had a full unit of Sarmatians.

The Sarmatian presence in the north of Britain was long-lived. An inscription from the time of the Gordians (AD 238–44) is dedicated to Apollo Maponus for the welfare of the *Numerus Equitum Sarmatorum Bremetennacensium Gordianus*. By the fourth century the Ribchester *Numerus* had become the *Cuneus Sarmatarum* (*Notitia Dignitatum*; Richmond 1945). The Sarmatians had thus continued to employ their typical shock tactics in warfare as attested by the descriptive term *cuneus*, a title originally given to shock cavalry fighting in the wedge formation, a tactic that found favour in the Later Empire.

In the same way that Rome made use of all the people that fought against her and were finally defeated, so she made use of the talents of her auxiliaries, however acquired. The entry of 5,500 horsemen into Britain in AD 175 must have made an immense impact, when it is considered that only 50 years earlier the total number of cavalry in Britain, as worked out from Hadrian's Diploma of AD 122, was approximately 11,200 men in *alae*, *cohortes equitatae* and legionary cavalry (see Ch. 7).

In the following centuries, right down to the final phases of the Empire, the Iazyges continued to make repeated incursions across the Danube, and to prove a constant thorn in the Romans' side. Rome treated them harshly, devastating Iazygian territory eight times between AD 290 and 313. Though weakened by continual Roman reprisals the Iazygians never knuckled under completely to Roman forces. It was another tribe of similar origin, the Alans, pushing them ever harder for territory, that brought about their fall from supremacy in the Sarmatian tribal hierarchy (Sulimirski 1970, p. 180).

Ammianus Marcellinus makes several references to the Sarmatians and the Quadi, with whom they were linked, referring to the campaigns of AD 358 and 372 (*Res Gest.* 17.12; 29.6). Later in referring to the Alans (ibid., 31.2) he makes the same comment that Strabo made of the Roxolani (*Geog.* 7.4.6): 'that they considered it beneath their dignity to walk'.

Down the centuries the two nations which kept much of the Roman armed forces continually employed in campaign after campaign were the Parthians and the Sarmatians, and their successors. Both were mounted warrior peoples – the Parthians in massed and glittering array, the Sarmatians, true to nomad spirit, constantly pushing to new frontiers while being pressured in turn, and fighting in a series of razzias. The Romans learnt from, used, periodically conquered, but never wholly mastered either race. They in their turn cost the Empire dear in men and natural resources.

14
Development of cavalry

The growth of Roman power has been well documented. The tangible remains are incorporated in hundreds of settlements from village to large modern metropolis, and the masking soil and sands of Africa, Europe and Asia Minor still yield new traces of where her armies forged conquest into habitat. The growth of Roman cavalry is not nearly so well illustrated, yet growth there was. Taken as a continually evolving sector of the Roman army, the cavalry had a defined growth pattern. Its stages were highlighted by the punctuation marks of major battles; small but vital engagements where the horse was the focal point; and military giants who recognized the role the horse should play.

When Rome burst out of her Italian confines and the Empire mushroomed, the cavalry expanded rapidly from its token complement of legionary horse and *socii* cavalry to the auxiliary *alae* of Augustan days, and then the vexillations and *cunei* of the Later Empire. Always an inveterate copier and adaptor of what worked well, Rome utilized her client and conquered kingdoms, many of whom had a history of superb horses and vigorous horsemen.

In Rome's early days quality stock was the province of the wealthy, and the knight or *eques* took his own animal to war. Cavalry, as depicted by Livy in his *Early History of Rome*, was no more than mounted groups of skirmishers dignified by the name of troops. It was first put on a formal footing with the alleged creation by Romulus of three centuries of knights – the Ramnenses, Titienses and Luceres (Livy, I.13). Later Tarquin expanded the cavalry, increasing the numbers to 1,800 (ibid., I.36). Such a number constituted a reasonable strike force for the still fledgling nation.

Under Servius, the cavalry was put on a proper footing, 18 centuries being organized. The state furnished cash for the purchase of mounts, and a levy on rich widows footed the feed bill (ibid., I.43). Livy tells us that cavalryman were conscripted from among the most prominent and wealthy citizens, so the 10,000 *asses* per century allocated for horse purchase was presumably only a partial payment, either for remounts as needed, the initial animal accompanying his rich owner, or as payment towards each animal submitted; 100 *asses* would hardly cover the whole cost. Taken in context with the property requirements of 100,000 *asses* for the highest class of infantry, it seems even more likely that this was a partial payment only. It is supported by Varro's use of a horse's value in *asses* in one of his examples of correct grammar, where he states that a cavalry horse is worth 1,000 *asses* (*de Ling. Lat.* VIII.71). Even taking inflation into account, between the time of which Livy was writing and that of Varro, horse prices, particularly those relating to the top category of horse, would not show such a wide divergence.

In the early centuries of Rome's history, supply of equines would have depended largely on the breeds either indigenous to Italy and/or those imported into Italy from Greece. Breeding, and therefore supply, would have been in the hands of large landowners. Supply would have been augmented by capture after skirmishes. Lack of saddles at this stage would have meant that more cavalrymen were unseated than after the four-horned retaining saddle had been developed. As Rome evolved from a city state to a nation, taking as her allies the surrounding tribes within Italy, her cavalry was augmented by warriors from the various geographical areas (Ch. 5). Once Rome became, in effect, Italy and burst out of those narrow confines, a massive input of available horse and rider power, particularly from the Celtic area to her north, became available. She had felt the weight of Celtic cavalry in 387–386 BC when Rome rumbled to the beat of their hooves.

By the time of Polybius cavalry structure had changed yet again and become in essence, if not in actual construction, the forerunner of the cavalry of Early Empire. To each legion, 300 cavalry were attached, selected on a property basis. Polybius gives us an inkling that a realization of the importance of cavalry was beginning when he stresses that the cavalry were enlisted before the foot (*Hist.* VI.20). Along with the new induction methods went better cavalry weapons – a more robust lance, pointed at both ends, and a larger, better-constructed shield, both patterned on those used by the Greeks (ibid., VI.25). Better organization of the horse lines was employed (ibid., VI.29) and fodder allocated per horse, or rather a specified amount of barley was allocated to each trooper for feeding his horses. A legionary cavalryman received 7 *medimni* of barley and an allied cavalryman 5 per month, (ibid., VI.39). This works out to almost 700 lb and 500 lb (315 kg and 225 kg), which would allow generous basic nutrition for a small string which a trooper could call on for remounts. The main drawback for the legionary cavalry was that they were chosen on the basis of wealth rather than for their horsemanship. However, the two were likely to go together because part of a wealthy young man's upbringing included being taught to ride, as Plutarch makes clear in his *Lives*. Obviously there would be a proportion of indifferent horsemen, even though they were given every opportunity to learn. The allied cavalry were contingents of real horsemen drawn from tribes with an equestrian background.

The Hannibalic Wars brought home to the Romans their deficiencies in cavalry. The ratio of horse to foot in the Roman sphere was low. Publius Cornelius Scipio (Africanus' father) was sent to Spain with a total of 22,000 foot and 2,200 horse (Polybius, *Hist.* III.40), a ratio of ten to one, whereas Hannibal entered Italy, after his marathon in the Alps where he had already sustained massive losses, with 20,000 foot and 6,000 horse – a ratio of ten to three. In addition the native Africans, Carthaginians and Numidians were natural horsemen. Hannibal also operated a higher standard of horsemanship, as shown by the rest and care given to the animals (ibid., III.60).

Even after the lessons in the use of cavalry at Ticinus and Cannae, Rome had much else to absorb in this department. Though not ranked as a major episode in Rome's military history, the equestrian content of the Jugurthine Wars must surely have shown Rome that she needed to assess and radically re-organize her approach to mounted warfare. The Jugurthine Wars stretching from 112 to 106 BC and taking place on the foreign soil of Numidia were a masterpiece of the tactics of hit, run, disperse, regroup and sting again, delivered by the descendants of those same Numidians who had aided and then finally opposed Hannibal at Zama. For seven years Jugurtha rapped the knuckles first of Bestia, then Metellus, followed by Sulla and Marius whose superior generalship, aided by the treachery of the Mauretanian king, Bocchus, finally turned the tables. What made Jugurtha's run of success possible was undoubtedly tactics, superb horsemanship, and an unending supply of lean, tough, nimble Numidian horses ridden bridleless in harmony with their riders. The Romans used imported Italian stock, unacclimatized to rapid desert warfare or the moisture-sucking conditions. True, in the final stages of hand-to-hand combat described by Sallust the cream of Rome's riders bested the Numidians, but running throughout Sallust's narrative are comments on Numidian tactics, their supply of equines, and scarcity of water hampering the Romans while the Numidians knew where it was available. It is a fact that heavy fleshed animals such as the Romans preferred lose more fluid and therefore need greater replenishments than wiry, 'dry', desert-bred animals. (I have used both types on endurance rides – one runs with sweat, while the other hardly has a damp skin, and at water stops the intake varies greatly from animal to animal.)

Shortly after the Jugurthine Wars a general who really understood the role of equines burst on to the scene. As a strategist Julius Caesar must have been aware of the underlying reasons as well as the obvious ones for most cavalry failures. He could be said to be the outstanding horseman in a military sense. Not only a superb horseman (Plutarch, *Lives*, vol. II, p. 189), he was also a breeder of note (Suetonius, *Caes.* 61), and as both horseman and general recognized the need for mounted troops. His Gallic and African Wars are liberally sprinkled with equestrian feats, and he made heavy use of allied tribes' cavalry as well as levies of stock. He knew how to use available local cavalry to best effect and, for regularly enlisted cavalry especially, purchased horses suited to the needs of warfare from Italy and Spain. The latter, of course, had a history of breeding the 'dry' type of horse, with sparser frame and greater resistance to dehydration.

Caesar's main homegrown adversary, Pompey, also knew how to hamper the enemies' cavalry as is shown by his cunning tactics and night attacks against Mithridates of Armenia in 66 BC (Dio, XXVI.47.2–3; 49.1–6). Against Oroeses of Albania he used copycat tactics – turn tail and run, then wheel and encircle the enemy out of retreat (ibid., XXXVII.54.2–3). Later, against Caesar, he drew on many sources for his cavalry in the manner of future auxiliaries. The African/Libyans, Moroccans and Numidians had already shown their worth against Rome in Italy, allied with them at Zama, and against the Saluvii in 125 BC. Additional cavalry which Pompey drew from the steppes – Sarmatians and Massagetic Huns – were later on to cause the Romans heavy losses (Lucan, *Pharsalia* 75–6).

In Augustus' time the organization went much further, and from his reign light is shed on much cavalry practice, and on the place of the equestrian class and those of lower rank. Horses were a very important part of any religious or civil procession, and the equestrian class, it can be inferred, were obliged to present themselves on horseback on certain occasions. This is borne out by the consideration shown by Augustus, who had revived the custom of making them ride in procession. He tempered this requirement by allowing the old or infirm to send their riderless horses to the procession's starting point and appear on foot themselves. Later he amended this so that any knight over 35 years of age who did not wish to retain his charger could surrender it privately (Suetonius, *Aug.* 38). This implies that the knights' chargers were provided by the state who retained ownership, the horses being given back when knights no longer required them. This is corroborated by the fragment of Dio (XXVIII.951–3) referring to an incident in 99 BC:

> The son of Metellus besought everybody to such an extent . . . to let his father return from exile. . . .
> Furius cherished such enmity against Metellus because the latter when censor had taken his horse away.

Publius Furius, under indictment for the acts he had performed while tribune, was slain by the Romans in the very assembly. He richly deserved to die . . . for he was a seditious person. . . .

Presumably a knight could ride his own horse if he preferred to, but was entitled to claim a charger from the state. Confiscation of the horse constituted not only punishment but also massive loss of face. Caligula also punished knights guilty of wicked or scandalous behaviour by the disgrace of publicly dismounting them (Suetonius, *Gaius* 16). These incidents place in context the social importance attached to riding a horse.

While a saddle became part of cavalry equipment from at least Julius Caesar's day, when the Germans considered the use of them effete (*de Bello Gall.* IV.4), the parading knights had no such security or comfort. In the earlier annual reviews they must have paraded bareback as the use of saddle cloths appeared for the first time in the reign of Nero (Dio, LXIII.13.3). There was some improvement in equipment, but civilian saddlery was not on such an elaborate or advanced level as that used by the military. Diocletian's *Edict on Prices* gives quite a comprehensive list of horse and mule harness and the top price that could be charged for each item. Civilians were still riding in the pad saddle that cost 100 *denarii*, the article being stuffed and weighing three Roman pounds (2.2 lb or 1 kg). If they wished they could be more adventurous and buy a more fashionable version of the same weight but adorned with gold for 250 *denarii*. In comparison, a military saddle cost 500 *denarii*, reflecting its more advanced construction (Leake 1826). No doubt if a civilian wished to spend the same amount he too could ride in the infinitely more secure rigid-tree saddle.

Legionary cavalry was now down to a token 120 per legion. Allied, client and beaten enemies, as part of the price for acceptance into the Empire, provided almost the total cavalry force. They fought under Roman officers and became the mounted auxiliary arm of the Roman army. In the same way as breeds were classified, many of the *alae* bore the name of country of origin, and their story is outlined in Chapters 5 and 13.

Many of the peoples, for instance Thracians, Sarmatians, Celts from Spain, Gaul and Northern Italy, and Syrians, provided mounted masses. Some, as we have seen with the Sarmatians, hired themselves out as mercenaries and could be found fighting for and against Romans in the same conflict (Tacitus, *Ann.* VI.34): in Trajan's Dacian Wars, the Roxolani fought against and the Iazyges with the Romans. The Sarmatians also brought with them the iron- (and/or leather-) clad horse, although as we saw the Romans had been introduced to cataphracts as early as 190 BC at the Battle of Magnesia (Plutarch, *Lives*, vol. II, 26, 62). Trajan fielded a massive army of 30 legions, 10 praetorian cohorts, 4 urban cohorts and 300 auxiliary units. Cavalry formed a great part of the latter. Barbarian units using their own weapons, customs and methods were also included (Rossi 1971, p. 142). These units added some of the nationalistic verve that the other auxiliary units had lost since being drafted into the Roman sphere.

As has been mentioned, the auxiliary units, both mounted and foot, were initially ethnic groups raised on home ground and sent to serve away from home. During the Flavian/Trajanic period this began to change, the units retaining the name of their country of origin but losing ethnic content and serving both at home and abroad (Holder 1980). The equine element, from being standardized according to breed in early auxiliary *alae*, must therefore have altered just as radically and consisted of a mixture of breeds. This dual change applied mostly to western units, with eastern units being largely unaffected, enlisting and serving mainly in that theatre of war; although occasionally eastern and African units were posted west (hence we find the head of a Libyan type of horse at Newstead which gives a whole new slant to the origins of the purebred Arabian (see Chs. 1, 5).

Numbers were also rising by leaps and bounds. Instead of a packed mass of locally recruited tribesmen as used in Caesar's day, the cavalry were now formally organized into *alae quingenaria* and *milliaria*. In the Vespasianic period 180,000 auxiliaries of horse and foot were mustered, and by the mid second century AD this had risen to 220,000, of which 80,000 were cavalry (Cheesman 1914). This did not include legionary cavalry, and the 30 legions in Trajan's day would have added at least another 3,600 to the total, plus the several hundred from his other regiments of Praetorian and Urban troops.

However, it was not only numbers that were escalating. Hadrian employed cataphracts in the Roman cavalry, although it is not certain how many. The role of the horse was changing as selective breeding improved the size and weight-carrying capacity. The vast distances involved in the stretched Empire called for speedier movements that only a mounted force could achieve, while the foot came up slowly. Gallienus spearheaded this by creating a very fast mobile strike-force composed largely of Dalmatian, Moorish and Osrhoenian horsemen armed with their native missile weapons (Williams 1985). Cheesman gives the number of his select cavalry force as between 50 and 60 *alae* (Cheesman 1914). At the very least this meant 25,000 troopers and was only a small part of the cavalry. It was based at Milan in a pivotal position, able to launch a very rapid attack by covering 50 miles (80 km) per day. This distance could be easily exceeded if pressed. Because such speed became the norm it was not as noteworthy as earlier isolated forced marches by the cavalry had been. Mounts must have been selected and trained with great care. It gave the Emperor a double-edged weapon – guarding him, providing his senior cavalry officers remained loyal, but deadly if power went to their heads. Gallienus was assassinated by his cavalry commanders in AD 268.

Succeeding emperors continued to utilize fast, mobile cavalry to great effect during their war-torn reigns. Claudius II destroyed a huge army of Goths in successive battles at Naissus and in the Haemus Mountains (Williams 1985, p. 29), and through his victories earned the title *Gothicus*. Yet these were only some of the Gothic and other incursions. The expanded Empire, relying largely on foreign cavalry mainly from Germanic sources, was to be repeatedly punctured by aggressive inroads of hostile armies, mostly mounted.

Diocletian greatly expanded the whole army by between 30 and 50 per cent (Jones 1964, pp. 679–80). The cavalry was approximately one-third of the total force and able to act independently as a major element of the army, rather than as an adjunct whose full potential was not harnessed, as in earlier centuries. During his reign Diocletian had great need of this fast, hard-hitting force for the massive troop movements, particularly between AD 287 and 298. The Illyrian emperors were beset by revolts and troubles. Britain freed herself from Rome under Carausius and then Allectus, but was regained successively by Maximian and Constantius in 296–7. Then Maximian departed for Africa to suppress the Moors in 297–8. In between, Diocletian was on the Danube fighting against Sarmatians, Goths and Alamanni during 293–4, then off to Syria in 295 and Egypt in 296. Galerius had his hands full on the Danube in 295, and rode against the Persians in 297. All in all, the Tetrarchy was constantly in the field and mobile cavalry was absolutely essential to nip revolts in the bud before they took too firm a hold.

At crucial sectors of vulnerable territory, cavalry came to be stationed in strong detachments close enough to render aid to a beleaguered fort at a scant hour or two's notice. The map shows that the most threatened sector was well covered by border troops, two vexillations each probably 500 strong, and the legions at Palmyra and on Danaba. Other vexillations, placed at the closest 20 miles (32 km) from the border and thereafter at 20-mile intervals, could be directed where needed very rapidly. The extensive road system crisscrossing the Empire enabled horses to travel at sustained speed. Using the less harsh, cleared roadside a rolling 16 m.p.h. plus (25 k.p.h.) canter would take only a moderate amount out of a fit, well-fed horse. If necessary the horse could travel in excess of 20 m.p.h. (32 k.p.h.) under full gear for two hours and come to no harm. He would still have enough reserve left to be useful as a warhorse when he arrived at the destination under threat.

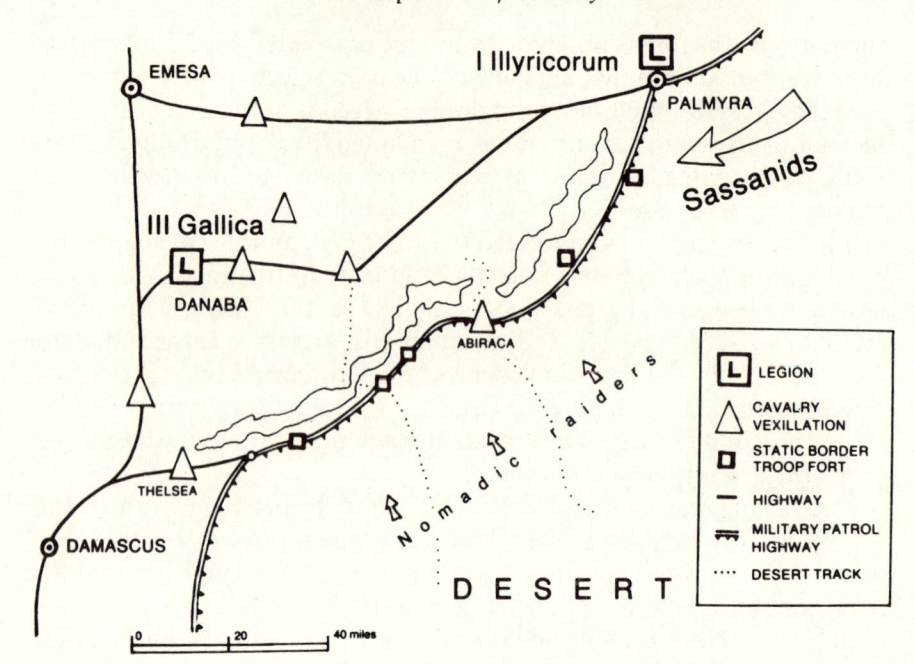

6 Map showing the Emesa, Palmyra, Damascus triangle

A modern example of such speed in adverse heat conditions can be used to substantiate this claim. The 1986 South African National Endurance Champion won the Fauresmith 130-mile (210-km) ride in 8 hours 17 minutes, with one 50-mile (80-km) section ridden at over 18 m.p.h. (30 k.p.h.). To compete in these Championships the horse must carry in excess of 160 lb (73 kg) and must finish in good veterinary condition. This means he is sound and has sufficient reserve left for a further distance under the same conditions (Hyland 1988). Temperatures in South Africa compare well with those of the Damascus/Palmyra/Emesa triangle. Fifty-mile races there are frequently won in little more than three hours, often in mountainous terrain. Records are often being broken for the same distance done in less than three hours.

Though the above Roman and South African examples are isolated they show what is feasible and possible. The Roman example also shows how the expectations of cavalry usefulness had risen over the centuries from the earliest days to Diocletian's time and after, when the force had expanded in size to something in the region of 200,000 horse, if we take the premise that a third of the force was mounted, and that the total number at any one time was about 600,000 (Jones, 1964, pp. 679–80). This of course was not necessarily the operative number but what would have been available if every unit was up to full strength. It gave a chance for considerable abuse in taxes levied on provincials, and to the army as well to claim allowances for men and horses not actually in use. This upgraded cavalry was a whirlwind force capable of putting many swift miles behind them in a very short space of time. As has been shown the use of a proper saddle with a secure seat facilitated this, as well as the higher physical standards required of the cavalry mount (*Codex Theo.*, 6.31.1). The general improvement in physique and stature of horses specifically bred for a certain role, as opposed to those running in a herd with little culling of inferior stock or prevention of inbreeding, enabled cavalry to fulfil its duties far more effectively. A small, weedy horse would be exposed to danger through many causes – lack of sustained speed, poor endurance, and inability to bear weight both of man and his developing armour, plus the horse's own armour in the case of partially or wholly mail-clad equines. The latter was a mixed blessing, as has already been shown, but covering of certain vital points such as head, eyes and chest were an unqualified advantage and not overburdening (even for a 'weed').

After a period of respite in the latter years of his reign Diocletian retired and was succeeded by Constantine. He also increased the mobile cavalry vexillations, creating the posts of *Magister Peditum* and *Magister Equitum* in overall command of the two military spheres. His crack cavalry were termed *scholae* with each unit 500 strong – seven units in the east and five in the west. Descriptively named, they were:

East:	1st and 2nd *Scutarii*
	Scutarii Sagittarii
	Scutarii Clibinarii
	Sen. and *Jun. Gentiles*
	Jun. Armaturae
West:	1st, 2nd, and 3rd *Scutarii*
	Senior Gentiles
	Senior Armaturae

From these regiments came the 40 white-uniformed *candidati* of the emperor's personal bodyguard. Originally the *scholae* were chosen from the elite cavalry with Roman citizenship, but eventually the posts were largely filled by Germanic peoples (Jones 1964, p. 613). As the softening process set in these crack troops tended to lose their martial qualities, becoming merely parade troops. With more and more foreigners, particularly in the cavalry, fighting in return for payment, the pride of nationhood must have decreased. The borders weakened and the rot set in, with repeated incursions of hostile bands carried into the Roman sphere by droves of steppe peoples mounted on steppe-bred horses. In the middle of the fourth century AD, two nations – the Ostrogoths (Ukraine) and Visigoths (Romania) – posed a greater threat. The Huns coming in from the steppelands had overrun their territories in the 370s AD, and so a multitude of Visigoths 200,000 strong poured over the Danube, and applied for and were granted the right to stay by Theodosius I (Grant 1981, p. 18). Ammianus Marcellinus described both the Huns and their horses exceptionally vividly, almost as if he had the smell of unwashed bodies and the reek of sweaty horses under his nose (*Res Gest.* 31.2). The men had squat bodies, strong and thick limbs, and were extremely ugly, bent and fixed centaur-like to their horses who were equally strong, hardy and ugly, as well as very adept at placing their riders in the most opportune position for lassoing opponents from their saddles.

Such incursions of stock had a far-reaching effect on the future of many of Europe's horses. Vegetius' analytical description of the Hunnish horse gives a superb picture of a less than beautiful but very tough piece of horseflesh. It bears out Ammianus and expands on his description (see Ch. 1). The large Hunnish horses, once moved to a more settled environment with better and more regular feeding patterns and crossed with the finer, better-bred horses already available from centuries of specialization in horsebreeding, enabled the future generations to show the characteristics that gradually evolved into the huge equines of later centuries. The superb sketch by Albrecht Dürer dated 1498 shows a man-at-arms mounted on an ill-conformed rouncy that would have easily fitted Vegetius' unflattering description of a Hunnish horse, as would the equally ugly splay-hooved equine sketched by Pisanello (1395–1455).

The eastern Empire had the even better-mounted Sassanians on its borders, so that the Empire was being squeezed by nations whose prime transport was the horse, each nation being mounted on horses with varying amounts of aesthetic appeal, but both types having an inbred ability to withstand hardship. Vegetius confirms the Hunnish horse's durability, and long before him Dio Cassius had been well aware of the Persian or Nisaean stock's superiority.

As with nations evolving into Empires, a breed of horse takes time – many decades – to fix a type that in turn becomes an individual breed. Careful management and clever use of prepotent sires and dams able to impart desired qualities achieve this. Once established a breed can flourish for centuries, using different bloodlines within the breed to prevent incest breeding. The Huns and their nomadic neighbours had the one breed, the Sassanians the other, and however it is argued there can be no doubt that the major external enemies of Rome's Empire were aided in great measure by their possession of superior stock and their skill in horsemanship and horsebreeding. Over the centuries Rome had made use of her cavalry auxiliaries mounted largely on horses indigenous to the auxiliaries' country of origin. As her cavalry arm grew, Rome had been forced to raise sufficient stock within her own borders to keep up the supplies. As the Empire drew in the barbarian elements to swell the cavalry ranks, outside genetic impulses were available from stock that survived the battle zones and tours of military duty. In any battle where cavalry was employed, loose mounts would be rounded up and go to the day's victors. Thus there would be a constant intermingling of genes. When what is termed in horsebreeding parlance a 'good nick' resulted, and even more importantly was recognized as such, a further impetus to desired quality would become available.

From the equine stance the eventual fall of the Empire to hordes of horse-borne barbarians on uncouth steeds opened the way for future generations of equines. The strong, large, brutish specimens blended with the refined produce of Greek and Roman stockbreeding to change the types of equines available to later centuries. This European, steppe, and eastern blood gave Europe the genetic pool from which the palfreys, rouncies, amblers, destriers, and very humble stotts and affers emerged. Medieval horses owed much to their Roman ancestors and the stock which Rome's eventual conquerors rode into battle.

Part Three

THE HORSE IN STATE AND CIVILIAN USE

15
The Roman circus

Racing at Rome and racing on today's modern track have many points of similarity. Two in particular stand out. The most obvious one, faithfully recorded by almost every Roman and Greek historian of the era, was the frenetic passion the circus and its equine and human stars aroused. This is mirrored today in the media, and by coverage given both in the sporting and equestrian press and in the racing pages of all daily newspapers. In Britain, every aspect of Flat, National Hunt, Hurdling, and Point-to-Point racing is reported. Ancient Romans, like modern punters and knowledgeable horsemen, could discourse on the horses' merits, pedigrees, speed and track performances, the drivers' and jockeys' tactics, and the ratings in winners' tables. Today's sport viewed at the saddling enclosure, parade ring, and rail-side is just as electrifying as the hurly-burly of the Roman circus.

Dio Chrysostomos, a writer of the second century AD, describes the manic behaviour of spectators, in this case those of Roman Alexandria:

> This passion for horses which infects the city . . . But of the people of Alexandria what can one say, a people to whom one need only throw bread and give a spectacle of horses since they have no interest in anything else. When they enter a theatre or stadium they lose all consciousness of their former state and are not ashamed to say or do anything that occurs to them. (*Orat.*, 32)

Dio then goes on to describe their parody of urging the horses themselves, and other overt actions:

> constantly leaping and raving and beating one another and using abominable language and often reviling even the gods themselves and flinging their clothing at the charioteers and sometimes even departing naked from the show. The malady continued throughout the city for several days. (*Orat.*, 77)

Today's racing buff is more restrained, but Dio's picture is all too often mirrored in the football stadium.

The other major link between then and now is commercial. Today all racing, particularly flat racing, is a huge industry generating vast influence. There are massive financial investments in bloodstock breeding, with the focal point in Britain being the Newmarket Sales; racetracks and stables with all their ancillary buildings; training facilities; stud farms, with productive land given over to livestock support; expensive veterinary care for racehorses and constant research into their ailments; large amounts of fodder and grain; and the essential farrier's, loriner's and saddler's crafts. The industry provides work for tens of thousands, either directly or indirectly. In Rome the expenditure was on an equally massive scale for the same basic necessities, although very different in structure, as the sport was maintained on a compulsory basis. Personnel involved came from all sections of society, from the Emperor, who owned vast estates where prime horseflesh was bred, down to the slaves who formed the *familia* of each faction.

In his *Life of Publicola*, Plutarch gives evidence for the early incidence of harness racing, placing it firmly as a regular occurrence in the last days of Tarquin. He recounts the portentous tale of a chariot race taking place at Veii, which 'was observed as usual', except that as the victorious charioteer drove gently out of the ring the horses were startled and bolted towards Rome, finally flinging the charioteer from his chariot at the Ratumena Gate. This was taken as a sign of Rome's future greatness, based on an earlier soothsayer's prediction linking the runaways with the chariot designed to stand over the top of the temple of Jupiter Capitolinus in Rome (*Lives*, vol. I, p. 62). Plutarch does not say if it was a four- or a two-horse hitch, yet earlier he mentions that Publicola was the first consul to make his entry in a triumph in a chariot and four (ibid., p. 59). From this we know that both two- and four-horse hitches were used.

As with much else in Roman society the Greeks had a great influence on Roman racing. No doubt this stemmed from the very early days when southern Italy and Sicily had a large Greek presence and was known as Magna Graecia. The Etruscans have left many representations of racehorses both ridden and in harness (usually hitched to a *biga*), showing Greek influence, which they had absorbed from their southern neighbours.

The Etruscan paintings give a fair idea of what the horses looked like, although the colours are not always true to life, maybe because available pigments were not able to portray colours exactly, and also because of some measure of artists' licence. The horses are somewhat stylized but do bear a striking resemblance in some points to the pictorial representation of medieval Italian horses of the Gonzagan period. The paintings clearly show the fine limbs, high heads, crested necks and high tail carriage of well-bred horses, with the lean body and powerful quarters of racers. It is possible to identify certain gaits that have been accurately portrayed, namely the four-beat walk and the two-beat lateral pace, the latter being unusual in today's horses except in harness racing where many Standardbreds pace, mostly in the USA and Australia. However, lateral gaits were common in many horses in antiquity, as is made clear by Pliny's description of the Asturian horse of Spain (*Nat. Hist.* VIII). The Etruscan paintings have a wide range of normal colourings – among them chestnuts with white stockings and ubiquitous greys – as well as blues, which could be meant to represent blue roans or dark greys, and a black with a pale mane and tail, which could be a very very dark liver chestnut with flaxen mane and tail – a combination that is uncommon today but spectacularly beautiful in the few I have seen. The size ratio of man to horse is enlightening. For once we can see representation with accurate artistic proportions, and it was obvious that the horses were not that small. Even allowing for the smaller stature of humans, and Latins in particular, at that time it would appear that the animals were close in size to the smaller category of modern horses. Today, 14.2 hh (147 cm) is used to separate horse from pony when differentiating on grounds of height, although the real difference is in breed and species characteristics. Some horse breeds, for example the Arabian, have many specimens under 14.2 hh. Of course it must be realized that today there are so many breeds registered that one cannot generalize, and a horse can range from the 14-hand (142-cm) small Arabian to the type used by top show jumpers which might be well over 17 hands (173 cm).

The massive Circus Maximus, the longest track in the Roman 'fixture list', was begun in the days of Tarquinius Priscus, the fifth king of Rome, and was planned and the early structures erected for the games given by Tarquin to celebrate victory in his first war against the Latins. The main attractions were horses and boxers, both from Etruria, and thereafter these games became an annual affair (Livy, I.35). In the early period of racing it was much as it is today, the province of the wealthy man, with individual owners running their own horses and gaining the acclaim when their animals won.

Over the centuries as racing developed, and the increase in popularity demanded ever more and more races, monumental edifices with the ancillary buildings needed were set up in all major cities of the Roman Empire, with smaller towns and cities boasting lesser tracks. The Circus Maximus, only one of five tracks in Rome itself, continued to hold premier place. As Rome was the hub of the Empire this is understandable, but from the horse's point of view it took a top-class animal to compete continually and successfully on such an extended track. The dimensions of the arena were approximately 2,150 × 725 ft (650 × 220 m). The *spina*, the central barrier around which the horses turned, was 770 ft (233 m) long. As each race was normally seven laps, this meant that at the very least, with a strong team well handled and not obstructed throughout the race, the winner, if he had drawn and kept a favourable position, would travel in excess of 2 miles (3 km). This hypothetical perfection would be virtually impossible to achieve, and the reality with a good driver would be closer to 3 miles (4.5 km). A poor driver who was always pushed to the outside and obliged to cover maximum distance would have raced for closer to 4 miles (6.5 km) per event. Modern flat races of major importance in prestige value range from the Kentucky Derby at 1¼ miles (2,000 m); the Epsom Derby at 1½ miles (2,400 m); and the St Leger at 1¾ miles (2,800 m); to the Grand Prix de Paris at 1 mile 7 furlongs (3,000 m) and the Melbourne Cup at 2 miles (3,200 m). All these fall far short of the Roman top-class racing distances and they are run on surfaces better suited to maintaining sound legs on a horse. Although arenas differed in track length most major ones were at least 1,450 ft (440 m) long (Humphrey 1986, p. 1). Other dimensions would have been proportionate.

The descriptive name *arena* tells us that the tracks were constructed of sand. J. H. Humphrey, in his exhaustive survey of the constructions of Roman circuses throughout the Empire, describes a compacted layer, with drainage incorporated where necessary, with an overlay of cushioning sand (Humphrey 1986). Modern harness racetracks in America have an extremely hard surface without a cushioning sand layer. (Many years ago when visiting a winter training centre for Standardbreds, I was told by one of the grooms that it was quite common for two out of three horses to have leg problems of one kind or another, and I could see this clearly myself.) Pelagonius in his *Ars Veterinaria* devotes many chapters to cures for various leg, back and shoulder ailments, most of which would happen on a racetrack. A footing with an unyielding base would cause joint concussion. The cushioning layer of sand would need to be very deep to avoid this, yet a deep layer would not be suitable for horses travelling at speed and pulling a vehicle, because then instead of concussion they would suffer tendon and muscle strain. Consequently any cushioning layer would only be of token or minimal depth. Concussion caused by constant pounding would have been exacerbated by the frequent turns at high speed which would add to joint and tendon stress in the legs, and cause back and shoulder injuries by wrenching.

That Pelagonius was operating as a track vet is confirmed by his references to accidents that happened during chariot races. Chapter XV.233 deals with a cure 'for a blow on the feet [hooves] occasioned by a wheel', and Chapter XVI.252 'for bony excrescences or insensitive tendons or numb tendons or if by chance the horse has been struck by an axle with resultant hardness'. This is a very accurate description of what happens if a horse's limb gets struck hard on a part with no flesh to absorb the initial impact. (A showjumper of mine was out of jumping competitions for seven months because after a kick on the hock a hard lump formed, and he could only be used in gentle work while we waited all that time for it to re-absorb.) In his opening preamble dealing with back injuries Pelagonius addresses 'advice to breeders and managers of public chariot horses, as well as to private owners who, while having no interest in the public spectacles of the circus, appreciate chariot horses for their beauty'. He offers advice on the 'care of the back in order that these horses may remain unharmed and free from injury'. He also implies that knowledge of such care is more important to the public charioteers than to the private owner (ibid., VIIIII.163).

At that time racing had been in the hands of factions for 400 years, at least since 70 BC, when, Pliny notes, faction colours were first recorded (*Nat. Hist.* 7.186). Racing was surrounded by a mass of rules and regulations, with religious and civil implications. The racing establishment was split into four factions, each designated by a colour and dedicated to the seasons and the gods, according to Tertullian. He tells us that at first there were only two, the Whites and Reds, Winter and Summer, and that luxury and superstition were responsible for rededication and amplification of the Reds to Mars, Whites to Zephyrs, Green to Mother Earth, and Azure to Sky and Sea or Autumn (*de Spect.*). It is clear from historians that Blues (Azures) and Greens came to dominate, for rarely are the exploits of the Reds and Whites recorded in literature, and they became merged, the Whites with the Greens and the Reds with the Blues, though each still retained a specific colour identity. The charioteer inscriptions confirm this. From the selection given by Dessau (*ILS*), four charioteers had wins for each of the colours, and as Table 6 shows no faction performed particularly badly.

Table 6. Number of wins for selected charioteers

ILS reference	Charioteer	Whites	Reds	Blues	Greens
5286 (1)	Polyneices	17	739	55	655
5286 (2)	Tatianus	7	125	24	89
5288	Gutta	102	78	583	364
5287	Diocles	81	925	205	216

It has to be said that the inscriptions lauding charioteers' wins are not always accurate, as frequently the totals given do not match the sum of the breakdowns recorded by faction. Diocles' 925 wins for the Reds is not actually recorded, but arrived at from his total of 1,462 wins. In the same year that Diocles won for the first time for the Whites, another charioteer, Teres, won for the same faction 1,011 times (*ILS*, 5287). Thus, in the Early Principate, from which these inscriptions mostly date, it is clear that all four factions were alive and doing well.

The Diocles inscription is the most extensive (*ILS*, 5287). It dates to the mid second century AD and gives a complete breakdown of this Lusitanian driver's 24 years as a charioteer, starting with his first race at the age of 18 in AD 122. Over the 24 years he accumulated 1,462 wins out of 4,257 starts, and must have held the reins of countless four-horse teams in that time. The inscription names only six of his horses. These were obviously his big winners, maybe only from one period of his career, most probably from his years with the Reds. He first won for them in AD 131, and obviously remained a top driver, as his inscription makes repeatedly and abundantly clear, racking up 925 wins. Charioteers passed from faction to faction, by what system is not stated, but it is hardly likely that they would take their top string with them as most were of slave status, and the factions, not the drivers, owned the stock. During his career, as well as driving possibly hundreds of horses, Diocles 'made' nine horses winners of at least 100 races apiece, and one a winner of at least 200 races; we know that some won well in excess of these figures. The operative word here is that Diocles 'made' these winners: '*Equos centenarios fecit* n. 9 *et ducenar* 1'. It is well known in competitive equestrian circles that one rider/driver can get a horse to perform seeming miracles, while a change of rider/driver could spell disaster. Of these top ten horses, the only horse whose actual winning total is given is Pompeianus with 152 wins. The other named horses are Abigeius (Reiver or Rustler), Lucidus (Brilliant), Paratus (Ready), Cotynus and Galata, possibly the only mare amongst them. In one year Diocles' three top horses were Abigeius, Lucidus and Pompeianus, who between them won 103 out of his total for the year of 127 victories.

Naturally there were a great many other horses who shared these victories, maybe many who were almost as good, but the prestige of winning rested on the inside trace horse, the *funalis*, who was not yoked, but only attached by a rein to the centre pair, or yoke horses. There are divided opinions as to the most important horse in the team, whether the *funalis*, the yoke horses or *iguales*, or, in the Greek sphere of racing, the outside trace horse. Each horse had a definite job to do, but in my opinion the *funalis* would have had to be the most versatile and also the strongest member of the team. Not only would he have had to corner carefully around the *meta* or turning post, slowing down just sufficiently and then speeding up once clear of the turn, but he would have had to be able to impose his will on the other horses to a great degree. Because of the sharper angle of his turns and the jarring of sudden contractions in stride, followed by strains of immediately lengthening stride, his muscles, joints, tendons and spine took more of a battering than those of the rest. Also he would be more at risk in a crash, being pinned between *meta* and *spina* and the other team horses. The outside horse would need just that little bit of extra speed on the turns, while the yoke horses would have had to be the steadiest, as they actually hauled the chariot and kept the pace even. So the named horses of Diocles, and other charioteers, would most likely be the *funalis* of the winning team (unless the charioteer had any particular reason for naming another, possibly from affection?).

The tremendous popularity of the sport throughout the Empire meant that there was definitely a sellers' market, with breeders being in the happy position of finding a ready sale for almost all bloodstock. If horses failed to make the grade for the major tracks at Rome and other large cities such as Antioch, Alexandria, Caesarea, or Byzantium/Constantinople, or for the many great centres in North Africa, Spain and Portugal, they would find their way to the minor tracks that graced any city of even moderate importance. Roman Africa alone had upwards of two dozen circuses. Some of these were monumental, some partly stonebuilt, others attested but with no known permanent structure. Close behind came Spain and Portugal with 21 main circuses (Humphrey 1986). What stock was left on the breeders' hands as unsuitable for the track would have found its way into the army, which had a steadily increasing need for cavalry remounts.

There was, supposedly, a shortage of cavalry horses early in Augustus' reign, thought to be caused by the demands for horses for the circus. According to Dio Cassius, Maecaenas, poet, friend and adviser to Augustus, incorporated a passage in his speech on recommendations for reform of government practices:

> Secondly the cities should limit themselves in erecting public buildings to what is strictly necessary both as regards their number and their size, nor should they waste their resources in providing a large quantity or variety of public games. . . . Certainly they should hold a number of festivals and spectacles, with the exception of the horse-racing we have here in Rome, but not on such a scale that the public treasury should be impoverished, or the estates of private citizens ruined, or that any stranger resident there should be compelled to contribute to their expense, or that every victor in every contest should be granted free subsistence for life. . . . As for those horse-races which are not associated with gymnastic contests, I consider that no city other than Rome should be permitted to hold

them. The purpose of this regulation is, first, to prevent huge sums of money from being thrown away to no purpose; secondly, to discourage the public from becoming demoralized by its obsession with this sport; and above all to keep those who are serving in the army supplied with the best horses. It is with these factors in mind that I would prohibit outright the holding of such races anywhere other than in Rome. (Dio, LII.30)

From this passage it seems that at the end of the second century AD members of the city aristocracies were dipping heavily into their funds to pay for the racing fixtures; that the city treasuries also bore a share of the cost; and even temporary residents found themselves supporting the financial side of the races. Victors in athletic contests were awarded pensions, in effect entitling them to live off the state. The majority of charioteers, though not so entitled due to their slave status, would also have expected some financial gain from their wins. The sport had evidently reached the stage where it exerted a drug-like influence on the populace, keeping them from more useful occupations.

Dio appears to provide evidence that in his time the army was being denied suitable horses for the cavalry. This helps to answer a point not *explicitly* dealt with anywhere else in Roman histories – exactly where the army obtained the bulk of its horses, on a yearly basis. It is known that there were Imperial studs for raising racing stock, and also breeding operations specifically for providing army mounts, although not much light is thrown on the latter. The *Codex Theodosianus* contains strict legislation for horse levies (see Ch. 5 above) in the Later Empire. Private individuals with sufficient wealth, land and an interest in horsebreeding raised stock for the track, as many of the mosaics scattered throughout the Empire attest. Many of the horses depicted are named and have the breeder's brand clearly shown, usually on their flanks. The Sorothi horses from Sousse (Hadrumetum) illustrate this very well, as do many other African and Spanish racehorses.

Common sense tells us that not all horses raised for the track would be suitable. Some of the reasons for being unsuitable for racing might be just the reverse of unsuitability for the cavalry: lack of speed; lack of competitive spirit; intractability in harness – some good saddle horses will not tolerate driving harness and are terrified of the cart behind them, no matter how much time is expended on their training; and disparity in size. A horse that grew excessively would not be compatible in harness, for unless he was evenly matched with his team-mates his stride would not conform to theirs. A four-horse hitch would not always be composed of the same four animals. Animals do not always breed true to expected size (although purebreds usually have similar conformation dimensions): my mare Magnet Regent had nine foals by the same stallion, the smallest of which matured at a scant 15 hands (152 cm), and the largest at 16.2 hh (167 cm) – a size difference of at least 6 inches (15 cm), and a stride difference when extended of several feet, as the small horse had a fairly choppy gait, the large one a really reaching stride.

Modern practice is for horses that are initially bred for the track but are found to be unsuitable to find their way into the general riding horse area, either bypassing the racehorse trainer altogether, as not worth the investment of a season's training bills, or quickly being sold off after trials, as not worth continued expense. They frequently make excellent hunters, hacks, and showjumpers. It would have been no different in Roman days, the racing industry and the cavalry both absorbing thousands of horses each year. Both sections would have had a natural wastage, and a very high accidental one due to track breakdowns, injuries and fatalities, and battlefield injuries, deaths and viral epidemics. The fact which seems to confirm the existence of dual purpose ranches is that many of the army's cavalry horses came from the same provinces that also raised noted racehorses – Africa and Spain in particular.

Diocles tells us that he was the best driver of African horses, and though his inscription does not state that the named horses were African – indeed some of the names are non-African but this need not be considered evidence for origin – it is probable that as they were his best performers they were of African blood, even if bred in Italy. His remark is very revealing for another reason. It implies that such stock needed much skill to drive and to achieve optimum performance. If, as I believe, the African, Numidian and Libyan horses had much the same genetic makeup as today's modern Arabian this is very understandable. Arabians are extremely intelligent, do not suffer fools gladly, will not tolerate insensitive handling, but respond magnificently to riders (and drivers) with whom they have a rapport. The average Arabian is desperately keen to give 110 per cent. The conformation of the Arabian head allows for greater brain capacity, and the attitude has to do with quickness of mind linked with the desire to cooperate, plus the sensitivity of well-bred horses where the nerve endings lie close to the skin surface, which in coarser, thick-skinned horses are buried deeper. Diocles quite clearly found he had a better rapport with African hotbloods.

The unknown fourth-century traveller who wrote a World Travel Guide for his son after an extensive Grand Tour seems to have spent a large amount of his time visiting the various circuses and studs scattered around the Empire. Almost every provincial capital boasted a thriving circus, packed to capacity with ardent fans watching horses from many countries compete against each other. A rich racing buff wanting to get involved in breeding horses for the track, and be rewarded later by seeing them run successfully, albeit maybe not in his ownership, could well have profited by reading this traveller's *Expositio Totius Mundi et Gentium* before he set off on a buying spree. It lists the main centres where good horses could be obtained, and does so in a non-partisan manner. Highly recommended were the Cappadocian (no. 40), Spanish (no. 59), Numidian (no. 60), African (no. 61), Pentapolitanian (no. 62), Sicilian (no. 65) and Sardinian (no. 66) stock, while the writer also affirms that the best charioteers came from Laodicea (32). The value of this from the equine angle is that for centuries literature had been pointing to these sources as areas where top-class animals could be purchased, mostly in isolated references recounting single instances of noteworthy breeds.

From the charioteer inscriptions further information can be culled. The breed of horse is sometimes given, along with the nationality of the drivers. Only the best would be recorded, but that need not surprise us. Even the person who has no interest in racing in general will often know who owns, trains and rides the winners of the major races – in Britain the Grand National and the Derby, in Australia the Melbourne Cup, in France the *Prix de l'Arc de Triomphe*. The also-rans go mostly unrecorded, as do their jockeys and trainers, until such time as a rank outsider captures a major prize and the media limelight. In Rome it was no different. Although in early days the honours went to the owner of the winning horses, this changed fairly rapidly and the real adulation went to the drivers and the horses themselves. Today honours are shared by the trainer, who would be paralleled by the *domini* of a faction. The actual owner, although taking the bulk of the money prize and a handsome trophy, does not receive a proportionate share of recognition.

In those charioteer inscriptions where breed of horse is mentioned, we can get an idea of the current trend in what would be equated with today's bloodline preference. A contemporary of Diocles, Aulus Teres, listed 42 successful horses on the wall of the Castel St Angelo in Rome. Of these 37 were African, 2 Spanish, 2 Greek, 1 Gaulish. The same driver records that he drove two African horses called Callidromus and Hilarus to 100 and 1,000 wins respectively: '*Palmas sibi complemit centesimam Callidromo Afro, millesimam Hilaro Afro*' (quoted in Cameron 1973, p. 66). African (Libyan) horses were noted, especially by Oppian, Nemesian, Gratius Faliscus and Aelian, as being very tough, enduring horses. To run, let alone win, 1,000 times means staying sound over many years and racing well beyond the age most such successful horses today would have been retired to stud. Diocles, as we have seen, also had a high success rate with African horses. P. Aelius Gutta Calpurnianus, a very successful driver, seemed to drive African horses to the exclusion of all others. He names four African horses with a total of 309 wins between them for the Blues – Germinator (92 wins), Silvanus (105), Nitidus (52) and Saxon (60) – followed by his wins for the Greens with the African Danaus (19), Oceanus (209), Victor (429) and Vindex (157). The last three do not have the breed appended, but I think we can fairly safely assume the same origin for these as all his others, particularly as breeds tend to have physical characteristics that match, and height and length of stride would be very important in a racing foursome (*ILS*, 5288). In the lines immediately before his claim to being the 'best driver of African horses', Diocles gives the usual comparisons and comments on the other eminent drivers of African horses. Pontius Epaphroditus won with his Bubalo 134 times, and Pompeius Musclosus won with another African horse, whose name is illegible, 115 times. Epaphroditus was driving in or about Domitian's day, as he drove for the Purple faction which was started by Domitian along with the Gold faction (*ILS*, 5282). Both these factions had a short-lived popularity (perhaps because Domitian was murdered after a tyrannical rule and suffered the *damnatio*, his factions probably ceased functioning immediately he was dead).

These records point to a long span when African horses were at the top – from at the very latest the demise of Domitian in AD 96 to the mid-second-century career of Gutta, and probably for far longer than this. Other indications of specific breed popularity are given from literary sources as well as pictorial evidence. The latter comes primarily from North Africa and Spain and would naturally depict mostly native stock, but not to the complete exclusion of other breeds as there was a very lively trade in horses, several countries being known for exporting bloodstock. It was quite common to ship horses in specially constructed horse transports. A mosaic from Medeina in Tunisia shows three racehorses named Ferox, Icarus and Cupido on board, and the type of ship is described by the Latin inscription *Hippago* written underneath, followed by the Greek equivalent (Toynbee 1973, p. 182).

Confirmation that breeders exported horses to foreign tracks can be found in a Barcelona mosaic that shows four *quadrigae* racing with the owners' or breeders' names branded on the horses' flanks. Two of the names are C. Sabinus and Sorothus. Another mosaic, this time in Algeria, shows a horse called Muccosus standing idle. He is branded 'Pra' for the Green faction, and 'Cl. Sabini' for owner or breeder Claudius Sabinus, thus showing that Claudius Sabinus from Cherchel in Algeria either raced his own stock in Spain, or sold horses to the authorities there. The Sorothi brand was worn by horses bred at a stud farm owned by the Sorothi family. J. H. Humphrey places this farm exactly in the hills near Souk Ahras, not far from the Algerian border, as a result of the discovery of an inscription mentioning the Saltus Sorothensis. The owner had a principal residence in Hadrumetum (Sousse) (Humphrey 1986, p. 320). Sousse has a marvellous collection of mosaics depicting racehorses, and one panel with three such mosaics contains two circular discs each showing two horses standing one on each side of a palm tree signifying victory. They carry the Sorothi brand. The central mosaic is a pastoral scene with eight horses of various ages. Two are broodmares with foals at foot; one is obviously a yearling; another a two year old; and one pair is of a very tolerant mare with a young stallion attempting an initial covering and getting it wrong – a quite common occurrence until they learn how and where. The mosaic hints at a practice of pasture breeding which would be in line with keeping a very large band of broodmares. This and Varro's advice to grooms on how to cope with a mare and stallion during an 'in-hand service' suggest that both methods were used, as they are today, although a stallion running with his mares does sustain painful batterings as a youngster until he learns which mares are receptive and which are saying 'keep off'. The main Sorothi stud is 200 miles as the crow flies from the Sousse country residence and racing centre, indicating that this wealthy owner travelled his horses extensively in their racing careers.

Humphrey says that Spanish racing was not normally run according to Roman factions except at Tarragona, where a full range of training facilities was available (1986, p. 238). Factions are attested at Tarragona through the incription put up to Fuscus of the Blues (*ILS*, 5301). The alternative would have been racing by privately owned strings of horses. Brands would be more likely to reflect the breeder than the owner, or both if they were the same, and would be a free form of advertising if the horses were highly successful. Most horses branded in Europe today are marked with a breed brand, such as the seven-branched elkhorn brand of the registered Trakehner, but in America brands often signify the owner, with a second brand being added if a horse changes hands.

Although it seems as if the African and Spanish horses held precedence, other breeds were also popular. Gratius Faliscus, an Augustan poet, adds Sicilian and Mycenaean Greek racers to African (*Cyn*.). Oppian of Syria, writing in the early third century AD and dedicating his *Cynegetica* to Caracalla, gives a more complete picture. He rates Spanish horses as the fastest but says they had no stamina. The Libyans (Africans) were endowed with endurance and exceptionally hard feet (Appian says the Spanish have soft feet, and we shall see why this could affect continued performance). Next in speed to the Spanish are Sicilian steeds, followed by the Cappadocian, which Oppian says have courage or in other words the will to win. A horse that is a battler is always termed 'courageous' in racing parlance. Tuscan and Cretan horses are given a good rating but are not as fast as the others. Nemesian, at the end of the third century AD, rates the Cappadocian, Spanish and Greek horses highly (*Cyn*.).

It appears that it was during the third century AD that Cappadocian horses, always highly rated, began to rise to supremacy. Prior to his election as Emperor in AD 238, and while still Pro-Consul of Africa, M. Antonius Gordianus, later Gordian I, sent 100 Sicilian and 100 Cappadocian horses to be shared out amongst the factions at Rome (Humphrey 1986). Sicilian horses must have been having a comeback as they were one of the very early breeds to succeed on the track, right from the days of the early Tyrants of Syracuse. Strabo says that Dionysius of Syracuse collected his stud of prize horses from the Heneti of Cispadana (*Geog.* 5.1.4), and in 398 BC Dionysius sent several Sicilian teams to race at Olympia (Harris 1972, p. 173). It is worth remembering that Sicily also had a very lengthy involvement with Carthage, and wherever Carthaginian troops went so also would there be Numidians with their nimble African horses, these providing valuable outcrosses on Sicilian stock.

Spanish horses were highly regarded in some racing circles during the fourth century. In AD 360 when the army in Gaul acclaimed the Caesar Julian as Augustus, he initially refused the title and wrote a letter to the Emperor Constantius explaining this and at the same time laying down conditions he knew would not be to the liking of the Emperor. He began, however, with a hopeful sop, trying to avoid censure, by offering to send the Emperor a consignment of Spanish horses (Ammianus, *Res Gest.* 20.8). But his ploy failed. As the Emperor was wintering in Cappadocia it is hardly likely that a gift of Spanish horses would arouse delight when he had the finest racers on his doorstep. The high value placed on Cappadocian horses is made abundantly clear only a few years later in AD 371 when Valentinian, Valens and Gratian jointly sent a direction to Ampelius, Prefect of Rome, ordering keep to be supplied to the racehorses from the Hermogenian and Palmatian studs in Cappadocia when they were no longer able to race as a result of either old age or injury. Spanish horses could be sold off, from which we can infer that they were not considered worth maintaining (*Codex Theo.*, 15.10.1). Under the same title it was ordered that Greek horses sent to the circus at Rome should not have their names changed (ibid., 15.10.1.1). In his notes to the translation of the *Codex Theodosianus* Pharr states that this was done to avoid misrepresentation since Greek horses, at that time, were considered inferior. To me it also suggests very good documentation of all racing animals, and that branding with the mark of the stud where they were raised was not a universal practice.

Under the heading 'Imperial herds', a law of Arcadius and Honorius to Caesarius, Praetorian Prefect, dated to AD 396–7, imposed fines for appropriating horses from the Imperial herds. Hermogenian or Palmatian horses rated a fine of one pound of gold (12 oz. or 339 g).

Other horses were rated at half a pound of gold, or half the value of the Hermogenian and Palmatian stock (*Codex Theo.*, 10.6.1). This shows the extent to which the Emperors by the Later Empire controlled the best racing stock available, and how loath they were to let anyone else gain possession. It could almost be seen as an indirect tax on the very wealthy. By Late Empire the Imperial Studs supplied the bulk of the racehorses to the factions at the tracks. The aspiring high official was obliged to put on expensive race meetings, and in order to avoid gathering the necessary horses and charioteers himself he contracted out to the factions, who in turn would pay for horses supplied by the Emperor. It is unlikely that the price of Imperial horses would be haggled over. There were exceptions to the rule, but great problems were encountered in obtaining stock. Spanish horses had to suffice for the rest, even for the not-so-ordinary man, as the Consul Quintus Aurelius Symmachus found when he started his quest for horses several years in advance of his son's praetorship games of AD 401 (Cameron 1976, p. 8). References to African horses seem most frequent in the Early Empire, and to Spanish and Cappadocian horses in the later era. Thus the inscriptions and the historians and poets spanning several centuries give us a good idea of the standing of breeds at specific times in the history of racing.

Naturally with the huge demands made on breeders even moderate horses would find their way to the minor tracks. Most of the horses raced were stallions, as relatively few names for mares occur in comparison to the hundreds for males. The mares would be mostly kept in the studs for breeding and only those found barren would be sold into the active market. Mares would also start with two slight disadvantages. Stallions are generally speedier than mares, not by much, but enough, although this is not to say that all stallions would beat all mares. The other disadvantage would be when the mares came into oestrus. It would be disruptive to the stallions, a fact a clever charioteer could use to his advantage, and frequently a mare on heat becomes cantankerous and unreliable for a few days.

Early handling of racehorses must have followed much the same lines as those of other horses and diverged when it became apparent which section of the market each horse was best suited for. A stud specifically geared to producing racing stock would hope all its colts would turn out to be Secretariats or Mill Reefs. Virgil tells us that 'racers and chargers are both a job to breed; for either it is youth, mettle and pace that trainers first demand' (*Georgics* III.118–20). Later, he says, well before the training proper begins, a trainer will accustom the horse to 'bear the squeal of dragging wheels and hear the jangle of harness in stable' (ibid., III.183–4). During the breaking-in process the horse might be kept on short rations, because Virgil also states:

when they're broken in, fill out their bodies with coarse mixed mash, for until you break them, their hearts are too high flown, they jib at handling, refuse to bear the lash or obey the cruel curb. But the most effective way to reinforce their strength is to bar them off from the passion and blinding goads of lust. (ibid., III.205–10)

Keeping a horse on minimum rations is still occasionally and wrongly thought to make the breaking job easier. It may help initially, but once well fed, if the horse is of an argumentative disposition the job has to be done again. Virgil's lines give some idea of procedure and imply that no disobediences were brooked, and that harsh handling was resorted to in order to subdue young colts.

Pelagonius gives us a more reassuring picture. Horses intended for the track were not raced in the circus until they were five years of age, but their training started in the third year, that is as a two year old. The best could still be racing at 20 years of age (*Ars Vet.* I). This speaks highly of the soundness of the best animals and the knowledge of the trainers and vets that putting a horse under pressure before he was mature shortened his useful life. A racehorse would need to be accustomed to certain conditions not met with by saddle horses, and the Greek system operating in parts of the eastern Empire continued some races for ridden animals.

One of the first things a young horse is taught today is to work on the lunge-line. The horse works around the handler in a circle with a radius of up to about 20 feet (6 m). He obeys verbal commands to change pace and gait, and to start and stop. Stopping is reinforced by the rein attached to either a cavesson, halter or bit. Occasionally a strong arm is needed when a youngster erupts. A horse well taught becomes obedient, smooth in his paces, and supple on the bends – a very necessary attribute for a chariot horse. That this system was known to the Romans is hinted at by Aelian, who says it is a method employed by Indians: 'Indians compel them [the horses] to go round and round returning to the same point. Now if a man would do this he requires strength of hand and a very thorough understanding of horses. Those who have perfected this try the same method of driving a chariot in circles' (*de Nat. Anim.* XIII.9). It was considered very clever to be able to do this. Although Aelian's collection of anecdotes about all sorts of animals was a real miscellany, some of which was very fanciful, some just repeating what he had heard or read, his reporting here suggests that he may have been acquainted with the process. This belief is strengthened by his previous remark about Indian horses being controlled by spiked muzzles (nose-bands) which allowed their tongues and the roof of their mouths to go unpunished (ibid., XIII.9). Few riders understand the complex action of severe bits, and this shows that Aelian had considerable knowledge of the complexities of such bit action. However, even though he shows such understanding, one may suspect that Aelian took this extract from Arrian's *Indica* and quoted it incompletely, because Arrian goes on to explain the actual bit action which is added to the spiked noseband favoured by the Indians (*Ind.* XVI.10–12). Nasal pressure is a common way of controlling horses today in either bosal or hackamore restraint, luckily without the spikes. Of course, Aelian may also have seen the Indian noseband used without the bit.

The other vital steps in the training of a circus horse would be to accustom him to the feel of the yoke, the pole and the traces. The latter can be done very simply through long reining (see Ch. 7), during which the horse gets accustomed to his sides being touched by the reins, and his turns indicated by a pull on one rein accompanied by a slight slackening on the other. Failure to obey a signal for a turn can be corrected by sharply swinging the animal around and thus teaching him to obey the bit before he is hitched for the first time. Today a light cart would be used as a training vehicle, sometimes with slightly longer shafts than normal so the horse is not frightened by too close a proximity to the body of the cart. He also has to learn to turn either with shafts in a single hitch or a pole in a double hitch. All these things take time and the process would have been roughly the same in Roman days. There are plenty of carvings, usually tombstones of cavalrymen, showing horses being long reined, proof that the technique was well understood.

The padded and contoured horse collar was not invented until well after the Roman era and draught animals were fitted to their vehicle by a neck yoke, which put severe strains on that part of their anatomy and meant that they could pull less poundage than today. Depictions of chariot horses show them harnessed variously, sometimes at the chest and sometimes midway between chest and gullet, but this is often due to lack of artistic accuracy. There are many illustrations and carvings, coins, and so on, from the Greeks, the Romans, and much earlier cultures to show that a breast harness was normally employed. Harness racehorses today wear a similar rig that is light, strong and supple and suited to the extremely lightweight sulky they draw. It would have been impossible to elicit any speed if the gullet was constricted, as the horse would be denied adequate oxygen. The only puzzle is why the obvious advantages of maximum traction via the shoulder took so long to develop.

Once through basic training the young racehorse would be consigned to the racetrack. It is not known how the system operated, but it is a fair assumption that speed and suitability were tried out. Pelagonius implies that the training process was a lengthy one. The young racehorse would learn to pull in partnership with another horse and for this he would be started in a *biga*, before proceeding to the more difficult *quadriga*. Parity in stride and amenability in temperament would be vital in a team. Common and horse sense would dictate that team speed trials would come much later, when horses were working in concert. Speed is always the last thing scheduled in any sensible training programme, and flighty colts could get excited and pull against each other with disastrous results. There would be enough upsets in real competition without having unruly horses to start with.

The next stage would be the introduction to the race itself. It is not known if races were organized at grass-roots level, but large studs would have had their own training tracks so that they could make an initial selection. This would have been narrowed further by competing at local tracks. The popularity of racing was such that almost every town would have some sort of facility, even if only a dirt track on a level bit of ground. This would have been ideal for small-time breeders to test their animals on, hoping to catch some talent scout's eye with a view to later dealings. Juvenal informs us that in his day small studs were common. Writing of the yield of a provincial farmstead he describes 'a few yoke of oxen, one stallion kept for stud, a small herd of broodmares' (*Sat.* VIII). For the largest studs the system of sales would be somewhat different. They would have had the power and prestige to breed from the best stock and to have the buyers flock to them. Some studs probably had supply contracts with factions. This is strongly suggested by the mosaic at Cherchel, Algeria, where not only the owner or breeder's name Sabinus is branded on the horse, but that of the faction also – *pra(cina)* for Greens.

We know that racing at Rome, as well as at other large cities was organized in factions. The smaller centres would not have had the means to operate such a large establishment, particularly when official racing would only happen on a few days each year. This argues for private enterprise at the smaller tracks, with horses either entered by individual owners or, when the official races took place, being hired by the magistrate, who had to foot the bill.

With their immense purchasing power the factions would have bought direct or by contract from top breeders. Other sources of racing stock would be by political gifts such as Gordian I made. Civic-minded wealthy men, who nearly always had town and country estates, would also make occasional gifts, particularly if such generosity helped their political careers.

In early times the annual race days were few, mostly falling on religious festivals. In the time of Augustus, races were run on 17 days a year and by the fourth century this had risen to 66 (Cameron 1976). The number of races per day provided a very full race card by modern standards. Claudius sanctioned running as many as possible in a day to celebrate his British triumph, but Dio tells us that not more than ten could be run (Dio, LX.23.5). Not long afterwards a consul, Asiaticus, resigned because of the expense of footing the bill for the Circensiam Games, where the daily number of races had risen to 24 (ibid., LX.27.2). This increase in races was having a far-reaching economic effect on the senatorial class. An official's political success often depended on the lavishness of the races he offered the public, so his pocket would frequently be called on to a far greater extent than he could afford. Added to this it was the custom that should any mistake be made in the format of presenting the games, the whole event had to be run again.

> It had been the custom that if any detail whatsoever in connexion with the festivals was carried out contrary to precedent, they should be given over again, as I have stated. But since such repetitions were frequent, occurring a third, fourth, fifth, and sometimes a tenth time, partly, to be sure, as the result of accident, but generally by deliberate intent on the part of those who were benefited by these repetitions, Claudius enacted a law that the equestrian contests in case of a second exhibition should occupy only one day; and in actual practice he usually prevented any repetition at all. For the schemers were not so ready to commit irregularities now that they gained little by doing so. (Dio, LX.6.4–5)

At its height, such abuse must have greatly profited breeders and dealers in horses, but put a very real strain on the animals themselves. It would also have hugely raised the number of days' racing the public could enjoy if the additional days were added to the official number. How much of the Empire's fiscal and agricultural resources were consumed by the races would be hard to work out, but it must have been a very real burden on the economy as it was not just bread and circuses for the idle populace, but barley, beans and hay for the hundreds of horses maintained in major cities and the smaller, though still considerable numbers kept elsewhere.

It is clear from many of the historians, Dio Cassius and Suetonius in particular, that the racing mania gripped both high and low. Many of the emperors were just as addicted as the plebs were to horseracing. Gaius, Nero, Domitian, Commodus, Caracalla and Elagabalus in particular spent fortunes on the sport. With the exception of Domitian, who is not recorded as actually racing himself, the others frequently took the reins. On his Grand Tour of Greece, Nero even tried his hand at driving a ten-horse hitch with unfortunate results, as he fell out of the chariot and his considerable bulk had to be crammed back in (Suetonius, *Nero* 24). Other emperors were also keen race-goers but restricted their participation to watching from the 'Royal Box'. Nero increased the number of races to such an extent that racing went on until nightfall. Faction managers no longer thought it worth while to bring out their teams except for a full day's racing (ibid., 22). Obviously delighted with the increase in business, they felt they could turn down less profitable engagements. Domitian went even further with his introduction of the two new factions, Purple and Gold.

He is also credited with increasing the number of races to 100 per day, and to fit them in reduced the number of laps from seven to five (ibid., *Dom.* 4). It has frequently been assumed that this increase was a general one, but Suetonius clearly states that the number was increased to 100 for the Saecular Games of AD 88, a religious festival at which equestrian games were given and which was only supposed to happen once every 100 years – although as Claudius had celebrated them in AD 47 Domitian was somewhat ahead of himself. A hundred races in a day, even over a shorter distance, would be almost impossible to stage on a regular basis. The horses' legs just would not stand such punishment, and the sheer organization, however much money could be spent, would result in chaos with literally hundreds of horses and handlers crowded around. I should think it very likely that once was enough, when it was realized just how over-ambitious it was. The horses were not stabled at the Circus Maximus, or at the other four racing centres in Rome, but at the Campus Martius, which also incorporated the Trigarium where they were exercised and trained. The Circus Maximus is at least a mile away and taking horses across the city in veritable herds would have posed a huge logistical problem! Martial confirms this as an exceptional occurrence when he describes the games of Stella given in honour of Domitian's triumph over the Sarmatians, where 'Caesar gave 30 prizes of victory, which are more than even both the consuls give' (*Epig.* VIII.78). Martial was an avid race follower with his witty pen on the pulse of Rome, and he highlights the norm which would appear to be 15 per day. However, there were so many exceptions to the average, and so many pretexts for giving games, that it would seem that the number of races depended on a man's wealth and generosity, and the frequency of race days must also have been erratic as every major happening seemed to be an excuse for a day's racing. An impromptu day was even given by Caligula for the asking, for he was besotted with racing and horses in general (Suetonius, *Gaius* 18).

The day before a race a trial was held – *Probatio Equorum* (Rawson 1981, pp. 1–16). Presumably this was a selection from the bulk of stock held at the faction stables to determine which horses raced the following day. It may have taken the form of a veterinary inspection to make sure they were sound. Before most stressful competitions today there is such an inspection to safeguard animals against possible injury. It would have made sense to race the fittest, and we know from Pelagonius (*Ars Vet.*) that faction stables had their own qualified vet, so this would have been one of his duties.

Much has been written about the pomp and ceremony of the circus and the actual racetrack, but little about the goings on behind the scenes. There must also have been provision for sufficient stalls to accommodate the number of animals entered for the races, particularly as festivals often took place over several days. There would have been a steady supply of fresh horses from the stables to the circus and return of horses entered in one race only, or injured or lamed animals. The number on a card implies that for races held over a number of days most animals would be expected to enter several events during the festival, especially when the card was expanded to huge proportions. The number of wins clocked up by some horses virtually confirms this, as they would be unlikely to win every time out. Horses winning hundreds of victories, like Fortunatus' Tuscus with 386 wins, would have to run multiple races during a festival even in a racing career spanning many years (*ILS*, 5287).

In the Circus Maximus there were 12 starting stalls, or *carceres*, each wide enough to take up to seven horses. The most common type of racing was with *quadrigae*, but *bigae* must also have been common in Domitian's day as Suetonius tells us that he 'gave many extravagant entertainments in the Colosseum and Circus and besides the usual two-horse chariot races he staged a couple of battles, one for infantry and one for cavalry' (Suetonius, *Dom.* 4). The inscriptions left behind concerning the careers of various leading charioteers of the period do not bear out the preponderance of *bigae*. Diocles in his 1,462 wins only had three wins with *bigae* (*ILS*, 5287); Scirtus had all his wins with *quadrigae* (*ILS*, 5283). One charioteer whose name is illegible had 47 wins with *quadrigae* and nine with *bigae* (*ILS* 5284); Crescens first won with *quadrigae* in AD 115 and names his four horses, plus all his wins with the type of teams running – there is no mention of *bigae* (*ILS*, 5285). Scorpus named his whole team of four horses, whereas usually the named horses are the number one horse in a team. Two inscriptions (*ILS*, 5291, 5291a) with pictorial representation show respectively four *quadrigae* and two *bigae* with drivers and the top horse named. Other inscriptions name wins and places but not the type of hitch used. The only charioteers that are firmly dated in Domitian's day are Epaphroditus, driver for the Red and Purple factions (*ILS*, 5282), and Scorpus, immortalized by Martial's epitaph for him: 'O Rome, I am Scorpus, the glory of thy noisy circus, the object of thy applause, thy short-lived favourite. The envious Lachesis, when she cut me off in my twenty-seventh year, accounted me, in judging by the number of my victories, to be an old man' (*Epig.* X.LIII). The others lived on both sides of Domitian's reign. Obviously both hitches were popular, with *quadrigae* the most common.

As well as straightforward racing variations were occasionally introduced. One of these was the *Diversium*, which was restricted to two drivers and involved the winner swopping places with his beaten rival. As some horses will only perform their best for their own driver it was a test of driving skill to get the maximum out of teams which had already given their energetic best. Constantine, a driver racing at Constantinople in the late fifth century, once won 48 out of 50 races held in a day (Cameron 1973). They were all *Diversium* races, and his superlative skill is shown with 23 out of 25 teams belonging to his opponent responding to him. It also highlights that on that day alone 200 horses were performing for just two drivers, as presumably two hard-run events were all a team could be expected to do in one day. *Pedibus ad Quadrigam* was a type of race where, when the horses finished their race, the driver jumped out and sprinted around the track himself. The first combination home was the winner. (Today's near equivalent is the Ride and Tie race, consisting of one horse to two riders/runners with the first team home the winner.) In the *ILS* collection only Gutta is shown as a winner of this speciality, but he won 40,000 *sesterces* for it so it was probably an unusual inclusion of considerable importance on that occasion.

Racing in the circus has many links with modern flat and harness racing in America (see Ch. 7). We think of starting stalls as an American innovation, but the Roman *carceres* operated in much the same way, all opening at once at the pull of a lever. The track was left-handed, as are most American tracks, and the surface was of a hardpacked construction such as is found in modern trotting tracks.

The curved starting end of the arena did not allow all horses to be started at an equal distance from the *creta*, or white line, which stretched across the track. The actual distance covered would eventually be the same: the outside *carceres* would be closest to the *creta*, whereas those starting furthest from the stands had to take an oblique line to the *creta*, as the *spina* had to be given clearance at the start of the race. However, those drawn nearest the *spina* would have a theoretical advantage as they would already be placed well for the first turn. No horse was allowed to break for position before it crossed the *creta*, but then it was every driver for himself. Lots were drawn for starting position and the charioteer who drew first chose his position first. As it went down the list the position chosen by subsequent drivers could affect the outcome of the race. Those drawing in the middle of the pack would have a greater chance of advantage by being able to avoid too close a proximity to certain adversaries, or if they drove a very disciplined team they could possibly upset a rival merely by placing their team too close to another known to become fractious at such proximity. Those with late draws would take what was left of the *carceres*. (A similar situation can be seen today when lining up in the show ring, particularly if riding either a stallion or a mare in heat. Being in the centre of the pack courts disaster with susceptible animals.) Being able to maintain his team's equilibrium would have given a driver an early advantage over other horses, many of whom reacted violently while in the stalls. As a trumpet was used to sound the approach of the race, a track-wise horse could become very excited. Several authors, Ovid, Lucan and Sidonius Apollinaris among them, tell of the horses' excitement as they fretted behind the *carceres* doors. No poetic licence is taken when they describe horses rearing and battering their hooves against the bars and lunging forwards. This is quite normal for some over-excitable horses.

Maybe the description by Sidonius Apollinaris of a *quadriga* race entered by the young court bloods in the fifth century is the most enlightening of all. He is describing what he had seen to one of the participants, his young friend Consentius. It fixes certain facts concerning formula and the way the race was run and is worth quoting at length:

> you chose one of the four chariots by lot and mounted it, laying a tight grip on the hanging reins. Your partner did the same, so did the opposing side.... Servants' hands hold mouth and reins and with knotted cords force the twisted manes to hide themselves, and all the while they incite the steeds, eagerly cheering them with encouraging pats and instilling a rapturous frenzy. There behind the barriers chafe those beasts, pressing against the fastenings, whilst a vapoury blast comes forth between the wooden bars and even before the race the field they have not yet entered is filled with their panting breath. They push, they bustle, they drag, they struggle, they rage, they jump, they rear and are feared; never are their feet still, but restlessly they lash the hardened timber. At last the herald with loud blare of trumpet calls forth the impatient teams and launches the fleet chariots into the field.... The ground gives way under the wheels and the air is smirched with the dust that rises in their track. The drivers, while they wield the reins, ply the lash; now they stretch forward over the chariots with stooping breasts, and so they sweep along, striking the horses' withers and leaving their backs untouched... Now... you had traversed the more open part, and you were hemmed in by the space that is cramped by craft, amid which the central barrier has extended its long low double-walled structure. When the farther turning-post freed you all from restraint once more, your partner went ahead of the two others, who had passed you; so then, according to the law of the circling course, you

had to take the fourth track. The drivers in the middle were intent that if haply the first man, embarrassed by a dash of his steeds too much to the right, should leave a space open on the left by heading for the surrounding seats, he should be passed by a chariot driven in on the near side. As for you, bending double . . . you keep a tight rein on your team and with consummate skill wisely reserve them for the seventh lap. . . . Thus they go once round, then a second time; thus goes the third lap, thus the fourth; but in the fifth turn the foremost man, unable to bear the pressure of his pursuers, swerved his car aside, for he had found, as he gave command to his fleet team, that their strength was exhausted. Now the return half of the sixth course was completed and the crowd was already clamouring for the award of the prizes; your adversaries . . . were scouring the track in front with never a care, when suddenly you tautened the curbs all together, tautened your chest, planted your feet firmly in front and chafed the mouths of your swift steeds. . . . Hereupon one of the others, clinging to the shortest route round the turning-post, was hustled by you, and his team, carried away beyond control by their onward rush, could no more be wheeled round in a harmonious course. As you saw him pass before you in disorder, you got ahead of him by remaining where you were, cunningly reining up. The other adversary . . . ran too far to the right, close to the spectators; then as he turned aslant and all too late after long indifference urged his horses with the whip, you sped straight past your swerving rival. Thus the enemy in reckless haste overtook you and fondly thinking that the first man had already gone ahead, shamelessly made for your wheel with a sidelong dash. His horses were brought down, a multitude of intruding legs entered the wheels, and the twelve spokes were crowded, until a crackle came from those crammed spaces and the revolving rim shattered the entangled feet; then he, a fifth victim, flung from his chariot, which fell upon him, caused a mountain of manifold havoc, and blood disfigured his prostrate brow. . . . (*Carm.*, XXIII)

The passage illustrates that it was not only individual hitches that raced with four horses harnessed, but teams of, in this case, two hitches. Teams of three and occasionally four are recorded. Individuals were the most common, but when it became a team race more tactics could be engineered between the drivers of the teams who would be from the same faction. In the final stages of the race, however, it was every driver for himself. It was similar to having a pacemaker entered in a race, as happens today, to encourage the stable's main contender, the pacemaker not being expected to win.

The passage also highlights the deviousness of Roman racing tactics. Today there is a camera to support a Stewards' enquiry if one contestant is thought to have deliberately fouled another. From many descriptions of Roman racing such tactics were considered part of the normal play – cutting across, crowding out, riding on the tail of another chariot, even whipping another driver's team. Pelagonius has many remedies for eye injury, some of which are for blows to the eyes (*Ars Vet.* XXX.410, 411, 412) and one for eyes scarred by striking from whips (ibid., XXX.413). These clearly suggest that one tactic was hitting an opponent's horses. A blow to the head makes a horse shy away, draw back, or throw his head up to avoid the blow, all of which would be liable to cause a nasty accident when done at full speed. Another remedy for 'recent blows to the eyes' (ibid., XXX.422) implies that sight would be affected for a considerable time after the initial injury was sustained. Out of 35 cures for various eye disorders, covering the whole range of ailments from cancer to keratitis, 14 are for use in conditions specifically occasioned by racing – 11 for blows to the eyes and scars, and three for inflammation which would of course be very common and caused by the flying sand thrown up. Many of the remaining cures are all-purpose salves and unguents.

Other tactics, such as cutting across, could cause what in Roman racing parlance was termed a *naufragia* or 'shipwreck'. The horses would be brought down, tangled in a welter of harness straps and possibly also the shards of a splintered chariot. The driver might have been fortunate enough to cut himself free of the reins, which were wrapped around his waist, and been thrown clear. If not he would be dragged, which would further panic his team who would be a danger to every other team on the track as well. The small amount of protective clothing worn by a charioteer – breast protection, a leather, felt or even metal cap, and some sort of leg wrappings – would afford little real protection under thrashing hooves. Many drivers lost their lives on the track, and though the writers do not tell us about the horses very often, there must have been a tremendous wastage, with horses with broken legs, ruptured tendons, torn backs, or total loss of nerve making further racing impossible.

Great skill was needed to survive the hurly-burly of the track, and the drivers no less than the horses needed strength. In driving a *quadriga* four sets of reins would have to be handled. It is not known if each horse's reins were dovetailed into one, as is the case in a multiple hitch today. They must surely have been for the fancy, spectacular hitches of six to ten horses. *Quadrigae* could conceivably have had all eight reins as single lines, particularly as they were wrapped around the charioteer's waist. The weight of the leather alone would have been considerable, and as the charioteer used his body weight and movement to control and guide his team to a great degree, using some slack in the reins for individual reining, he must have been either of a sturdy physique or the type that is wiry and extremely strong.

That such strength and savage use of reins was employed we learn again from Pelagonius. His treatment for a cut tongue was merely to stitch it up and then wash it with wine and smear honey on the cut each day until it was healed (*ibid.*, V.66). To cut a tongue so badly that it needs stitching takes a tremendous amount of bit pressure. The normal bit for racing would probably have been a snaffle, which works on the bars of the mouth and the tongue (see Ch. 10). Though considered a mild bit today some ancient snaffles were quite vicious, but even so great pressure would have had to be exerted to cause that degree of damage. There are Celtic examples of pairs of snaffle bits used for chariot ponies (Mann 1975, p. 13). Curb bits, as indicated by the quotation above (*Carm.* XXIII.289), were also used. *Lupatus* (curb) is described in the dictionary as a bit with sharp wolf teeth (studs) (Lewis & Short 1966). These could be either on the canons of the bit inside the mouth, on the branches outside the lips, or both, as in the most vicious examples. Today we understand a curb to be a bit that has a long branch outside the mouthpiece and is operated by bit, poll and chin groove action. I do not think this applied so rigidly in Roman days, modern translators, who are not necessarily horsemen, taking curb to mean any severe bit. This is important in the context of racing. A true curb would be very impracticable to use on a four-horse team that needed direct contact with the bars and lips of the mouth for the hauling associated with strong driving tactics, especially on the turns. Assyrian snaffles clearly show the wolfs' teeth incorporated on the canons.

One danger to the charioteer that was minimized was that which could be caused by flying tails. Some representations of chariot horses show the tails bound into a club effect. It was the practice with horses who swished their tails to any great extent, as some do particularly when angry or excited, to nick the muscles part way down the dock to prevent this. Pelagonius actually states that part of the tail was removed from the vertebrae, meaning the muscular part, but specifically adds that the tail is not cut off, the wound will heal and the switching cease (*Ars Vet.* XXI.292). Long hairs wrapping themselves around the reins could prove fatal, as when a horse has something caught under his dock his reaction is to clamp down his tail and panic. The driver would have been rendered powerless as he lost all directional control. The tail muscles are exceptionally strong and it would not have been simple to extricate the reins. When the muscles are cut the tail becomes very limp.

Hooves abraded by constant pounding and friction on the sand of the arena caused considerable trouble, a point I mentioned earlier in discussing the good and bad attributes of various breeds. The faction's veterinary surgeon must have had considerable influence when it came to accepting horses into the racing ranks. Soft hooves would not only abrade quickly, but the laminae would break down as a result of incessant pounding on the track. The veterinary manual has several treatments for such abraded hooves, and for improving the quality of the horn. Accidents apart, abraded hooves must have been the commonest problem with which the grooms had to contend, as the more an animal raced the more his hooves abraded, even if they were strong healthy ones. Hooves only grow from a quarter to half an inch (1.1–2.2 cm) a month. This can be helped by superb feeding, and frequent exercise improves blood supply to the hooves, thus promoting healthy growth. The hoof factor would have been responsible, or at least be one of the main reasons, for keeping a large batch of horses at each faction stable. We have already noted that the most renowned racers came from countries with a dry climate and either sandy or rocky going, both conditions that will produce hard hooves; and we have also seen that the Celts are credited with using shoeing as we know it before other peoples, and also that hardly any racehorses from moist Gaul appeared in the Roman circus.

Mosaics sometimes show horses with leg bandages. One in Sousse has four horses so equipped. This information, plus that contained in Pelagonius' work concerning ruptured and fevered tendons, indicates that such injuries and strains were common amongst racehorses. The Sousse mosaic shows the leg bandages affixed in exactly the same manner as support wraps are used today for jumping and eventing horses, as well as horses with susceptible tendons. Another indicator from this mosaic is that all four horses are stallions, shown by the very pronounced muscular jowls which are absent in mares and geldings.

Another hazard for horses and one with which the faction vet was all too familiar was the tying-up syndrome, or azoturia. Some horses subjected to extreme physical stress literally seize up, and the muscles of the hindquarters become rigid. Urine appears bloody, though we know that this is due to chemical action with myoglobin being present in the urine (Hayes 1968, p. 20), not as Pelagonius thought being actual blood. It is due to lactic acid build-up, and over-exertion. Failure to urinate often accompanies tying up, and as the poisons in the system increase the muscles sustain damage. Chapter VIII of the *Ars Veterinaria* gives a very confused list of symptoms, some of which equate with the ailment we understand, some of which are incorrectly diagnosed, but the core of information indicates this very severe condition, brought on as Pelagonius says by 'too much running and frequent journeying and not having the chance to urinate' (*Ars Vet.* VIII.141). Other ailments linked to it by Pelagonius are obviously colic and dysuria (ibid., VIII.140). Azoturia is one of the worst troubles that can plague an endurance horse. A Roman racehorse was put under very similar pressures, particularly those animals that were raced too frequently. The accumulated mileage covered by both types of horses, and the speeds at which the two types of races were run, are closer than in any other equestrian sphere.

Races were scaled according to importance, either by prestige or by the amount of money riding on the winners. It was considered a most prestigious win if a driver won the race held immediately after the *pompa*, or ceremonial entry, in which everything and everybody took part, from the multiplicity of gods, members of Roman high society, and performing acts, as well as the charioteers who were to take part in the day's races. Presumably they were already driving their top teams in preparation for the first race. Other races were classified by prize money, with 60,000 *sesterces* at the top end of the scale and other major prizes decreasing by tens of thousands to 30,000 *sesterces*, which seems to have been the lower limit of the major prizes. Diocles also mentions 15,000 *sesterces* won with *triga* on several occasions, but not amongst his major wins (*ILS*, 5287). The *annagonum* was a race for what we would consider novice or maiden horses. In Rome it was for first-time runners. Today a maiden stays in that category until it has won, and then becomes a novice. Presumably in the Roman circus the distance would be shortened for such horses, but there is scant mention of these events. Gutta, who was a driver for all four factions during his career, only records two such wins out of a lifetime's victories, variously but not always accurately estimated (*ILS*, 5288). Complementing the novice status of racehorses was the apprenticeship of young drivers who were only allowed to drive *biga*. An inscription from Tarragona in Spain is dedicated to a young driver named Eutyches, who died while still a *rudis auriga* (Humphrey 1986). A few of the inscriptions mention victories won *remissus*. This must have been the occasions when races had to be re-run for a multitude of reasons, mostly connected with a lapse in following the traditional pattern. That so few are mentioned must have been proof that Claudius' edict, against what was becoming an engineered abuse, was continuing to be successful (Dio, LX.6.4). Then comes the *revocatus* which must surely be equated with a disqualification, which today usually follows on a Stewards' enquiry into fouling, rule infringements, or doping. If so it implies an attempt at some form of judging and an element of fairness in running the games. Martial supports this when he comments on a charioteer of the Green faction winning races even though Nero is dead, proving that victories were earned by merit, not by rigging a race to appease an emperor known to support that faction (*Epig.* XI.XXXIII).

Presumably the tactics we would consider foul play were just part of the risks accepted by participants.

Money, of course, could be a massive incentive. To keep a driver racing for a faction, a cut of the purse must have come the charioteer's way. If he was a freedman or of free birth he could transfer his talents to the highest bidder. This could well be the reason that so many of the top drivers drove for all four factions during their careers. Juvenal puts it very neatly: 'you'll find that a hundred lawyers scarcely makes more than one successful jockey' (*Sat.*, VII). Nero's father, Gnaeus Domitius Ahenobarbus, considered an unpleasant character who had purposely run down a lad with his equipage, also tried to cut his expenses, when praetor, by swindling victorious charioteers out of their prize money. When the managers complained he decreed that all future praetors had to pay prize money in cash on the spot (Suetonius, *Nero* 5). Having saved himself the cost he made sure all the others got lumbered with it. The cost of putting on the races was just about the heaviest liturgy a man could bear, and it broke many a rich man. Juvenal captures the essence of the races, the prestige, the cost, the frenzy of the crowd, the chance to flirt:

> Now the spring races are on; the praetor's dropped his napkin and sits there in state but those horses just about cost him the shirt off his back one way or another; and if I may say so without offence to that countless mob, all Rome is in the Circus today. The roar that assails my eardrums means, I am pretty sure, that the Greens have won, otherwise you'd see such gloomy faces, such sheer astonishment as greeted the Cannae disaster after our Consuls had bitten the dust. The races are fine for young men; they can cheer their fancy and bet at long odds and sit with some smart little girl friend, but I'd rather let my wrinkled old skin soak up this mild spring sunshine than sweat all day in a toga. (*Sat.* XI)

As the sport continued to escalate in popularity the urge to outdo previous quaestors, praetors and consuls in the magnificence of 'their own' games finally brought legislation to bear on the amount that could be spent on such events; who could be held liable to pay up; who was exempt, along with the fines such persons were to pay if they tried to wriggle out of their obligations. There were a great many laws passed, all codified in the *Codex Theodosianus*, and a few will be sufficient to give an idea of the legal structure, and also the expense. Although this was in the latter half of the Empire it was the abuses and the unfair burdens that had gone before and were escalating that made such laws necessary.

(1) No person under twenty years of age was to be liable for any obligation to pay for games (*Codex Theo.*, 6.4.2).

(2) All men of the rank of Most Noble who dwelt in the diocese of the Praetorian Prefect were to be compelled to come to Rome with cash in hand for the games (ibid., 6.4.4).

(3) Praetors who were elected several times were liable to diminishing amounts (ibid., 6.4.5): for the first (Flavial) praetorship they had to pay 25,000 *folles* and 50 pounds of silver; for the second (Constantinian), 20,000 *folles* and 40 pounds of silver; for the third (Triumphal), 15,000 *folles* and 30 pounds of silver.

If senators liable for the expenditure tried to escape their obligations, they were to be fined 50,000 measures of wheat. Paying the fine did not absolve them from also paying for the games. These laws were passed during the reigns of Constantine and Constantius. By the time of Gratian, Valentinian and Theodosius, the burden had become so heavy that additional praetors were appointed and the cost shared between the parties (*Codex Theo.*, 6.4.25):

(4) The functions of the Constantinian and Constantian praetorship to cost 1,000 pounds of silver shared between two praetors.

(5) The functions of the Theodosian praetorship to cost 1,000 pounds of silver shared between two praetors.

(6) The functions of the Triumphal and Augustal praetorship to cost 450 pounds of silver and to be shared between two praetors.

(7) The functions of the Roman and Laureate praetorship to cost 250 pounds of silver and to be shared between two praetors.

There was even a law passed to make sure each paid his appointed share, and if he failed, he faced an even greater burden of paying the whole bill for a day's racing:

> of the five praetors who had been assigned to the Theodosian Aqueduct [by a law of the previous day moneys for games had been diverted to the Aqueduct project] I command that the one who limits his share to 100 lb silver shall be assigned to the festivities of the birthday of the Emperor Honorius. (*Codex Theo.*, 6.4.30)

There are other laws enacted but the above gives an idea of how the system operated and how onerous it was.

There were also stringent laws against magic, much of which was connected with the circus. Many lead curse tablets have been found, specifically alluding to the circus, whereby a curse would be put on a driver and his horses by a rival. One such comes from Hadrumetum (Sousse):

> I adjure you, demon whoever you are, and I demand of you from this hour, from this day, from this moment, that you torture and kill the

horses of the Greens and Whites and that you kill in a crash their drivers Clarus, Felix, Primulus and Romanus and leave not a breath in their bodies. (*ILS*, 8753)

There were many more, some summoning up demons, others showing charioteers pierced with nails, a precursor of the type of witchcraft we usually associate with medieval times.

Ammianus Marcellinus gives three instances of prosecutions for witchcraft involving charioteers. The City Prefect, Apronian, was prosecuting sorcerers partly because he had lost an eye as a result, he thought, of witchcraft, and partly because there had been a great increase in practitioners of black magic. Hilarinus, a charioteer, was convicted of apprenticing his own son to a sorcerer so that he could eventually help his father in secret. Condemned, he was duly beheaded (*Res Gest.* 26.3). Four men of senatorial rank, Tarracius Bassus, his brother Camenius, Marcianus and Eusaphius were tried on charges of being the patron and accomplice in sorcery of a charioteer called Auchenius, but the evidence was insufficient and they were acquitted (ibid., 28.1). Athanasius, a popular charioteer, was found guilty of sorcery and burnt at the stake (ibid., 29.3). These trials took place, along with a general purge of all sorts of civil disorders, followed by savage reprisals, under Valentinian between AD 364 and 372.

While the law governed the finances of horseracing and legislated against corruption, the Church, once it had got over its own initial problems, began to fulminate against the idolatry and extravagance. Tertullian, a third-century Church Father, inveighed against everything to do with the races, seeing demons in every statue, and instructing Christians to avoid places tenanted by diabolical spirits. He berated racegoers for allowing the excitement of the races and partisanship for a charioteer to take the place of prayer; warned against the temptations of gay attire and the chance for men and women to meet and passions to be aroused. Yet in his writings he gives such a good picture of all phases of the spectacle, from the detailed description of the *pompa* to the dress of the charioteers and the behaviour of the restless, excitable mob, that it is quite clear that he was a regular racegoer on many occasions, and one suspects that he earlier appreciated every nuance of the day's sport before he became a bigoted convert (*de Spect.*, VII–VIII).

Fortunately for the masses employed in the circus and its ancillary occupations, the religious rantings were completely ineffectual and at least some clergy were able to appreciate the finer equestrian points on display, as Sidonius Apollinaris made clear in the obvious enjoyment of his young friend Consentius' skilful debut.

16
Daily life

Mules and donkeys

Although the army, the circus and the public post used the greatest proportion of the horse and mule population, both of which held a fairly high monetary value, the wheels of commerce and the sporting pleasures of the moneyed classes kept another large section of the equine population busy. Of the very humble donkey there is scarcely a word in the literature, although the better-bred Reatine ass gets a favourable mention by Varro (*de Re Rust.*). Cato places the little animal firmly in its niche as beast of all work on a farm raising olives (*de Agri Cult.*). Here a donkey rotated the mill for crushing fruit, while others hauled the olives to the press, carted manure, and so on. All such farm duties other than heavy ploughing could be done by donkey, mule or horse power. City streets, great highways, and country roads must have been thronged with pack mules and donkeys, as well as the larger mules and oxen used for traction. Varro stated that herds of asses and mules are not usual, except where large numbers are needed as pack animals around Brundisium and Apulia where the bulk of farm produce is taken for onward movement by ship, but the countless smallholders and market gardeners in urban areas would have owned their string in order to pack perishable foodstuffs to market.

As cities continued to expand, with more and more buildings being erected, one of the commonest sounds must have been the braying of protesting mules accompanied by the thwack of sticks on rumps as the teamsters drove their mule trains from kilns to sites. Horace describes the builder hurrying along with his mules and porters (*Epist*. II.II) A century later Martial complains bitterly of negotiating a steep hill, the crush of mules, and skeins of ropes hauling marble blocks, in addition to being plagued by an always filthy footpath, and all to visit a friend who was never at home (*Epig.* V.XXII).

Not only perishable footstuffs but all of life's commodities would have been brought in by baggage or harness beast. Even if bulk transport was possible by river or canal the short haul from dock to local shopping centre would have needed a never-ending supply of animals. The sheer numbers of animals can never be accurately worked out, but some idea can be grasped when it is realized that a donkey load was assessed at 300 Roman pounds (225 lb or 100 kg), and a camel load at 600 pounds (450 lb or 200 kg). Mules were considerably more common as baggage beasts than camels were, and would have carried closer to a camel than a donkey load. Diocletian's *Edict on Prices* listed transport charges by wagon and by pack at so many *denarii* per mile. A donkey load commonly cost 4 *denarii* per mile, and a camel (or mule) load 8 *denarii*, while a wagon load of 1200 pounds (900 lb or 400 kg) cost 20 *denarii* (Jones 1964). However, this could be varied in some localities, as the Aphrodisias copy of the *Edict* shows, in which a camel load is only half the cost shown above, though the wagon load remains the same (Erim & Reynolds 1973, pp. 99–110). This made vehicular transport considerably more expensive than pack transport, as one such wagon would need at least two and more likely up to four animals to pull it. Two yoke comprising four oxen were allowed for each wagon for transporting sick soldiers (*Codex Theo.*, 8.5.11). As the weight of the carts would be comparable the same estimate would apply to civilian cargo. Even though oxen are less expensive to feed than horses, the difference would not be enough to pay for the lower cost of ox transport. In any case it is likely that mules would not receive such good care and feeding as the more prestigious horse.

Today considerably greater weights can be drawn by mules and horses hitched to a wagon. As we have seen, lack of a suitable collar in the Roman era prevented maximum efficiency. The neck yoke, which seems all right for oxen although still preventing maximum power being applied, constricted the mule's gullet, denying sufficient oxygen to the animal. It also made the animal raise its head and this also reduces pulling capability. Should a wagon be overloaded, with such a system the mules would have ended up with dislocated necks and other disabling disorders. The *Codex Theodosianus* laid down the maximum loads permitted in various carriages in order to protect the public post animals and also, no doubt, road surfaces (8.5.28). Although this applied to a governmental department, private hauliers would also have been bound, if not by law by practice, to similar weights: in contravening the laws they ran the risk, at the very least, of crippling their animals.

The crush of animals in the cities caused traffic jams, tremendous pollution of road surfaces, and the resulting aversion of the lawmaking upper strata of society to wading ankle deep in donkey dung, and being assailed by malodorous smells and a cacophony of noise. Unlike horses, donkeys are extremely and powerfully vocal. Various laws were passed over the years to minimize the problem. Caligula, while in Germany, sent a courier post-haste to Rome with a florid dispatch containing the news of the defection of Adminius, the son of the British king, Cunobelinus, and instructed the courier to drive through the city to the Senate House, even though wheeled traffic was forbidden in the city during daylight hours (Suetonius, *Gaius* 44). Claudius banned mounted travel or wheeled conveyances in Italian towns (Suetonius, *Clau.* 25). The various bans on wheeled traffic and horse riding within city limits were honoured more in the breach, as many references make clear. Severus Alexander allowed senators to use carriages in the city (*SHA*, Sev. Alex., XLIII.1), but that hard taskmaster Aurelian kept to the letter of the law, changing his carriages for a horse on entering Rome (*SHA*, Aur., V.4). Later on Ammianus Marcellinus tells us that the young bloods were still running riot, galloping their horses 'at the speed of the Public Post' throughout the city (*Res Gest.*, 14.6). A law of AD 386 permitted all dignitaries of high civil or military rank to use carriages in town (*Codex Theo.*, 14.12.1). As the capital city had a high concentration of VIPs, their two-horse carriages considerably expanded the city's equine population. There were obviously other exceptions to the ban so that the public transport system could operate. Suetonius tells us that Caligula crippled this for a short time when he went on a private fund-raising spree, selling off items from the palace in Gaul and appropriating all the public conveyances in Rome, as well as draught animals from the bakeries, to haul the load north. Lack of public transport meant that folk outside town could not appear in court when summoned and lost cases by being unable to defend themselves, while the city population went hungry because no flour was being ground in temporarily powerless mills (Suetonius, *Cal.* 39). This one incident highlights the dependence upon equines, rather like the City of London becoming paralysed in a rail strike where no office personnel are able to travel to work.

Ammianus' tale of youths galloping pell-mell through the streets gives another picture of the young, wealthy riff-raff upsetting everyone else by their inconsideration, and scattered throughout Roman literature we find many references to how the rich used the horse for pleasure, sport, exercise and travel.

The Golden Ass of Apuleius, while being a thoroughly good comic novel, also instructs us on second-century equines in everyday life. The fact that mounting blocks were placed outside the houses of the well-to-do implies that their general method of getting about was on horseback (p. 87). Those wealthy enough could afford well-bred horses to ride. Apuleius specifically mentions 'Thessalian Thoroughbreds' and 'Pedigreed Gallic Cobs' (p. 214). The picture of town life thus includes a variety of equines, from the large white Thessalian horse to those of stuffier conformation implied by the word cob, probably for the more elderly riders. By that time it was normal to be riding *in* a saddle rather than *on* a saddle pad or cloth (p. 23). Although the adventures of Lucius were in the guise of an ass, much of what happened to him also concerned horses and equines in general, such as the warranty required on sale which guaranteed the animal to be quiet to ride or drive (p. 168). The poor ass was terrified on seeing gelding irons (p. 151), from which we learn of more than one method of gelding. Vegetius (*Mulom.* I.23) describes a method of castration by depriving the testicles of blood supply, causing them to atrophy and drop off, while Apuleius, by referring to gelding irons, suggests the method used today of surgically severing the testicles. The former method was frequently used in veterinary medicine up until the Second World War, before the advent of modern drugs which anaesthetize the horse, resuscitate him, and prevent future infection.

On one of his forays, Lucius in the guise of an ass was set on by dogs (p. 78), an occurrence familiar today which can cause serious accidents. On another occasion he was commandeered by a centurion for use on army business. This must have been a widespread nuisance to private owners, who would not dare refuse. From the many prohibitions in the *Codex Theodosianus*, we know that military and government personnel were in the habit of demanding services they were not entitled to, such as maintenance for their animals when billeted on private individuals. The billeting was permitted, but not fodder exaction (*Codex Theo.*, 10.2 and 7.8.5.1). Lucius even touches on the lustful behaviour of the ass (p. 216). This was also an unpleasant facet of the arena games under the more depraved emperors, and not all that far-fetched as certain stallions, if not watched and handled strictly, are not particularly choosy about their mates. That this was not an uncommon occurrence is borne out in other writings: Aelian, for one, puts it succinctly in his tale of a horse 'who fancied its groom and got talked about when the horse became too reckless' (*de Nat. Anim.* VI.44).

Shoeing also gets several mentions in Apuleius. In his ass's guise Lucius complains that his unshod hooves were worn down to the quick (p. 82), and later on that he had no shoes to protect his hooves from the hard edges of the frozen ruts, or the projecting pieces of broken ice (p. 192). There are examples of hipposandals for use in icy conditions, and the *solea spartea* was known. A similar kind of rushy hoof covering has been in fairly recent use in Japan. In addition the nailed on shoe was known from the Celtic area, but the practice was not general until much later, towards the end of the Empire.

Apuleius obviously did considerable research for his novel, as his descriptions of animal behaviour and the appalling conditions met with by the dejected mill beasts are so accurate. His ass got a wicked beating for stealing the goddess Epona's rose garland (p. 78). On the donkey level of his mind he ate it because he was starving, having been kicked away from the manger by the Thessalian horse and the other stable occupant. On the Roman level, he hoped he would be transformed back to a human by absorbing the votive offering to the horse goddess.

The harrowing description of the end of the road for worn out beasts is worth quoting:

> As for my fellow animals, what a string of wornout old mules and geldings and how they drooped their heads over their piles of straw! Their necks were covered with running sores, they coughed ceaselessly and wheezed through their nostrils. Their chests were raw from the galling of the breast ropes, their ribs showed through their broken hides from the continual beating and their hooves had lengthened into something like slippers from the everlasting march round and round the mill. Every one of them had the mange. (p. 180)

Several interesting points emerge. The mention of breast ropes suggests that the principle of maximum power and traction was understood. If so, it is curious that a proper collar was not devised until many centuries later. The coughing and wheezing implies the conditions known as broken wind, heaves and roaring. And the overgrown, elongated hooves! Such hooves are frequently seen on donkeys, where the unpared growth forces the animal back on to its heels so that the toes are inordinately lengthened. Donkey hoof horn, being harder than that of most horses, does not break off and splay out as it would with neglected horses' hooves. Juvenal gives a similar picture of the fate of an unsuccessful racehorse who repeatedly changes hands at knock-down prices and ends up turning a mill wheel, neck galled from the collar and fit for no other work (*Sat.* VIII).

The law

Throughout history possession of a horse implied that the owner was a man of means and rank. Possession of mules and donkeys did not, as they were merely the tools of the trade for the farmer and teamster and artisan. Therefore few people were in the fortunate position of actually owning horses, and most references to the civilians possessing them are to *equites*, senators and the wealthy man about town or his sons sowing their wild oats. The right to own and ride horses for other classes of people was largely governed by their trade, and eventually even by law. Varro says that two herdsmen are needed to control a herd of 50 mares, and for this they are to be supplied with riding mares so they could drive the herd mares to their stables at night. Horse and mule breeding must have been on a fairly large scale as he specifically mentions that in Apulia and Lucania this is often the case. Other areas would also have been involved.

Horses were also one of the tools of the trade for nefarious activities such as rustling, and to guard against this it was found necessary to restrict the right to own horses to certain classes, irrespective of whether the man could afford to own a horse. In AD 206–7 an Italian called Bulla headed an elusive robber band, terrorizing and plundering Italy for two years (Dio, LXXVII.10.1–7). To remain at large and continue operating successfully he must have led a mounted force or he would have been easily apprehended. Brigandage and rustling was obviously a major and continuing problem in Italy, particularly in the southern and central districts, for a whole set of laws were promulgated in AD 364 and 365 by Valentinian and Valens. Additional legislation was enacted by Arcadius and Honorius in AD 399. Ownership of horses and mares was restricted to senators and dignitaries, administrators of provinces, veterans who had performed under arms, and decurions (civil). The writ ran in Picenum, Flaminia, Apulia, Calabria, Bruttium, Lucania and Samnium. Any person breaking the law was punished as a cattle thief (*Codex Theo.*, 9.30.1). It is significant that most of these areas were renowned for raising horses, mules, cattle and sheep. A further law denied shepherds employed on the Imperial estates the use of horses in their job, and this restriction was extended to senators' procurators and overseers (ibid., 9.30.2). A year later in AD 365, a similar law was enacted, covering lands as far north as the Rubicon. The only persons permitted to ride a horse were those whose position and rank 'freed them from the suspicion of such crime'. Swineherds were exempt, but were held liable if any thievery broke out in the district in which they were operating. In areas free of brigandage the sanctions did not apply (ibid., 9.30.3). Class distinction did not even permit the idea to take root that the upper classes could be guilty of any such crime, and the poor swineherds must have felt very on edge herding their pigs to Rome, at least until they reached a 'crime free' area.

This law throws a little light on to the importance of pigs to the cities, where the idle populace relied on the bread and pork dole, which was instituted on a daily basis in the reign of Aurelian (*SHA*, Aur., XXXV.1–2). Anyone who has tried herding animals on foot and without the use of trained dogs will know how frustrating and well-nigh impossible it is. A good horse is of enormous value in such work. Pigs can also be extremely vicious and will attack a man. Maybe this fact was also recognized and the swineherd was judged safer aboard a horse. Today, even in Britain, horses are essential in herding jobs (the New Forest has yearly round-ups of both cattle and ponies, and the colt round-ups in particular are very exciting to both horse and rider). These laws were extended even further in AD 300 when shepherds were denied the use of any equine animal under pain of exile (*Codex Theo.*, 9.30.5).

While on the subject of laws relating to the horse, it is interesting to note that the beginnings of the British bridleways system is embedded in Roman law. Under the Praedial Servitudes certain rights do not lie solely with the owner of the land but may be shared by others. One of these, coming under Rustic Servitudes, allowed the right of passage either by riding, driving a herd animal, or driving a carriage over the lands of another. Also under Praedial Servitudes comes the right of depasturing stock on the lands of another, similar to the commoners' rights in the New Forest today. However, if the men who had these rights bought the property, the right did not pass on to the new owner at a subsequent resale, as would be the case in the New Forest (Curzon 1966).

The *Justinian Digest* shows that horses, or rather their owners' vested interests, were also protected. Under the *Lex Aquilia* concerning damages, if a person wilfully caused injury to a man's horse he had to pay the owner the animal's highest value during the previous 30 days (*Dig.* 9.2.27). If the animal died he had to pay the highest value it had attained over the previous year. If the person causing the accident denied liability and was subsequently proved guilty he had to pay double damages (ibid., 9.2.2). If a horse bit someone other than his owner damages could be levied, but if the animal was surrendered damages could be avoided. However, the animal had to be acting out of a character, and if it had been provoked no damages were payable (Curzon 1966).

Many other equine aspects came under the *Lex Aquilia*. For the purposes of law, a slave was lumped into the same category as a horse, mule, or any other animal designated as cattle. It behoved anyone handling, driving or riding mules or horses to know what he was doing and have them under proper control. If they caused injury to another it was deemed negligence and damages were payable. A horse running out of control, or lack of strength or experience on the part of rider or driver was also construed as negligence (*Dig.* 9.2.8). If one member of a mule team or a chariot team was injured not only was damage payable for the injured beast, but for the decrease in value of the un-injured members of the team (ibid., 9.2.22). Striking another's in-foal mare or pregnant slave and causing her to miscarry was also liable to an action for damages under the *Lex Aquilia* (ibid., 9.2.27). Even when animals strayed on to another's land the owner of the land had to treat the animals as if they were his own, particularly in the case of in-foal mares, for should he either drive her harshly or beat her off his land and cause her to miscarry he was also liable to pay damages, even though she was trespassing on his land (ibid., 9.2.39).

With such strictures under Roman law the animals were much better protected than similar animals are today, when cases of wilfully hurting animals are rarely prosecuted, and if they are punishments do not reflect the severity of the injury. This concern shown by Romans was of course not due to sentiment on the part of Roman owners, but mostly concern for protection of property. Equines, particularly horses and mules, were a very expensive commodity, with quality mares only rearing a foal every two years and being considered past prime breeding age by 10 years old, though some still bred up to 15 years of age.

Religion and superstition

The state maintained a considerable number of horses for ceremonies connected with the circus, religious feasts and military triumphs. From scattered references we know these were usually grey, or as they are more commonly termed outside horse circles, white horses. Marcus Furius Camillus, commander of the victorious Roman army against Veii in 396 BC, used white horses in his triumphal procession and was supposedly banished because he had infringed the rights of the gods to whom their use was sacred. In fact he had been guilty of peculation (Dio, LII.13). When Domitian rode in his father's Judaean triumph he was mounted on a white horse, which was the usual steed for princes on such occasions (Suetonius, *Dom.* 2). It was also an exceptional animal of superb breeding, or as Josephus says, 'a steed that was itself a sight' (*Bell. J.*, VII. 152). Under a law of Valentinian and Valens promulgated in AD 372, praetors holding games were entitled to four horses each to pull their ceremonial chariot in the *pompa*. These horses were to be selected from the Imperial herds in Phrygia (*Codex Theo.*, 6.4.19). Emperors had studs in various parts of the Empire, most notably Cappadocia where racehorses were bred. State- (or Emperor-) owned horses were also raised on estates in Thrace and in other parts of Asia Minor (Jones 1964, p. 671). Thracian horses were noted as being huge and white (Homer, *Iliad*), and therefore would have stood out in a crowd. Their other attributes made them suitable for war. As the state produced 'horses for courses' it can be assumed that the Phrygian herds were also white, and also more suited for ceremonial duties than racing. Most civil and military ceremonies and celebrations also had their religious side (or rather the Romans played safe and included some god or other in all ceremonies!), and it would have made sense for all the horses to be able to double up on these duties, and so would therefore have been drawn from a breed showing true consistency in type and colour. Use of white horses was not peculiar to the Romans. Tacitus remarks on the sacred white horses of the German tribes, who used them to predict and warn of future dangers. They were kept at public expense and never worked a day in their lives (*Germ.* 10). We have inherited the legacy of white horses in Britain's Windsor Greys pulling the Queen's coach on state occasions; in America, where the Caisson horses at a President's funeral are white; and in Spain, where the ceremonial horses used on state occasions are also white.

From religion to portents is a fairly short step, and though the Romans may have used their religion more as a political matter than in a really spiritual sense, they were rabidly superstitious and many of the omens involved equines. To us, portents appear ridiculous, but some, emperors most notably among them, placed great stock in them. Others, having more sense, only used the portents to their advantage. Augustus was surrounded by a whole set of omens regarding his birth and future greatness. The most outstanding and graphic must surely have been that dreamt by his father of his son crowned, armed with Jupiter's thunderbolt and sceptre, and drawn in a chariot by 12 dazzling white horses (Suetonius, *Aug.* 94). Even more fortuitous was the donkey called Nicon (Victory), driven by a peasant called Eutychus (Fortune), whom he met prior to Actium. Augustus is supposed to have erected a statue to the pair after winning the battle at sea (Plutarch, *Lives*, vol. I, p. 65). Mule portents appear repeatedly and are interpreted as a good or bad influence according to what subsequently happened, or how the recipient of the news wished to use it. Galba's 'mule' tale harked back to his grandfather's disbelieving statement that when a mule foaled he would achieve greatness. When it did, he was spurred to grasp the purple (Suetonius, *Galba* 4). (Chapter 1 above explains how this so-called miracle is possible because of the chromosome count.) Another gloomy portent that supposedly foretold Julius Caesar's doom concerned a herd of horses which he had dedicated to the Rubicon. They were reputed to be showing repugnance to the pasture and shedding bucketsful of tears (Suetonius, *Caes.* 81). The logical explanation is they must have been off their feed through a virus, one of whose symptoms was runny eyes. Viruses and chromosomes were not understood in Roman times.

In AD 363 Julian was very quick to note a useful portent. He was in the throes of a Parthian campaign when one morning his favourite charger, Babylonius, was brought to him already tacked up; the horse had an attack of colic and, following normal behaviour for colicking horses, got down and rolled, damaging his expensive gear. Julian quickly exclaimed:

'Babylon lies low, stripped of all her finery' (*Res Gest.* 23.3). There were plenty of other portents deduced by the Etruscan soothsayers in Julian's retinue, but this one really shows his opportunistic attitude. One wonders whether Julian was honestly superstitious, as has been supposed. Finally, among a host of other equine portents, a very funny one told by Ammianus Marcellinus occurred in the town of Pistoia (Pistoria) in the mid 360s AD. A donkey mounted the tribunal before a crowd and brayed persistently. No one could fathom what this portended until later Terentius, a baker, was rewarded with the governorship of the province for accusing the ex-prefect Orfitus of embezzlement (ibid., 27.3). Tongue in cheek about plebeian credulity, or merely recounting what he had heard, Ammianus was merely giving a picture of what comes most naturally to donkeys – being where they shouldn't be and making a lot of noise about it.

Private riding

The range of private riding enjoyed by men of means from the rich merchant to the emperor is quite wide. The riding mule and the horse provided the easiest means of getting about outside a town. Vehicular traffic needed several animals and must have been fairly uncomfortable with slow, springless conveyances. Today it is rare to find mules used for riding, most being either the smaller type used as multi-purpose farm animals or beasts of burden, or as in parts of the southern states of America the heavy draught type used for ploughing, which are massively built. Occasionally the smaller, finer type is broken to saddle (I have ridden a rather elegant mule in the USA and a saddle mule is Australia's endurance mileage champion; see Ch. 2). In the Roman world it was very different. Mules were not considered second-grade, plodding saddle animals. Martial has several references to both type and cost, and a well-bred animal could set its purchaser back the price of a house (*Epig.* III.LXII). If it was spirited, it could give a lively ride to a gentleman whose purple cloak marked him as a member of the upper classes (ibid., IX.XXII). For timid riders who feared riding a lofty steed there was a breed of dwarf mule (ibid., XIV.CXCVII).

Martial also refers to gaited horses: 'the small Asturcan horse who picked up his swift hooves in such regular time' (ibid., XIV.CXCIX), apparently a syncopated four-beat gait which is or resembles either a rack or an amble and is ideal for riding without stirrups. Riders of gaited horses such as American Saddlebreds, Peruvian Pasos or Tennessee Walking Horses sit close in the saddle and the horse appears to glide smoothly over the ground. Pliny the Elder describes the Spanish breeds bred by the Gallaic and Asturian tribes, saying that the 'Romans call the horse type a Theldones, though when it is more of a pony it is called a cob! These horses do not have the normal gaits but a smooth trot, straightening the near and offside legs alternately from which they are taught to amble' (*Nat. Hist.* VIII.67). This informative passage, although jumbled as to nomenclature, tells us that the Romans considered an animal a horse or pony according to its size, not its species, and that what Pliny called the trot was in reality the pace, which is a lateral gait. Many *naturally* gaited horses both rack and pace and can be taught to develop either gait, as is also implied by Pliny. (The gelding Katchina, used for much of my practical research into military riding, can do both under certain circumstances – he has to be asked to rack, but on the lunge-line, instead of a true four-beat walk he often paces automatically.) The Emperor Nero set the seal of approval on Asturian horses, as one was his favourite mount (Suetonius, *Nero* 46). In his case he would have needed a smooth ride as his bulk would have bounced off a trotting or cantering horse. Pliny's nephew wrote to his friend Attius Clemens about the death of the son of Regulus. The boy had been thoroughly spoiled and given all sorts of pets, among them Gallic ponies which he used to ride and drive, most probably the same breed mentioned by Pliny the Elder (Pliny the Younger, *Epist.* 4.2). Therefore it would seem as if Spain supplied horses for all uses – racing, military, and for the civilian rider.

There are sufficient references in various works to attest that covered ways and special riding grounds were constructed for the wealthy man to exercise his carriage horses, or take a ride himself without having to cross rough ground or, in the case of a covered way, without getting wet or being exposed to burning sun.

Juvenal is scathing in his comments on the profligate waste of money for luxuries – how teachers worked a full year for what a jockey could earn from one race; how for self-aggrandizement an advocate erected a four-horse chariot statue, and had himself portrayed aboard a charger; and how a magnate spent thousands on a private bath and even more on a covered way, for 'you couldn't expect him to wait till the weather clears, or let his pair get muddy. Better to ride where those polished hooves will keep their lustre undiminished' (*Sat.* 16).

For the country equivalent the description Pliny the Younger gives of his estate in Tuscany and its environs is marvellous (*Epist.*, 5.6). He had an oval carriage drive, similar to a circus track, and in addition a riding ground that would be the envy of anyone who wished to enjoy the exercise and the companionship of his horse, ride in exquisite surroundings with winding, turfed pathways lined with shady trees and flowering bushes, and meander down other tracks scented with rose beds. As a change from the gentler ambling in a sylvan setting more serious training of horses could be done in the central, tree-shaded arena. All this was overlooked by a spectator area provided with dining facilities, individual fountains at each bench. The riding ground even had a suite of rooms, so that someone temporarily confined to bed could oversee equestrian activities (the description is too long to give in full, but it is worth the trouble to look it up). This sensational equestrian complex was all for a man who was not even a dedicated whip or horseman. His use of the carriage drive was moderate, and while driving around it Pliny kept his thoughts on his writing. Occasionally, if his concentration had been great and prolonged, he rode rather than drove but only in order to get it over with more quickly. Just occasionally he hunted, but took his notebooks along with him – a very gentle form of hunting, although in his earlier letter describing his estate he says the Tuscan countryside afforded good hunting (ibid., 9.36).

Aurelian was reputed to have liked living in the Gardens of Sallust, where he built a portico 1,000 ft (305 m) long in which he exercised his horses and himself every day (*SHA*, Aur., XLIX.2). Though much of this work is thought to be spurious and far-fetched, certain elements can be taken at face value. Those which are grossly exaggerated can at least shine a light on to certain customs. The length of this covered way, around a third of a mile, is far in excess of anything that is erected today for exercising horses under cover. Covered linear tracks are not usually built today, though one of the training stables at Newmarket has a covered track built on a huge circle, wide enough for two horses abreast, and the whole roofed with timber, so that ice or heavy going outside need not disrupt training of racehorses. Augustus, on the other hand, had entirely more abstemious habits. In the early years of his reign he rode and fenced on the Campus Martius, but as he got older he took gentler exercise, merely hacking out or going fishing (Suetonius, *Aug.* 83).

Naturally it is emperors who we know most about, including details of their private recreations and personal exploits. As well as the addiction many emperors showed to the races, some were quite tough individuals when it came to riding. Many writers comment on Julius Caesar's superb horsemanship, Suetonius and Plutarch among them. Suetonius also says that Titus rode a horse as well as any man living, and had a horse killed underneath him in battle but mounted another (*Titus* 3 and 4). The emperor who wins the highest accolade in the masochistic equestrian stakes must surely be Caracalla, who as a boy raced his brother Geta in a pony hitch, fell out and broke his leg (Dio, LXXVII. 7.2), but not dismayed continued in adult life upgrading his pony racers to high-priced circus horses and taking part himself (ibid., LXXVIII.10.1–3). Not content with that, he would ride as many as 100 miles on horseback (ibid., LXXVIII.11.3). Riding in 100 mile competitions is a popular sport today, and the distance is perfectly feasible in one day provided proper training is given to the horse and sensible precautions are taken. The world record is held by Australia for 100 miles in under nine hours' riding time. Of course, Caracalla may have used a string of horses, in which case the endurance would have been more of a personal triumph for him. The only time 100 miles is specifically mentioned as being covered by one horse is in the reign of Probus. In booty taken from the Alans, a horse was found that was reputed to be able to travel 100 miles a day and to repeat it for eight or ten days running. On being offered it Probus is said to have declined it, with the comment that such a horse was best suited to a soldier on the run (*SHA*, Prob., VIII.3). A not altogether unbelievable tale, especially as 100-mile rides are now frequently run, whereas only 25 years ago it was considered an impossible feat for a horse. The Alans were noted for their tough horses, and in later years it was considered normal for Mongol ponies in Batu Khan's army invading Europe to cover 60 miles a day in the depths of winter in mountainous terrain, and 80 miles a day was not at all unusual under normal conditions (Hyland 1988, pp. 35–6).

Hunting played a great part in the sporting pastimes of the rich. It was conducted not as we know it, with a pack of hounds but, according to Arrian, with the hounds in leashed couples and a few horsemen. There was a strict code of hunting conduct, mostly concerned with hunting the hare, but the parallels with today's foxhunting are uncanny. Change the quarry and it could be the same sport. Arrian deplored chopping the quarry in covert, but preferred it to get a start and give a good hunt. If it gave good sport he was best pleased by seeing it go free at the end. Each hound was to be known by name, as is the practice today, and praised and fondled after a good chase. He describes the best hare hunting as conducted by a single horseman with a line of beaters handling hounds to be unleashed at the appropriate time. For stag hunting he is very explicit, outlining the danger to hounds, and recommending that in open plains where the going is suitable Scythian and Illyrian horses, as used by the Getae and Mysians, are best. He notes that these horses are uncouth and would win no prizes in the beauty stakes, which would go to the fast and large Thessalian, Sicilian and Peloponnesian horses. But in the hunt the rangy Scythian and Illyrian horses wore the stag down until he stood panting and could be despatched or lassoed and taken away (*Cyn.* 23). Arrian accurately describes the supremacy of the lean, tough, racy endurance horse over the heavier fleshed animal who does well on parade or in the show ring. The exact situation occurs today when the overweight show hunter does well in the show ring but breaks down under stress.

It is from the various treatises on hunting that most information is culled, but apart from Arrian, who concerns himself mostly with hounds, there is little specific information on the hunting horse. Oppian advises riding a stallion as they are swifter than mares, and too much mixed company and the stallion would be likely to scare the prey off with lustful neighing, he comments. Gratius Faliscus says the colour is more important than the breed, and to a degree he is right. He recommends black legs and a brown body – in modern terminology bay; and those whose backs resemble burnt embers – a dun horse with a dorsal stripe and black legs. As we saw in Chapter 1 horses of these colours are known to be hardy and to possess very tough hooves. Both attributes would be necessary, as hunters go where the quarry runs regardless of ground conditions. Much of the Roman hunting territory was stony, unlike the lush shires of typical British hunts. A springtime treatment for hunters recommended by Nemesian is to lance a vein to let old-standing ailments flow out with tainted blood. On bringing a hunter up from grass at the end of summer the old-time English stud groom purged it to cleanse the system – different process, same reason, different seasons. Roman hunting took place more in the summer than during winter, and the majority of hounds were gaze-hounds. Foxhounds would not do very well for scent in the height of summer, which is also when fox cubs are raised. Arrian names three types of quarry with their relative values. The Celts sometimes offered thanks to Artemis in the form of cash payments – 1 obol for a hare, two for a fox, and four for a deer. A wide range of other animals were also hunted. Oppian names several to be taken on horseback: for hunting sheep and wolves a net was used; for hunting hares on horseback the weapon was a special trident; for tigers and bears two long javelins and a hunting bill or knife.

Lions were also hunted, and, in the Dura Europos papyri, hunting lions is mentioned as part of cavalry duties, presumably in a slack period (Fink 1971, no. 1, p. 18). Of course it may be that they were being hunted for the arenas, or because they were causing damage locally, in which case the hunts were necessary. The net result, however, must have been something akin to the pig-sticking or boar-hunting that kept the British cavalry occupied in leisure time in India. Cavalry must occasionally have been a law unto itself, arrogating privileges which no disciplined force would dare to take. On his Parthian campaign, Julian's cavalry came upon the Parthian king's hunting park near Seleucia. It was enclosed by a fence and inside various dangerous beasts roamed – lions, boars, bears, and a host of others. The cavalry broke the fence down and went on the rampage, killing indiscriminately with hunting spears and missiles, presumably arrows (Ammianus, *Res Gest.* 24.5). This account is echoed centuries later by the Mongolian method of teaching young Mongolian cavalrymen manoeuvres and instilling courage into them. Hunting on a front as much as 80 miles (130 km) wide was conducted on a massive scale each year, the animals being gradually driven into a smaller and smaller space. As anyone who understands animals well knows, when those which have any weapon other than sheer speed are trapped they turn at bay and are then at their most aggressive. Some Roman hunting definitely needed a foolhardy brand of courage from man and horse.

Boars were a favourite quarry, needing great skill from the rider, allied with equal courage from the horse when faced with such a lethally armed animal which is so angry when cornered. The most noted Imperial hunter was Hadrian, who was known to be addicted to it, and to have an inordinate affection for both his horses and his hounds – a somewhat rare and endearing characteristic when animals in those days were so often *ballista*-fodder. Hadrian broke his collar bone out hunting and almost had a leg maimed (Dio, LXIX.10.2); the collar bone is still about the most common fracture received out hunting or in steeplechasing, and bad falls cause plenty of leg fractures. Dio records that Hadrian had named a town in Mysia 'Hadrianotherae', or Hadrian's hunting grounds, and that when Borysthenes, his favourite hunter, died he had it buried there with an inscription above the tomb. A highly suspect poem is attributed to Hadrian:

> On his favourite hunting-horse.
> Borysthenes the Alan
> Was mighty Caesar's steed:
> O'er marshland and o'er level,
> O'er Tuscan hills, with speed
> He used to fly, and never
> Could any rushing boar
> Amid Pannonian boar-hunt
> Make bold his flank to gore
> With sharp tusk whitely gleaming:
> The foam from off his lips,
> As oft may chance, would sprinkle
> His tail e'en to the tips.
> But he in youthful vigour,
> His limbs unsapped by toil,
> On his own day extinguished,
> Here lies beneath the soil.
> (*Minor Latin Poets*, p. 447)

It may be bad poetry, but the sentiments are right, and the text informative. It names the breed – an Alan, no doubt similar to a Hunnish horse, from an area noted for tough horses. Borysthenes, swift, courageous, and never bested by the quarry, travelled everywhere Hadrian went in his many peregrinations.

Other riders were not so skilful as Hadrian and paid the penalty. Martial offers timely advice to his friend Priscus who was evidently an adventurous rider in a hare hunt, galloping hell for leather across any type of going. Martial warns of the danger of riding spirited horses recklessly, saying that such speed often kills the rider sooner than the hare. He considers boar hunting safer, since traps were set to lessen the risk to the rider (*Epig.* XII.14). There must have been several methods of hunting boar – the risky Hadrian method that needed courage from man and horse to face an enraged boar, and the uneven contest where the animal stood no chance; also different types of horses – the swift hunter and the more plebeian sort that went at a steadier pace. It would seem that the term 'hunter' in Roman days meant much the same as it does today: any horse on which one hunted, from the elegant Thoroughbred to the stuffy cob.

Many of these wealthy landowners who enjoyed their leisure-time hunting did so in districts far removed from Rome, sent there by the Emperor to act as governors of the Roman provinces. With each governor went a lengthy train of staff and servants, their baggage on wagons and pack mules provided by the state. The system must have given rise to much abuse, governors indenting for non-existent animals. Augustus attempted to remedy the situation by awarding governors a fixed mule and tent allowance (Suetonius, *Aug.* 46). Presumably if they were too extravagant in fitting out their baggage train, the extra cost had to be born by the appointee. By the time of Severus Alexander this had reverted to the old system of supplying judicial personnel with the actual goods. The equipage a governor departing for his province could expect to take with him included 20 pounds of silver, six she-mules, one pair of mules, a pair of horses, ceremonial garments, 100 gold *aurei*, one cook, one muleteer, and, the icing on the cake, a concubine for an unmarried man. All but the latter had to be returned when his tour of duty was finished (*SHA*, Sev. Alex., XLII.4). Just over a century later, the perquisites had increased immensely, and though the letter written by Valerian to Zosimus, a fictitious procurator of Syria, is spurious and the list of contents probably grossly exaggerated, it shows the munificence an officer with Imperial favour could expect to receive. This time the bounty devolved on Claudius, later Emperor (AD 268–70). Supposed to be posted as a tribune, he was to receive from the state treasury vast quantities of wheat, barley, bacon, vintage wine, oil, wax, and as much hay, straw, and cheaper wine as needed. His equine allowance was to be repeated each year to the tune of six mules, three horses, ten camels and nine she-mules. There was also a large quantity of expensive table-ware, clothing, armour and arms – the list continues, but in this case, though Valerian is supposed to have said it was a special case, Claudius was not to commute it all to cash (*SHA*, Claud., XIV.2ff). Tongue-in-cheek, Juvenal gives another description of the lengthy train following a governor to his province. If his wife went with him a herd of she-asses would travel with them so that their milk could freshen her complexion (*Sat.* VI).

Language and literature

Equines occupied a niche in the lives of every class of Roman: the humble donkey turning a mill wheel or carting manure; the prancing saddle mule and his stockier kin weighted with panniers in the winding baggage trains; the aristocratic horse munching hay and barley in a wealthy man's stables. They even found a place in the catch-phrases of the day. A man down on his luck was said to 'have Seius' horse in his stable', alluding to the massive horse bred in Argos at the stud of Gnaeus Seius and sold consecutively to Dolabella, Cassius and Mark Anthony, all of whom had a turn for the worse as soon as the horse entered their ownership. Another, concerning people discontented with their lot, ran: 'an ox wishes to wear a saddle and the horse to pull a plough' (Vigneron 1968). Livy gives us a proverb describing the disposal of a useless animal. During the Hannibalic Wars, a Campanian cavalryman challenged a Roman counterpart to a fight. Evenly matched on horseback, Taurea, the Campanian, challenged Asellus, the Roman, to fight in the confines of a ditch where neither could avoid the other. Asellus immediately jumped off his horse into the ditch at which Taurea lost his nerve and slightingly refused with the phrase: 'what, a gelding in a ditch. I think not' (Livy, XXIII.47). An easy victory, which we would term 'winning in a canter', came out on the Roman tongue as 'to outstrip with white horses', again elevating the white horse symbol. The ubiquitous little donkey also managed to butt his way into daily speech. 'Because an ass peeped' arose from an actual lawsuit where a donkey peeped into a potter's window and broke some pots. The potter then sued the donkey's owner – a rather amusing case of third-party liability. The other, 'all because of an ass's shadow', quoted by Plato concerned another dispute over a donkey. The hirer had dismounted and rested in the shade cast by the donkey and the miserly owner complained that he had hired out only the donkey, not his shadow (Apuleius, *Metamor.*, p. 200).

Games and spectacles

Our last glance at equines in everyday Roman life is not nearly so amusing. Horses were frequently used in the arena spectacles for a variety of acts, rarely as the target, although that occasionally did happen, but more usually as the unwitting prop. Julius Caesar was extremely lavish with the games he gave to win public favour and to celebrate his various triumphs. Suetonius gives a description of the contents of his spectacles. In addition to normal circus races he also had young noblemen competing in chariots, trick-riding as *desultores* where they jumped from horse to horse. Mock battles were also held in which cavalry took part (Suetonius, *Caes.* 39). Caesar was also credited with introducing chariot fights, where two gladiators fought each other from the back of moving chariots. These continued to be popular turns, and there would be teams of chariot horses, slave driver, and the gladiator known as an *essedarius*. In Caligula's reign, a chariot fighter called Parius drew such tremendous applause for freeing his slave driver after a victory that Caligula, enraged at the reception given to what he considered an insignificant act, left in a huff, tripped, and fell headlong (Suetonius, *Gaius* 35). Claudius was rather more generous to his *essedarii*. When four brothers pleaded for their father's discharge as chariot fighter, Claudius complied amid cheers, and had a proclamation read out loud: 'you now see the great advantage of having a large family' (ibid., *Claud.* 21).

No mention is ever made of the horses that drew these fighting teams. Any violent fracas is very upsetting to a horse, who is basically a timid animal relying on speed to escape, so arena horses must have been especially valued for their steadiness under mental pressure. They also needed to be fast and extremely nimble so the driver could place his fighter advantageously for a telling blow to be struck and then rapidly escape from any retaliation.

One arena exploit is exactly matched today. The Roman Thracian bullfighters were the equivalent of the modern bulldoggers, riders who gallop up alongside a bull, jump off the horse and bring the bull down by twisting its neck. The only difference between the Roman and the rodeo event is that today the bull gets up and walks away. The danger in both is very real, and the horses used have to be courageous, fast and very well trained (ibid., 21). Other events were held more for the appreciation of talent in the horses than for the gore spilt. In the days of Titus, 100 days of spectacles to celebrate the opening of his father's Colosseum used horses that were trained to dance in water alongside bulls (Dio, LXVI.25.2–5). This type of entertainment was only a small part of the whole enormous affair in which many thousands of animals were killed.

The Emperors Gordian I and III had a whole zoo from which to choose their animals, but when they were succeeded by Philip the whole stock was slaughtered in the arena at the last holding of the Saecular Games in AD 248. Among them were 20 wild asses and 40 wild horses, along with dozens of elephants, lions, tigers and many other rarer animals – elk, hyenas, hippos and a rhinoceros (SHA, Gordian, III.7; XXXIII.1). No wonder that during the Roman Empire so many animals species came to the verge of extinction.

The slaughter was so enormous and so frequent that one wonders what happened to the remains. Obviously some were used as food to keep those next in line fit for exhibition, but the shambles outside the arenas must have been vast and not all the by-products capable of being used. It would not have been long before putrefaction set in and destroyed some useful parts. Eating horsemeat was repugnant to Romans, as it is to many civilized people today, and only done in the emergency of famine. Horsehair would have been used to form ropes, helmet crests, and so on. Today the strongest lariats and many of the very beautiful mecate ropes used in American hackamores are made of different coloured strands of horsehair and fetch very high prices. Skins could have been used for leather, and the hooves were useful in a travelling medicine kit as receptacles not liable to breakage.

One is left with a picture of equines as absolutely essential in most phases of Roman life, but in that picture there is little of the esteem with which we regard horses today. True, the charger was extolled for the glory he shed on the warrior, and the racer won many plaudits in the circus, but as a companion we hear very little of the emotional bond that can be formed between man and horse and which can be an extremely rewarding one of love and trust. Hadrian had this rare talent and rapport with animals. Arrian through his writings shows that he was very much in tune with both dogs and horses, and even with the quarry he hunted. Maybe the most telling episode of all is that described by Dio concerning the punishments which Severus meted out to the Praetorian Guard members who had murdered Pertinax, executing all those who had been actively involved, and taking their chargers away from the rest and banishing them from Rome. One horse, on being separated from his rider, kept following him and neighing, and in desperation the rider killed both the horse and himself (Dio, LXXV.1.1–2). It sounds extravagant and may be an unlikely tale, but bonding can sometimes be exceptionally strong between man and horse, and in this case the extreme stress of the severity of the punishment compounded by the loss of a friend and companion of many years meant to the man that his last hope was gone.

17
Transport and the Cursus Publicus

We have seen how the equine population was employed in daily civil life, and that the suburbs of major cities and country towns and rural roads hummed with heavy traffic of baggage, cart and ridden animals trotting up and down. On a much wider scale this fanned out into one of the best organizational and operative achievements of the Roman Empire – the *Cursus Publicus*.

The network of trunk roads covering the Roman Empire amounted to a staggering 53,625 miles (85,000 km) (Chevallier 1976, p. 131) by the time of Diocletian. Most evidence for the part played by animals in the *Cursus Publicus* comes from the Later Empire. In Chapter 8, Title 5, of the *Codex Theodosianus*, but also contained in a scattering of laws in other chapters, a mine of information is revealed. Most laws were passed after gross abuse of the system had resulted in the organization being overstretched, its animals overworked, and fodder either priced too high, not available where needed, or stocked to excess in other locations. Several laws were passed repeatedly, which suggests that abuses were widespread, difficult to stop, and even once they had ceased they appeared again somewhere else. The main body of laws passed covered a period from AD 315 to 407.

By the early fourth century the *Cursus Publicus* had already been in operation for well over three centuries, steadily developing and expanding. Augustus is credited with implementing the first system. He kept in touch with the provinces first by relays of runners, and later by organizing a chariot service, based on posting stations, so that the same messenger could travel the whole way (Suetonius, *Aug.* 49). However, well before his day, most of the main roads in Italy were already constructed, and in 148 BC the Romans built their first road outside Italy, the Via Egnatia in Greece (Chevallier 1976, p. 140). They also improved roads as necessary wherever the army was in occupation, and after that initial 'foreign' route, more and more routes criss-crossed the landscape wherever the tramp of armies was heard. Even before Augustus' innovation these roads were already fulfilling what became one of the most important functions of the *Cursus Publicus* – facilitating the transmission of despatches and information. Government officials had their own despatch carriers during the Republic and one inscription (*CIL*, I.551; *ILS*, 23) relates how a praetor, thought to be the later Consul P. Popilius Laenus who held office in 132 BC, 'made the road from Rhegium to Capua and on this road placed all the bridges, milestones and couriers'. (Ramsay 1920, pp. 81–2). This confirms the existence of a postal service and in so doing suggests that there were other regions that had a similar facility. Capua to Rhegium and thence to Sicily and on to Africa would have been a vital route for transmission of information. The army used despatch riders who pounded along the softer edges of the roads. When Pompey was in Spain, he had couriers strategically placed so he could keep watch on Caesar's movements. Caesar reciprocated with a similar mounted courier service. The idea was not new: the Assyrians and Persians had pioneered the system, and Augustus followed by instituting the national postal service for Rome.

As the service mushroomed, so did the cost. At first an Imperial expense, it soon devolved upon the *civitates* in the provinces through which the routes ran. Attempts were made by several emperors to lessen the burden and even to make the treasury totally responsible for expenditure. Nerva freed Italy of the cost of the Imperial post and a *sestertius* of his reign commemorated the event. It is one of the few coins that faithfully reproduces an equine with correct conformation. The delightful scene shows two mules, released from their duties, at pasture. Around the edge are the words *vehiculatione Italiae Remissa* (*RIC*, Nerva, 93 and 104). *SHA* also gives information from several reigns. Hadrian shifted the cost from the towns to the fiscus (Had., VII.5), and his successor Antoninus Pius mitigated the burden by very careful management (ibid., Pius, XII.7). Half a century later Septimus Severus had another try at relieving the people of the cost (ibid., Sev., XIV.2). These repeated attempts show how ineffectual the treasury was in assuming the enormous cost. Without incoming taxes in cash or kind the fisc just could not find the wherewithal, and inevitably the cost reverted back to burdening the private sector.

In addition to its main function of expediting military and government despatches, the *Cursus Publicus* carried important but non-urgent information; ensured promulgation of laws; carried official personnel on their journeys; and hauled state-owned baggage such as Imperial freight, gold and silver, and military supplies, such as armour and clothing. The *annona* and payments in kind also trundled along via the *Cursus Publicus* (*Codex Theo.*, 8.5.13), and sick soldiers were transported in *cursus* wagons (ibid., 8.5.11). To service this enormous organization stops for changing animals were set up every few miles. These were divided into two types: the *mansiones*, about 20–30 miles (32–48 km) apart, which as well as offering fresh animals catered for overnight stops; and *mutationes*, about 8–12 miles (12–20 km) apart, which were merely change-over places. There were also *stationes* for soldiers who were to act as deterrents to the gangs of highwaymen that infested the roads. Escorts to protect valuable shipments of coin were provided by *palatini* (officers of the *comes sacrarum largitionem*) and these drew their mounts from the post stations, not from the military, so it is clear that there was cooperation between the military and civilian operations (*Codex Theo.*, 8.5.48). If the *Cursus Publicus* officials had difficulty in raising whatever was needed to run the system adequately, they brought the army in to help. This happened in Phrygia during the continuous squabble between two villages over who should supply how many beasts (Davies 1967; Frend 1956). An inscription from Gebze (Dakibyza) in Bithynia where the *Cohors VI Equestris* was stationed mentions the presence of muleteers and an agent in the Imperial Procuratorial Service on the staff of the *Cursus Publicus*, showing that the same location was shared by military and *Cursus Publicus* (Davies 1967). This would presumably be one of the larger *mansiones* and it can further be taken that similar situations occurred elsewhere, such locations serving two arms of government.

There cannot have been many people untouched by the greedy maw of a system that literally had to feed tens of thousands of beasts, provide their replacements on a four-yearly rota, and supply the muleteers to work the animals, the vets to see to their health and hooves, the blacksmiths, carpenters, saddlers and wheelwrights to keep the wagons and harnesses in good order.

Travel and shipment of goods by the *Cursus Publicus* was only permitted for officials carrying a valid permit. These came in several varieties, the main ones being:

Evectiones – warrants for use of pack animals/riding animals
Angariae – warrants for use of post wagons (also the post wagons themselves)
Tractoriae – warrants for use of transportation and the right to food and lodging

Warrants also stipulated how many animals could be commandeered. Demanding extra animals was forbidden, and if a person insisted on being supplied with a 'supplementary' post horse, he stood in danger of being severely punished (*Codex Theo.*, 8.5.29). With *tractoriae*, the number of days was also stipulated to prevent travellers extending their stop-overs at government expense (ibid., 8.6.2.). An example of numbers permitted is given below in a law dating from AD 389 issued by Valentinian, Theodosius and Arcadius to Caesarius, the Master of Offices:

> The governors of provinces shall inspect the post warrants, from whatsoever region the travellers may come, and for the service of their vehicles they shall allow counts to employ four posthorses with a supplementary posthorse; tribunes of soldiers, three posthorses each. All other persons, members of the household guard, the imperial bodyguard, and secret service shall be allowed to use only two posthorses each. (ibid., 8.5.49)

Constantine had cause to complain to Acindynus, the Praetorian Prefect, in AD 316, because so many packhorses and extra post horses were being used that insufficient were left for his own retinue. He tried to stop excessive demands being made on the provincials by stipulating that extra horses could only be demanded in emergencies, and on production of an official warrant or, using the legal jargon, 'unless their trustworthiness is recognized'. Presumably they had to carry an identifying badge when requisitioning. It is also made clear that public post animals were only to be used on the official routes, not on side or military roads. The Praetorian Prefect was specifically told that he could use the public post but only in the line of duty, and should it become necessary to deviate he must limit his diversion and the number of animals so used as far as possible (ibid., 8.5.3).

Half a century later, the procurement of unwarranted supplementary post horses had not abated, and in the reign of Constantius had assumed such alarming proportions that many provincials were being ruined by having an inordinate number of extra horses demanded of them over and above what their taxes stipulated. That corruption was involved is shown by the wording: 'has fattened the avarice of some' (ibid., 8.5.7). In this case it was the Praetorian Prefect who was to blame for including the addition of supplementary post horses in the warrants he issued. It was customary for the bulk of warrants to go through the Praetorian Prefect's office and be issued in batches to various officials, governors of provinces, and so on, so he was in an excellent position to milk the system. The only exemptions from the supplementary restriction were the members of the Secret Service who oversaw the movements of troops, another link between the military and the civilian departments. Infringements brought punishment on both the one who released and the one who used the supplementary post horses (ibid., 8.5.7).

Another abuse that put considerable pressure on the *Cursus* was the use of legally warranted animals for the permit-holder's private journeys that he was crafty enough to tie in with his official trip. With the animals already being required to cover considerable distances, and no doubt fed according to that requirement, such abuses would have resulted in many horses being lamed, having condition worn off them, or generally being unfit for immediate duty when their turn next came round. The practice must have been widespread for legislation to bear on it, and punishments were in store, even for high-ranking members of the Imperial service, if they deviated from the route by over 500 paces (ibid., 8.5.25).

This brings us to the distances which these animals would be expected to cover, and the speeds to which they were pushed. In open flat country, distances between stages would be longer than in tough hilly going, so the energy expended would level out. Procopius tells us that between eight and five stages a day, depending on the terrain, were expected to be covered by an Imperial courier on horseback. These couriers were mounted on extremely good, fast horses, and could, if their news was urgent, complete a journey of 240 miles (384 km) in one day (*Secret History*, p. 188). This distance was normally expected to take 10 days, suggesting that an average day's journey consisted of 24 miles (38 km). Even the slowest plodder could manage more than that, but maybe the unfit rider could not, and many of the more usual travellers would not be physically tough. But 240 miles a day for one fit person with repeated change-overs of mount is quite feasible. The ancient world had its own precedent: a courier was expected to do the 1,600-mile (2,575-km) Sardis to Susa run for the Persian kings in a week (Hyland 1988, p. 50). In modern times, the American Pony Express witnessed many hair-raising rides by their talented young riders. William Frederick Cody, later known as Buffalo Bill, made a non-stop 384-mile (618-km) ride in conditions far tougher than that faced by Roman couriers in a well-policed state. Cody ran the gamut of Indian attack when the killing of his intended replacement riders necessitated his epic ride (ibid., p. 58).

The distances given by Procopius would only have been approximate, and a better guide is the itinerary left us by a pilgrim travelling from Burdigala (Bordeaux) to Jerusalem and back (Jones 1964, p. 831). The journey was split into five main sections and his report details the towns, *mansiones* and *mutationes* of the distinct countries crossed. The traveller went by way of France, Italy, Illyria (Yugoslavia) and Thrace, crossed from Constantinople to Chalcedon and thence across Asia Minor to Cilicia, and from Tarsus down to Jerusalem. The journey was just over 3,300 miles (5,300 km) and the pilgrim noted 305 stopping places. This works out at approximately 11 miles (18 km) per stage. In the first section across France the stops were closer by 2 miles (3 km), and from Tarsus to Jerusalem they averaged 12½ miles (20 km) apart. Obviously in more difficult sections they would be closer together, and on easier routes further apart.

Most pilgrims would have to use the equivalent service provided by privately run establishments that complemented the government set-up. There the rules governing the use of animals and the prices for hire of both animals and vehicles would have differed according to location, demand, and to some extent according to what the market would bear, Diocletian's attempt at regulating costs notwithstanding. These establishments would have needed to be similarly equipped to the *Cursus Publicus*, but probably on a much larger scale, as they catered to the majority of travellers from the private person to the merchant and his string of pack-mules. Many users of the commercial operation would have been using their own stock and been in need of stop-over facilities and fodder and grain for their beasts. There must also have been a nucleus of animals available for hire, as continuous stressful work by a string of mules, couriers' horses, or oxen pulling wagons would have taken too great a toll if the animal never got a day's rest. Transport would have been disrupted either by the pace being set far too slow to save stress, or hampered by a percentage of animals becoming unfit through a variety of reasons, of which the most common must have been lameness through soreness, harness galls, and exhaustion. As a result replacement beasts must have been available, and it is sensible to speculate that some code of practice or agreement governed the return of animals from one station to another. If abuse of animals was to be minimized, possibly a deposit was required over and above the normal hire, refundable if the animal was returned in reasonable condition. This would imply co-operation between private entrepreneurs when each facility was owned by one person, and also suggests that big business would enter into the haulage market by one 'firm' having many depots.

Excessive wear and tear on animals was a constant problem, and must have occurred in the private sector rather more than in the *cursus*. Here it was severe enough for legislation to be enacted over the use of 'persuaders'. 'Very many persons' were using 'knotty and stout clubs' to bludgeon animals into excessive speed early in their journey, thus putting them under stress and using up excessive energy. Constantine decreed that only a switch, or at the most a whip with a prick in its end, might be used so that 'the lazy limbs of the animals may be tickled into action'. Soldiers who disobeyed were deported, officers demoted (*Codex Theo.*, 8.5.2). Anyone who knows about whips realizes that a switch or goad is far more effective than a blunt club which serves to bruise, but the picture does arise of animals being subjected to excessive demands which shortened their lives.

The normal road life of a *cursus* horse was about four years, and replacements were organized on that basis (ibid., 8.5.34). Under this same provision an exception was made for Africa, where animals were to be replaced only as necessary. Should fewer animals be needed the taxpayers were not to be forced to pay the balance. This throws a light on to the use and probably the type of animal used in Africa. As has been discussed in Chapter 1, African horses were generally of an extremely tough strain, their qualities very much akin to those possessed by today's Arabian, two of whose best characteristics are its longevity and durability. The law also highlights the very real stress that *cursus* animals worked under, as a four-year working life is exceptionally short. True, some use might still be made of discarded animals, but in an era when soundness and serviceability were vital, a horse for what we would term 'light hacking only' would be a burden and treated accordingly. In the heyday of coaching in England and Europe, where a four- or six-horse hitch pulled a three-ton coach plus freight and many passengers, the coach horse was lucky to last longer than three years in harness (Hyland 1988, p. 55). The horses or mules pulling the vehicles on the *Cursus Publicus* at least fared better in that the weight of loads according to the type of vehicle was strictly laid down, as were prohibitions against excessively heavy vehicles. The number of animals per vehicle was also stipulated. On the plus side for the coach horse was a superior harness using the shoulder collar that permitted maximum traction without constricting the windpipe. On the plus side for the *cursus* were the infinitely superior roads of the Roman Empire.

Many laws were enacted with regard to these weight tables, some just reiterating earlier ones, others slightly altering the weights, broadening the scope and/or making exceptions for gear going to court for state or personal use by the emperor. In AD 357 the maximum load for a post carriage was considered to be 1,000 Roman pounds (720 lb or 326 kg); for a two-wheeler, 200 pounds (144 lb or 65 kg); and for baggage on a horse in addition to the rider, 30 pounds (22 lb or 10 kg), for 'it appears that they cannot support heavier burdens' (*Codex Theo.*, 8.5.8). This says quite a lot about the type of animal that was being used, as 30 pounds in addition to a rider is not very much if adequately and well positioned. A horse of similar height used in ranching today would quite easily carry a man of 6 ft (1.82 m) or more weighing upwards of 200 lb (90 kg), plus a 40–50 lb (18–22.5 kg) saddle. Many horses for endurance riding in the heavyweight division carry over 240 lb (110 kg) over 100 miles (160 km) in one day. Without stirrups, however, the rider would be more of a deadweight and possibly a lumpish burden bouncing about with resultant sore backs and stressed limbs (for both horse and rider). A gaited horse would be far preferable to a walk/trot/canter mount but such horses, though smoother for the rider, do tend to use more energy when artificial gaits are induced by training, as Pliny affirms, and therefore are not as economical for the horse. Mule power was multiple, a carriage needing eight in summer and ten in winter, and a two-wheeled vehicle three (ibid., 8.5.8.1). In a two-wheeler the mules were hitched abreast. So many animals for such a small weight! As well as the less efficient method of yoking and harnessing, the design of ancient vehicles lacked the advantages of superb construction which today's modern horse-drawn carriages enjoy.

A law of AD 368 reiterates riding horse and carriage weights and adds the restriction of 1,500 Roman pounds (1,080 lb or 490 kg) for a post wagon. This was drawn by oxen and is outside the scope of this book. It must have been an infuriatingly slow means of transport as an ox in top gear reaches all of 2 m.p.h. Nearly 30 years later in 385 and 386 other laws came into force, augmenting the above and slightly altering the baggage allowance in saddlebags (ibid., 8.5.47):

For travel by post carriage: maximum freight weight	1,000 pounds
For travel by cart: maximum freight weight	600 pounds
For travel by riding horse:	
saddle and bridle shall not exceed	60 pounds
saddlebags and contents shall not exceed	35 pounds

For the carriage of Imperial gold and silver special arrangements were made and the type of vehicle not left to chance or choice. Obviously because less weight was carried, it facilitated a faster journey. One carriage was used per 500 pounds (360 lb or 163 kg) of gold or 1,000 pounds of silver. If it was the Emperor's personal money, it went even faster with 300 pounds (216 lb or 98 kg) of gold or 500 pounds of silver per carriage. The accompanying outriders were permitted heavier saddlebags of up to 50 pounds (36 lb or 16 kg) (ibid., 8.5.48). By the same law the military supplies were now to go by the slower wagon or boat, but clothing for the court could still travel in the 1,000 pound freight of a post carriage.

Size of vehicles was also regulated. It was forbidden to build enormous vehicles (ibid., 8.5.17). As shown by the wording of the law this had become an abuse. Presumably the carriage makers were profiteering by charging high prices for overlarge carriages. Oxen and mules would have suffered stress and certain strains, particularly in the spinal area, if overburdened by these. The Aphrodisias copy of Diocletian's *Edict* lists many of the prices for whole carriages and wagons and for spare parts, and shows a wide divergence in cost and quality of product. Valentinian sought to curb the abuse by sending a freemen guilty of breaking this law into exile, and slaves to perpetual labour in the mines. One would have thought the slaves' owner should have gone there instead!

The burden for supplying the *cursus* with sufficient animals fell mostly on the provincials. Many of the laws refer to them supplying post horses;

others to prohibitions against requisitioning plough oxen for *cursus* duty (ibid., 8.5.1). Horses were also bred on the Imperial studs, though it is to be doubted that the Emperor actually provided the animals gratis to the *cursus*. As time went on, the payment of levies in kind was commuted to cash payments, along the same lines as for army horses. These payments in turn found their way back into the pockets of breeders and dealers in horses and mules, though the price levied was probably not the price paid out, the profit going into the fisc. It would also permit the haggling so beloved of horsetraders and provide a further avenue of pecuniary abuse.

One state stud is mentioned in an inscription concerning Angareia (Frend 1956). On the map, the towns concerned are Synnada, Docinum and Polybotus, set in a rough triangle whose sides measure approximately 25, 15 and 30 miles (40, 24, 48 km), connecting the towns contained within the estate. On this estate, it is highly probable that the horses for the ceremonies connected with state functions were raised (*Codex Theo.*, 6.4.19). On such a huge estate many thousands of animals would form the herds of horses, mules and oxen, and those not destined for court and religious functions would go to help swell the ranks of post and army horses. It is doubtful if any horses sent from an Imperial stud would be rejected. The estimate of a yearly crop of calves and foals in the thousands is no exaggeration: Gregory the Great complained of finding the Church's estates in Sicily unprofitable and drastically reduced the size to 400 mares being kept (Jones 1964)!

This Phrygian triangle was also set strategically for many of the important post roads, and the map gives some idea of the burden that a relatively small area would carry in providing animals and fodder, and maintenance services – grooms, mule-drivers, and so on. There would also be a positive side: excess crops would find a ready market, although in the immediate vicinity of the Imperial stud the beneficiary would be the Emperor himself.

Other influential people also supplied equines to the public and civil sector. Suetonius tells us that when Vespasian was financially embarrassed by the heavy demands on him as Governor of Africa, he mortgaged his estates and went into the mule trade (Suetonius, *Vesp.* 4). But from these sources some animals would be rejected. The *manceps*, or supervisor, of the post station took the blame if the wrong type of animal was purchased: 'Even the supervisor of the post station shall have the unrestricted right with the knowledge that it is at his own risk to purchase robust and healthy animals and prepare them by his own care for the use of the public post' (*Codex Theo.*, 6.29.9.1). This is a crucial law. It highlights several aspects of the organization of the *Cursus Publicus* and the care and training that was entailed in preparing animals for their duties. It also shows one of the main reasons why acting as *manceps* was so distasteful. This was a post that in the Early Empire was auctioned to the highest bidder. In the Later Empire it was a civil appointment which could not be evaded by a man of sufficient rank and means. Many of these appointees had already served a term on the proconsular staff or in civil service posts and been discharged, or what we would call retired (ibid., 8.5.34.3). Once appointed he had to serve for a period of five years, but was then exempted from any further compulsory services and given the title of *perfectessimus*. During his five-year stint he was not allowed to be absent from his post for more than two days in any 30-day period (ibid., 8.5.36).

To have to absorb the cost of any deficient animals for that period would break any man, so the *manceps* must have either known a good deal about horses himself, or put great trust in the state-owned slaves who worked under him, caring for the horses and mules. The state-owned slave with *mulomedicus* status would have had to vouch for the animals' usefulness and soundness, though the *manceps* was ultimately held responsible. He would certainly have insisted on the legally binding warranty as to soundness, docility and suitability for work mentioned by Varro and Pelagonius (*Ars Vet*. Int. 3). It also suggests that these slave grooms, or at least a proportion of them, were above the ordinary if they could train animals to go under harness, work as a team, and also break the riding animals in to a degree of safety so that inferior riders holding warrants were secure. A horse is very quick to realize if he has a tyro aboard, and almost without exception will take quick advantage. The fact that at least some of the larger stations had animals going through the training process suggests that some depots were of very considerable size. Each groom had three animals assigned to his care (*Codex Theo.*, 8.5.33.1) and there were slave veterinarians in attendance, as well as wagoners who saw to the maintenance of the vehicles (ibid., 8.5.31). There would also have been a blacksmith at larger posts to attend to any metal parts of the vehicle, mostly wheel rims.

Farriers would not be needed as the *mulomedicus* pared horses' feet as part of the veterinary profession (and vets still have to be able to do this today). Hipposandals, which have been found in sufficient quantities and types to substantiate their use, would be employed for carriage and wagon animals in very stony areas, but most ridden animals would have followed the unpaved verges of roads and would not have needed shoeing except in areas of very abrasive going. As the *Cursus Publicus* was a service with many centuries of operation to its credit and ran well into the period when horseshoes were starting to be more common, it is worth speculating that some at least of the *cursus* animals were shod in the same way as today. Evidence, however, would be hard to come by; a shoe thrown miles from any depot, if found, might not be linked to the

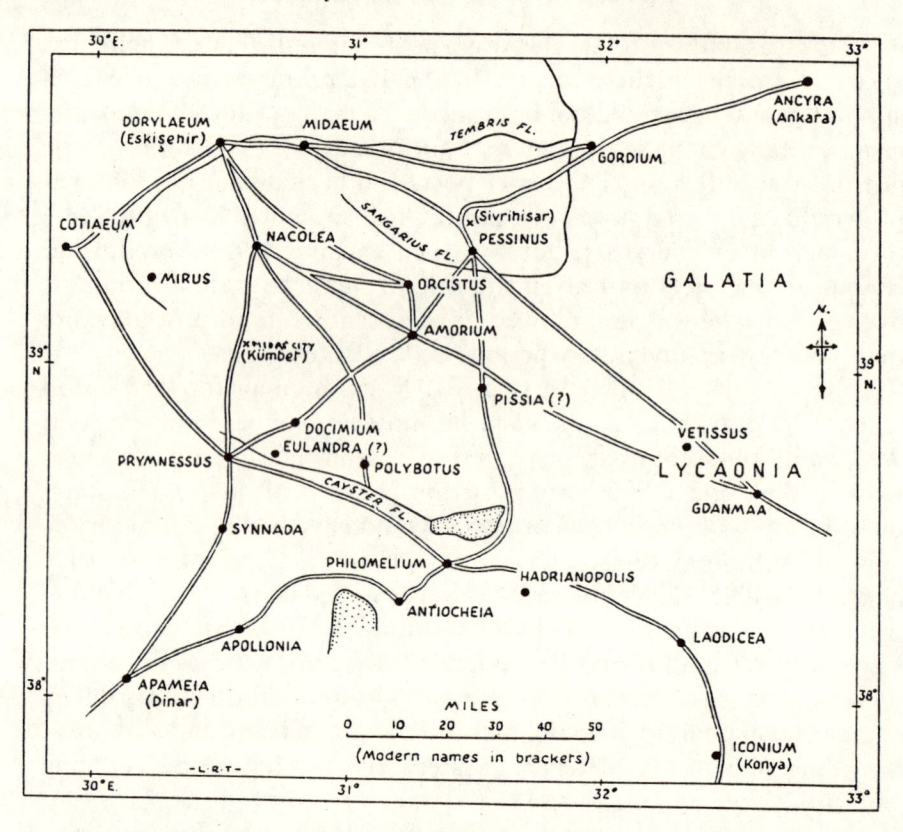

7 Map showing the Roman roads in Phrygia

cursus before ending up on a modern rubbish dump. Worn out animals, or animals that died in service, would not leave evidence of being shod as their remains would be utilized for hair, hide, glue, and so on. No proof of the large-scale use of shoes, even in the Later Empire, is available. If it had been the norm, large stations would have yielded evidence, but such lack does not preclude the possibility of the occasional use of shoes on the public roads, particularly in the areas known to use shoes in the private sector, such as Gaul and Britain where shoes have been found. Suetonius, in one of his racy tales about Vespasian, tells of a journey where the mule-driver dismounted and began shoeing the mules, and Vespasian, suspecting it was an excuse for dallying for a chat with a friend met *en route*, enquired as to the cost of the shoeing and demanded half for himself (Suetonius, *Vesp.* 23). This implies that various additional charges were made over and above the hire of transport – a parallel of today's car hire when mileage is also charged. Presumably on this occasion, Vespasian was travelling in a hired carriage from the private sector, not one procured by warranty from the *Cursus Publicus*. It must also have been before his days as Emperor, when as a private citizen he was not entitled to such a privilege except on state business.

Slave personnel were not permitted to accept tips. It was considered that their food and clothing was sufficient remuneration (*Codex Theo.*, 8.5.31), and should any mule-driver abscond or be enticed away he was to be sought out and returned, and the enticer fined. If any provincial governor had the temerity to free such a man because of old age or disability he was to be fined one pound of gold. Even old and feeble men were to be dragged back with their families (ibid., 8.5.58). Conditions were harsh for both man and beast in the *cursus* service.

Procopius tells us that up to 40 horses were held ready at each station (*Secret History*, p. 188). There would also have been a large number of mules and a complement of oxen. It is not known how many stages every class of animal was expected to cover. Harnessed animals probably covered far fewer than ridden animals as their pace would be slower, and maybe they only did one stage at a time before being unhitched and rested. But only one stage of approximately 11 miles (see p. 254 above) would be nothing for a horse. Distance worked must have depended on the severity of the terrain, the load carried, the urgency of the mission and, for a man riding, his own ability as much as the animal's speed or capacity for work. The five to eight stages for a courier only give us a very broad outline for one class of *cursus* user. The average walking pace of a very athletic, eager horse is 4½ m.p.h. (7 k.p.h.). Most dawdle at around 3 m.p.h. (5 k.p.h.) or even less. Inefficient riders do not get the maximum out of horses, and in fact put maximum stress on them. If a two-wheeled carriage travelled at an *average* of 5 m.p.h. (8 k.p.h.) that would be very good going, necessitating considerable speed in some sections, as even five minutes walking drops the average more than is generally realized. Even for an experienced long-distance rider one of the main challenges is to average the required speed: to average 8 m.p.h. (13 k.p.h.) over 50 miles (80 km) means flying along for much of the route! In this context the eight-day chariot trip by Caesar from the Rhône to Rome is highly commendable (Plutarch, *Lives*, vol, II. p. 189). The 1,000-mile (1,600-km) ride of Icelus, Galba's freedman, from Spain to Rome in a week, with no stirrups, was even more remarkable (Plutarch, *Life of Galba*, p. 342).

The *Codex Theodosianus* frequently mentions the 'wearing out of the public beasts', so demands must have been fairly heavy. To ameliorate this somewhat there was a limit to the number of horses (and correspondingly other animals, it is implied) that were allowed out each day, varying from five to six (*Codex Theo.*, 8.5.33, 40). Despatch of carriages was limited to one per day. The laws made provision for exceptions to the rule if more animals were required. Therefore if the stations held up to 40 horses at each post, or even only half that, it would seem as if the exception was the rule, if the pressure on services and animals was as great as the constant attempts to reduce it imply.

From the time of Constantine the *cursus* was used extensively to mount the hurrying clergy, who seem to have been very peripatetic men. They were also a very dissentient group, with various sects and heresies springing up, so that numerous synods were convened to sort things out: 'public transport hurried throngs of bishops hither and thither to attend what they called synods, and by his attempts to impose conformity Constantius only succeeded in hamstringing the post service' (Ammianus, *Res Gest.* 21.16). Although the clergy loved to travel and made abundant use of the *cursus*, the religious life was also an escape from liturgies, and so many men were disappearing into the cloistered life that the *cursus* was left short of supervisors. To remedy this there was the threat of sequestering a cleric's property (*Codex Theo.*, 8.5.46.1). It would be interesting to know if the rush to take Holy Orders suffered any shortfall in AD 285 when this law was enacted.

The actual numbers of animals can only be arrived at by a very rough computation. With over 53,000 miles (85,000 km) of trunk road served by the *cursus* and a station every 11 miles (18 km) or thereabouts, there would have been around 4,800 stations to stock with animals. As well as the 40 head of horses per depot there would have been even more pack animals plus the oxen. In addition there were the private establishments, also with huge numbers of animals. The trackways would have buzzed in more ways than one, and the surrounding land have been rather more fertile than usual.

The need to produce enough fodder must have been a constant worry. Animals need high quality grain and hay to work efficiently, and bad harvests would have hit both the tax-payer and the stock. The men would not have had the grain to pay taxes, and when the taxes were commuted the money from sale of produce would not have made sufficient return to meet obligations. The animals would not have had enough to eat, would become debilitated and unable to work efficiently, and replacements would have been needed more often. Travel and transport would have ground down to a much slower pace and the demands of travellers outstripped the ability of the *cursus* to cope. Bad harvests would have created a vicious circle. That the *cursus* managed to overcome many of these difficulties was another example of Roman thoroughness and sense of order.

Select glossary of Roman and equine terms

Ala Cavalry regiment.

Ala quingenaria 16 *turmae* = 512 men.

Ala milliaria 24 *turmae* = approx 1,000 men.

Azoturia A build-up of lactic acid in the horse, causing swelling of the muscle fibres, followed by degenerative changes, locomotor inability, passage of myoglobin into blood plasma and its excretion into the urine.

Barding Armour covering body of horse.

Bosal A type of rawhide hackamore used in Western riding.

Broken winded A horse with a chronic respiratory condition.

Calcaneus Bone in the hock to which the Achilles tendon is attached.

Cohors equitata Infantry unit with a cavalry element.

Contus Heavy lance.

Cuneus Wedge-shaped heavy mailed cavalry formation.

Decurio (military) Commander of a *turma*.

Diagonal (gait) Movement of the horse's legs in diagonal pairs at a trot.

Duplicarius Decurion's second-in-command.

Ewe neck upside-down neck – poor conformation.

Gaited Specifically referring to horses which have other gaits in addition to the normal walk, trot, canter, gallop, variously known as rack, singlefoot, pace, amble, triple, foxtrot, slow-gait, running walk.

Gyrus Round training arena, a larger version of the American round-pen breaking corral.

Hackamore (*Jaquima*) American term for a bitless bridle that works by nasal control, originally from the Spanish.

Hasta   Spear.

Heaves   A form of broken wind with a double respiratory lift in the flank.

Horrea   Grain store.

Incest breeding   In-breeding; in horses, very close breeding in the same family: mother to son, father to daughter, siblings.

Laminitis   Lameness due to vascular congestion in hoof, usually a serious condition.

Lateral gait   Where the offside and nearside legs work together as a pair, e.g. in the pace.

Leads   Term used for the leading leg when a horse is cantering.

Line breeding   Breeding horses which have many close crosses to the same ancestor(s), but not their immediate family as in incest breeding.

Loose box   Accommodation for one horse untied, large enough for him to lie down.

Loriner   Bit maker.

Meta   Roman circus (racetrack) turning post.

Mutton-withered   Low, fleshy withers that will not hold a saddle well.

Naufragia   Literally, shipwreck; term used for collided chariots in the circus.

Outcross   Use of a different bloodline whether from within the same breed or from a different breed.

Phalerae   Metal disc or boss for the forehead and breast of horses.

Prata   Grazing lands for the Roman cavalry, owned by the military.

Psalion   Roman type of hackamore of metal construction with action similar to a dropped noseband. Called after the Greek for 'scissor' because of its action.

Razzia   Raid.

Rig   Cryptorchid (stallion in which one testicle has not dropped, usually infertile, nearly always a nuisance around others).

Roach back   Horse's spine raised in a convex form towards the loin area – bad conformation.

Roaring   Another form of broken wind (after the noise it makes).

Spatha   Cavalry sword.

Spina   Central barrier in Roman circus racetrack.

Splint   Bony enlargements on the cannon bones, can cause lameness.

Stall   Accommodation where the horse is tied and divided from others by a partition.

Select glossary

Strator   Groom, usually head groom or manager.

Tying up   Myoglobinuria (akin to azoturia, but usually found in fit horses after a hard day's work), affects loins and croup the most. There is a lactic acid build-up and the horse has difficulty moving. This would have been common in cavalry horses after extended fast trips.

Thrush   Necrotic, foul-smelling condition in the underparts of a horse's hoof, usually due to dirty, constantly wet conditions.

Turma   30–32 man cavalry troop.

Weed   Scrawny, narrow, badly conformed, and usually leggy horse.

Wrangler   Rough rider who takes the risks with young horses.

Horse breeds noted in classical literature and grouped according to geographic area

Italy
Tuscan
Apulian
Sicilian
Venetian (Henetian)
Rosean
Reatine
Ligurian

Africa
Moorish
Mazician
Libyan

Crete
Cretan

Spain
Iberian
Cob
Asturian (Asturcan)
Theldones

Arabia
Erembian
Arab (modern name)

Greece
Achaen
Argolic (Argos)
Epeian
Elein
Ionian
Arcadian
Epidaurian
Epirote
Aetolian
Acarnanians
Magnesian
Aenian

Kindred Greek (but specially noted for horses)
Macedonian
Boetian
Thessalian
Thracian

Asia Minor
Cappadocian
Phrygian
Parthian ⎫
Medean ⎬ interchangeable as to type (larger than most)
Nisaean ⎭
Persian
Armenian
Syrian

British/French
Gallic horses

Various
Sarmatic
Hunnish
Frisian
Burgundian
Thuringian

Bibliography

Abbreviations used in the text and bibliography
AHS   Arab Horse Society
CIL   Corpus Inscriptionum Latinarum
ILS   Inscriptiones Latinae Selectae
JRS   Journal of Roman Studies
JRGZM   Jahrbuch des Römisch-germanischen Zentralmuseums, Mainz
PBSR   Proceedings of the British School at Rome
RIC   Roman Imperial Coinage
SHA   Scriptores Historiae Augustae

Original works consulted
AELIANUS, *de Natura Animalium*
AMMIANUS MARCELLINUS, *Res Gestae*
APPIAN, *Roman History*
APULEIUS, *Metamorphoses*
ARRIAN, *Ars Tactica*
ARRIAN, *Cynegetica*
ARRIAN, *Indica*
CAESAR, *de Bello Africo*
CAESAR, *de Bello Civili*
CAESAR, *de Bello Gallico*
CALPURNIUS SICULUS, *de Carminibus Bucolicis*
CATO, *de Agri Cultura*
CELSUS, *de Medicina*
CHIRON, *Mulomedicina*
Codex Theodosianus
COLUMELLA, *de Re Rustica*
DIO CASSIUS, *Historiae Romanae*
DIO CHRYSOSTOMOS, *Orationes*
DIOCLETIAN, *Edictum de pretiis*
DIODORUS SICULUS, *Biblioteca historica*
DIONYSIUS OF HALICARNASSUS, *Roman Antiquities*

Expositio Totius Mundi et Gentium
FRONTO, *Epistulae*
GRATIUS FALISCUS, *Cynegetica*
HELIODORUS, *Aethiopica*
HERODOTUS, *Historia*
HOMER, *Iliad*
HORACE, *Epistulae*
HORACE, *Saturae*
JOSEPHUS, *Antiquitates Judaicae*
JOSEPHUS, *Bellum Judaicum*
JUSTINIAN, *Digesta*
JUVENAL, *Saturae*
LIVY, *Ab Urbe Condita*
LUCAN, *Pharsalia*
LUCILIUS, *Carminum Reliquiae*
MARTIAL, *Epigrammaton*
NEMESIAN, *Cynegetica*

Notitia Dignatatum
ONASANDER, *The General*
OPPIAN, *Cynegetica*
PALLADIUS, *de Re Rustica*
PELAGONIUS, *Ars Veterinaria*
PLINY, THE ELDER, *Naturalis Historia*
PLINY, THE YOUNGER, *Epistulae*
PLUTARCH, *Lives*
POLYBIUS, *Historiae*
PROCOPIUS, *Secret History*
SALLUST, *Bellum Jugurthinum*
SCRIBONIUS LARGUS, *Compostitiones*

Scriptores Historiae Augustae
SIDONIUS APOLLINARIS, *Carmina*
SOPHOCLES, *Electra*
STRABO, *Geographica*
SUETONIUS, *de Vita Caesarum*
TACITUS, *Agricola*
TACITUS, *Annales*
TACITUS, *Germania*
TACITUS, *Historiarum*
TERTULLIAN, *de Spectaculis*
VARRO, *de Lingua Latina*
VARRO, *de Re Rustica*
VEGETIUS FLAVIUS RENATUS, *Epitoma Rei Militaris*
VEGETIUS PUBLIUS RENATUS, *Digestorum Artis Mulomedicinae Libri*
VIRGIL, *Aeneid*
VIRGIL, *Georgics*
XENEPHON, *On Horsemanship*

Secondary sources and editions used

AELIAN, *On the Characteristics of Animals*, trans. A. F. Scholfield, 3 vols., Loeb Classical Library, Heinemann, 1958-9.

AMMIANUS MARCELLINUS, *The Later Roman Empire: AD 354-378*, trans. Walter Hamilton, Penguin, 1986.

APULEIUS, *The Transformations of Lucius, Otherwise Known as The Golden Ass*, trans. R. Graves, Penguin, 1950, reprinted 1976.

Arab Horse Society News, Winter 1987, correspondence from Peter J. Whybrow, Dept of Palaeontology, British Museum.

ARRIAN, trans. E. Iliff Robson, 2 vols., Loeb Classical Library, Heinemann, 1966-7.

BELL, H. I., MARTIN, V., TURNER, E. G. AND VAN BERCHEM, D., *The Abinnaeus Archive: Papers of a Roman Officer in the Reign of Constantius II*, Clarendon Press, 1962.

BISHOP, M. C., 'Cavalry equipment of the Roman army in the first century AD', *BAR International Series*, no. 394, 1988, pp. 67-196.

BRANIGAN, K., *The Roman Villa in South-West England*, Moonraker Press, 1977.

BUTLER, D., *The Principles of Horseshoeing*, D. Butler, Texas, 1974.

Caesar: Alexandrian, African and Spanish Wars, trans. A. G. Way, Loeb Classical Library, Heinemann, 1955.

CAESAR, JULIUS, *The Civil War*, trans. Jane F. Mitchell, Penguin, 1967.

Caesar: The Gallic War, trans. H. J. Edwards, Loeb Classical Library, Heinemann, 1970.

CAMERON, ALAN, *Porphyrius the Charioteer*, Clarendon Press, 1973.

CAMERON, ALAN, *Circus Factions*, Clarendon Press, 1976.

Cato On Agriculture; Varro On Agriculture, Loeb Classical Library, Heinemann, 1934.

CHEESMAN, G. L. *The Auxilia of the Roman Imperial Army*, Clarendon Press, 1914.

CHEVALLIER, R. *Roman Roads*, Batsford, 1976.

COLUMELLA, *On Agriculture*, 3 vols., Loeb Classical Library, Heinemann, 1941-55.

CONNOLLY, PETER, 'The Roman saddle', *BAR International Series*, no. 336, 1987, pp. 7-27.

CURLE, JAMES, *A Roman Frontier Post and its People: The Fort of Newstead in the Parish of Melrose*, James Maclehose, 1911.

CURZON, L. B., *Roman Law*, Macdonald & Evans, 1966.

DAVIES, R. W., 'A note on P. Dura 64', *Latomus*, no. 26, 1967, pp. 67-72.

DAVIES, R. W., 'The training grounds of the Roman cavalry', *Archaeological Journal*, no. 125, 1968, pp. 73-100.

DAVIES, R. W., 'The supply of animals to the Roman army and the remount system', *Latomus*, no. 28, 1969, pp. 429-59.

DAVIES, R. W., 'The Roman military medical service', *Saalburg Jahrbuch*, 1970, pp. 84-104.

DAVIES, R. W., 'Cohortes equitatae', *Historia*, no. 20, 1971, pp. 751-63.

DENT, A., *Encyclopedia of the Horse*, Octopus, 1977.

DIO CASSIUS, *Dio's Roman History*, 9 vols., trans. Earnest Cary, Loeb Classical Library, Heinemann, 1961–70.
DIO CASSIUS, *The Roman History, The Reign of Augustus*, trans. Ian Scott-Kilvert, Penguin, 1987.
DIOCLETIAN, 'Edictum Diocletiani et Collegarum', *CIL*, vol. III, pp. 801–41.
DIODORUS OF SICILY, 12 vols., trans. C. H. Oldfather, Loeb Classical Library, Heinemann, 1933–67.
DIONYSIUS OF HALICARNASSUS, *Roman Antiquities*, trans. Earnest Cary, 7 vols., Loeb Classical Library, Heinemann, 1961–8.
EADIE, J. W., 'The development of Roman mailed cavalry', *JRS*, no. 57, 1967, pp. 161–73.
ERIM, K. T. and REYNOLDS, JOYCE, 'The Aphrodisias copy of Diocletian's *Edict on Maximum Prices*', *JRS*, no. 63, 1973, pp. 99–110.
Expositio Totius Mundi et Gentium, trans. Jean Rouge, Les Editions du Cerf Sources Chrétiennes, Paris, 1966.
FINK, ROBERT O., *Roman Military Records on Papyrus*, American Philological Association, 1971.
FOL, ALEXANDER, and MARAZOV, IVAN, *Thrace and the Thracians*, Cassell, 1977.
FRANK, TENNEY (ed.), *An Economic Survey of Ancient Rome*, 5 vols., Johns Hopkins Press, 1933–40.
FREDERIKSEN, MARTIN W., 'Campanian cavalry', *Dialoghi di Archaeologia*, 1968, pp. 3–31.
FREND, W. H. C., 'Angareia in Phrygia', *JRS*, no. 46, 1956 pp. 46–56.
GARBSCH, JOCHEN, *Römische Paraderüstungen*, Munich, 1978.
GRANT, M., *Dawn of the Middle Ages*, Weidenfeld & Nicolson, 1981.
HARRIS, H. A., *Sport in Greece and Rome*, Thames & Hudson, 1972.
HAYES, CAPT. H. M., *Veterinary Notes for Horse Owners*, 16th edn, Stanley Paul, 1968.
HERODOTUS, *History*, trans. Aubrey de Selincourt, Penguin, 1974.
HICKMAN, J., *Farriery*, J. A. Allen, 1977.
HOLDER, PAUL A., 'The auxilia from Augustus to Trajan', *BAR International Ser.*, no. 70, 1980.
HOMER, *Iliad*, trans. R. Fitzgerald, Penguin Classics, [1950].
HORACE, *Satires and Epistles*, trans. C. Smart, Bohn's Library, 1859.
HULL, DENISON BINGHAM, *Hounds and Hunting in Ancient Greece*, University of Chicago Press, 1964.
HUMPHREY, JOHN H., *Roman Circuses and Chariot Racing*, Batsford 1986.
HYLAND, A., *Beginner's Guide to Endurance Riding*, Pelham, 1974.
HYLAND, A., *Foal to Five Years*, Ward Lock, 1980.
HYLAND, A., *The Endurance Horse*, J. A. Allen, 1988.
Inscriptiones Latinae Selectae, ed. H. Dessau, 3 vols., Weidmann, 1892–1916.
JONES, A. H. M., *The Later Roman Empire, 284–602*, Basil Blackwell, 1964.
JOSEPHUS, vols. II–X, Loeb Classical Library, Heinemann, 1967–81.
JUSTINIAN, *The Digest of Roman Law*, trans. C. F. Kolbert, Penguin, 1979.
JUVENAL, *The Sixteen Satires*, trans. P. Green, Penguin, 1974.
KARAGEORGHIS, VASSOS, *Excavations in the Necropolis of Salamis I*, Department

of Antiquities, Cyprus, 1967.
LAWSON, ANNABEL (née TAYLOR), 'Studien zum Römischen Pferdegeschirr', *JRGZM*, no. 25, 1978, pp. 131–72.
LEAKE, W. M., *Edict of Diocletian AD 303*, John Murray, 1826.
LEWIS, C. T., and SHORT, C., *A Latin Dictionary*, Clarendon Press, 1966.
LEWIS, N., and REINHOLD, M., *Roman Civilization – Sources*, vol. II: *The Empire*, Harper & Row, 1966.
LINDSAY, JACK, *Arthur and His Times*, Frederick Muller, 1958.
LIVY, *The Early History of Rome*, vols. I–V, trans. Aubrey de Selincourt, Penguin, 1960.
LIVY, *The War with Hannibal*, trans. Aubrey de Selincourt, Penguin, 1965.
LOCH, S., *The Royal Horse of Europe*, J. A. Allen, 1986.
LUCAN, *Pharsalia*, trans. R. Graves, Penguin, 1956.
LUCILIUS, *Carminum Reliquiae*, F. Marx, 1905.
MACLEOD, G., *Treatment of Horses by Homeopathy*, Health Science Press, 1977.
MANN, J. *The Romans in the North*, University of Lancaster and Durham, 1975.
MANN, R. D., *Modern Drugs Use: An Enquiry on Historical Principles*, MTP Press, 1984.
MANNING, W. H., *Catalogue of the Romano-British Ironwork in the Museum of Antiquities, Newcastle upon Tyne*, Department of Archaeology, University of Newcastle, 1976.
MANNING, W. H., *Catalogue of the Romano-British Iron Tools, Fittings and Weapons in the British Museum*, BM, 1985.
MARTIAL, *The Epigrams*, Bell & Daldy, 1865.
MATTINGLY, H., *Roman Coins*, Methuen, 1928.
MEEK, A., and GRAY, R. A. H., 'Report on the 1910 excavations at Corstopitum: animal remains', *Arch. Ael.*, 3rd series, no. 7, 1911, pp. 220–67.
Minor Latin Poets, trans. J. Wight Duff and A. M. Duff, Loeb Classical Library, Heinemann, 1968.
MORGAN, M. H. (ed. and trans.), *Xenephon, The Art of Horsemanship*, J. A. Allen, 1962.
MORRISON, J. S., and COATES, J. F., *The Athenian Trireme: the History and Reconstruction of an Ancient Greek Warship*, Cambridge University Press, 1986.
NOBIS, GÜNTER, 'Zur Frage Römerzeitlicher Hauspferde in Zentraleuropa', *Zeitschrift für Sängetierk*, no. 38, 1973, pp. 224–52.
OPPIAN, trans. A. W. Mair, Loeb Classical Library, Heinemann, 1928.
PELAGONIUS, *Ars Veterinaria*, ed. M. Ihm, Leipzig, 1892.
PLINY, THE ELDER, *Natural History*, Loeb Classical Library, Heinemann, 1937.
PLINY, THE YOUNGER, *Letters*, Penguin, 1969.
PLUTARCH, *Lives*, trans. W. and J. Langhorne, Chandos Classics, Frederick Warne, 1884, vols. I and II (Roman).
POLYBIUS, *The Rise of the Roman Empire*, trans. Ian Scott-Kilvert, Penguin, 1979.
PROCOPIUS, *The Secret History*, Penguin, 1966.
RAMSAY, A. M., 'A Roman postal service under the republic', *JRS*, no. 10, 1920, pp. 79–87.

RAWSON, ELIZABETH, 'Chariot racing in the Roman republic', *PBSR*, no. 49, 1981, pp. 1–16.
REYNOLDS, P. J., *Iron-Age Farm: The Butser Experiment*, British Museum Publications, 1979.
RICHMOND, I. A., '*Bremetannacum Veteranorum* and the *Regio Bremetennacsis*', *JRS*, no. 35, 1945, pp. 15–29.
RIDGEWAY, WILLIAM, *The Origin and Influence of the Thoroughbred Horse*, Cambridge University Press, 1905.
Roman Imperial Coinage, ed. H. Mattingly and E. A. Sydenham, vol. II: *Vespasian to Hadrian*, Spink, 1926.
ROSSI, L., *Trajan's Column and the Dacian Wars*, Thames & Hudson, 1971.
ROSTOVTZEFF, M. I. et al., *The Excavations at Dura-Europos, Preliminary Report of Sixth Season of Work*, Yale University Press, 1936.
RUDENKO, S. I., *The Frozen Tombs of Siberia*, J. M. Dent, 1970.
SALLUST, *The Jugurthine War*, Penguin, 1963.
Scriptores Historiae Augustae, Loeb Classical Library, Heinemann, 1921.
SIDONIUS APOLLINARIS, *Poems and Letters*, trans. W. B. Anderson, Loeb Classical Library, Heinemann, 1968.
SOPHOCLES, *Electra*, Penguin, 1953.
SPARKES, IVAN, *Old Horseshoes*, Shire Publications, 1976.
STENICO, ARTURO, *Roman and Etruscan Painting*, Weidenfeld & Nicolson, 1963.
STRABO, *Geography*, Loeb Classical Library, Heinemann, 1961.
SUETONIUS, *The Twelve Caesars*, Penguin, 1957.
SULIMIRSKI, T., *The Sarmatians*, Thames & Hudson, 1970.
TACITUS, *On Imperial Rome*, Penguin, 1956.
TACITUS, *Agricola and Germania*, Penguin, 1970.
TACITUS, *The Histories*, Penguin, 1975.
TAYLOR, ANNABEL, 'Römische Hackamoren und Kappzäume aus Metall', *JRGZM*, no. 22, 1975, pp. 106–33.
TERTULLIAN, *de Spectaculis*, T. & T. Clark, 1869.
The Theodosian Code, trans. C. Pharr, Princeton University Press, 1952.
TOYNBEE, J. M. C., *Animals in Roman Life and Art*, Thames & Hudson, 1973.
TREVELYAN, G. M., *English Social History*, Pelican, 1967.
VARRO, *On Farming*, trans. L. Storr-Best, Bell, 1912.
VARRO, *De Lingua Latina*, Loeb Classical Library, Heinemann, 1938.
VEGETIUS FLAVIUS RENATUS, *The Military Institutions of the Romans*, Greenwood Press, 1985.
VEGETIUS PUBLIUS RENATUS, *Digestorum Artis Mulomedicinae*, ed. Ernestus Lommatzsch, Leipzig, 1903.
VIGNERON, P., *Le Cheval dans L'Antiquité Greco-romaine*, Nancy, 1968.
VIRGIL, *Georgics*, trans. C. Day Lewis, Cape, 1943.
VIRGIL, *Aeneid*, Loeb Classical Library, Heinemann, 1960.
WALKER, R. E. Appendices in Toynbee, 1973.
WEBSTER, GRAHAM. *The Roman Imperial Army of the First and Second Centuries AD*, 3rd edn, A. & C. Black, 1985.

WHITE, K. D., *Roman Farming*, Thames & Hudson, 1970.
WILLIAMS, STEPHEN, *Diocletian and the Roman Recovery*, Batsford 1985.

Index

Abinnaeus Archive 85, 158, 160
Abinnaeus Flavius 85
Aelian 14, 177, 210, 215
Afranius 169
Africa 177
African (breed) (incl. map) 11–14
African cavalry 173
Agricola 166
Agrippa 165
Ailments, care of 38–40, 49–60
    passim
Ala Flavia Afrorum 26
Ala I Gallorum et Pannoniorum
    Catafractorum 151
Ala I Pannoniorum 106, 119
Ala Quinta Praelectorum 160
Alamanni 193
Alans 185
Alexander Severus 149
Allectus 193
Ammianus Marcellinus 63, 73, 80, 90, 93
Ammianus, on
  Batnae 93
  Cataphracts 149
  German tactics 126
  Huns 112
  hunting 244
  Persians 112
  public post (use of) 164
  Quadi 80
  Sarmatians 80
  strators 73
  witchcraft 230
Annona 93
Anthony 181–2
Antiochus III 148, 179
Antiochus XII 76
Antoninus Pius 151
Aorsi 183
Appian 212
Apulian horses 178
Apsyrtus 5, 14, 54
Arabian, modern breed of 24–27
Araxes river 182
Arch of Orange 131
Arenas
  Alexandria 201, 207
  Antioch 207
  Caesarea 207
  Constantinople 207
  North Africa 207
  Portugal 207
  Rome 203–4
  Spain 207
Aretas 76
Aristarchus of Samothrace 25
Armenia 178
Armenian cavalry 179–180
Arminius 75
Army *see under* Cavalry
Arrian
  Cynegetica on grooming 39
    hunting 243
    Numidia 112
  Indica on bitting 216

Tactica 45, 101, 107, 109–12
    passim, 116, 120–1, 151–2,
    168
Ars Veterinaria see Pelagonius
Artavasdes of Armenia 181–2
Artybius 81
Asia Minor 178–9
Assyrian dung pharmacopoeia 49
Asturian horses 115, 203
Augustus 165, 190, 242, 250–1
Aulus Atticus 79
Azoturia, description of 226

Babylonius (Julian's horse) 239
Bactria 178
Barding *see* horse armour
Basilica Exercitatoria 107, 119–20
Bestia 189
Bishopping 45
Bocchus 189
Bone evidence from
    Colchester 68
    Corbridge 68
    Krefeld Gellup 68, 82
    Newstead 25, 68
    Pazyryk 22–3
Borysthenes (Hadrian's horse) 245
Brands 212
Brecon 120
Breeds, cavalry *see under* charger
Breeds, list of 266
Breeds, main
    African 11–14
    Arabian 24–7
    Armenian 15
    Cappadocian 11, 29
    Gallic 20
    Greek 17
    Hunnish 27–8
    Libyan 11–14, 24–6
    Median 15
    Nisaean 15
    Numidian 11–14, 24–6
    Parthian/Persian 14–15, 24
    Sarmatian 22–3
    Spanish 14, 29

Thessalian 16, 177
Thracian 16, 177
Breeds, race *see under* racehorse
Brough on Noe 95
Bullfighting 248

Calpurnius Siculus 5
Caltrops 110
Campanian Cavalry 171–2
Camp Prefect 87
Campus Martius 219
Cannae 166, 175, 181, 189, 228
Cantabrian Gallop 106, 120, 168
Canusium 163
Carrhae 180–1
Carthaginian horsemen 172–3
Cato the Elder 30, 32, 231
Cavalry, of
    Agrippa 75
    Antiochus of Syria 75
    Aretas of Nabatea 76
    Constantine 195
    Gallienus 192
    Hamilcar 172
    Hannibal 74, 166, 172–4 *passim*
    Hasdrubal 172
    Julius Caesar 74, 166, 169, 182
    Malchus of Arabia 75
    Maxentius 156
    Numidians 74, 172–7 *passim*, 189
    Persians 149
    Roxolani 156, 184
    Sarmatians 78, 183–4
    Soeamus of Emesa 75
Cavalry chargers from
    Africa 78
    Campania 73, 171–2
    Dalmatia 192
    Gaul 75, 156
    Germany 75
    Morocco 192
    Osrhoeni 192
    Palestine 78
    Panonnia 77–8
    Sicily 171–2
    Spain 74, 75, 77, 78

Syria 78
Cavalry duties 160–2 *passim*
  ambula 162
  animal capture 160–1
  courier 162
  escort 160–2
  general policing 160
  guard 161–2
  military 160
  scouting 162
  tax collection 160–1
Cavalry logistics
  Annona 93
  barley 94
  Basilica Exercitatoria 107, 119
  beans 94
  dehydration effects of 96
  fodder
    allowance 73
    issue of 90
    quantity per *ala quingenaria* 91
    quantity per horse 90
    rations – Polybian 188
    supply of 87–94 *passim*
  grain yield – ancient 93–4
  grain yield – modern 93
  grazing – *pratae* 91
  grazing – seasonal value 92
  harness requirements
    leather 97
    saddler 98
    tanner 98
  hay 90–3 *passim*
  Horrea 93
  marching camp 97
  parade grounds 119
  pasture
    management of 96
    Vegetius on 96
  picketing 37, 97
  stabling at 94–7 *passim*
    Brough on Noe 95
    Dormagen 95
    Hod Hill 95
    Krefeld 95
  stabling, drainage of 96
  stabling, size of 96
  structure of cavalry acc. to Polybius 188
  transports – *trieres* 98–9 (diagram and text)
  water consumption 96
Cavalry numbers
  Anthony *v* Parthians 181
  Aretas of Nabatea 76
  Capua 172
  Celts 74
  Diocletian's day 30, 194
  German 75
  Hannibal's 173–4, 189
  list of (Cheesman) 77
  Mons Graupius 166
  Roman 74–5
  Sarmatians to Britain 78
  Scipio's (Publius Cornelius) 189
  Vespasianic 192
Cavalry organization
  deployment – actual (Josephus) 165
  deployment – text book (Vegetius) 164
  entry to 113
  harrying 166–7
  postings 76, 163–4
  recruitment 163–4
  speed of 193
  tactics 165–7
Cavalry – supply of equines to 71–86 *passim*
  Campania 73
  Codex Theodosianus – cost 158
  Cohors XX Palmyrenorum 73, 157
  dealers – Pelagonius 71
  Dio Cassius on (inferred) 207–8
  importing
    by Celts 71
    by Germans 75
    by Julius Caesar 74
  levies 73–4
  methods of acquisition 77, 83
  price/value 83–6, 157–8, 188

purchase 74
Saltus 76
Servius Tullius' day 73
taxation 84–5
tribute 84–5
Cavalry Units/types in Roman army
  Ala Quingenaria 76, 159–60
  Ala Milliaria 76, 159
  Alae 75
  allied 191
  auxiliary *alae* 76, 112, 192
  baggage animals 71, 88–9
  British units 88–9
  Candidati 195
  Cataphractarii 75, 149, 152, 154–5, 178, 192
  Clibinarii 149, 152, 154–6, 178
  Coh. Eq. Quingenaria 89
  Coh. Eq. Milliaria 89
  Cohortes Equitatae 71, 76, 106, 160, 165, 167
  Cuneus 187
  ethnic units 76–7
  legionary cavalry 191, 192
  mailed – description of (Heliodorus) 149
  Numerus Equitum 185
  Praetorian 192
  remounts 88–9
  sagittarii 153, 178, 182
  scholae, list of 195
  urban 192
  vexillations 195
Celtic cavalry 172–3, 188
Celtic dispersal 172
Celtic imports 71
Celts (under Julian) 164
Chamfron 145–8
Charioteers
  Crescens 220
  Diocles 205–7 *passim*, 209, 227
  Epaphroditus 211
  Eutyches 227
  Fortunatus 220
  Fuscus 212
  Gutta 205, 210–11, 227

Laodician 210
Polyneices 205
Pompeius Musclosus 211
Scirtus 220
Scorpus 220
Tatianus 205
Teres Aulus 206
Cherchel, Algeria 217
Chester 120
Chiron 50
Cincibulus 21, 173
Circensian Games 218
Circus *see* Racing
Circus Maximus 203–4, 219–20
Claudius II Gothicus 193
Codex Theodosianus 11, 29, 42, 55, 69, 72–3, 78, 83–6, 88, 90–1, 93–4, 113, 158, 160, 195, 213, 228–9, 232–4 *passim*, 236–8 *passim*, 250–62 *passim*
Coh. VI Equestris 252
Cohors I Hispanorum Veterana Quingenaria Equitata 160–2 *passim*
Cohors XX Palmyrenorum 73, 82–3, 85, 157, 161
Colic 51
Columella 5–6, 30–3 *passim*, 37–8 *passim*, 40, 47, 72
VI Commageniorum Cohors Equitata 106, 119
Conformation 6–10
Constantine the Great 5, 195, 253, 262
Constantius 164, 193
Crassus 148, 180–1
Cuneus 187
Cuneus Sarmatarum 185
Curse Tablets 229–30
Cursus Publicus 51–2, 72, 250–62 *passim*
  animal data
    abuse of 255
    distances travelled 254
    numbers (Procopius) 261
    supply of 257–8

weight carried 256–7
weight pulled 256–7
depots
  mansiones 252
  mutationes 252
  stationes 252
laws pertaining to 250–262 *passim*
permits for use of
  angariae 252
  evectiones 252
  tractoriae 252–3
personnel
  grooms 259, 261
  Manceps 259
  Mulomedicus 259
  slaves 261
structure system 252
uses of 251
Cyrnus River 180

Dacia 184
Dacians 183
Dacian Wars 78, 164, 184, 191
Damascus 194
Danaba 193–4
Danube 183, 185, 193
Decurio 111
Delphi 24
Desultores 248
Diocletian 30, 193–5 *passim*
Diocletian's Edict on Prices 191, 232
  Aphrodisias copy of 257
Dionysus, Tyrant of Sicily 20
Distance capability 162–3
Domitian 184, 211, 238
Donkeys 36, 231–3
  jacks 35
  mares 35
Dura Europus 73, 82, 149, 153, 162
Dura Europus housings 153

Elephants, Dio Cassius on 108–9
  Hannibal's 177
Emesa 194
Emperor's private riding/driving
  Dio Cassius on 242
  SHA on 242–3

Suetonius on 242
Epona 173, 235
Eques 187
Equine responses in battle 167–9
Equi phalerati 21
Equipment *see under* horses, *see under* trooper
Equites Catafractarii Ambianses 152
Equites Catafractarii Pictavenses 152
Erembian Horse 25
Essedarius 248
Etruria 170–1
Etruscans 170–2

Fabricae 149
Factions 205
  colours of 205, 211
Flavian/Trajanic 192
Founder (colic) 51
Fronto 102
Fulvius Flaccus 74, 172, 177, 192

Galerius 193
Gallic breed 21
Gallic horse 181
Gallienus, assassination 193
  mobile cavalry 192
  upgrading cavalry 14
Games 248–9
  Circensian 218
  Saecular 219
  of Stella 219
Gardens of Sallust 242
Gauls 181
gelding 80
gelding irons 234
Georgics (*see also* Virgil) 5
Germanicus 75, 157
Golden Ass (Apuleius) 233–5
Gordian I 213, 217
Goths 193
Gratius Faliscus 5, 16, 78, 210, 212
Greek cavalry 171
Gundestrup Cauldron 133
Gyrus 103, 105

Hadrian
  Adlocutio 106

Cataphracts 151, 192
Diploma 88–9, 185
horse 245
hunting 245
Lambaesis 119
Roxolani 184–5
Wall 183
Hadrumetum 176, 208, 211
Haemus mountains 193
Haltonchesters 120
Hannibal
  baggage train 87
  cavalry of 74, 123, 173–4
    at Cannae 166, 175, 189
    at Ticinus 189
    at Trasimene 123, 175
    at Trebbia 129, 175
Hanno 174
Hasdrubal 163, 173, 176–7
Health *see under* horse
Heneti 17, 20
Hermundurii 184
Hippago 211
Hippika Gymnasia 112, 116
Hod Hill 82, 95
Horrea 93
Horse data
  age of (*see* teeth) 45–6, 82
  branding 83, 211–12
  castration 80–1, 168
  conformation 6–10
  education of (basic) 46–8
  hooves
    condition of 36, 225–6
    growth of 124–5, 163
    hipposandal 124, 259
    shoeing 36, 123, 226
    solea ferrea 103, 124
    solea spartea 103, 124, 234
  mentality 66–7, 167–9 *passim*
  physiology 66–70 *passim*
  physique 69
  psychology 66–70 *passim*
  sex of
    geldings 81, 95–6
    mares 81, 95–6
    racehorses 214
    stallions (treatment of) 81, 95–6
  transport 98–9, 211
  weight carrying ability 153–5
Horse equipment (military)
  armour
    advantages 152
    chamfron 145–8, 149
    crinet 151
    disadvantages 153
    Dura Europus finds 149–51
    estivals (greaves) 151
    eye guards 148
    leather (Ammianus) 149
    mail (Heliodorus) 149
    peytral 148
    sarmatic 183
  bitting 136–140 *passim*
    curb bit 136–7
    Newstead 137–8
    Santa Barbara 137
    size of 139–40
    Thracian – severity of 139
  bridle (lapithae) 104
  hackamore – roman 140–4 *passim*
    psalion 103, 104, 140–4 *passim*
    Flavius Bassus *psalion* 143
    Vindolanda *psalia* 143
  long reins 105
  muzzles 80, 142
  phalerae 103, 136
  saddle – military 109, 116, 131
    benefits 133–4
    construction 132–3
    disadvantage 134
    Pazyryk 132
  saddle accessories
    breast harness 135
    breeching straps 135
    girth 135
    girth buckles 135
  total weight of equipment 154
Horse health
  colic 51, 128
  dehydration 128, 155
  endemic illnesses 129

fibulae 126
heat stress 155
injury 125–7 *passim*
lameness 122–4 *passim*
veterinary *see under* Pelagonius
Horse's reactions
  aggression of 66, 168
  anger 169
  battle 167–8
  fear (horse's) 68, 108, 169
  fear (rider's) 169
  launched weapons 167–8
  mares in oestrus 81, 214
  speed 167
Horse's training 101–10 *passim*
  Arrian – *Tactica* 101, 107, 109, 110, 111
  Basilica Exercitatoria 107
  Cantabrian Gallop 106, 120, 168
  Career 107
  Cohors XX Palmyrenorum 104
  elephants – accustoming to 108–9
  Gyrus 103, 105
  jumping – Arrian on 109
  long reining 105–6
  Lunt, the 104–5
  probatio 104
  swimming, Tacitus on 109
    Vegetius on 109
  testudo formation 110
  Toloutegon 107
  Vegetius on training 101–2
  Virgil on training 104, 108
  weight carried 109
  Xenophon on training 101, 104
Horsemanship – Strabo on 15
Huns 195–6
  Ammianus on 112
  Massagetic 190
Hunting
  Ammianus on 244
  Arrian on 243
  boar hunting 245
  Gratius Faliscus on 244
  Hadrian 245–6
  Martial on 246

  Oppian on 244

Iazyges 78, 183–5, 191, 193
Iazygian horses 185
Icelus 261
Igel monument 35
Illerda campaign 169
Imperial post 251
Imperial studs 208
Inchtuthil 120

Jewish wars 75, 165
Josephus 75–6, 165, 167
Jotapata 75
Jugurtha 157, 189
Jugurthine wars 157, 189
Julian (emperor) 118, 164, 213
Julius Caesar 14, 21, 70, 109, 157, 182, 189–92 *passim*, 251
  on cavalry 74, 75, 77–8, 166
  on draught horses 71, 88, 173
  on forage 90
  at Illerda 169
  as patron of games 248
Justinian Digest 237–8
Juvenal 36, 72, 228

Katchina 68, 116, 131
Krefeld Gellup 68, 82

Laelius 177
Lambaesis 106, 119
Lapithae 104
Latifundia 40, 103, 159
Lepidus 179, 237
Lex Aquila 237
Libyan – breed 11–14, 24, 177
Libyan – cavalry 172–3, 190
Libyans – Aelian on 177
Lilies 110
Livius – consul 163
Luceres 187
Lucius Quietus 164
Lucullus – Dio Cassius on 179
  Plutarch on 148

Macedonians 171
Macedonian cavalry 175
Magister Equitum 195

Magister Peditum 195
Magna Graecia 17, 171
Magnesia, battle of 179
Mago of Carthage 54
Marches of note, Nero (consul) 163
　Publius Scipio 171
Marcommanian wars 185
Marcus Aurelius 78, 183
　column of 151
Marius 189
Massinissa 176–7
Mauretanian cavalry 164
Maximinian 193
Medes 171
Median plains 23
Mesopotamia 179
Metaurus 163
Metellus 189
Milan 192
Mileage 162–3
Mithridates of Armenia 179–80
Moesia 184
Mons Graupius 79, 166
Mount Olivet 167
Mules 24, 35, 231–2
　breeding of 35–6, 71–2
　riding of 240
　value of 72

Nabatea 24, 76
Naissus 193
Nemesian 5, 210
Nero (consul) 163
Nero (emperor) 218
Newstead 25, 120
Newstead chamfron 145–6
Newstead curb 138–9
Nisaean horses 16, 41, 196
Nisibis 179
Notitia Dignitatum 149, 151, 156, 185
Numerus Equitum Sarmatarum Bremetennacensum Gordianus 185
Numidian – breed 11–14
Numidian – cavalry 74, 172–7 *passim*

Aelian on 177
　under Fulvius Flaccus 74, 172, 177
　under Hamilcar 172
　under Hannibal 74, 172, 174
　under Hasdrubal 172
　under Jugurtha 189
　under Julius Caesar 74
　under Massinissa 176–7
Nutrition 40–5 *passim*
　barleys 40
　beans 94
　coarse mix – modern 41
　coarse mix – Roman 41–2
　farrago 43
　hay (lucerne/alfalfa/medick) 41, 171
　Medica 41
　oats 40
　wheats 40

Oppian 5, 11, 14, 25, 33, 210, 212, 244
Orodes 180
Ostrogoths 195

Palladius 10
Palmyra 193–4
Parade armour 116
Parade grounds 119
Parthian cavalry 178, 180–3
Paullus Lucius Aemilius 166
Pazyryk burials 22–3, 132–3
Pedanius at Mount Olivet 167
Pelagonius (*Ars Veterinaria*) 5–11 *passim*, 32, 37–40 *passim*, 52–60 *passim*, 82, 108, 125–6, 204–5, 215, 220, 224–7 *passim*, 259
Perseus of Macedonia 108
Persia 22
Persian 171, 193
Persian cavalry 171
Persian horse 23, 96
Petulantes 164
Phalerae 103, 136
Pharnaces 180
Philip IV of Macedon 179

Phraata, battle of 181
Phraates IV 182
Phrygia 260
Phrygian herds 238
Picket line 37
Pliny the Elder 5, 31–2
Pliny the Younger 5, 111
  on riding facilities 241–2
Plutarch on
  Anthony 181
  Crassus 180
  Julius Caesar 180, 190
  Pompey 180
Points of the horse 7
Polybius – cavalry structure 188
  horse rations 188
  picket line 37
Pompey 109, 128, 169, 190
  Dio Cassius on 179–80
P. Popilius Laenus 251
Portents 239–40
Postal service 251
Postings *see under* cavalry
Praedial Servitudes 237
Probatio 104
Probatio Equorum 219
Procopius 254, 261
Prorostratum – meaning of 83
Proverbs 247
Psalion 104, 140–4 *passim*
Punic Wars 173–8 *passim*

Quadi 80, 185
Quintus Pedius 70

Racehorses of note
  Abigeus 206
  Bubalo 211
  Callidromus 210
  Cotynus 206
  Cupido 211
  Danaus 211
  Ferox 211
  Galata 206
  Germinator 210
  Hilarus 210
  Icarus 211
  Lucidus 206
  Muccosus 211
  Nitidus 210
  Oceanus 211
  Paratus 206
  Pompeianus 206
  Silvanus 210
  Tuscus 220
  Victor 211
  Vindex 211
Racehorse breeds of note
  African 209–10, 212, 214
  Cappadocian 210, 212–4
  Cretan 212
  Gallic 210
  Greek 210, 212, 213
  Mycenaean 212
  Numidian 210
  Pentapolitanian 210
  Sardinian 210
  Sicilian 210, 212–3
  Spanish 209–10, 212–4
  Tuscan 212
Race frequency under
  Augustus 217
  Caligula 219
  Claudius 218
  Domitian 211, 219–21
Race length 204
Racing
  Dio Cassius on 207–8, 218, 227
  Dio Chrysostomos 201
  Juvenal 228
  Martial 219, 220, 227
  Plutarch 202
  Sidonius Apollinaris 222–3
  Suetonius 218–20 *passim*, 228
  Tertullian 205, 230
Racing terminology
  Annagonum 227
  Arena 204
  Biga 217, 220
  Carceres 220–2
  Creta 221
  Diversium 220
  Domini 210

Factions 205, 211
Funalis 206
Igualis 206
Meta 216
Naufraga 224
neck yoke 216
Pedibus ad Quadrigam 220
pole 216
Pompa 227, 230, 238
Probatio Equorum 219
Quadriga 217, 220
Remissus 227
Revocatus 227
Rudis Auriga 227
Spina 204, 207, 221
traces 216
Triga 227
yoke 216
Ramnenses 187
Reproduction (of horses) 31–6 passim
   chromosone count 35
   covering 32
   foaling 31
   genetics 32
   oestrus 31
   teaser 32
Ribchester 78, 185
Roads
   builder (first) 251
   length 250
   Phrygian 262 (map)
   Via Egnatia 250
Rock paintings 172
Romulus 187
Roxolani 183, 191
Ruspina 100
Rustic Servitudes 237

Saddle cost of – civilian 191
   cost of – military 191
Saecular Games 219
Sagittarii 178, 182
Saltus 76
Sarmatians
   Aorsi 183
   Ammianus on 185
   Dio Cassius on 185
   Iazyges 78, 183–5, 191, 193
   in Britain 185
   Roxolani 183, 191
   Strabo on 23, 186
   Tacitus on 23, 184
Sassanians 196
Scipio Africanus 74, 175–6, 179
Scipio Lucius 179
Scribonius Largus 52
Seius' horse 247
Seleucids 78, 179
Seleucis Nicator 179
Sena 163
Servius Tullius 73, 187
Severus 128
Sicilian cavalry 171–2
Soaemus 165
Sophocles 24
Spanish cavalry 172–4
Spectacles 248–9
Stabling – cavalry 94–7 passim
   Pelagonius on 37
   Varro on 37
Strabo 5, 11, 76, 78, 80, 177, 180
strator 51, 73, 151
Strymon river 16
Stud groom, duties of 37–8
Studs of horses
   Hermogenian 213–4
   Imperial 213
   Juvenal on 217
   Palmatian 213–4
   Phrygian 238
   Sabini 211, 217
   Sorothi 208, 211, 212
Suebi 184
Sulla 189
Superstitions 239–40
Surenas, the 180
Symmachus Quintus Aurelius 214
Syphax 176
Syria 75–6, 178
Syrian cavalry 75, 102, 178

Tactica see under Arrian
Tactics *see under* cavalry
Tarquin 187
Teeth – ageing by 45–6, 82
Tertullian 205, 230
Tetrarchy 193
Theodosius I 196
Thessaly 171
Thrace 171
Tiberius 182
Ticinus 189
Tigranes 180
Titienses 187
Toloutegon 107, 111, 120
Training *see under* horse, *see under* trooper
Traffic abuses 233
Traffic laws 233
Trajan 71, 78, 162, 191–2
Trajan's Column 35, 131, 183
Trasimene 123, 175
Trebbia 129, 175
Trigarium 219
Trooper, *Codex Theodosianus* on 113
Trooper equipment
  bracae 116–7
  cataphract's armour 118
  contus 118
  cuirass 117
  hasta 118
  pilum 154
  shield – battle 116
    boss 118
    parade 118
    rim 118
  spatha 110
Trooper height 159
  suitability 160
Trooper training
  basics of 114–6
  Hippika Gymnasia 112
  Vegetius on mounting 112

Troy Games 111–2
Turma 111
Tychaeus 176

Ubii 159
units *see under* cavalry
Utica 176

Valkenburg 131
Varro 5, 30–2, 34–5, 37, 46, 48, 50–1, 79, 80, 82, 168, 212, 231, 236
Vechten 131
Vegetius Flavius Renatus 64, 86, 101–2
Vegetius Publius Renatus 11, 14
  on gelding 234
Vercingetorix 75
Vespasian 75, 258, 260
Vespasianic 192
Veterinary medicine 49–60 *passim*
  immunes 50
  mulomedicus 50
  veterinarius 50
Vibilius 184
Vindolanda chamfron 145–7
Vindolanda *psalia* 143
Virgil 5, 30, 33–4, 39, 47, 79, 82, 104, 108, 214–5
Visigoths 195–6
Vonones 183

Warranty 48, 259
White horses, use of
  religious 238–9
  state 238–9
  superstitions about 239
Wolf breed 17, 20
Wu Ti 22

Xenophon 45, 101, 103–4, 142
Xerxes 24

Zama 74, 176, 179
Zeuxis 179